The Handbook for Microcomputer Technicians

Books from QED

Database

Managing IMS Databases
Building the Data Warehouse
Migrating to DB2
DB2: The Complete Guide to Implementation
   and Use
DB2 Design Review Guidelines
DB2: Maximizing Performance of Online
   Production Systems
Embedded SQL for DB2
SQL for DB2 and SQL/DS Application
   Developers
How to Use ORACLE SQL*PLUS
ORACLE: Building High Performance Online
   Systems
ORACLE Design Review Guidelines
Developing Client/Server Applications in an
   Architected Environment

Systems Engineering

Software Configuration Management
On Time, Within Budget: Software Project
   Management Practices and Techniques
Information Systems Architecture:
   Development in the 90's
Quality Assurance for Information Systems
User-Interface Screen Design: Workstations,
   PC's, Mainframes
Managing Software Projects
The Complete Guide to Software Testing
A Structured Approach to Systems Testing
Rapid Application Prototyping
The Software Factory
Data Architecture: The Information Paradigm
Software Engineering with Formal Metrics
Using CASE Tools for Practical Management

Management

Developing a Blueprint for Data, Applications,
   and Technology: Enterprise Architecture
   Planning
Introduction to Data Security and Controls
How to Automate Your Computer Center
Controlling the Future
The UNIX Industry
Mind Your Business

IBM Mainframe Series

From Mainframe to Workstations: Offloading
   Application Development
VSE/SP and VSE/ESA: A Guide to
   Performance Tuning
CICS: A Guide to Application Debugging
CICS Application and System Programming
CICS: A Guide To Performance Tuning
MVS COBOL II Power Programmer's Desk
   Reference
VSE JCL and Subroutines for Application
   Programmers
VSE COBOL II Power Programmer's Desk
   Reference
Introduction to Cross System Product
CSP Version 3.3 Application Development
The MVS Primer
MVS/VSAM for the Application Programmer
TSO/E CLISTs: The Complete Tutorial and
   Desk Reference
CICS: A How-To for COBOL Programmers
QMF: How to Use Query Management Facility
   with DB2 and SQL/DS
DOS/VSE JCL: Mastering Job Control
   Language
DOS/VSE: CICS Systems Programming
VSAM: Guide to Optimization and Design
MVS/JCL: Mastering Job Control Language
MVS/TSO: Mastering CLISTs
MVS/TSO: Mastering Native Mode and ISPF
REXX in the TSO Environment, 2nd Edition

Technical

Rdb/VMS: Developing the Data Warehouse
The Wonderful World of the AS/400:
   Architecture and Applications
C Language for Programmers
Mainframe Development Using Microfocus
   COBOL/2 Workbench
AS/400: A Practical Guide to Programming and
   Operations
Bean's Index to OSF/Motif, Xt Intrinsics, and
   Xlib Documentation for OSF/Motif
   Application Programmers
VAX/VMS: Mastering DCL Commands and
   Utilities
The PC Data Handbook
UNIX C Shell Desk Reference
Designing and Implementing Ethernet Networks
The Handbook for Microcomputer Technicians
Open Systems

QED books are available at special quantity discounts for educational uses, premiums, and sales promotions. Special books, book excerpts, and instructive materials can be created to meet specific needs.

This is Only a Partial Listing. For Additional Information or a Free Catalog contact
QED Information Sciences, Inc. • P. O. Box 812070 • Wellesley, MA 02181-0013
Telephone: 800-343-4848 or 617-237-5656 or fax 617-235-0826

The Handbook for Microcomputer Technicians

Peter N. Bernstock

QED Publishing Group
Boston • Toronto • London

Many of the designations used by manufacturers and sellers to distinguish their products are claimed as trademarks. Where those designations appear in this book, and QED was aware of a trademark claim, the designations have been printed in initial caps or all caps.

© 1993 QED Information Sciences, Inc.
P.O. Box 82-181
Wellesley, MA 02181

QED Technical Publishing Group is a division of QED Information Sciences, Inc.

Library of Congress Catalog Number: 92-11611
International Standard Book Number: 0-89435-424-8

Printed in the United States of America
93 94 95 10 9 8 7 6 5 4 3 2

Library of Congress Cataloging-in-Publication Data

Bernstock, Peter N.
    The handbook for microcomputer technicians / Peter N. Bernstock.
        p.   cm.
    Includes index.
    ISBN 0-89435-424-8
    1. Microcomputers—Maintenance and repair—Handbooks, manuals, etc. 2. Microcomputers—Upgrading—Handbooks, manuals, etc.
    I. Title.
    TK7887.B47   1992
    621.39'16—dc20   92-11611
                                                                CIP

Contents

Introduction

Many people are involved with computers these days. The involvement may be as a casual user, a power user, a technical support person, or a service technician. The purpose of this book is to provide guidance to those who wish to become more deeply immersed in the repair and upkeep of computers. This book will not make you into an instant technician or computer guru. It will, however, enhance your knowledge and understanding of microcomputers and the MS-DOS operating system.

The text makes reference to *technicians* and *customers*. Technicians are the people who service and repair the computers, while customers are those who own or use them. In some cases, technician and customer are one and the same. There is discussion on certain manufacturers and models, but the majority of the book is generic. If you are a customer who likes to solve his or her own problems, or a technician with a minimum of experience, this book should provide a valuable reference. It is not meant to be a substitute for hands-on training. Of course, experience is the best teacher.

The author has been involved in the computer service industry since 1983. During this time, he has attended trainings conducted by many of the major computer and printer manufacturers. During these sessions, the manufacturers provide training on their own equipment, with the attitude that competition does not exist. In the real world, computer systems are a combination of hardware and software provided by a multitude of vendors. This book addresses the multi-vendor aspect of systems service.

The first chapter discusses the relationships among the customer, the technician, and the technician's employer. Technical training rarely discusses this aspect of the business, which is so important in today's competitive market.

There is a chapter that explains what a computer is and how it works. Anyone with more than a casual interest in computers will find this information interesting, and hopefully, useful.

The chapter on systems and their manufacturers discusses compatibility issues, authorizations, and manufacturer support.

The next chapter lists many of the MS-DOS commands, syntax, and usage. There is a discussion about the uses of some of the commands to assist the technician in troubleshooting a system.

Another subject that is rarely dealt with in training classes or technical schools is software. The software chapter examines some problems and solutions. The reader is guided through a series of suggestions for dealing with these problems and working with unfamiliar applications.

A chapter is devoted to diagnostic methods. Use of manufacturer-supplied and third-party diagnostics is examined.

There is an in-depth look at module (component) repair. Some insight is given to set-up costs and possible problems of getting involved in this phase of the business.

The chapter on networks gives the technician enough information to troubleshoot or, at least, localize a problem. Networks are complicated systems, especially when they are encountered for the first time. The basic information provided here should give an inexperienced technician enough confidence to meet the challenge.

The chapter on installing peripheral devices and upgrading systems provides hints and techniques for all systems from the original PC through current platforms. Attention is given to both older systems as well as the current 386 and 486 machines.

A section is devoted to hard drives. Concepts include interfacing, interleave factors, low-level formatting, partitioning, and reasons why hard drives fail.

Techniques and general problems that cause components to fail are discussed. There are hints to remember when disassembling systems and some situations that a technician is bound to encounter.

There are several appendixes that provide information not usually found in a single source. There is a comprehensive listing of POST error codes, an extensive list of floppy drive and hard drive characteristics, ROM BIOS tables for hard drive installation, some part number listings, and a wealth of miscellaneous information that includes switch settings for various boards. There is also a resource list containing the names and addresses of suppliers of systems, parts, tools, components, fourth-party services, software publishers, cables, connectors, drive repair specialists, and many other related products and services.

Customers, Technicians and Responsibilities

DEALING WITH CUSTOMERS

This chapter deals with the part of service that is neglected by technical schools—fixing the customer. A well-trained technician has little difficulty repairing a machine. Repairing the customer, however, is a skill that is acquired through experience and common sense. Most technicians leave school looking forward to their first position, with no experience in dealing with people. The ability to satisfy the customer is more important than a quick repair.

Customer Satisfaction: The degree to which a customer's level of expectation in buying a product or service has been met or exceeded.

Customer satisfaction is how the customer perceives the manner in which he or she has been treated. As a person who deals with customers, you want to maintain the highest possible level of customer satisfaction. A happy customer is a steady customer. A satisfied customer will tell a few other potential customers, which is good free advertising. The bottom line is that *the customer pays your salary*.

Customer Relations: The respect that we show someone with whom we are dealing as a buyer of products or services.

Customer relations is how the customer is treated, as seen by the technician. All too often, the technician's view of customer relations is very different from that of the customer. A dissatisfied customer will not continue to do business with you. A dissatisfied customer will tell his story to the whole world—also free advertising, but not the kind that you want. Remember, *the customer pays your salary*.

Regardless of your knowledge, training and experience, or the lack of same, there are many factors that contribute to a high level of customer satisfaction. You must maintain a professional appearance at all times. Dress in a neat, clean manner. An open collar and loose tie or a shirttail hanging out of your belt does not make a good impression. Neither do jeans and a tee shirt, or worn-out or torn apparel.

Conduct yourself in a professional manner. Do not smoke, chew gum, eat, or drink while in a customer's place of business. Don't fraternize with the customer, the customer's employees, or the customer's patrons. Maintain excellent communication skills, both written and verbal. Speak to the customer in plain language. Avoid using slang expressions, and don't get technical. Use mouthwash or brush your teeth, especially after meals. Stay away from garlic, onions, and other spicy foods. Never drink any alcoholic beverages during working hours. Above all, show respect to the customer.

There are many negatives in dealing with customers. You must be aware of those negatives, and retain your composure. Remember that the customer is always right . . . even when he isn't. The customer may think that you are a fool, but you know that you are not. The customer thinks that he knows more than you do. Be patient. If the customer really knows more, why does he need you? The customer thinks that the problem can be fixed without you. If this is true, why didn't they fix the problem and save the cost of a service call?

Follow up on your service by calling the customer a day or two after your visit. They'll appreciate the fact that you are interested.

RESPONSIBILITY OF THE SERVICE REPRESENTATIVE

The word *representative* is used because you are representing your employer wherever you go and to whomever you meet in the course of performing your job. Your job is to complete the service in a timely, accurate, and professional manner.

Your responsibility is to your customers, your employer, your co-workers, and yourself. When you receive a service call, speak directly with the customer immediately. Gather as many facts as you can regarding the problem or trouble. Make an appointment for a service call (for on-site service), and keep it. Be on time for your appointment. Notify the customer if you will be delayed. Be prepared to perform the service based upon the facts that you have obtained, but be flexible.

Take as much time as is necessary and be as thorough as you can. A little extra time and testing now is better than coming back and performing the repair a second time. Repair or replace only those parts that are necessary. Charge the correct amount for your time and materials. You were called to perform a service, and the customer expects to pay a fair price.

Responsibility to your employer includes reporting for work on time, and in a neat, clean, sober, and presentable condition. Give a day's work for a day's pay. If your employer's business thrives and prospers, you should be rewarded. If the business declines, it may be a result of the actions and attitudes of the employees. Problems should be addressed directly with the employer. Discussions with other employees are not professional and may be counterproductive.

Responsibility to your co-workers is a two-way street. You should help them whenever possible, and they should help you. Do not return defective parts to stock marked as good parts. Would you want to try to repair a machine using a bad part? Document your service activities. It is helpful to have a history for each customer and for each system. Share any information that you may acquire. The person who has the most secrets does not win the game.

You also have a responsibility to yourself. Put yourself in the place of your customer, your employer, and your co-workers. Are you confident in the ability of the person that you really are? Do you really see yourself as others see you? Are you satisfied with your appearance? Are your communication skills, verbal and written, better than average? Are you competent in your job? Do you follow up on seemingly minor details? Do you return telephone calls or call customers when you promise to do so? Do you take an interest in your work and the well-being of your employer? Are you part of the team? If you were the boss and had an employee like yourself, would *you* keep *him*?

SOME ADVICE

Some service people prefer to travel light. The better service representatives will carry a full set of tools, extra cables, fuses, cable ties, power cords, diagnostic floppy disks, blank floppy disks for testing, an extra copy of DOS, RAM chips, miscellaneous nuts and bolts, and those other little items that prevent embarrassment, needless return visits, and extra traveling back and forth.

2

What Is a Computer? How Does it Work?

A computer is a machine that stores and processes data (information). Data is input, processed, and output. Components include a processor (CPU), ROM(s), RAM, input/output (I/O) devices, and storage.

FUNCTIONAL UNITS OF A COMPUTER

The processor (also called the CPU or Central Processing Unit) executes machine-coded instructions (or programs), one instruction at a time (see Figure 2.1). The processor also performs arithmetic and logical operations, and handles data transfer 8 bits, 16 bits, or 32 bits at a time. A processor chip is composed of control circuitry, registers, and an ALU (Arithmetic Logic Unit). Microchannel and EISA (Extended Industry Standard Architecture) computers operating under OS/2 (and perhaps other operating systems) will be able to utilize two or more processors. This is called "distributed processing."

Many computers have an optional coprocessor (also called a math coprocessor or floating point coprocessor) installed. A companion to the processor, this chip has specialized capabilities for performing floating point math. Math coprocessors contain specialized registers and perform complex operations that free the processor, decrease operating time, and increase bus availability. The application software must support the math coprocessor, or operation of the system will not be affected.

The ROM (Read Only Memory), also called the BIOS (Basic Input Output System) is a chip or set of chips that is preprogrammed by the

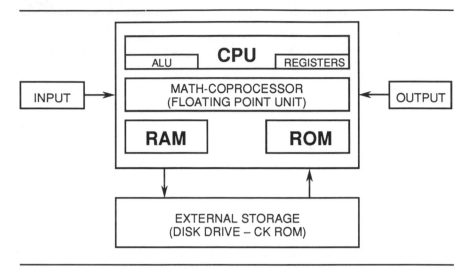

Figure 2.1   The EDP cycle—input . . . process . . . output.

manufacturer. The contents of the ROM can not be changed. If problems occur as a result of a defect in the BIOS, there are several remedies.

Because the BIOS is actually software, it can be rewritten and burned into new chips. The manufacturer will then offer a replacement or upgrade, usually for a nominal cost. For example, the original IBM PC did not support a hard disk. At the time that the original BIOS was written for this computer, the company was not offering a hard disk as an option. Hard drive kits, consisting of the drive, controller, and necessary cables, appeared on the market for upgrading the PC. IBM was also offering equipment to upgrade these machines. In order for the hard disk to be recognized, the correct DOS version was required, with the proper BIOS.

A series of interesting problems was found in the early PS/2 microchannel computers[1] (Models 50 and 60). IBM found that the BIOS was the cause. Instead of replacing the BIOS ROMs, IBM created a driver (DASDDRVR.SYS) to be added to the CONFIG.SYS.

Some computer companies such as Compaq® or IBM® manufacture their own BIOS ROMs. Other computer companies use BIOS ROMs manufactured by Phoenix®, AMI®, or other "third-party" suppliers. A

---

[1]See Miscellaneous Information in the Appendix for a discussion of these problems.

ROM is considered to be permanent storage (data is *not* lost when power is removed). The ROM contains start-up instructions for the computer and the basic input/output system (BIOS). The ROM occupies the highest portion of the address range.

If an upgrade to a system, such as replacing the hard drive with a drive of higher capacity or adding a 3½" drive, does not work, verify that the correct version of the BIOS is installed and the version of the operating system supports the upgrade.

RAM (Random Access Memory) is temporary storage (data is lost when power is removed). The contents of RAM can be altered or changed, either by the operating system software, application software, or the activities of the customer. During normal computer operation, the RAM contains parts of the operating system, application programs, and customer data. Sometimes called "user memory," portions of RAM can be used for disk buffers or print spoolers. RAM occupies the lowest portion of the address range.

The input/output (I/O) channel is an extension of the processor. The

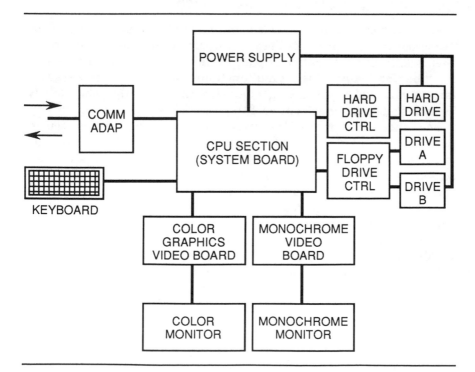

Figure 2.2   Functional Block Diagram of a Microcomputer.

I/O channel is divided into four main groups: power and ground (+5, –5, +12, –12 VDC), control lines, address lines (I/O and memory), and the data bus. This is the bus that permits expansion boards (or cards) to be added to a computer and allows them to communicate with the processor.

I/O boards permit interfacing between a device (such as a video monitor) and the processor. These devices can be either internal[2] or external to the system, as long as the I/O board is connected to the bus. Devices can be either input only (such as a mouse), output only (like a video monitor), or both input and output (a modem).

Storage devices for application software and data are also connected through interface boards. These devices include floppy disk drives, hard disk drives, and CD-ROMs. Floppy and hard disks are called read/write devices. The information stored on these disks can be changed or erased. A CD-ROM, as the name states, is "read only" memory. The information stored on a CD-ROM can not be changed or erased.

BASIC SYSTEM INITIALIZATION SEQUENCE FROM COLD-BOOT OR POWER-ON RESET

The events that take place inside a computer when it is switched on are numerous and complicated. They also occur in a definite sequence (see Figure 2.2). Little attention is paid to these events when a computer functions normally. When a malfunction develops, it is important to know what events are taking place and the order that they follow. Troubleshooting is much easier if the technician knows what has happened, and what has not. The processor is reset, and system control passes to the BIOS (in the ROM). The BIOS initialization routine begins, and the POST (power on self test) is loaded into the first memory segment of RAM. The POST routine begins. The system board and interface boards are checked for failures, and the I/O devices are initialized. Configuration and set-up information is read (from the CMOS[3] chip) and is then written to the first segment of RAM where it is stored in a configuration table. POST checks for the presence of external ROMs (such as on a hard disk adapter). POST does not perform any extensive testing of components or devices. It merely detects the presence or absence of devices that it expects to encounter and executes a

---

[2]Some internal devices, such as a modem, are actually part of the board.

[3]Systems using a "set-up" routine instead of configuration switches for items such as the amount of RAM, number and types of disk drives, and so forth, use a CMOS (complimentary metal oxide semiconductor) backed up by a battery to store this information.

limited functional test. If POST completes successfully, one short beep (two short beeps on some Compaq® systems) is heard and a completion statement is displayed on the screen. This indicates that the system is ready for use, but it does not guarantee that the system and all devices are functioning 100 percent. The sequence that follows a successful POST is much the same as a warm boot.

An unsuccessful completion of POST is indicated by an incorrect or missing audio response, a displayed error code, no display, or a blinking cursor. A critical malfunction will halt all testing. A noncritical malfunction will suspend the POST and display an error code and a message requesting that the "F1" key be pressed. The system will then continue testing. A completely dead system (no display or audio error) may result from a defective module in the first memory bank or a defective ROM. Increasing the memory or adding peripheral devices to a system will mean a longer POST time. Different device interfaces may produce erroneous audio errors.

WARM-BOOT (CTRL-ALT-DEL) SEQUENCE

A warm boot produces an interrupt different from a cold boot. A warm boot does not initiate the POST. When a warm boot is initiated, instructions from ROM are loaded into RAM. The instruction set begins to load the operating system into RAM from a boot device (usually a hard disk). The boot record is loaded from the boot device. A file called the device handler (IO.SYS for the MS-DOS operating system[4]) is loaded into RAM, replacing the boot record. Another file called the file manager (MSDOS.SYS for MS-DOS) is loaded into the next available RAM address. Portions of the command processor or command interpreter (COMMAND.COM) are loaded into the next available RAM address. Other portions of the command processor are loaded as needed. The CONFIG.SYS file (if present) is read, information is loaded, and the system is reconfigured if necessary. The AUTOEXEC.BAT file, if present, executes. RAM resident programs are loaded if configured to do so by the AUTOEXEC.BAT file. An application program loads into the next available RAM address if configured to do so by the AUTOEXEC.BAT file. The application program may replace some portions of the command interpreter. In this case, when the application is exited, it will reload the command interpreter. The remainder of the RAM is available as the user work space, such as data files.

---

[4]The IBM version of the operating system is called PC-DOS. The two hidden files in PC-DOS are IBMIO.COM and IBMDOS.COM.

I/O ADDRESSES AND IRQ ASSIGNMENTS

Each device in a computer system needs an address (or range of addresses) for communicating with the CPU (microprocessor). Some devices allow their address to be changed, within a limited range, through jumpers or DIP switches. The ability to change a device's address is important, as two or more devices can not use the same address. Each device must communicate with the processor through its own unique address. If two (or more) devices are set to the same address, an "address conflict" is created. When an address conflict exists, results can be unpredictable. Sometimes, one of the devices functions normally and the other does not function at all. Sometimes, neither device will function.

In most cases, the addresses are combined with an interrupt request level (IRQ). The IRQ level sets the priority for devices requiring the attention of the processor. The lower the number, the higher the priority. It is sometimes necessary to set or alter the IRQ level, in addition to the address, when a device is installed. Proper instructions should be included with the device.

A typical example is the Microsoft bus mouse. Before installing the bus card, the IRQ level must be set. Microsoft has a list of conditions in the installation literature. Depending upon the configuration of the system (number of parallel ports, number of serial ports, presence of a hard drive, etc.), a jumper location is suggested. Setting the jumper actually changes the IRQ level.

IRQ assignments were created when the original PC was designed. These machines could support only eight interrupt levels, IRQ0 through IRQ7. When the 16-bit (and higher) systems were designed, an additional eight levels, IRQ8 through IRQ15, were added. The first eight IRQs are designated as "master," and the second eight IRQs are called "slaves." The second group of IRQs is tied to IRQ2, so the priority levels become IRQ0–IRQ2, IRQ8–IRQ15, followed by IRQ3-IRQ7.[5]

When adding a device to a system, verify the existing addresses and IRQs. Be sure that the new device is not using an address that is already in use. Some older devices do not permit altering their addresses. If it is necessary to change the address of a device, all of the devices in the system must be tested. The change may have affected an item that had been functioning normally until the new device and address become active.

---

[5]IRQ assignments and I/O addresses (in hexadecimal) appear in the Appendix.

3

Systems and Their Manufacturers

SIMILARITIES AND DIFFERENCES BETWEEN MODELS

In 1981, IBM brought their "PC" to market, along with the new PC-DOS[6] operating system. A hardware platform and operating system standard was established. If any manufacturer planned to remain in the micro-computer business, IBM compatibility was necessary for survival.

Along with compatibility came enhancements. Higher-quality video, better color graphics, more memory, larger storage, faster pro-cessing speed, bigger, better, faster. More and more bells and whistles began to emerge. The next computer era arrived in 1987, when IBM announced their second generation of systems, called the PS/2. The higher-end PS/2 computers (Model 50 and greater) incorporated the Microchannel, a completely new and sometimes faster bus structure. This time, the rest of the industry did not follow IBM. Compaq, Hewlett-Packard, and several other major manufacturers stated that they did not see any benefits to the Microchannel. This group of manu-facturers developed an extension of the Industry Standard Architec-ture and called this EISA (Extended Industry Standard Architecture). EISA is a 32-bit bus that is "downward compatible." That means that any existing 8-bit or 16-bit expansion boards could be used in a system

---

[6]PC-DOS is the IBM version of MS-DOS.

with an EISA bus. The Microchannel bus was physically different from the ISA bus, and none of the older expansion boards could be used.

With the introduction of the PS/2 series of machines, IBM changed from the industry standard 5¼" floppy disk to a 3½" disk. The 3½" drives are smaller and have a higher density than the 5¼" drives. The industry became divided over the issue of the size of the floppy disk drives. The majority of the industry remained with the 5¼" drives. Many machines are now available with both 3½" and 5¼" drives so that data on floppy disk can be moved from one machine to another. Portable computers and "lap tops" also used the 3½" format because of its size. Software publishers were forced to make their products available on both formats, which caused them some concern.

The basic compatibility issues of transfer of information between systems and a uniform operating system, which were solved with the introduction of the PC, have been carried along thus far. Other operating systems such as UNIX, XENIX, PICK, and OS/2 are available, but MS-DOS (formerly PC-DOS) is still the most popular and widely used.

PARTS COMPATIBILITY

Compatibility issues include cosmetics (color, matching knobs, face plates or handles, size), physical fit or mounting, electronic attributes (8-, 16-, or 32-bit bus, CPU speed, BIOS, power supply capacity), environmental (physical shock), and software acceptance.

The bus architecture, either ISA, EISA, or Microchannel, is a standard. Interface boards are easily moved from one system to another (ISA to ISA, ISA to EISA, Microchannel to Microchannel), with few compatibility issues other than address conflicts that must be resolved during installation. Some multipurpose boards will have to be reconfigured so that they don't conflict with features that are internal to a particular system. There are many generic or compatible peripheral devices on the market that will work with almost any system, such as video monitors and keyboards. These items are not sold as part of the system unit. Some are necessary for the system to function, such as a video monitor. Others are accessories or enhancements such as expanded or extended memory boards. Boards or devices made by a system manufacturer may need to be installed in specific systems (and sometimes in specific slots) in order to function to their fullest capacity and provide the full range of available features. A specific version of the operating system may be required, or special utility software may be available only from the manufacturer of that system.

Some generic devices, such as hard and floppy disk drives, will function in the majority of systems, but there may be cosmetic differences. Physical differences are usually provided for by including one or more sets of mounting hardware and face plates. Electronic differences can often be handled by a modification, such as changing a jumper or switch, or configuring the system through a software driver. The environmental factor of physical shock could be a problem if a hard disk drive is installed in a portable computer that will be transported frequently. Many manufacturers are using plastic or metal rails for mounting their drives. Installation of a generic drive may still require rails supplied by the system manufacturer.

Most Compaq 5¼" floppy disk drives are either half-height or third-height. The half-height drives fit into the Deskpro series of desk top computers, while the third-height drives are for the newer desk top (small footprint) systems and the portables. The third-height drives use two different latches, as they are supplied to Compaq by different vendors. Still, the strategy of using fewer unique parts and a small group of vendors decreases manufacturing costs, reduces stocking levels, and permits servicing of a broader product line. In comparison, IBM used full-height floppy disk drives for their PC and XT, and half-height drives for the XT-286 and AT systems. The drives for the XT-286 systems were also a different color than the AT drives.

The newer machines are more powerful but physically smaller. The trade-off is that the smaller machines have more built-in features, but they contain fewer parts. The system boards on the PS/2 line have the hard disk circuitry, floppy disk controller, parallel, serial, mouse, and video ports all built in. This means that the compatibility of devices is far less flexible than the larger system board with all the plug-in interface cards. Compaq and several other manufacturers have followed this strategy, producing machines with smaller footprints that fit in better with the present decor found in the workplace.

Since each of these fully integrated system boards is different, parts-stocking strategy is changed. The wider variety of available systems, with their 8086, 286, 386, and 486 processors, 8-, 16-, and 32-bit architecture, and clock speeds from 5 to 40 MHz, added floppy disk formats, and higher hard disk capacities increase the variations to an almost unmanageable amount.

MANUFACTURER'S SUPPORT

Manufacturers rely on their base of authorized dealers to support customers. Manufacturer's support is a serious problem for the nonauthorized (third-party or corporate internal) service provider.

Most of the major manufacturers provide telephone support or on-line support for their authorized service providers only. Each authorized location is assigned a code number, which must be given to the support person each time that assistance is requested. Some of the manufacturers have opened limited lines of communication for their customers as a result of problems with their dealers.

Technical support, from the point of the manufacturer, is meant to aid authorized service personnel in solving unusual problems. The manufacturers feel that the service force should be factory trained, equipped with the proper documentation, and use technical support in cases where there is a problem that can not be solved through use of the service manuals and diagnostics.

Authorized service providers are repeatedly cautioned not to give out technical support numbers or dealer ID numbers to unauthorized persons and especially not to customers. Unauthorized use of tech support facilities creates a backlog for those who are authorized.

The manufacturers want to maintain the highest possible level of customer satisfaction, and they will recommend that an end user take the problem to an authorized service provider.

OBTAINING SERVICE AUTHORIZATION

Authorization procedures vary from manufacturer to manufacturer. Generally, the dealer who sells the product is required to provide service. In many instances, a manufacturer will authorize a service center that is in the service-only business (does NOT sell any hardware). These authorized service-only centers are often given a contract different from a dealership service center. These differences may include spare parts pricing, lack of technical support, inability to perform warranty service, no advertising support, higher cost for training, and other inconveniences used to discourage the relationship. Some initial requirements include the size of the service area, size of the showroom and sales area, space for parts and backup stock, an outbound sales force, size and experience of the in-house sales department, location, visibility, accessibility, proximity of the nearest competitor, experience of the company and management, length of time the company has been in business, financial stability of the business, floor planning (inventory financing) for another vendor, a business plan, other authorizations of the business, the product's place in the product line, possible competition from other products presently being sold, and the manufacturer's need for a dealer in this location.

There are also ongoing requirements to be considered. What will be the annual dollar commitment to this vendor? Will you sell, service, and support the manufacturer's entire product line? Will you service and support obsolete equipment from this manufacturer? Can you (and will you) meet the inventory requirement (and quotas) of the vendor? Will you meet the service parts and documentation requirement of the vendor? You must keep the sales and service staff trained on new and current products. Will you support customers who purchased their equipment from another vendor? You must service equipment covered under a warranty. Can you compete with other dealers in your area who sell this line? Manufacturers such as IBM issue a limited number of "medallions" to dealers, and these manufacturers will not authorize a dealership until a medallion becomes available (an existing dealer surrenders a medallion). Dealers can not transfer authorizations between locations, or from one dealer to another. If one store in a chain is authorized to sell a product, this does not mean that another store in that chain is automatically authorized. Each location must be individually authorized to sell and service a particular product.

4

MS-DOS and the Technician

WHAT IS AN OPERATING SYSTEM?

When a computer is powered on (booted), the operating system is loaded (the exact sequence of events will be discussed later). The operating system is a group of programs that allow a human using the English language (here in the United States anyway) to communicate with the computer through a keyboard or other device. The most commonly used operating system for microcomputers is MS-DOS (MicroSoft Disk Operating System). Some other operating systems will be mentioned later.

Functions of the operating system include handling interrupts and servicing devices through the device handler (IO.SYS), controlling I/O operations through the file manager (MSDOS.SYS), and providing user access to the system via the command processor (COMMAND.COM). The operating system also loads application programs through the command processor, file manager, and device handler. For a system to boot under MS-DOS, the boot disk (either the hard disk or a floppy disk) must contain the two hidden system files IO.SYS and MSDOS.SYS and the command interpreter COMMAND.COM. Once the system has booted and the prompt (or start-up message or program) is displayed, the system is expected to be functional. If the system has not reached this point, a malfunction has occurred. Appropriate action must be taken based on error messages or other indications of the difficulty.

The majority of computer hardware manufacturers will supply (either included with the system or for a charge) their own version of an operating system, which must support the hardware in the system. For example, PC-DOS prior to version 3.3 did not support 3½" floppy disk drives. When IBM brought the PS/2 series to market, they also introduced DOS 3.3. Compaq DOS 3.31 supported hard drive partitions of up to 512Mb, while PC-DOS did not add this capability until version 4.0. The differences in the versions supplied by computer manufacturers frequently contain enhancements that are specific to their hardware. Some of these enhancements include controlling the clock speed (such as normal and "turbo") and enabling or disabling video features.

In late 1991, Microsoft released MS-DOS 5.0 which contained many enhancements. An upgrade was made available directly from Microsoft (and dealers) so that customers could update to 5.0 with a minimum of trouble. This was the first time that Microsoft marketed their product directly and the first time that updating of the DOS operating system was so simple. A full-blown 5.0 was made available to hardware manufacturers to sell with new systems. IBM, Compaq, and other systems manufacturers have their own versions of 5.0.

A BRIEF HISTORY OF MS-DOS

Prior to 1981 there were many computer manufacturers working to make their products the "industry standard." Each of these computers had their own architecture, their own operating system, and their own special features. Information generated on one system, in most cases, could not be used on another system. The disk formats were different.[7] Often the format of the data itself was different. Application software available for one type of system was not always available for other types. The video systems were different and keyboards were different. There was no compatibility.

The only transportable operating system being used on microcomputers at the time was CP/M[8]. CP/M was cryptic in terms of today's operating systems, but it worked on dozens of computers using the 8088 or Z80 microprocessors. CP/M had several major drawbacks. Some of the problems were the result of how CP/M was designed and written,

---

[7]There were companies that could transfer files from one type of disk format to another. This was often expensive and time consuming, and not without problems.

[8]Control Program for Microprocessors, written by Digital Research.

while others resulted from lack of communication and compatibility between hardware manufacturers.

The maximum addressable RAM was only 64K, which resulted in extensive delays in program execution while information was written to and read from disk. Most of the systems were floppy disk based, as the price of hard disks was extremely high. Hardware manufacturers used different disk encoding and read-write schemes. A disk written on one kind of CP/M computer could not be read on a different model without the use of some type of format conversion software.

Format conversion software such as Compat® or Uniform® was reasonably inexpensive, but the reliability factor was not always 100 percent. Machines such as the Zorba® had a conversion routine built in. When the computer booted, a menu would appear on the screen asking which format should be assigned to the B drive.

Video systems were different from machine to machine. Color did not exist. Video RAM was limited and graphics were either very crude or impossible. The hardware design of the CP/M systems was similar to that of a dumb terminal. The video portion was devised to emulate a particular video terminal. Screens were refreshed and addressed differently, depending upon the specific terminal. Software had either to be written specifically for the terminal that the system emulated or include special (often confusing) installation routines.

In 1980, IBM announced that they were developing a desk top microcomputer system to be released in 1981. Most of the other manufacturers (an exception was Apple) stopped what they were doing in the area of research and development of new systems. They all knew that corporate America would be buying IBM (and eventually, something compatible). Unfortunately, there was no way to manufacture a machine that was compatible with something that did not yet exist. IBM had contacted Digital Research to ask them about developing an operating system for the new computer, but they were not interested. IBM then contacted Microsoft who agreed to write a new operating system, which IBM called PC-DOS. In 1981, the IBM PC and PC-DOS were introduced. Shortly thereafter, some former IBM people began a company called Compaq (COMPatibility And Quality). Other compatibles began to appear on the market, coming from both domestic and foreign manufacturers.[9] IBM owned PC-DOS, and the other manufacturers needed a compatible operating system, so they contacted Microsoft. Microsoft was able to sell an operating system called MS-DOS which was compatible with PC-DOS but did not infringe on IBM's copyright.

---

[9]Some early compatibles were manufactured or sold under the names of Leading Edge, Epson, Kaypro, and Mitsubishi.

With one or two differences, PC-DOS and MS-DOS are virtually the same. The major difference is that IBM used a version of the BASIC[10] programming language that resides partly on disk and mostly in ROM. The same BASIC in MS-DOS, using non-IBM hardware, is called GWBASIC and is disk based. Some early application software was written for the IBM version of BASIC. When the compatibles appeared on the market, software publishers quickly realized that their product had to be suitable for use on all systems.

WHY 640K?

IBM designed their system around the Intel 8086 microprocessor. The 8088 was very similar and inexpensive due to the quantities produced for use in computers using the CP/M operating system. One of the major differences between these processors is that the 8086 could function with a 16-bit data bus, while the 8088 is limited to an 8-bit bus. When Microsoft began working on the new operating system, an analysis was made of the 8088, the microprocessor that was being used in the IBM computer. The 8088 is effectively an 8-bit processor with 20 address lines. Having 20 address lines, the processor can support 2^{20} or 1,048,576 addresses. Since 1,048,576 is a bit unwieldy, it was rounded down to 1,000,000 or 1Mb. CP/M computers contained only 64k of RAM, as previously stated. The first version of the IBM PC contained 16K of RAM, which could be upgraded to 64k on the system board.[11] Microsoft wrote PC-DOS with the ability to address 640k of RAM. That was ten times the amount of RAM found on any desk top computer at the time. The balance of the addresses between 640k and 1Mb were reserved for system functions. The 8-bit data bus also meant that RAM had to be increased in 8-bit[12] increments.

When Intel introduced the 80286 processor, several things changed. The 286, as it was called, contained 24 address lines and could support 2^{24} or 16,777,216 addresses. This is commonly rounded down to 16Mb. The 286 contained a true 16-bit data bus and was referred to as a 16-bit processor. The architecture of 16-bit machines requires that RAM be increased 16 bits at a time.[13]

---

[10]Beginners All-purpose Symbolic Instruction Code.

[11]A later version, the model B, had 128k installed on the system board that could be expanded to 256k. This became the more common configuration and the model A was dropped from production.

[12]8 chips plus 1 parity chip for each 8-bit bank.

[13]A bank of RAM consisted of 16 bits or chips plus 2 parity chips.

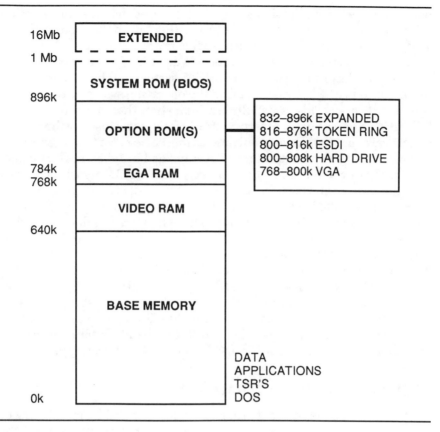

Figure 4.1   Memory address usage map.

The Intel 80386 soon followed. The 386 was a 32-bit processor with 32 address lines and used a 32-bit data bus. It was capable of addressing 4 gigabytes (4,096Mb) of RAM and required memory upgrades in increments of 32 bits. See figure 4.1.

MINIMUM REQUIREMENTS TO BOOT A SYSTEM

A minimum of 128k of RAM is necessary to load MS-DOS.[14] A system may have an undetected memory problem, load DOS normally, and still

---

[14]The majority of systems have the first 128k of RAM soldered to the system or memory board for this reason. One exception is the original IBM XT.

not function with application software. Advanced diagnostics will often not catch this type of memory failure either. If applications will not load, part of the RAM may require replacement.

The majority of desk top computers in use today will attempt to boot from a hard disk or floppy disk. (An IBM system will boot directly into ROM-based BASIC if it does not find the operating system on any of the bootable devices. This is usually an indication that there has been a failure. It is necessary to ascertain if this failure is caused by hardware or software and to take appropriate action.) One exception is specially dedicated network workstations that have no hard disk or floppy disk drives. These work stations boot directly from a ROM which is located on the network interface board.

For a system to boot successfully, three files must be present on the boot disk and in the proper location. These files are the device handler (IO.SYS), the file manager (MSDOS.SYS), and the command processor (COMMAND.COM). The first two files, IO.SYS and MSDOS.SYS, are hidden files. The names of hidden files will not be displayed in the directory of the boot disk. The CHKDSK command will verify that there are two hidden files present on the disk. These three files are copied to a hard disk or floppy disk each time the disk is prepared as a boot disk using the /S switch with the FORMAT command. Before proceeding any further, a discussion of MS-DOS commands is necessary.

WHAT ARE MS-DOS COMMANDS?

An MS-DOS command is a word, sometimes followed by mandatory or optional switches, arguments, or parameters, that is entered into the computer (usually through the keyboard) that initiates an action or function.

There are two types of commands, internal and external. An internal command is a command that is built into the command processor, COMMAND.COM. As long as COMMAND.COM is present in RAM (which it must be except when an application is executing), any of the internal commands can be activated. Internal commands do not display in the directory. An external command is a command that is not part of the command processor. These commands must be accessible (in the current directory or through the PATH command) and be loaded (copied) into RAM before they can execute. Changes in versions of MS-DOS have changed the status of some commands. Commands that were external at one point have become internal, and some infrequently used internal commands have become external. As COMMAND.COM must be present in RAM for MS-DOS to function, its size is a factor. By eliminating unnecessary internal commands, the size of COMMAND.COM has been reduced.

CONVENTIONS OF NAMING FILES

Conventions of naming files are very strict and must be followed. A file name may have up to eight letters, numbers, or special characters, followed by an optional extension of up to three characters. For example: FILENAME.EXT. The following characters can not be used when naming a file: * ? " = / : ;] [, \ . | < > or a space.

Some applications allow a file to be created without following the rules, which results in difficulties at a later time. An example is an application that will accept a space as part of the file name. Since the space is an invalid character, the file can not be manipulated (copied, erased, or backed up) through MS-DOS. It would be impossible to make a complete backup of a hard disk that contains a file with an invalid character, as the backup function would cease when the invalid file is encountered. The application that allowed the creation of a file with an invalid name may not recognize the file once the application is exited.

The optional three-character extension is used to specify the type of file or the application to which the file belongs, or to group files together. Files that can be run, executed, or called upon to function directly from the operating system have extensions of either BAT, COM, or EXE. A file with the extension BAS is a BASIC program and can only be run when BASIC, BASICA, GWBASIC, or a compatible version of a BASIC interpreter is running. Files with an SYS extension are device drivers. They are used to alter the operating system or BIOS routines when called by the CONFIG.SYS file. BAK files are backup files that are automatically created by some applications as a safety function. Files with no extension or an extension other than those mentioned above are either part of a larger program, data files, or a file created by a word processor or editor. An example is dBase, which creates DBF database files.

There are two wild card characters, * and ?, which may not be used in naming files. Wild card characters may be used when working with groups of files, using commands such as COPY, DELETE, BACKUP, RESTORE, DIRECTORY, RENAME, or SORT. This is not a complete list, and caution must be used when working with wild cards, especially in conjunction with the DELETE command. The * (asterisk) is used to replace a group of characters. To copy all files ending in EXT, you would use the command COPY *.EXT. To copy all files starting with FI and ending with EXT, the command is COPY FI*.EXT. All files starting with FI would be COPY FI*.*.

The ? (question mark) is used to replace a single character. The command COPY FILE?.EXT would copy all of the files named FILE(any legal character).EXT, such as FILE1.EXT, FILE2.EXT, FILEA.EXT, and so on.

MS-DOS COMMANDS FROM A TO Z

The following list of commands is from IBM PC-DOS Version 3.3 and Compaq MS-DOS Version 3.31 Revision E. This is not a complete listing of all of the files that are included with these versions. Some version 5.0 commands have been included, which are either frequently used or have substantially changed from earlier versions. These commands and configuration file information will be sufficient to support a customer in most cases when software trouble is suspected.

This information includes some of the switches necessary to implement the commands. A commentary is included with many of the commands to describe their use as a trouble-shooting tool. For complete information, refer to the appropriate MS-DOS or PC-DOS user manual. Usage has been shown in most cases, and appear in UPPER CASE.

COMMAND	INT/EXT	PURPOSE AND USAGE
ANSI .SYS	External	A device driver to control the display attributes and reassign keyboard functions. Device drivers are used to reconfigure the system through the CONFIG.SYS file. (See CONFIG.SYS.)
ASSIGN .COM	External	To transfer requests for a specific drive to another drive. ASSIGN A=B causes the system to transfer all commands for drive A to drive B. This is handy when software must be installed from a floppy disk. For example, if the system has a 5¼" A drive and a 3½" B drive, and the software comes on a 3½" disk and must be installed from the A drive, the ASSIGN command is very useful.
ATTRIB .COM	External	To display, set, or reset the read-only and archive attributes of a file or group of files. ATTRIB +R filename.ext sets the read-only attribute of a file. To set

the attribute to read/write, use the command ATTRIB -R filename.ext. In some installations, the AUTOEXEC.BAT, CONFIG.SYS, or a menu may have been given a read-only attribute. It may be necessary to change this to read/write for maintenance or software installation.

AUTOEXEC.BAT   N/A   This file name is reserved for a file that is executed by the command processor when MS-DOS is loaded through a warm or cold boot. AUTOEXEC.BAT consists of standard MS-DOS commands which execute in the order that they are directed to do so by this file. This file can be executed by typing AUTOEXEC at the DOS prompt and pressing the "Enter" key. (The AUTOEXEC.BAT file is customized and created for each particular machine. This is not part of MS-DOS but appears on almost every system.) It is not necessary to have an AUTOEXEC.BAT file unless a particular application requires one.

A typical AUTOEXEC.BAT file will contain a PATH directive such as PATH C:\DOS (see PATH) or a PROMPT directive such as PROMPT PG (see PROMPT).

For example:

```
@ECHO OFF
PROMPT $P$G
PATH C:\DOS
CD\MYDIR
FILENAME
```

The AUTOEXEC.BAT file takes care of these "housekeeping" chores. The AUTOEXEC.BAT may also have the system boot directly into a menu, into an application, or on to a network.

The AUTOEXEC.BAT file is created and modified with a word processor or text editor such as EDLIN.

Errors in the AUTOEXEC.BAT file can cause systems to lock up or perform in an erratic fashion. Errors in the AUTOEXEC.BAT can be caused by commands being out of order, or typing errors such as striking the "Alt" or "Ctrl" key while modifying the file. Sometimes renaming the file and carefully recreating it can be a solution.

BACKUP .COM	External	To back up files from one drive (usually a hard disk) to another (usually floppy disks). BACKUP C: A:/S will back up all files on drive C from the current directory and all subdirectories below this to drive A. (See RESTORE.)
		Files that are backed up using the BACKUP command are archived. The files MUST be restored using the RESTORE command in order to be accessed. Files can also be backed up from one hard disk to another.
BREAK	Int/Bat	BREAK=ON or BREAK=OFF tells MS-DOS when to check for a ^BREAK or ^C (Control-C). This may appear in the AUTOEXEC.BAT file.
BUFFERS	Config	To set the number of disk buffers allocated for use by an application, as BUFFERS = 20. Some applications will require a specific number of buffers to be allocated. Do not set the number of buffers higher than the largest number required by all of the applications installed on a system, as allocating buffers reduces the amount of RAM available to the system. (See CONFIG.SYS.)

CALL	Int/Bat	A BATCH command used to execute a batch file from within another batch file: CALL WP. If the CALL command is not used, the first batch file will not resume execution when the second batch file completes. If a software application starts from a batch file, and the customer wants the application to be run directly from the AUTOEXEC.BAT, a CALL command must be used in order for the AUTOEXEC to continue execution after the application is exited.
CHDIR or CD	Internal	To change the current directory. CD\DOS changes to the DOS directory. CD\ changes to the root directory.
CHKDSK .COM	External	To provide a disk and memory status report. CHKDSK will provide information for the current drive. CHKDSK A: will provide information for the A: drive.
		This command also corrects errors in the directory and helps repair fragmented files using the /F switch, eg: CHKDSK/F.
		CHKDSK should be used occasionally to maintain the hard disk. Fragmented files slow down the performance of the disk.
		If you use the /F switch and there are lost clusters, the following message will be displayed:
		Convert lost chains to files (Y/N)?
		Responding with "N" will cause the cluster to be ignored.
		A "Y" response will cause CHKDSK to recover the clusters and place them in files named NNNN.CHK (where NNNN is a sequential file starting with 0000). These files will be located in the ROOT directory and can be examined and renamed or erased.

From the prompt, enter the command CHKDSK C:

CHKDSK will report statistics in the following format:

```
42496000  bytes total disk space
   55296  bytes in 2 hidden files
  129024  bytes in 60 directories
11804672  bytes in 712 user files
   30720  bytes unavailable
30476288  bytes available on disk

  655360  bytes total memory
  532656  bytes free
```

The first line indicates the formatted capacity of the hard disk (drive C in this case).

The second line gives the sizes of the hidden files (the two hidden system files and any other hidden files that may be present).

The third line is the number of directories on the drive and the amount of space needed to maintain those directories.

The fourth line shows the number of files and the space required for them.

The fifth line is the size of any bad tracks that have been detected during the FORMAT process and are mapped as unusable. This line does not appear if the disk does not contain any bad tracks.

The sixth line shows the amount of space still available.

Line seven shows the total amount of RAM that is available for MS-DOS. Since MS-DOS only recognizes 640k, this will be the maximum number displayed regardless of how much RAM is installed in the system.

Line eight is the amount of RAM available after the system files, command processor, and any RAM resident programs have been loaded, based upon the 640k maximum.

Obviously, each system will show different information. Use CHKDSK to determine how much free space is available on the hard drive. Some applications create temporary files on the hard drive. If sufficient work space is not available, these applications will be unable to execute properly.

CLS	Internal	To clear the screen—CLS. Usually found in a bat file such as the AUTOEXEC. If screens change too rapidly to read, remove the CLS. Inserting a PAUSE command (see PAUSE) will also aid in reading screens that flash by too fast.
CONFIG .SYS	N/A	This file consists of directives and device drivers. It is used to reconfigure the system or provide configuration information needed for some software or devices to function. (This is not part of MS-DOS but is created and customized for each individual system. It is found on most systems.)

Device drivers are added to the CONFIG.SYS by using the statement DEVICE = FILENAME.SYS. The syntax would be DEVICE = ANSI.SYS. If the ANSI.SYS driver is not in the root directory, it would most likely be found in the DOS directory. In this situation, the statement in the CONFIG.SYS file must be modified to show the location of the driver. The line would then read DEVICE=\DOS\ANSI.SYS. This driver is required by some software applications. If an application appears to be causing a problem, try adding this driver. The driver can always be removed at a later time.

A typical CONFIG.SYS file will contain directives to increase the number of buffers available, the maximum number of open files, and one or more device drivers as required:

For example:

BUFFERS = 30
FILES = 30
DEVICE = ANSI.SYS

The CONFIG.SYS file is created and modified using a word processor or text editor such as EDLIN.

If the CONFIG.SYS file is changed, the system must be either warm booted or cold booted for the changes to take effect. The CONFIG.SYS can not be run from the system prompt. Each directive in the CONFIG.SYS directly affects the usage of RAM. Allocation of too many buffers or open files, as well as utilizing unnecessary device drivers, uses RAM that would otherwise be used for applications and data. Be sure that the CONFIG.SYS contains only those items (and quantities) necessary for proper system operation.

| COPY | Internal | To copy one or more files, or transfer data to a device. COPY A:MYFILE.EXT C:, or COPY A:*.DTA C:, or COPY A:*.* C:. |
| COUNTRY | Config | Sets country-dependent information ough as date and time format, currency |

symbols, and so forth. COUNTRY = 001 is the default for the U.S., and it is not required. In some IBM PS/2 systems, using the directive COUNTRY = 001 in the CONFIG.SYS causes problems with the keyboard.

DATE	Internal	To display or change (temporarily) the system date. Permanent changes in the system date must be made through set-up.
DEBUG .COM	External	The DEBUG utility allows you to perform activities in areas of memory including viewing, assembling, relocating, changing, and executing files or programs. DEBUG also allows you to read or write a disk file.

Partial listing of DEBUG commands:

D   Dump

To display the memory contents of a memory address or range of addresses.

F   Fill

To fill a range of addresses with values in a specified list.

G   Go

To execute a program in RAM or ROM.

L   Load

To load a file, disk sectors, or information from the keyboard into a specified range of addresses.

Q   Quit

To terminate DEBUG.

W   Write

To write to a disk file.

DEBUG is used most frequently by technicians for making software modifications when directed to do so by the publisher's technical support personnel. Another common use is for low-level formatting of some hard disks through a routine included in the ROM on the drive controller. This varies with the brand and type of drive and controller. Additional information on ROM-based formatting is included in the Appendix. Caution is necessary when using DEBUG, as the contents of files can be permanently changed, rendering them useless.

DELete   Internal   To delete a file or group of files. DEL *.DTA will delete all files with a DTA suffix on the current drive. Use CAUTION when DELeting files, especially when using a wild card character.

NOTE: The DELete (or ERASE) command does not actually DELete the file(s). The file or files are marked as deleted and do not display in the directory. The file is not actually affected until the disk space is needed for other files. If a file is accidentally erased, do not write or save anything to the disk. A utility such as Norton Utilities, PC Tools, or SafetyNet will "unerase" the file(s) by removing the deletion marks from the file header. The UNERASE command included with MS-DOS 5.0 can also resurrect an erased file. See UNERASE.

DEVICE   Config   Instructs MS-DOS to load a device driver through the CONFIG.SYS file. Some drivers are included with MS-DOS, while others will be included with peripheral devices. For example, when you purchase a mouse for use with your system, you will also receive a disk with a mouse driver such as MOUSE.SYS to be installed in the CONFIG.SYS file. The driver is added using the command DEVICE = MOUSE.SYS (if the MOUSE.SYS driver is not in the root directory, use DEVICE = \dir\MOUSE.SYS where dir is the directory containing the file MOUSE.SYS). See CONFIG.SYS.

DEVICEHIGH	Config	Version 5.0 and later. Used to load device drivers into upper memory. Consult the MS-DOS 5.0 manual.
DIR	Internal	To list the files in a directory. DIR A: lists all files on drive A. You can use the /P switch to display one page at a time as DIR/P. Wild cards can also be used with this command.
DISKCOPY.COM	External	Copies an entire floppy disk including hidden files. Will format a disk that is being copied to if the disk is not formatted already. Disks must be of the same size and capacity. DISKCOPY A: B:.
DOS	Config	Version 5.0. The DOS = HIGH directive in the CONFIG.SYS allows MS-DOS to load in the high-memory area, freeing conventional memory for applications and other uses.
DRIVER .SYS	Config	A device driver that allows you to add external floppy disk drives to a system. It must be used with the ENHDISK.SYS driver.
DRIVPARM	Config	A configuration directive used in the CONFIG.SYS. This does not appear as a file in the directory. This directive is not valid in some versions of PC-DOS. DRIVPARM is used to specify or modify

the parameters of an existing drive. The directive DRIVPARM= must be followed by the /D: switch and the number of the drive, A being 0 as DRIVPARM = /D:0. Other switches include /C (the drive can detect whether the door is closed); /F: (factor that can be 0 through 9); /H: (heads); /I (electronically compatible 3.5-inch drive); /N (nonremovable device); /S: (number of sectors); and /T: (number of tracks). The drive controller must support the specified parameter in order for the drive to function normally. See the MS-DOS manual for additional information.

ECHO	Int/Bat	To suppress the display of commands, or to allow information to be displayed on the screen, ECHO or ECHO OFF. Placing the @ character before the ECHO command (DOS 3.3 or higher) will suppress the echoing of the ECHO command on the display. Most AUTOEXEC.BAT files begin with @ECHO OFF. It may be useful to turn the ECHO ON to observe the commands as they are executed.
EDLIN .COM	External	The line editor utility. This is a text processor used for constructing and altering text files such as batch files and configuration files. EDLIN must be used in conjunction with a file name, for example, EDLIN FILENAME.EXT.

The following are the most frequently used EDLIN commands:

L   List—Lists the file being edited. Each line is numbered.

D   Delete—To delete one or more lines. To delete line 6, enter 6 D. To delete a range of lines, enter 3,5 D which will delete lines 3 through 5. When a line is deleted, all the lines that follow are renumbered.

I   Insert—To insert a line or group of lines. If the command I is given, a line will be inserted before the present position and all lines will be renumbered. The command 6 I will insert a line prior to line 6.

Q   Quit—To abort the editing session. No changes will be saved.

E   End—To end the session and save all changes. The old file will be named with the BAK extension.

It is important that the technician have a working knowledge of EDLIN. It is often necessary to edit or modify the AUTOEXEC.BAT and CONFIG.SYS files, and use of EDLIN provides the simplest method.

ENHDISK .SYS	Config	If used, this MUST be the FIRST device driver in the CONFIG.SYS file. The ENHDISK.SYS driver makes it possible to access multiple partitions on hard disks that were partitioned using FDISK with versions of MS-DOS prior to Version 3.3. It is not practical to deal with mixing or combining versions of MS-DOS. It will benefit the customer to upgrade to a current version of the operating system.
ERASE	Internal	See DEL or DELETE.
EXPAND	External	MS-DOS 5.0 files are compressed on the distribution disks. EXPAND is used to retrieve files that are included with MS-DOS 5.0 installation or update disks.
FASTOPEN	External	The FASTOPEN utility decreases the amount of time needed to open

		frequently used files. This command may be used in the AUTOEXEC.BAT file. FASTOPEN has no effect with many applications. It is most effective with applications that open and close files frequently such as databases. Including FASTOPEN in the AUTOEXEC may not be the best way to implement this utility as it uses conventional memory.
FDISK .COM	External	To partition the hard disk prior to formatting. FDISK must be run from a floppy disk. FDISK is a menu-driven utility that allows multiple partitions to be created and accessed. Early versions of MS-DOS (and FDISK) provided a maximum partition size of 32Mb. COMPAQ version 3.31 and IBM 4.0 and later versions permitted partitions of 512Mb.
FILES	Config	Specifies the maximum number of file handles that can be open at one time. This is governed by the needs of application software. The greater the number of file handles, the more RAM required, which reduces the amount of free memory for applications and data. The number of file handles should not exceed the maximum number required for any of the applications on the system: FILES = 20.
FOR	Int/Bat	To repeat a command for several variables in a batch file.
FORMAT .COM	External	To prepare a disk for use with MS-DOS. FORMAT A: formats the floppy disk in the A: drive as a data floppy disk.
		FORMAT C:/S will prepare the hard disk C:. The /S switch also tells the FORMAT utility to transfer the three

system files, making C: a system (bootable) disk.

Other switches allow formatting of a low-density floppy disk in a high-density drive.

Attempting to format a hard disk will result in a warning message on the screen. The message will tell you that the hard disk is about to be erased and asks you if you want to continue.

At the conclusion of the FORMAT process, the disk statistics will be displayed, and you will be asked if you want to FORMAT another (floppy disk). For example, the command FORMAT A:/S (using a 5¼" 360K floppy disk) results in the following information:

C>FORMAT A:/S

Insert new floppy disk for drive A:, and strike ENTER when ready

Head: 0 Cylinder 0

The head and cylinder count will continue until the last head and cylinder is reached. Head 1, cylinder 39 is correct for a 360k 5¼" floppy disk.

Head 1 Cylinder 39

Format complete

System transferred

```
362496   bytes total disk space
 80896   bytes used by system
281600   bytes available on disk
```

Format another (Y/N)?

MS-DOS version 5.0 will ask for a volume name, which is optional. 5.0 also includes switches for performing a quick format (/Q) which deletes the previous

FAT (File Allocation Table) but does not scan for bad tracks.[15] Another switch (/U) specifies an unconditional format that destroys all existing data and negates the use of the UNFORMAT command. The size switch (/F:) specifies the capacity of the disk such as 160, 180, 320, 360, and so on. This allows low-density disks to be formatted in high-density drives. The /F: switch supersedes the use of the /T: (tracks) and /N: (sectors) switches used in previous versions of DOS. It is important to note that low-density disks formatted in high-density drives may not perform reliably. See the MS-DOS manual for a complete listing and explanation.

GOTO	Int/Bat	In a batch file, to transfer control to a different label (conditionally skips a line or lines).
HELP	External	Included with MS-DOS 5.0 is an on-line HELP utility. Typing HELP [command] or [command] /? at the system prompt will provide on-line assistance.
IO .SYS	System	This is the device handler. It handles interrupts and services devices. This file is one of the two hidden files necessary for DOS to function. It is transferred using the SYS command as SYS C:.
MSDOS .SYS	System	This is called the file manager, which controls the I/O (Input/Output) operations. It is the second hidden file that is necessary for DOS to work. This file is also transferred using the SYS command.
IF	Int/Bat	To execute conditional commands in a batch file.

---

[15]Quick format can only be used on previously formatted disks.

LABEL .COM	External	To create, change, or delete a volume label. A volume label consists of up to 11 valid characters. LABEL C:MYVOLUME.
LASTDRIVE	Config	Sets the last valid drive letter that MS-DOS will accept. This is required in some versions of DOS where the default is "E" (five drives) and additional hardware (such as a CD-ROM changer with multiple drive addressing) is added: LASTDRIVE = J. A quantity of memory is allocated for each logical drive specified, even if there is no actual drive.
MKDIR or MD	Internal	To create a new subdirectory: MD\MYFILES.
MODE .COM	External	To change some features in the system such as video attributes or redirect communications. Some commands are dependent upon the system combined with specific versions of MS-DOS.

The most common use of this is to direct the system to use the serial port for a printer. This command requires two lines. The first line sets the parameters for the transmission of the data. The second line redirects the data from the parallel port to the serial port. The typical syntax is MODE COM1:9600,N,8,1,P where COM1 is serial port #1, N = no parity, 8 data bits, 1 stop bit, and P means that time-out errors are retried continuously. The next line, MODE LPT1:=COM1, redirects the output from the parallel port (LPT1) to the serial port #1 (COM1).

Another frequently used command is for controlling the clock speed. This command may be in the form of MODE

		= HIGH or MODE = TURBO, depending upon the system. Other attributes that can be controlled via the MODE command are video (40 or 80 column, monochrome or color), video emulation on an LCD,[16] or control of an internal MODEM on some portables.
MORE .COM	External	To display data one screen at a time. This is a "FILTER" command and is used with the "pipe" (|) character: DIR|MORE.
PATH	Internal	Specifies a search path for files and commands not in the current directory: PATH C:\DOS. See AUTOEXEC.BAT.
PAUSE	Int/Bat	To suspend execution of a batch file. The user is prompted to press a key to continue. As a troubleshooting tool, placing one or more PAUSE commands in the AUTOEXEC.BAT will aid in observing the effect of each command as it is executed. Remember to remove the commands after the trouble is cleared.
PROMPT	Internal	To change the MS-DOS command prompt. The normal prompt is (C:>). To change the prompt to display the current directory, enter PROMPT GP. The result is C:\MYDIR> (if the current directory is MYDIR on drive C). There are various other ways of manipulating the prompt.

The following are the most frequently used PROMPT commands:

$ = the parameter delimiter and MUST precede each command.

---

[16]Liquid Crystal Display, as found on many lap top and portable computers.

MS-DOS AND THE TECHNICIAN

t = current time (HH:MM:SS).

d = current date.

p = current directory of the default drive.

g = greater than (>) character.

RECOVER .COM	External	To recover one or more files from a disk with bad sectors. Files that are recovered will be named FILENNNN.REC where NNNN represents a number ranging from 0001 to 9999. It is safest to recover one file at a time and rename the file back to the original name. If you recover a group of files (RECOVER A:*.*), there may be some confusion about which file is which.
		If an application seems to be functioning but can not retrieve a file that it has previously created, try using RECOVER.
REM	Int/Bat	Allows REMarks to be inserted into a batch file. REM This is a batch file.
REN or RENAME	Internal	To rename a file or group of files. Note: Be safe. REName one file at a time. REN MYFILE NEWFILE renames MYFILE to NEWFILE. MYFILE no longer appears in the directory.
RESTORE .COM	External	To RESTORE files that were backed up using the BACKUP command. The /P switch should be used. This switch will prompt you before restoring read- only files (including the hidden system files) or files that were modified. This prevents new files placed on the affected disk from being overwritten by damaged or corrupted files that were backed up. The /S switch is used to RESTORE all files in the subdirectories below the current

directory. It is best to BACKUP and RESTORE files using the same version of DOS.

RMDIR or RD	Internal	To remove a directory. Before removing a directory, it must be empty (all files and any subdirectories within the directory must be erased). You can not remove the directory in which you are working, even if it doesn't contain any files.
SETVER .EXE	External	Some applications require a specific version of DOS or they will not run under 5.0. SETVER allows software to think that the operating system is the required version.
SORT .EXE	External	To SORT information, such as files in a directory. SORT is a filter command DIR|SORT.
SYS .COM	External	Transfers the two hidden system files IO.SYS and MSDOS.SYS to the specified disk. The command SYS C: does NOT transfer the command interpreter (COMMAND.COM).
TIME	Internal	To display or temporarily set the time.
TREE .COM	External	Displays the structure of the drive, including all levels of subdirectories. TREE. This will aid in understanding the structure of a customer's hard disk. It also helps in finding applications and nested directories. Be sure that the structure agrees with the PATH statement in the AUTOEXEC.BAT file.
TYPE	Internal	To display the contents of a text file: TYPE A:MYFILE.TXT. Using the TYPE command with a nontext file will produce strange sounds and peculiar characters on the display. Using the pipe and MORE displays one screen at a time.

Many applications contain a filename.TXT or READ.ME file or something similar. These files have corrections or additions to the documentation and should be read.

UNDELETE	External	An MS-DOS 5.0 utility, the UNDELETE can restore a file or group of files that was removed using the DEL or ERASE command under certain circumstances. Refer to the MS-DOS manual for a full explanation.
UNFORMAT	External	Another version 5.0 utility, UNFORMAT can restore a disk that was erased by the FORMAT command or restructured by the RECOVER command under certain circumstances. Refer to the MS-DOS manual. There is no guarantee that UNDELETE or UNFORMAT will function in all situations. Backups must be made before using these utilities.
VDISK .SYS	Config	Allows a portion of the computer's memory to be used as a disk drive: DEVICE = VDISK.SYS. This reduces the memory that is available to applications and data.
VER	Internal	To display the MS-DOS version. Helpful if an application must run under a particular version of MS-DOS.
VERIFY	Internal	VERIFY ON or the /V switch after the COPY or DISKCOPY command verifies that the files written to a disk during a copy operation are correct and complete. The tradeoff is that the copy procedure is slower.
XCOPY .EXE	External	Copies files or directories, or can create a directory if necessary: XCOPY A: C:. XCOPY does not copy hidden files.

INSTALLING MS-DOS

In 1981, a hard disk was an expensive device, and the majority of systems contained only floppy disk drives. As the use of microcomputers increased and technological advances led to the lowering of costs (and prices), more systems were sold with hard disks. Currently, almost every system sold contains a hard disk. This discussion of MS-DOS installation will be limited to hard disks. It is assumed that the installation will be performed on a hard disk drive that is operating normally. It is also expected that a low level or physical format has been performed.

Installation requires the drive to be partitioned using the FDISK utility. Partitions are then formatted for MS-DOS. There is a detailed discussion of partitioning and formatting of drives in Chapter 9, Peripherals and Upgrades.

MS-DOS ERROR MESSAGES

MS-DOS error messages can be generated by missing or corrupted files, mixing DOS versions, hardware failure, user error, or software bugs. The error messages may be generated from the system level or from within an application program. Listed below are the most common MS-DOS error messages and suggestions for relieving the problems. This is not a complete listing, and the MS-DOS manual should be consulted when an error message appears on the display. The error messages are listed in UPPER CASE. The required action is then listed in normal text format.

ACCESS DENIED

Attempt to write to a read-only or write-protected file or disk.

ATTEMPTED WRITE-PROTECT VIOLATION

Attempted to format a write-protected floppy disk.

BAD COMMAND OR FILE NAME

Attempt to execute a command, where the command is not in the current directory, not in the root directory, can not be located through the path command, or is not a valid command.

BAD OR MISSING COMMAND INTERPRETER

COMMAND.COM is not in the root directory, or the file is corrupted.

BAD OR MISSING (DEVICE DRIVER NAME)

The device driver called for in the CONFIG.SYS file is not in the root directory or the path stated in the CONFIG.SYS file, or it is corrupted.

CANNOT DELETE EXTENDED DOS PARTITION WHILE LOGICAL DRIVES EXIST

You must delete all logical drives through FDISK before you delete the extended DOS partition.

CANNOT FIND SYSTEM FILES

When FORMAT is used with the /S switch, it must be executed from a drive that has IO.SYS and MSDOS.SYS in the root directory.

CANNOT LOAD COMMAND, SYSTEM HALTED

The COMMAND.COM file can not be located. MS-DOS may have to be reinstalled.

CANNOT START COMMAND, EXITING

Available memory is too small. May have to increase the FILES= in the CONFIG.SYS.

CONFIGURATION TOO LARGE FOR MEMORY

Adjust the BUFFERS= statement in the CONFIG.SYS file.

DATA ERROR READING <DEVICE>

ABORT, RETRY, IGNORE?

Retry the operation. If failure is repeated, test the device using the diagnostics. Could be a device failure, or defective media, or media not seated correctly (if removable).

DATA ERROR WRITING <DEVICE>

ABORT, RETRY, IGNORE?

See above.

DISK BOOT FAILURE

You tried to boot with a non-DOS disk, the system files have been corrupted, or there is a hardware failure.

DISK ERROR READING/WRITING FAT/DIRECTORY

FDISK attempted unsuccessfully to update the File Allocation Table (FAT). Retry the operation. A second failure indicates that the media must be reformatted or the media is bad or the drive is not functioning properly.

DISK FULL. EDITS LOST

The disk does not have enough space to save the file that is being edited.

Note: When an existing file is saved, the original file is not erased until the new file is written to the disk. This means that the disk must contain sufficient "work" space.

DISK UNSUITABLE FOR SYSTEM DISK

The area required for system files is damaged. Try reformatting. If this is a hard disk, it may need a low-level format or need to be replaced. If it is a floppy disk, it can be used for data but not as a system disk.

Floppy disk ERROR
REPLACE AND STRIKE ANY KEY WHEN READY

You have either a defective floppy disk or a drive failure.

DIVIDE OVERFLOW

Caused by an internal logic error, an error in the application software, or mixed versions of MS-DOS.

DRIVE LETTER MUST BE SPECIFIED

A command such as FORMAT was specified without a drive letter (such as FORMAT A:).

DRIVE NOT READY

Make sure that a floppy disk is inserted and that the drive door is closed.

DRIVE TYPES OR Floppy disk TYPES NOT COMPATIBLE
COPY PROCESS ENDED

Tried to use DISKCOPY (or DISKCOMP) with floppy disks of different capacities or densities.

DUPLICATE FILENAME OR FILE NOT FOUND

The file name entered in the RENAME command already exists, or it could not be found.

ERROR—INCORRECT DOS VERSION

You are using mixed versions of MS-DOS, or there are mixed versions or utilities from different versions on your disk.

ERROR LOADING OPERATING SYSTEM FROM HARD DISK DRIVE. INSERT DOS Floppy disk IN DRIVE A:

PRESS ANY KEY WHEN READY

The operating system can not be loaded from the hard disk or the partition is not active. Check the partition. It may be necessary to reformat the hard disk.

ERROR OPENING LOGFILE

MS-DOS can not open the BACKUP log file. Check the command syntax. There may be a problem with the floppy disk drive or the media.

ERROR READING HARD DISK

FDISK can not read the hard disk. A low-level format may be required. There may be a defective hard disk, adapter board, or cables.

ERROR READING PARTITION TABLE

Drive may have to be repartitioned.

ERRORS FOUND, F PARAMETER NOT SPECIFIED.

CORRECTIONS WILL NOT BE WRITTEN TO DISK.

CHKDSK was executed without the /F switch and has detected some errors. Run CHKDSK/F.

FILE ALLOCATION TABLE BAD DRIVE X (X = DRIVE SPECIFIER)

The disk may be incorrectly formatted, unformatted, or damaged. Try the operation again. Disk may have to be reformatted.

FILE CANNOT BE COPIED ONTO ITSELF

Target file name and drive is the same as the source. Check the syntax. Specify a different drive or file name.

FILE CREATION ERROR

The directory may be full or the drive or media is defective.

FILE NOT FOUND

No files were found that match the file specification. Check the file names and the path.

FORMAT FAILURE

There was an error during the FORMAT procedure. Check that the media is seated properly. May be caused by defective media or drive.

INCOMPATIBLE SYSTEM SIZE

The system size on the source drive is larger than the space available on the target drive. You can not transfer the system using the SYS command. Reformatting with the /S switch is necessary.

INCORRECT DOS VERSION

There are mixed versions of MS-DOS present. It is best to clean the drive and reinstall DOS.

INSUFFICIENT MEMORY

A command can not be executed due to insufficient memory. Free memory by removing memory resident programs or decreasing the BUFFERS = in the CONFIG.SYS file.

INSUFFICIENT MEMORY FOR SYSTEM TRANSFER

There is not enough memory to transfer the system files during a FORMAT/S operation. Free memory by executing this command from the system prompt, removing memory resident programs, or decreasing the BUFFERS = statement in the CONFIG.SYS file.

INVALID BAUD RATE SPECIFIED

In the MODE command, a baud rate was specified that is either incorrect or not supported.

INVALID COMMAND.COM

The version of COMMAND.COM does not match the version of the system files. This is another problem associated with mixing DOS versions.

INVALID DIRECTORY

An invalid directory or path was specified.

INVALID DRIVE IN SEARCH PATH

An incorrect drive specifier was entered in the PATH command.

INVALID DRIVE SPECIFICATION

An incorrect drive specifier was entered in a command or parameter.

INVALID DRIVE SPECIFICATION
SOURCE AND TARGET DRIVES ARE THE SAME

Attempt to BACKUP or RESTORE to the same drive.

INVALID DRIVE SPECIFICATION
SPECIFIED DRIVE DOES NOT EXIST OR IS NON-REMOVABLE

Attempt to DISKCOPY or DISKCOMP to an invalid drive specifier or a hard disk.

INVALID FILENAME OR FILE NOT FOUND

Attempt to RENAME a file that does not exist.

INVALID MEDIA OR TRACK 0 BAD—DISK UNUSABLE

Bad tracks were detected on the media in the area where the system must reside, or the drive density is not compatible with the media. Low-density media can be formatted in a high-density drive if the correct FORMAT syntax is used. If this error occurs on a hard disk, try to perform a low-level format. The disk may be unusable.

INVALID NUMBER OF PARAMETERS

Check the syntax of the command that you are trying to execute.

INVALID PARAMETER

An nonexistent parameter or switch was entered in a command.

INVALID PATH

An incorrect PATH (DIRectory) was entered.

INVALID PATH, NOT DIRECTORY, OR DIRECTORY NOT EMPTY

Attempt to remove a directory that still contains files, or the path specified is not correct, or you are logged into the directory that you are trying to remove.

INVALID PATH OR FILENAME

A nonexistent path name or file specification was entered.

INVALID SYNTAX

Incorrect syntax entered or there was a typing mistake.

INVALID SYNTAX ON XXXXXXXX.SYS CODE PAGE DRIVER

Improper syntax used in CONFIG.SYS file with the DEVICE command, where XXXXXXXX is the DEVICE that was to be loaded.

INVALID VOLUME ID

Attempt to FORMAT a disk with a VOLUME label, where the VOLUME label entered was incorrect.

LABEL NOT FOUND

Incorrect GOTO command in a BATCH file.

MEMORY ALLOCATION ERROR

The memory tracking area of MS-DOS has been lost or corrupted. Reload MS-DOS.

NO FREE FILE HANDLES

Increase the FILES = command in the CONFIG.SYS file.

NO PAPER ERROR WRITING <DEVICE>
ABORT, RETRY, IGNORE?

The printer is out of paper. Load paper and RETRY.

NO PATH

The PATH command can not find a path, or there is no PATH command.

NO ROOM FOR SYSTEM ON DESTINATION DISK

There is no room for the system files on the target floppy disk. You must use the FORMAT/S command, rather than the SYS command to transfer the files. This usually happens when a floppy disk is formatted as a data floppy disk (no /S switch), and then an attempt is made to transfer the system using the SYS command.

NO SYSTEM ON THE DEFAULT DRIVE

The system was not transferred correctly, or the system files have been corrupted.

NON-DOS DISK ERROR READING <DEVICE>

ABORT, RETRY, IGNORE?

The FAT contains invalid data, or the drive is not functioning properly. Try CHKDSK. If that fails, the disk must be reformatted.

NON-DOS DISK ERROR WRITING <DEVICE>

ABORT, RETRY, IGNORE?

See above.

NON-SYSTEM DISK OR DISK ERROR

REPLACE AND STRIKE ANY KEY WHEN READY

Attempt to boot from a floppy disk or hard disk that does not contain the system files in the proper place. Could be a drive error. Try booting with a known good MS-DOS system disk.

PARTITION SIZE CANNOT BE 0

A partition size of 0 was specified during the FDISK procedure.

PATH NOT FOUND

Check the command syntax.

PROGRAM TOO BIG TO FIT IN MEMORY

Free some memory by removing memory resident programs or decreasing the BUFFERS = in the CONFIG.SYS file.

READ FAULT ERROR READING <DEVICE>

ABORT, RETRY, IGNORE?

Verify that the device is connected and functioning properly.

REQUESTED LOGICAL DRIVE SIZE EXCEEDS THE MAXIMUM AVAILABLE SPACE

You tried to create a logical drive that is larger than the space available.

REQUESTED PARTITION SIZE EXCEEDS THE MAXIMUM AVAILABLE SPACE

See above.

RESTORE FILE SEQUENCE ERROR

A floppy disk is in the wrong order during the RESTORE function.

SECTOR NOT FOUND ERROR READING (OR WRITING) <DEVICE>

ABORT, RETRY, IGNORE?

The requested disk sector could not be found. This could be the result of a hardware failure or a media defect.

SEEK ERROR READING (OR WRITING) <DEVICE>

ABORT, RETRY, IGNORE?

The specified disk cylinder could not be located. This could be the result of a hardware failure or defective media.

SOURCE Floppy disk BAD OR INCOMPATIBLE

COPY PROCESS ENDED

Drive or media is defective, or floppy disk is not compatible with the drive (different densities).

SOURCE DOES NOT CONTAIN BACKUP FILES

Attempt to RESTORE from a disk where the backup files can not be found, are corrupted, or are in the wrong directory.

SYNTAX ERROR

An error in a command, specification, or parameter has been made.

TARGET CANNOT BE USED FOR BACKUP

The target disk for a backup is not properly formatted, or protected files exist.

TARGET floppy disk BAD OR INCOMPATIBLE

COPY PROCESS ENDED

The target floppy disk is either damaged or not compatible with the drive.

TARGET floppy disk IS WRITE PROTECTED

PRESS ANY KEY WHEN READY

The floppy disk is write protected, or the drive is defective.

TARGET floppy disk MAY BE UNUSABLE

There was an error during the DISKCOPY procedure. This may result from defective media or a drive problem.

TARGET IS FULL

System is unable to RESTORE all files due to lack of space on the target disk.

THE LAST FILE WAS NOT RESTORED

A file could not be restored due to an error condition.

UNABLE TO WRITE BOOT RECORD

The boot record could not be written during a FORMAT operation due to a problem with track 0. This could be caused by the media or the drive.

UNEXPECTED DOS ERROR

This is an error code for an unexpected error.

UNRECOGNIZED COMMAND IN CONFIG.SYS

Check the syntax for CONFIG.SYS and the command that is not correct or invalid.

UNRECOVERABLE READ ERROR ON DRIVE d: SIDE s, TRACK t

Data could not be read from the source floppy disk during a DISKCOPY, after four attempts. Check the floppy disk and retry the function.

UNRECOVERABLE WRITE ERROR ON DRIVE d: SIDE s, TRACK t

Target disk could not be written to during DISKCOPY after four attempts. The copy may be defective or incomplete. Reformat the floppy disk. The media may be defective.

WARNING! NO FILES WERE FOUND TO BACKUP (OR RESTORE)

The source disk did not contain any files that matched the specification, or there was a syntax error in the command. Verify that the correct syntax and path name are being used.

OTHER OPERATING SYSTEMS

UNIX/XENIX

UNIX is an operating system developed by AT&T to run on mainframe computers. XENIX, a derivative of AT&T UNIX, is the operating system designed and written for a microcomputer environment. XENIX was designed to function as a multi-user operating system or a single-user, multi-tasking operating system. Most applications running under XENIX are written in the C programming language. Most XENIX software runs under a menu shell. The actual operating system level is not accessed by the user. In other words, the users do not have to know any of the XENIX commands, as all of the normal functions are presented to them on a menu. When troubleshooting a XENIX system, determine if the system is multi-user or not. If the system is multi-user, first ascertain if the problem is cabling. Workstations may be either microcomputers or dumb terminals. If the cabling is not defective, verify that the workstations are set up, configured, and functioning correctly. If the hardware is behaving normally, get help from the resident software people.

MS-OS/2

MS-OS/2 (or OS/2) is a single-user, multi-tasking operating system for microcomputers, designed to run on a 286 or higher system. MS-OS/2 features multi-tasking (the ability for two or more applications to run at the same time), task switching (the customer can switch between any of the applications at any time), increased memory support (OS/2 can support up to 16Mb of RAM), virtual memory (by using space on the hard disk as an extension of RAM, OS/2 can use more memory than is actually available), protected mode operation (application programs run in a protected area of RAM, allowing two or more applications to execute without them having to share the same RAM area and conflict with each other), and interprocess communication (allows applications to exchange data while operating concurrently). Applications written by different software companies can share data under MS-OS/2 as long as a standard communication format and method is retained.

The original OS/2 supported a maximum hard disk partition of 32Mb. Version 1.1 and later support partitions of up to 2 gigabytes (a gigabyte is 1,000 megabytes).

Software written to run under the MS-DOS operating system can run in an area of OS/2 called the Compatibility Box, but available DOS memory is reduced from 640K to about 510K. MS-DOS applications can reside on the same drive as OS/2. Data files generated under DOS can be used with OS/2, provided that an OS/2 version of the application software is used.

OS/2 hardware requirements include a 286 processor or greater, 1.5Mb RAM minimum (up to 16Mb), 20Mb hard disk (up to 2Gb supported in version 1.2), and a mouse (recommended). To permit applications to run concurrently, the RAM must be increased. 1Mb per application is the minimum suggested upgrade.

MS-OS/2 was introduced in 1988 as an operating system that would increase productivity and enhance the capability of 286- and 386-based microcomputers. Customers required more memory and faster processing of applications. They wanted to be able to use their machines instead of sitting idly while the computer was processing data internally.

The multi-tasking feature of OS/2 enables processing of one application to continue while a customer is using a different application. The hardware was available with the introduction of 286-based machines, but there was a need for a "DOS-like" operating system. People using microcomputers with the MS-DOS operating system had become familiar with the command language and structure. Microsoft Corp., who had written the MS-DOS operating system, also wrote MS-OS/2. The command structure and syntax are similar, although OS/2 has additional commands. OS/2 also has (in version 1.2 and later), a "Presentation Manager," which is a graphical interface using icons on the screen. Commands can be entered using the presentation manager with pull down menus and a mouse. The idea is that users do not have to remember commands or program names. Everything is available on the menus for easy selection. (Apple provided this feature years before with the introduction of their Macintosh computer).

Though OS/2 has undergone several refinements and upgrades, it still has not become a popular operating system. The reasons are many. OS/2 will not function on an 8086 (or 8088) system; it needs an 80286 system or greater. This is because of the 1Mb RAM addressability limitation of the 8086 (and 8088). There are many 8086 systems currently in use with no reason to upgrade to a 286 just to use OS/2. Applications written for the MS-DOS operating system will not function under OS/2 unless they are run in the compatibility box. The compatibility box feature of OS/2 reduces available RAM from 640K to 512K, so some applications may not function. There is very little application software written specifically to run under the OS/2 environment. It is pointless for software developers to write applications for an operating system that is not widely used. It is also difficult to market an operating system for which there are few applications available.

Most computer users would not upgrade to a different operating system and new software unless they required a specific application that would not run on their current platform. People or businesses purchasing systems for the first time may purchase OS/2 over DOS if required applications were immediately available, as the enhanced features of OS/2 may be an advantage in the future.

OS/2 must be purchased from the hardware manufacturer. The OS/2 operating system is configured to work with specific hardware through a long and involved CONFIG.SYS file, using drivers for practically everything inside the computer.

As of this writing, Microsoft has abandoned further development of OS/2 to concentrate on Windows. IBM has stated that they would continue with OS/2 and support current and future users of this operating system. Several other vendors (Compaq among them) have previously supplied OS/2 and are currently providing support.

5

Software Problems

IS IT THE HARDWARE OR THE SOFTWARE?

If a system properly completes POST, a hardware problem can generally be ruled out. There are occasions when a RAM problem will not be detected by POST, but an application will freeze the system. This is rare, but it does happen. Video problems such as a dead display will not be detected by POST, even though it is obviously a hardware failure. Some disk problems can not be detected by POST, either, and may not arise until a read or write function is required. If the hardware is functioning properly, the operating system, application software, and the customer remain.

The effects of operating system problems on applications are also unusual, but they do occur. If a problem is suspected, the safest thing to do is regenerate the operating system using the SYS command.[17] This will not harm anything, but it could solve many a problem. Remember that the operating system consists of files residing on a hard disk or floppy disk, and it can be corrupted just like any other disk file.

Software problems can be the result of corrupted files, improper installation, or misuse. If files are corrupted or damaged, they can be recopied from the original distribution disks. Corrupted files may be the result of bad sectors on the hard disk (or floppy disk). It is advisable

---

[17]Be sure to use the same version of the operating system.

57

to back up the files, format the drive, restore the backed up information, and then recopy the files that were damaged from the distribution floppy disk.[18] Data files, the files that are created through application software, can become corrupted too. These files should be backed up on a daily basis. If the application software must be reinstalled, the data files may need restoring also.

If there are no backups available and the customer must attempt to salvage his or her data from the corrupted files, try examining the files with a text editor or word processor. Even if the files are readable with the word processor, there may be some problems. Do not permit the word processor to embed any formatting commands or control codes in the file. Most word processors have a nondocument or text-only (also called ASCII or DOS text file) feature for this type of work. Be careful of "End of File" markers. Do not insert any control codes or characters, as this marker must be at the end of the file. Do not delete the EOF marker or the application will not know where the file ends.

Even though the file can be repaired, indexes may have to be regenerated or the file may have to be reindexed. This must be done through the application software. It is a good idea to reindex the file as a safety precaution, even if the file appears to be correct. Some applications and earlier versions of DOS limited the size of files to 8Mb. Other versions limit the file size to 32Mb. Check the file size.

Correct software installation can then be verified. Some installations are a simple matter of copying the distribution floppy disks, while others require knowledge of the hardware. It is not unusual for the installation to ask for information about the printer, video adapter, display, computer, memory, coprocessor, and other peripherals and devices. Some applications present a menu, and the installer must indicate the hardware configuration based upon the available selections. Improper installation can freeze the system. If the exact components are not listed, it may be necessary to eliminate the selections on a trial and error basis until the correct combination is found. When the installation is complete, the software must be tested to see if it functions with the hardware. Test as many functions of the software as possible, including drawing graphs on the screen, printing graphics, and printing any forms that incorporate compressed or expanded characters. Certain combinations of hardware and software will never work! For ex-

---

[18]Hard disks should be maintained in this manner annually. Formatting will remove any bad sectors that have developed since the last time that the disk was formatted.

ample, it is not possible to view graphics on a system using the IBM "Monochrome/Parallel" video adapter. The adapter is not capable of this function.

Following the installation, it is necessary for the customer to test the software and attempt to duplicate the failure. They must try and duplicate the problem as it was previously encountered. The application should function properly if the problem was solved. If a problem persists, it is absolutely necessary to make sure that the software does not contain any bugs. If the software is an off-the-shelf product, it is most likely bug free. "Vertical" market applications that are not mass-merchandised could have problems with the application itself or the installation instructions or both. If the technician has verified the integrity of the hardware and the operating system, completed the installation according to the instructions, and is confident that the customer is not causing the problem, a call to the software publisher is the next step.

The publisher's tech support people will ask questions regarding the hardware environment, installation procedure, AUTOEXEC.BAT, CONFIG.SYS, and, possibly, about other applications that are installed, including TSRs.[19] It is wise to have this information handy and a telephone near the computer. It may be necessary to modify the CONFIG.SYS or the AUTOEXEC.BAT (or both). It may even be necessary to modify the application, using DEBUG.

Before formatting the drive or erasing any files, be sure that none of the applications have to be uninstalled. Also verify that the distribution software can be installed again. Some software allows a limited number of installations. In an effort to reduce unauthorized copies of their software, some publishers used unique methods, such as a limited number of installs, or having to uninstall the software in order to reinstall it. If correct procedures are not used, the software may become unusable. Backing up to floppy disks or tape does not get around the publisher's safeguards.

Some software requires the user to perform a customized installation. Before destroying the already installed version, find out which features are active. The user may be familiar with the customized version and will not be able to function if the new installation is different. *IF ALL ELSE FAILS. . .READ THE MANUAL!*

---

[19]Terminate and Stay Ready. Applications or utilities that are loaded into RAM, usually through the AUTOEXEC.BAT, and remain there to be used as needed and then sent back to the "ready" state. Examples are calculators, alarm clocks, telephone number lists, and so on.

APPLICATION SOFTWARE ERROR MESSAGES

Application software will generate its own unique error messages. If an error message appears on the screen, make a note of it or print it out by using the "Print Screen" key. Compare the error message on the screen with the DOS manual to determine if the error is generated by the operating system or the application. If the error message is generated by DOS, the manual will have an explanation and the appropriate action to be taken. If the error message is generated by the application, consult the appropriate user manual.

If the error message does not appear in either the DOS manual or the documentation for the application, there are several other possibilities. The MS-DOS manual contains all of the error messages generated by DOS. The error message may have been generated by some other software such as a RAM resident program (TSR). Remove the RAM resident application and try to duplicate the error. It is possible that the application itself has generated an error message that is either not documented or has been documented in a later version of the software or manual. A call to the publisher is probably necessary at this time.

TROUBLESHOOTING SOFTWARE PROBLEMS

The technician has been called to service a system that is "not working," and she is convinced (after testing) that the hardware is functioning normally. There must be some dialogue with the customer to help restore the system to its prior status. Ask the customer which applications he or she uses. If there are two or more applications being used, the isolation of the problem becomes simpler. Are there problems with one application or several applications? Problems with a single application lead right back to that application or to the operating system. Problems with multiple applications point to the operating system, a shared peripheral, or perhaps back to the hardware.

Verify that the correct version of the operating system is installed, and remove any duplicated operating system files on the hard disk (especially the command interpreter, COMMAND.COM). Regenerate the operating system by booting with a floppy disk containing the correct DOS version and issue the command SYS C:. Copy a fresh COMMAND.COM from the floppy disk to the root directory of the C drive. Remember, the operating system files, including the hidden files, can be corrupted just the same as any other file. Test the software again. Test the software each time a change is made. Document the changes so they can be reversed if a problem appears.

Confirm that the CONFIG.SYS file is correct, and that it does not generate any errors. With some of the newer (and faster) systems, error messages may fly by so quickly that they are missed or can not be read. Do the same with the AUTOEXEC.BAT file. These may become corrupted, too. Any file residing on a hard disk or floppy disk may become damaged or corrupted at any time. Some well-meaning person may have "modified" the AUTOEXEC.BAT or CONFIG.SYS with disastrous results. The AUTOEXEC.BAT file can load a TSR utility that is reacting unfavorably with an application. Many TSR's will specify exactly how or where in the AUTOEXEC.BAT file they are supposed to be loaded. The documentation that comes with the software will also indicate the order in which to load the application if other TSRs are being loaded. TSRs occupy RAM even when they are not being used. If a TSR is removed improperly, there will be an area of RAM (where the TSR was located) between the operating system and the current application that becomes a hole. This situation must be avoided because of problems that can emerge.

It may be necessary to change the AUTOEXEC.BAT file for testing purposes. Remember to return the file to its original condition after solving the problem (unless this was the cause of the trouble). If the AUTOEXEC.BAT file must be used, do not load any TSR's until after all testing has been performed and the problem has been located and eliminated. If the problem does not reappear, perhaps the TSR is responsible. Change the AUTOEXEC.BAT to load the TSR(s), one at a time if there are several of them, and observe any differences that occur. Ask the customer to duplicate their normal routine, including the use of the TSR.

Rename the CONFIG.SYS and AUTOEXEC.BAT files. A good name is AUTOEXEC.nnn and CONFIG.nnn, where nnn are your initials. Reboot the system and observe the results. Remember that the CONFIG.SYS file is loaded on a warm or cold boot, so the system must be rebooted (using Ctrl-Alt-Del) each time this file is changed. The AUTOEXEC.BAT file is executed upon booting, but it can be called from the keyboard by simply typing AUTOEXEC and pressing Enter at the system prompt. It is safest to reboot the system each time a change is made. Remember to make notes of the changes. Generate a new CONFIG.SYS or AUTOEXEC.BAT instead of using the nnn files if it is suspected that one of these files may be contributing to the problem. Use the EDLIN text editor. The order of the directives in the CONFIG.SYS is often important. Consult the DOS manual to verify the order and the syntax. The order of the commands in the AUTOEXEC.BAT can affect the functioning of the system. For instance, a command that is not in the

ROOT directory will generate an error message if it is called before the PATH command has executed or if the PATH does not include the directory where the command resides.

When the integrity of the operating system, the CONFIG.SYS and the AUTOEXEC.BAT files, has been verified, it is time to concentrate on the application itself. Applications consist of one or more files (or modules or programs) that work together. There will be either a BAT or EXE or COM file that must be called from the system level to begin the application. Some installation routines place the application in its own subdirectory and create a BAT file in the Root directory.

When the application is running, files (or subprograms) will call other files in order for the program to function correctly. The number of different modules necessary for an application to work depends on how the programs were written. If any of the necessary files are missing, corrupted, or in a place other than where they should be, the application will eventually crash. The missing or corrupted file may not be called until a specific function of the application is required. For example, some financial applications require close-out routines at the end of the month, quarter, and year. Defective or missing modules used only at the end of a quarter would allow the application to function for about three months before a problem was discovered.

Before attempting to diagnose the problem, ask the customer if there have been any changes made to the system. Has the printer, monitor, or any other internal or external hardware been serviced, replaced, added, or exchanged? Has any software been added or removed from the system? If the answer to any of these questions is affirmative, ask when the changes were made in relation to the discovery of the problem.

It is important to have each application reside in its own directory on the hard disk. An application may use subdirectories to store tutorials, data, or other files, but each main application should be in a directory one level below the root directory. Before erasing any files, verify that these files can be replaced or that they are unnecessary.[20] If the application performs some or most of the functions correctly but has problems with screen or video functions or printing, verify that the drivers have been correctly installed. If necessary, reinstall the software. Some application packages will allow a partial installation, such as changing the printer or video driver, while others require a complete installation.

---

[20]Some applications create BAK (backup) files that must be removed manually.

Confirm the type of video monitor and video controller that are installed. If the software does not have a driver for the specific controller that is being used, either try all of the combinations or call the publisher of the software for their suggestions. Sometimes the publisher will recommend an outside vendor that can supply the correct driver for the video controller. Some functions are just not possible, for example, displaying graphics with the IBM "Monochrome/Parallel adapter." This video adapter has no graphics capability whatsoever.

A similar situation exists for printers. The first step is to verify that the printer is configured properly. Do not assume that the internal switches or jumpers on the printer are set correctly. Some applications are not fussy about the way that a printer is set up, while others will have specific requirements. A deviation from these conditions can cause problems with printed output. Confirm that the software is not attempting to print to a nonexistent device, such as a serial printer, when a parallel printer is installed. Another problem that arises is PORT assignments. If there is only one parallel (or serial) port on the system, do not call it LPT2 (or COM2) instead of LPT1 (COM1 for serial). There must be a functioning LPT1 (or COM1) before there can be a secondary port. Once the printer is set up correctly, verify the software installation. Again, special drivers may be required. Some printers are said to emulate[21] other printers. The compatibility may not be 100%. If the printer is not included in the application as a compatible printer, call the software publisher. The publisher may require that the customer purchase a driver or, possibly, an upgrade of the complete application.

Do not expect that all of the components in a system will work together just because they were sold as a package. If problems still exist, try reinstalling the complete application. Make sure that the number of installations is not limited. It may be necessary to uninstall the application prior to the reinstallation. Above all, be sure that everything that is required to perform the installation is present and available. Before doing a reinstall, check the installed version to find out how it was installed originally. For example, the installation may ask which colors are wanted for certain screens, text, or background. The original installation may have been set up for the preferences of the customer. It is important to duplicate these characteristics. If the screen looks different, the customer may not understand why, which could lead to more

---

[21]Printer emulation refers to responding to a set of control codes These codes are used to turn features, such as compressed or expanded print, on and off. Many printers emulate the Epson.

problems. When a hard disk is initialized, bad sectors are written to a file so that they cannot be used. If any sectors are marginal and not detected, they may be used by the software. Marginal sectors are bound to deteriorate with time, to the point where they will cause problems. It is good practice to reinitialize the hard disk every 6 to 12 months in order to detect marginal sectors and prevent software difficulties. If the application software needs to be reinstalled, perform a backup of the hard disk, a low-level format, and reinstall the operating system. Restore the backed up files, and then reinstall the application from the original distribution floppy disks. If the problem persists, then there is either a problem in the original distribution floppy disks furnished by the publisher, the installation is faulty, or there may be a user error that is not detected. Remember to test the software each time that a change is made!

Test the software by loading the application from the operating system. Create a document or file. Save the file and exit to the operating system. Load the application again and recall the file. Print the file. Save the file and exit again. If these functions can be performed without any mishaps, then the system is operational. The next step is to have the customer perform the same group of functions. If the customer is successful, then try to duplicate the previous error(s).

It is possible that a document or data file has become corrupted. In this case, if it is a short file, it must be recreated. If it is a long file, contact the software publisher to see if they have a way to correct the problem.[22] As with applications, data files can become corrupted or reside on an area of the hard disk that has deteriorated. There is the possibility that the distribution floppy disks are defective, or that a bug exists in the actual code of the application that has not been discovered. These occurrences are few and infrequent. If these guidelines have been followed and there is still a problem, a combination of circumstances that produced an incompatibility may be the reason. The publisher may have to be contacted for assistance.

One thing that must not be overlooked is human error. Frequently, the customer is performing a mechanical function. In other words, they are operating the equipment without understanding exactly what they are doing. As long as everything happens as it is expected to happen, the situation is considered to be normal. If something happens that the

---

[22]Some publishers will provide utility software that can attempt to recreate a damaged file. Other publishers will ask that a copy of the damaged file be sent to them for repair. There may or may not be a charge associated with the service, and there are no guarantees of success.

customer does not expect or understand, then a service call is placed. A technician (or anybody for that matter) is not expected to have knowledge of every piece of application software that is currently available. It is important to have the basic concepts of how different types of software function. Technicians should have a working knowledge of a word processor, database management system, and spread sheet, as well as MS-DOS, as a bare minimum.

In word processing, for example, once the fundamentals are known there should be no problems using any similar application. The menus or commands will be different, but the basic function is the same. Printing, formatting, margins, and so forth will be of a similar nature, and a user error should be easy to detect. There are situations where the customer does not have the original manuals, documentation, or distribution floppy disks. This may be because the application was purchased by someone else, and the customer was given a copy. The application may have been installed on a system with a totally different hardware configuration (where everything was working perfectly). The customer installs a copy onto a system with a different hardware configuration, and problems develop. Some files or drivers may be missing that would allow changes in the configuration. Without the necessary files, the application can not be installed on the customer's hardware. Be aware that making copies of application software (and operating systems and manuals) is a violation of the Federal Copyright Law.

APPLICATION SOFTWARE

Applications are the programs or software that make the computer useful to a person or a business. They can be electronic analysis sheets (spread sheets), manipulate customer information (databases), allow you to prepare correspondence or manuscripts (word processor), or perform almost any task that requires (or required) a paper and pencil. The applications found on a system depend upon the specific requirement of the user. Troubleshooting software problems requires a working knowledge of the application. Working knowledge of common or popular applications is easily gained. It is not so easy to become familiar with software that is encountered infrequently, especially vertical or custom written applications. A technician must be able to install application software correctly, be able to start the application running, retrieve stored data for the application, verify that the application or data is displayed correctly, print a report or other available items (graphs or charts), save and store data that is generated, and exit the application properly. In each of the above instances, the technician should be able to perform the required function with the aid of the user manual or installation guide that is part of each software package.

INSTALLATION

The correct installation of application software often involves more than just copying the distribution floppy disks to the hard disk. Many current applications come in a compressed format, requiring the proper installation procedures to be followed. The minimum system requirements for the application to be installed and function properly are listed in the manual or on the package. Verify that the software and the computer system are compatible. Be sure that there is sufficient space on the hard disk for the software to be installed. Application packages consist of a manual and one or more floppy disks. At least one of the floppy disks is sealed in such a manner as to force the seal to be broken in order to remove it from the packaging. Breaking the seal is an indication that there is agreement to the publisher's printed software license. Once the seal is broken, the software can not be returned unless it is defective or if a special arrangement has been made with the vendor. If a problem arises after reading the installation instructions, the customer should be able to return the software package with the seal intact for a refund, exchange, or credit.

Before beginning an installation, be sure that the system has a floppy disk drive that is compatible with the distribution disks. Some software publishers provide both 5¼" and 3½" disks, while others provide only one size. It is also necessary to know how much RAM the system contains, how much free space remains on the hard disk, if the system has a math coprocessor, what type of video adapter is in the system, the characteristics of the video monitor (resolution, color, or monochrome), the type and speed of the processor, the make and model of the printer, the port assignments for I/O devices such as printers, plotter, mouse, and so on. Consult the manual that came with the application to see if it is compatible with the hardware. Does the application require a mouse or any additional hardware? Will the video work properly and completely? Is the specific printer supported?

The majority of applications available today have a broad range of hardware support built into them. There are some older systems still in use that may have unusual hardware configurations, parts of which may not be supported. Conversely, the customer may have an application that is dated and may not support current hardware. If a hardware support problem is encountered, contact the publisher. There may be an update available, or a new driver set, or even a third-party driver that may be purchased. Follow the installation instructions in the manual carefully. Most applications have an install program that uses a menu or a series of questions as a guide. The installation may make changes to the CONFIG.SYS file, which means that the system must be rebooted (a warm boot is sufficient) to activate the new configuration. It is a good idea to make notes as the installation is performed, so that if the application must be reinstalled at a later date, the information will be available.

PRINTER SETUP

Before testing a printer, verify that any switches or jumpers are set properly. If the printer is not supported by the application, check the printer manual to see if it can emulate a supported printer. The emulation mode may not support all of the available features, but it will produce acceptable output until another solution can be found. It may be necessary to adjust one or more switches or jumpers so that the printer can be used in the emulation mode. Verify that the changes will not conflict with any other applications that are currently installed.

Should a conflict occur, instruct the customer on how to effect the required changes. It is best to write down step-by-step instructions and then demonstrate the sequence of events necessary to make the change from standard mode to emulated mode, and to reverse the procedure. Have the customer perform the changes so that they can see how the procedure is accomplished, and verify the correctness of the written instructions at the same time. Have the customer return the system to the normal configuration and verify the instructions again. Remember to *turn the printer off* before changing any switches or jumpers. Some printers use a menu, accessed through the control panel, to effect changes. In this situation, the printer must remain on.

If there is more than one printer connected to the system, verify the port assignment for the printer that will be used. If using a switch box, tell the customer that the printers *must* be off line when the switch is activated in order not to damage the printer. This is especially necessary with Hewlett Packard and similar laser printers. Be sure that any changes to the hardware, the AUTOEXEC.BAT, and the CONFIG.SYS do not affect any other application that is installed on the system.

RETRIEVING INFORMATION

If the application includes test or practice files, one of these should be retrieved and examined. Create a practice file if none exists. A file that will fill several screens and require at least two pages to print will permit testing of the video system, printer pagination and margins. An easy way to create a practice file is to copy some information from examples shown in the user manual that came with the application.

When the file is created, save it to the hard disk. Give it a unique name that will be easy to remember. Clear the screen and retrieve the file from the hard disk. Examine the screen to confirm that the material that is displayed is the same as the file that was created. Check to see that the format and pagination are the same as when the data was entered. If the customer is not satisfied with the displayed data, see if there are any changes to the format or display that can be made. Sometimes, the colors or shading on the screen can be changed to make viewing easier. Keep notes of the changes so that the new settings can be duplicated, if requested, or the original settings can be reinstated. When the customer is satisfied, make the changes permanent by changing the defaults. All notes should become part of the documentation that came with the application. Repeat the save and retrieve functions several times, making changes to the data each time. Verify that the changes are saved each time.

Be cautious when working with software. Some applications, especially accounting packages, are very unforgiving and do not permit the random creation and deletion of data files. Any information entered into these files is permanent. Be absolutely sure that the process is reversible before altering any existing files. One way to work around this problem is to install the application and use it for practice or training. At the end of the training period, erase the entire application and the files that were created. Then, install the application again. Be sure that the customer knows when the live application is installed and that there is to be no more practice.

PRINTING REPORTS AND DOCUMENTS

Print a test file on the printer. See if the margins, pagination, and other features are as expected. Check for any special formats, characters, fonts, or other items that the application is capable of generating. Make note of any discrepancies and consult the manual for an explanation. Try utilizing the special features by changing the test file. Use as many of the features as possible, and keep a list of the changes to compare the output with the expected results. Some applications, especially word processors, contain a test file that demonstrates all of the features that the application is capable of producing. If the printer is not directly supported or is installed improperly, the test document will make it quite obvious.

SAVING A FILE AND EXITING THE APPLICATION

After a file has been created, saved, retrieved, and printed, exit the application and shut down the system. Try to exit the application without saving the latest changes. The application should display a reminder to save the work. Save the latest changes and exit to the system level. Even if there weren't any changes, the application must be exited through the sequence designed by the publisher. If the application is not exited properly, files may be left open. The exit sequence is designed to close all files and reset any changes made to the system that were necessary for the application to function. The exit sequence may also reload the command processor (COMMAND.COM), which would not be accomplished by aborting (unless the abort is performed through rebooting). Exiting from the application returns to the system level.

To conduct a thorough test, turn the system off, wait a minute or two, and then bring the system back up. This will test the CONFIG.SYS, AUTOEXEC.BAT, and PATH, if required. When the system is up again, repeat the entire sequence. Load the application, retrieve a file, print it, save, and exit. This will demonstrate to the customer that the system is behaving properly and that the newly installed application is functional. It is difficult to test each facet of an application, especially an unfamiliar one, but test as much as is practical. It is also good practice to check the existing hardware setup, especially if any device—such as a mouse or modem—has been installed along with the application. The possibility exists that a problem or address conflict was created during the installation that will surface later on. Having reached this point, it is safe to say that the application has been installed successfully and that the system is functioning properly. Remember to keep notes on all of the work that is performed until all of the problems have been cleared. This will prevent repetition of troubleshooting procedures and help in the event of a recall for a similar situation.

DATA RECOVERY USING MS-DOS UTILITIES

Data recovery is discussed here because it concerns the use of software to repair software. Recovering data from a damaged or partially damaged disk is often difficult. There are several firms that specialize in data recovery, and their charges vary depending upon the time required and the media from which the data must be recovered. In some cases, data that is recovered has been damaged and must be repaired. Without complete familiarity of the structure of the damaged file(s), attempting these repairs can cause additional problems.

MS-DOS includes three utilities, DEBUG, RECOVER, and CHKDSK, that can be utilized for data recovery. There are no guarantees that data can be recovered using any or all of these utilities, or that the information that is recovered will be usable. It is not necessary to have any special software or utilities, as these files are part of MS-DOS. As always, it is highly recommended that a backup of the hard disk be made before attempting to perform a recovery operation, and especially before using DEBUG.

DEBUG allows the user to display the contents of any memory location (address), move blocks of data between memory locations, change the contents of a memory location, read disk sectors into memory, write the contents of memory to disk, write and execute assembly language programs, display the assembly source code of a program, trace the execution of a program, display and alter the contents of registers (CPU), input from or output to an I/O port, and perform hexadecimal arithmetic. DEBUG is more of a programmers tool and requires intimate knowledge of the structure of the media as well as the file(s) that are to be repaired. Using DEBUG to recover data is beyond the scope of this book.

RECOVER is used to recover data from a damaged file and to mark the File Allocation Table (FAT) so that the area where the damage occurred will not be used. RECOVER will mark the damaged sector(s) as well as the sector preceding and following the damaged area. A minimum of three sectors will be marked. RECOVER is used when a SECTOR NOT FOUND error is displayed.

When the SECTOR NOT FOUND error is encountered, the following choices are available: *A*bort, *R*etry, *I*gnore, *F*ail? The normal response is to *R*etry. Retry should be attempted several times. If, after one or more retries, the file can be loaded, save the file under a different name. If the file can NOT be loaded, try to copy it to another file name such as C:COPY FILENAME.EXT FILENAME.NEW. If the error is displayed during the copying, respond with *I*gnore. The *I* will cause the bad sectors to be ignored, and the entire file will be copied. The area with the bad sectors will be either missing or garbled. After the copy is complete, mark the damaged sectors using the recover command; the syntax is C:RECOVER FILENAME.EXT. MS-DOS will respond with a message stating that XXXXX of YYYYY bytes recovered. RECOVER will create a file named FILE0001.REC, which is the recovered version of the original file.

There are several drawbacks to using this method. FILE0001.REC may not contain all of the information in the original file. There could be information missing from the area that resided on the damaged area of the disk, or the file may be truncated at the point where the bad sector was located. The file that was loaded and renamed as a result of the multiple *R*etries may contain a damaged area where the bad sectors were located. A file containing bad sectors that was copied with the bad sectors being Ignored, will be damaged or contain garbage within the file.

If a FILENAME and EXTension are not named when the RE-COVER command is initiated, MS-DOS will attempt to recover every file on the disk. The files may be scrambled or damaged, and there will then be several files on the disk named FILEnnnn.REC, where nnnn will be sequential from 0000 to however many files were found. It will be necessary to rename each file individually to its former file name, assuming that the file can be examined and the original name located. The original file will still be on the disk, but it will be damaged or truncated. The damaged file must be erased.

If the damaged file contained text or other ASCII data, it is possible to repair the damage using a word processor. If the file was in binary, as most program files are, it is not repairable and must be recopied from the original distribution disk. When working on database files, be careful of the structure of the records and the placement of delimiters. Most database applications have a utility to reindex the data files. Reindexing must be performed before the file is accessed through the application program, or errors will result, especially when part of the data is lost.

If situations involving bad sectors occur, the entire hard disk should be backed up and reformatted. The formatting process detects bad sectors and writes their addresses to a table on the disk so that these areas are not used. A disk that has been in use for a period of time may develop bad sectors. The reformatting should be construed as preventative maintenance and performed annually on systems that are used regularly.

The statistics displayed by CHKDSK are discussed in the MS-DOS section of this book and in any MS-DOS manual. In addition to statistics, the CHKDSK command may display the message "Errors found, F parameter not specified" and "Corrections will not be written to disk." In this case, the /F (fix) switch must be used (CHKDSK/F).

With the /F switch activated, the message "xxx lost clusters found in yyy chains" will be displayed, followed by "Convert lost chains to files (Y/N)?" A lost cluster is an area on the disk that the FAT pointer says is in use by a file, but none of the directory entries claim ownership of the cluster. Responding to the message with N results in the lost clusters being reclaimed, and the pointers are reset. Responding with Y causes the lost clusters to be converted to files, which are given names. The names are FILEnnnn.CHK, where nnnn will be a sequential number beginning with 0000. These files will be located in the root directory.

The resulting files (such as FILE0000.CHK) should be examined. If these files are useless, they should be erased. Should the files contain needed information, they can be renamed. These fragmented files are generally created when an application is aborted or interrupted, without following the proper exit routine.

If files are cross-linked, the message "AAAA.XYZ is cross-linked on cluster XXX" is displayed. Cross-linked files indicate that two or more files claim ownership of the same cluster and indicates that there is a problem with the FAT pointer(s). Several file fragments point to the same cluster on the disk, even though only one file can own the cluster. The remedy for this problem is to copy each of the files named in the message to a new file (C:COPY FILENAME.EXT FILENAME.NEW), and then delete the old files. Deleting the old files will reset the pointer(s), and repair the FAT. Examine the newly created files. With luck, one of the files will contain meaningful information and can be renamed to the original filename. The balance of the files will probably contain garbage and should be erased.

To examine the files on a disk for fragmentation, use the command CHKDSK *.*. The message "FILENAME.EXT contains nn noncontiguous blocks" will indicate the number of fragments. If the file is small, copy it to a floppy disk and then back to the hard disk. The copying process will defragment the file. If there are several severely fragmented files, or the fragmented files are too large to fit on a single floppy disk, use the MS-DOS BACKUP utility to back up the files. The backup process defragments the files, and they will be continuous when they are restored. Severe fragmentation may also indicate that the disk is reaching its capacity. Before disaster strikes, the disk should be cleaned. Obsolete files should be backed up and then purged from the hard disk.[23] There are some utility programs that will defragment the files and clean up the disk. It may take up to several hours to defragment a drive, depending upon the capacity of the disk.

OTHER DATA RECOVERY UTILITIES

There are many other utilities available through commercial channels to aid in the recovery of lost or damaged data. Often, a combination of one or more of these utilities is required to complete the task of recovering a lost or damaged file. Sometimes, the data will be lost permanently. Be sure to make copies of the damaged files before attempting a repair.[24]

---

[23]Additional information on fragmented files appears in Chapter 9.

[24]Refer to the sections on Data Recovery and Diagnostic Hardware and Software in the Resource List, Appendix E.

6

Diagnostics

NO TROUBLE FOUND (NTF)

No Trouble Found (NTF) can be frustrating for both the customer and the technician. Frequently, NTF or "Cannot Duplicate the Problem" can be traced to one or more of the following situations: lack of familiarity with the equipment or the manner in which the equipment functions by the technician, the customer, or both; hardware or software incompatibility; system not grounded; low line voltage or dirty power; intermittent problems caused by static electricity, power surges, or dropouts; user error (but equipment blamed); poor communication between the technician and the customer, or the inability of the customer to correctly describe the problem; or inability to duplicate the circumstances that caused the problem.

SERVICE METHODOLOGY

Do not underestimate the ability of the customer to cause a problem unknowingly. Customers will attempt hardware upgrades, software installation, move systems, or just be playing around. Never speculate on the cause of a problem or blame a customer.

Determine if a hardware problem exists. Does the system complete POST? Are any error messages displayed? Is there a prompt? Is there really a hardware problem? Is the problem intermittent? Can the customer duplicate the problem?

73

Approach the task with a clear mind and a relaxed attitude. Be thorough and methodical. If a technician is excited or panics (due to inexperience or pressure from the customer), the job becomes more difficult. Don't tear the system apart immediately. Always start at square one. Gather and note all known symptoms, information, and observations. Check for installation and configuration errors. Collect the proper maintenance manuals for the system and its options. Examine any external or exposed jumpers or switches and verify that they are set correctly.

If the computer must be opened, record chip speed and size, I/O port assignments, switch settings, jumper settings, location of all adapter boards, and the CMOS configuration before making any changes. Check for any address conflicts. Determine correct addresses, and reassign the conflicting devices.

Boot the system and monitor the audio and visual indicators. Check the environment—incoming power, airborne contaminants, blockage of the power supply air vents, or covers on heat dissipating components (VLSI and other power consuming chips). Does the monitor come on and work correctly? Are there any POST indicators or messages audible or displayed on the screen?

MODULAR FAILURES

A module is a device that is connected via a plug and socket. These include boards, cables, ROM and RAM chips, math coprocessor, and the CPU chip. Failing modules can sometimes be identified through POST error codes or the use of diagnostic software. When a system appears dead, or refuses to boot, turn the power off and remove all modules except the CPU, ROM, and the first 128K of RAM. Install the modules, one by one, until the system starts running (make sure that power is removed from the system when inserting or replacing any boards, connectors, chips, or devices).

If a module appears to cause a problem, replace it with a known good unit. Sometimes the problem is caused by the interaction of two (or more) defective modules. They will function normally as single units but cause a failure when they are combined. It may be necessary to replace several modules before the system is functioning properly.

INTERMITTENT FAILURES

Diagnosing intermittent failures (a here again, gone again problem) is the major headache for any technician. Intermittent failures may be the result of a combination of factors that only occur occasionally, such as when a specific application is running or when the accounting department is performing end of period processing. Obtaining an accurate description (symptoms) of an intermittent failure from a nontechnical customer is not often an easy task. What is the best approach? Where is the best place to start?

Ask the customer to write out the symptoms, the trouble, the effect, and when the problem occurred (time of the day and day of the week). Indicate which application was running at the time of the failure. Indicate if this failure has occurred before. If so, was a different application running at that time? Ask the customer to reproduce the failure. One of the best resources for fighting an intermittent hardware bug is the manufacturer's advanced diagnostics. Another method is to apply heat, which should cause the failure to become constant.

Pay attention to time-related failures. These can be caused by large amounts of AC noise on the incoming power lines. The sources for these can be large motors (air conditioners or elevators), photocopiers, or other power-hungry equipment. Be calm and observant. Properly diagnose the trouble. Formulate and ask as many questions as possible, no matter how farfetched they may be. This type of dialogue between customer and technician often leads to answers that are vital to the solution of the situation. Can the customer describe the malfunction? Can the problem be duplicated with regularity? Are there any error messages or POST information that is unfamiliar or not documented? Are the correct manuals, diagnostics, and tools available? Is there a plan of action? Above all, think about what is (or is not) happening.

What is needed to perform the service? Are these items available? Perform the required service, and test the system to verify that the trouble has been cleared. *Has* the trouble been cleared? Was there more than one problem? Did clearing one problem cause another? Is the system fully functional? If there was an intermittent problem, has it really been cleared? Complete the paperwork and inform the customer as soon as the service is completed. If the unit was brought into the shop, return it as soon as possible. Shop space is at a premium, and the customer needs the equipment. If the service is billable, the billing is not complete until the equipment is delivered in working condition.

Do not be afraid to educate the customer. Explain what the problem was and what had to be done to perform the repair. Tell the customer what (or who) may have caused the problem. Explain any warranty that is related to the repair. Provide proof to the customer that the machine has been tested and that it is fully functional. Take some extra time to demonstrate that the equipment has been repaired properly. Have the customer test the system to verify that the trouble is gone.

THEORY OF TROUBLESHOOTING

Prior to discussing the theory of troubleshooting and the use of third-party diagnostic or utility software, we should consider the following quote from *PCWeek* of September 24, 1990.

> Today's PC-based diagnostic software is in need of a diagnosis itself. The features in current packages vary so much that they "show little consistency about what there is to diagnose," according to *PCWeek*'s in-depth look at the packages. Features to look for are "locating problem areas, defective memory chips, surface areas gone bad on hard disks and serial and parallel ports that don't properly pass data."

DIAGNOSTICS TYPES

There are several types of hardware and software diagnostics, provided by either the hardware manufacturer or outside sources. Materials that are supplied by the manufacturer may be either machine specific or brand specific. For example, IBM provides a different diagnostic disk for each system or "family," while Compaq has one diagnostic disk to test all of their systems. Each time IBM markets a new system or family, it becomes necessary to add a diagnostic disk to the collection. Compaq will issue a revision of their diagnostics each time they bring a new system to market. The revision supersedes all previous revisions, so the collection is merely updated instead of increased. Using the incorrect version of the user or advanced diagnostics can lead to false error codes, improper testing, and possible damage to hard drives.

The POST is built into every system. POST is available to the customer and technician without any additional expense or charge. Observing the POST is the first step in testing a system. POST error codes or messages are often the only information needed to solve a problem.

Some manufacturers (usually the major companies) provide user diagnostic software with the system. User diagnostics are generally similar to the advanced diagnostics, with some important differences. The user diagnostics are interactive. This means that the system under test must be attended by a person who can respond to questions and directions displayed on the screen. The user diagnostics will permit a technician to perform some valuable tests.

The advanced diagnostics on disk are provided by the system manufacturer to authorized dealers and repair centers. In addition to all of the features of the user diagnostics, the advanced version includes multiple pass testing in the unattended mode and low-level hard drive formatting routines. Often, there are no advanced diagnostics available. The user diagnostics included with the computer will enable the technician to isolate the trouble in most cases.

Whether the user or advanced diagnostics are being used, they must be booted from a floppy disk. The diagnostics contain a special operating system that must be loaded in order for the tests to function. Diagnostic disks contain a utility to make backup copies. Use this utility if backups or extra copies are required. Never copy the material from a diagnostic disk onto a customer's hard disk.

There are a wealth of third-party diagnostics available including hardware-based (boards to insert into one of the expansion slots) and software. It should be unnecessary for an experienced technician to use anything other than the manufacturer-supplied advanced diagnostics and service manual, if available. In situations where there aren't any manufacturer-supplied diagnostics (such as when working with custom built or clone systems), third-party diagnostics may be required.

The major hardware manufacturers neither recognize nor guarantee compatibility of these third-party products. Manufacturers design their diagnostic tools to be compatible with their hardware (and BIOS). Third-party devices must be compatible with everybody. Some of these third-party products are so generic that they are useless in many cases. In some instances, use of third-party diagnostics or utilities have been known to damage applications or corrupt system information written on a hard disk. When Compaq released MS-DOS version 3.31, they included the ability to create hard disk drive partitions with a maximum size of 512 Mb. The maximum partition size that could be created using other MS-DOS versions (including IBM version 3.3) was 32 Mb. Compaq published the following in their *MS-DOS Version 3 Reference Guide*:

Compatibility Considerations

Some applications assume that the 32-Megabyte disk partition is the maximum partition size. This assumed partition size may cause these applications to produce unpredictable results when performing calculations for partitions greater than 32 Megabytes. For example, unpredictable results could occur when calculating values assuming a 32-Megabyte limit.

Unpredictable results may occur from applications that perform physical-level disk read and write operations. Older disk-management types of utilities may be included in this category.

MS-DOS Version 5 includes some of the "Norton type" and other utilities which heretofore were available as "third-party" products. Bear in mind that the ADVANCED DIAGNOSTICS are the BEST OPTION for diagnosing trouble. Hardware manufacturers make these available to Authorized Service Providers to reduce down time and to prevent or reduce Technical Support telephone calls.

Generally, some third-party diagnostics will perform some tests on some systems. Most third-party diagnostics are stronger in areas that are generic, such as diagnosing hard drive problems, and weaker in areas dealing with specific manufacturers such as BIOS controlled activities and memory management. If it is necessary to use third-party software, do not stick to one brand. Use several brands for thorough testing. One more point to watch is the version of the software. Hardware manufacturers don't always tell diagnostic software publishers when a change is made to the system or BIOS.

Another compatibility problem is when diagnostics are used with hard disks formatted under an operating system other than MS-DOS (or OS/2). Diagnostic software requires certain information that it reads from the disk in order to perform correctly. If the disk is prepared by software other than MS-DOS (or OS/2), the necessary information may be missing or located in a place where the diagnostic software does not search.

The main drawback with any software-based diagnostics is that the system to be tested must be able to boot from the floppy disk drive, and the video system must be operational. In other words, the system must be mostly functional (about 70 percent) in order to be tested.

DIAGNOSING FAILURES THROUGH THOUGHT AND OBSERVATION

In order to diagnose a trouble quickly and correctly, several materials are required. They include the owner's manual, a service manual with flow charts or trouble trees, and either user or advanced diagnostics. The following items will become increasingly valuable to the technician as his or her career advances: experience, intuition, knowledge, and the ability to reason. One of the most important tools that a technician can have is the notebook that he or she keeps. This notebook should contain information that is frequently needed, such as telephone numbers, switch settings, cable configurations, jumper settings, and DOS command syntax. Information that was once needed, and time was spent researching, may be needed again. Obscure information that will never be needed again (it was needed once . . .) should not be eliminated. The appendixes of this book (and other similar books) contain a lot of good information. Use this information as the beginning of the notebook. Be sure to use a looseleaf book, so that data can be inserted as necessary. Collect and share as much material as possible. It can be weeded from time to time if the book becomes too cluttered.

OBSERVATION AS A TOOL

Read the screen (for error messages or instructions). If messages disappear too quickly, ask someone else to read the screen and discuss the observations. Try to redirect the output to a printer so that the messages can be read as often as necessary. Insert pause statements in batch files (don't forget to remove them when they are no longer needed). Remove CLS statements if the screen clears too quickly.

Loose or open cable connections, or cards that are not fully seated cause all kinds of problems. Moving a system, or sometimes normal vibration from the cooling fan and hard drive, can cause connectors to

Never overlook the obvious!

vibrate loose. Sometimes vibration in connection with heat will cause chips (RAM, ROM, CPU) to "walk" out of their sockets. Hands are also a problem. A repair is made or a device is installed and a cable is inadvertently moved away from the mating connector.

Turn off or disconnect the power to the system. The technician should use an ESD (Electro Static Discharge) kit if available, or ground him- or herself to remove any static electricity that has built up on his or her clothing. Remove the cover, being careful not to catch it on internal cables (or clothing). Observe the interior of the system. Does anything look out of place? Are their any vacant sockets that look like they should be populated? Are their any cables or connectors that are not in the correct place or condition? Are any switches or jumpers set incorrectly? Remove all cards and reseat them. The friction of removing and reseating a card is enough to remove surface oxidation that has formed. Do the same with internal cables. Carefully press each socketed chip back into its socket. Be sure that while replacing the cover nothing (especially internal cables) is caught, moved, or damaged.

Are there any discolored resistors or diodes, burst capacitors, or similar visible component damage (these are usually found in a video monitor or power supply). Are any mechanical parts (metal or plastic) missing, twisted, or broken.

AUDIBLE OBSERVATIONS

One of the greatest assets of a technician is the ability to verbally communicate with the customer. Verbal communication includes speaking and listening. It is also a good idea to keep a written record of communication with a customer. If there is not enough room on a work order or service invoice, use a pad and attach the information to the service documentation. Have a list of questions to ask the customer (sometimes a simple checklist will suffice). Note how the customer responds to the questions, such as their tone, word usage, and listening skills. If the questions are too technical or confusing, they must be rephrased.

Other sounds that the technician must be aware of include the cooling fan (or fans). Are the fans running? Do they sound OK? Are there any motors that should be running? Are any motors running that should not be? Do any mechanical noises such as grinding or rubbing appear during power up, while the system is on and idle, or during a disk access? Are these sounds normal?

Are there any unexpected audio codes during POST? The normal sound is one beep. Some systems, such as the newer Compaq machines, produce two beeps. Some systems emit a sound during the RAM test portion of the POST. This can be quite annoying, and confusing if it is not familiar. Never assume that something is wrong when an unfamiliar sound is heard. Ask the customer first, to avoid embarrassment.

ODORS

Normal functioning of a computer system produces heat. The power supply gets hot. The hard drive gets hot. The chips, especially the RAM and CPU, get hot. Sometimes, when new components sustain normal operating temperature for a period of time, there is an odor. This is not as pungent or offensive as the odor of a burning resistor or transformer. If something is burning, the odor will be accompanied by smoke. This does not happen often. When a definite burning odor is detected, use caution. Disconnect power from the equipment immediately. After the equipment has had a chance to cool off, a visual inspection will probably locate the problem. Burning is almost always accompanied by a discoloration.

One note about offensive odors. Some laser printers produce ozone, which has an offensive odor. These printers contain an internal ozone filter. After a number of hours, the filters expire and must be replaced. If the odor of ozone is detected, check for a defective or missing laser printer filter before reaching for the fire extinguisher.

TOUCH

Use caution when touching the inside of any electrical or electronic device! Aside from the obvious peril of electric shock, the inside of a computer system contains moving mechanical parts and heat-generating devices. There is also the ever present problem of ESD. It is important to use extreme caution when exploring the interior of a system. There are, however, several observations that can be made by touching parts inside the computer. There should be heat given off by the RAM and CPU chips when the power is on. Cold chips indicate trouble. The hard drive motor should be active when power is on, even though there isn't any read or write activity. If the drive is touched, the vibration of the motor should be felt. Touch is also important when testing a keyboard. Keys that are stuck or sluggish can easily be detected.

EXPERIENCE AND INSTINCT

Experience is the best teacher. Instinct is a combination of training, thinking, and experience. It is not possible to be trained to solve every problem that can be encountered. It is possible to draw on experience when confronting a situation, and every situation will be a new experience.

Before tearing the hardware apart, review some basic possibilities. Is the problem caused by something obvious such as a blown fuse or circuit breaker outside of the computer? Is there a loose or defective power cord? Is the brightness control on the monitor turned down, or is the monitor turned off? Is there a cable or connector that is not properly fastened? Is everything connected properly? Use common sense. It is better to spend a few minutes assessing the situation than to jump to a hasty conclusion.

USING A FLOW CHART OR TROUBLE TREE

A flow chart or trouble tree is an excellent tool in helping to track down a problem. It will force the technician to structure his or her thinking along logical paths. Knowing the appropriate paths will aid in locating the failing module quickly. Some manufacturers include flow charts or trouble trees in their service manuals. Most of these tools present a series of questions that require a true or false (yes or no) answer. When a question is presented, the answer dictates the next step or leads to the next question. Sometimes it is necessary to take a reading or measurement using a meter or gauge. Again, the action that follows depends upon the results of the measurement or reading. When using these tools, there are two things that are extremely important to remember.

The first is to follow the path precisely. Never make any assumptions. Perform all tests and measurements. Do not skip over any steps, and follow the steps from the beginning. If the technician gets lost or confused, or strays from the path, it becomes necessary to start at the beginning again. Several restarts may be required before the solution to the problem is found.

The second thing to remember is that the tool may not fit the situation exactly. The answer to a true or false question may be either true, false, or may not apply. If this is the case, it is necessary to follow first one path and then the other. The result will be more time consuming, but the solution will be correct. It may be necessary to deviate from the path several times before reaching the end. It is important to make notes at each intersection so that steps will not be repeated unnecessarily.

POWER SUPPLIES

If a power supply problem is suspected, use an accurate VOM. Measure the five-volt and twelve-volt supplies. A disk drive is a good loading device for testing. The measurements will not detect intermittent, slow rising, or loading conditions. Many power supplies have charts on them listing the output voltages and test points. Replace the power supply if any of the voltages are incorrect. If a power supply is removed from the system for testing on a bench, the output must be loaded. A floppy disk drive can be used as the load. If the power supply is totally dead, look inside for a failed fuse. Some power supplies have fuses hidden within the bowels, requiring disassembly, while others such as Compaq make fuses easily accessible (if you know where to look).

SYSTEM BOARDS

Remove and reseat all connectors to ensure that they are properly connected. Check all switch settings and jumper positions. Exercise the switches to be sure that they are making contact. Monitor and interpret all POST codes by cold booting the system. Run all of the manufacturer's advanced diagnostics if they are available. Turn the system off, remove all adapter boards, reboot the system, and rerun diagnostics. A defective battery is usually indicated during POST by a 161 error code or a message telling the customer to run setup. Sometimes the system boots up in the 40-column mode (instead of 80-column). The battery affects the real time clock and information stored in CMOS. Disconnect the battery leads and measure the DC voltage (6.0 volts between pins 1 and 4). Replace the battery and run SETUP. On systems manufactured by Compaq, NEC, IBM, and some other major companies, SETUP is accomplished through software included with the diagnostic disk. Some AT compatibles have a built-in SETUP program in their BIOS, depending upon the manufacturer. Pressing the Del key during the booting process usually accesses the SETUP routines. For the others, you will find the SETUP program on the diagnostic floppy disk.

KEYBOARDS

Keyboard errors can be difficult to detect. Observe the POST codes for 3xx errors. Run the manufacturer's diagnostics and test the individual keys. Test the fuse for the keyboard power (found on some systems and located inside the system unit). Measure the DC voltages on the keyboard connector.

The majority of keyboard problems result from dust, dirt, food particles, staples, and paper clips, which are dropped into the keyboards. Inverting the keyboards often allows the debris to drop out, thus clearing the problem. If this fails, a strong vacuuming is recommended. Disassembly and cleaning is the next step, but this should be done with caution. Some keyboards (the original IBM PC and XT, for example) have small springs that will shoot out all over if they are not disassembled properly. There are companies selling ultrasonic cleaners for keyboards. These require that the keyboard be immersed in a liquid cleaner for a period of time. The ultrasonic method works well on most keyboards. One exception is the keyboard for the AT&T 6300. This keyboard contains small rubber insulators. Contact with liquids, such as the ultrasonic cleaning solution, will ruin the rubber.

Keyboard difficulties can also be caused by a defective cable or a broken ground wire. Check the ground from the connector to the inside of the keyboard (this requires removal of the keyboard cover). Verify that the keyboard is connected correctly and in the proper place. The original IBM PC had a cassette connector adjacent to the keyboard connector. The PS/2 series from IBM places the mouse port next to the keyboard connector. Both units use the same plug, and it is easy to connect the devices in the wrong order. A keyboard connected to the mouse port will not function or do any harm. A mouse plugged into the keyboard connector will blow the fuse on the system board when any of the mouse buttons are activated. A 305 POST error code should be generated as a result of a blown fuse.

Many keyboards have a switch on the rear of the case marked XT/AT or a similar designation. These keyboards will work with most systems, provided that this switch is set to the proper position. Verify the setting, and exercise the switch once or twice if trouble in this area is suspected.

VIDEO CONTROLLERS AND MONITORS

Video adapters come in several types, monochrome, CGA, EGA, and VGA. VGA adapters (and monitors) have 15 pin connectors. All of the other types have 9 pins. Mixing adapters with monitors, such as connecting a monochrome monitor to an EGA adapter, will result in either no video or garbage on the screen. Before replacing a video adapter or monitor, determine the type of system that is required. Sometimes a customer will switch monitors, causing a mismatch between the display and the adapter. Verify that they match.

A properly configured system will support one monochrome and one color video adapter. Check all switch settings and jumpers on the system board and the adapter. This is especially important if more than one video adapter is installed. Listen for audio error indications (IBM will be one long and two short beeps). Video POST Error Codes 4xx, 5xx,

24xx, 74xx. Run the manufacturer's advanced diagnostics. Note that some adapters may not be supported by the particular manufacturer's diagnostics, and test bad even though they may be good. Check the output DC voltages on the video connector. (For an IBM XT or AT, run the advanced diagnostics and measure the voltages as specified in the IBM flow charts.)

If POST completes normally, the problem may be with the monitor. Check for power by observing the pilot light on the front panel (if present). Look inside the vents on the top of the case to see if the rear of the VDT (Video Display Tube) is illuminated. If the tube is dark, a power problem exists. Check the controls on the monitor. Controls may be in the rear, the front, on the side, or hidden behind a front panel. If in doubt, set all the controls at their midpoint. They can be adjusted later. Be sure that the connections from the monitor to the power and video sources are tight and that they are connected to the proper places.

If a customer is having difficulty with one or more applications, but the diagnostics confirm that the video system is normal, check for video driver software. Many video controller cards require their own software drivers to function with or enhance specific applications. For example, the correct controller and driver combination can allow Lotus 1-2-3 to display 132 columns (or more) on the screen instead of the normal 80. These drivers are either activated through the CONFIG.SYS or installed into the driver set of specific applications. If a video controller is replaced with a different type, the drivers will not function correctly and cause video problems. Driver software, like any file, can become corrupted. It may be necessary to reinstall the application using a generic driver, or trying each available driver until the problem is solved.

There are software utilities that prevent the screen from being burned by a stagnant image. These can be independent pieces of software or part of a menu application. If a screen is not refreshed regularly, the information that is displayed can be burned into the coating on the inside of the tube. This is true for any type of CRT, including a home television set. If a customer leaves a monitor unattended for long periods of time without reducing the brightness, the image begins to be burned into the screen. If the screen is severely burned, the information can be read when the monitor is powered off. It is also difficult to use the monitor, because the images generated by the software must be read through or behind the burned-in image. The software utilities either blank the screen or cause a random pattern to be generated and displayed. The utility takes over if the keyboard has not been activated for a specific amount of time. The time, usually in minutes, is set by the customer. When the utility is functioning, strike a key to resume normal operations and return the screen to the proper display. The utility is generally a TSR, which is started from the AUTOEXEC.BAT. It may be necessary to deactivate the utility for testing or to eliminate a video problem.

HARD DISK SUBSYSTEMS

Hard disks are temperature sensitive. If the drive is cold, it will not boot. In some geographical areas, temperatures drop fairly low. A hard drive in a computer that is turned off over night (or over a weekend) may be reluctant to boot up in the morning, especially if the heat in the building was lowered or turned off. It is best to turn the system on and let it run for 20 or 30 minutes before attempting to reboot.

Hard disks rarely fail while in use. Do not confuse a software problem or bad sector error with a failed drive. If a hard drive is going to fail, it will most likely be while attempting to boot. If regular backups are performed, they should be done at the end of the work day, while the system is up and running. Leaving the backup for the first thing in the morning can be disastrous, as the system may not boot up. Often, problems are the result of corrupted information on the boot tracks of the disk. This is because the boot tracks and system areas of the disk are involved in a great deal of activity each time that a drive is booted or accessed. By backing up, reformatting, and restoring information at least once a year, the areas are renewed. Tracks or sectors that are in marginal condition will be bypassed through the formatting process, preventing a possible disaster.

Most modern drives retract the head to a landing zone unless a read or write operation is taking place. If power is removed from the drive during a read or write function, a head crash is possible. Head crashes may damage one or more of the read/write heads, the disk surfaces, or both. Disks that are damaged through crashes can sometimes be reformatted if the heads are not damaged. If a drive appears to be ruined as the result of a head crash, and the data must be recovered, there are companies that provide this service. See the appendix under Data Recovery.

In the event of a hard disk problem, a POST error code (in the 17nn group) will be displayed. The tests conducted by POST involve a signal sent from the BIOS to the disk controller. The controller then communicates with the drive, and the results are returned to the BIOS which generates a code if the responses are not normal.

These codes are not always reliable. If the controller attempts to communicate with the drive and a cable is loose, the controller will assume that the drive is defective because it is not responding. In the event of a 17nn error message, remove the system cover and perform a visual inspection. Check all switches and jumpers (Drive Address Selection) on the drive and the controller for proper position. Check all cables for seating, correct orientation (pin 1 on the connector to pin 1 on the cable), and a tight fit. Pin 1 on the cable is usually marked with a colored stripe. Pin 1 on the connector is usually marked on the device or adapter board. Pin 1 is closest to the key on the device and on the connector. Boot the system and monitor the POST codes. Test with the manufacturer's advanced diagnostics or user diagnostics if available.

If a failure exists after the visual inspection and testing with diagnostics, replace the drive, cables, and controller in that order. The drive is a mechanical device and is more likely to fail than the other components. Drives and controllers must be matched to each other in order to function correctly. If either the drive or the controller is replaced, a low-level format must be performed. In many cases, a good controller will not work with a good drive because of differences in manufacturing tolerances. A successful low-level format will insure that the drive and controller are compatible with each other.

It is sometimes possible to repair an apparently dead drive by replacing the circuit board with one from the same brand and model. If a spare drive is available, it is worth the effort, as the replacement is not very involved and takes only a few minutes. Some drive manufacturers—Seagate, for example—sells these boards as a separate item.

New or replacement drives should be allowed to run for 30 minutes prior to formatting, to allow the operating temperature to stabilize. Drives that are formatted when they are cold will behave erratically when they reach their normal operating temperature. Problems may not arise for several weeks, but eventually the drives will fail.

In recent years, the IDE (Intelligent Drive Electronics) drive has become very popular. The IDE system consists of a drive and controller physically attached to each other in a unit. These are connected to a system by an adapter board (not an external controller). Low-level formatting must be performed through special software available from the drive manufacturer. Attempts at low-level formatting through traditional controller ROM-based routines can cause permanent damage to these drives.

FLOPPY DISK SUBSYSTEMS

Most computers in use today either include an internal hard drive or are connected to a network. The floppy drives are used for connecting to the network, loading new applications, or performing backups. On some systems, the floppy disk drive is hardly used. Lack of use allows dust, smoke, airborne dirt, and oxidation to form on the heads. The environment in which the computer is installed contributes to the seriousness of these problems. Many floppy disk problems can be eliminated by an occasional cleaning, using one of the many drive cleaning kits that are currently available.

Before troubleshooting a floppy disk subsystem, be sure to validate the test disk. Media problems are often confused with drive problems. Be sure that the test disk is of the same density as the drive. Double-density drives can not read a high-density disk. A simple format, write, read test using a blank disk is sufficient for functional testing. If the functional tests are passed, then a compatibility test must be performed. Compatibility requires that the speed and alignment of the drive that is being tested conform to a set of standards. A simple compatibility test requires the use of two systems. Format, write, and read a disk on one system, and then see if the other system can read and write to the disk as well. Try switching disks back and forth several times. If a disk can be reliably read and written by two systems, either both drives are out of whack by the same error, or they are most likely both functioning normally. If disks prepared on one system can not be used by other systems, the drive should be repaired or replaced. Drive repair is discussed later in this book.

If a malfunction occurs and the media is not suspected, perform a visual inspection. Inspect all switches and jumpers (Drive Address Selection) for proper settings. Check all cables for seating and orientation. Check all cable connections for proper position, and the order of the connector on the cable. This determines the selection for drive 0 or drive 1. Verify that the correct cable is being used. Floppy drive cables look very much like hard drive cables, but the position of the twisted conductors are not the same. Boot the system and monitor the POST codes for the floppy disk subsystem (a 6nn code is displayed if a failure occurs). Measure the DC voltage at the disk power connector. Test with the manufacturer's advanced diagnostics or user diagnostics, if available. The floppy disk drive power measurements are the same as for the hard disk, 5VDC and 12VDC.

Since most floppy disk drives are open, debris (parts of disk labels), dust, or even a stray cable can inhibit proper mechanical functioning. Sometimes a customer will not insert the media properly. Ask to see the customer operate the drive. Sometimes the latching mechanism requires cleaning.

POWER ON SELF-TEST (POST)

POST is a series of diagnostic tests contained in the BIOS ROM, which run automatically when a system is powered on (cold boot). POST checks the system board, memory, system memory boards, keyboard, controller boards, and peripheral devices. These tests are to see if the devices detected by the BIOS are actually present and responsive. POST can not be construed as being a thorough or complete test. Tables 6.1 and 6.2 list the beeps or codes that indicate that POST has detected an error.[25]

Table 6.1   IBM systems audio codes.

Audio Code	Possible Failure
No sound and no display	Power supply
Click, but no beeps	Power good, can't run POST
Continuous beep	Power supply
Repeating short beeps	Power supply
1 long and 1 short high beep	System board (clock speed too fast)
1 long and 2 short beeps	Video board or display
1 short beep—bad or no display	Display problem
1 short beep and no boot	Hard disk, cable, or controller
1 long and 3 short beeps	EGA problem

Note: System size is displayed as it is being tested (except on the original PC). The final value is the maximum amount of RAM located. Error codes are displayed on the screen. Expanded memory is not tested on some systems.

---

[25]A full listing of POST error codes appears in Appendix A.

Table 6.2 Power on self-test (POST).

Error Code	System Component
01n	Undetermined
02n	Power supply
1nn	System board
2nn	RAM memory
3nn	Keyboard
4nn	Monochrome Display adapter
5nn	Color Graphic adapter
6nn	Floppy disk subsystem
7nn	Math coprocessor
9nn	Parallel Printer adapter
10nn	Alternate Parallel Printer adapter
11nn	Asynchronous Communications adapter
11nn	PS/2 System Board Asynchronous Port
12nn	Alternate Asynchronous Communications adapter
12nn	PS/2 Dual Asynchronous Communications adapter
13nn	Game Control adapter
14nn	Matrix Printer adapter
15nn	Synchronous Data Link Communications (SDLC) adapter
16nn	Display Emulation (327X, 5520, 525X)
17nn	Hard disk subsystem
18nn	I/O expansion unit
19nn	Hard disk drive backup (tape)
20nn	Binary Synchronous Communications (BSC) adapter
21nn	Alternate BSC adapter
22nn	Cluster adapter
23nn	Plasma Monitor adapter
24nn	Enhanced Graphics adapter
24nn	PS/2 System Board Video Graphics Array (VGA)
25nn	Alt. EGA or VGA adapter
26nn	XT/370 subsystem
27nn	A T/370 subsystem
28nn	3278/79 Emulation adapter
29nn	Color graphics printer

Table 6.2   (Continued)

Error Code	System Component
30nn	Primary PC Network adapter
31nn	Secondary PC Network adapter
32nn	Display adapter (3270 PC or AT)
33nn	Compact Printer adapter
35nn	Enhanced Display Station Emulation adapter
36nn	General Purpose Interface Bus (GPIB) adapter
38nn	Data Acquisition adapter
39nn	Professional Graphics adapter
44nn	Display Attachment Unit and Display
45nn	IEEE -488 Interface Adapter Card
46nn	PS/2 Multiport Interface Board
48nn	Internal modem
49nn	Alternate internal modem
56nn	Financial communications system
71nn	Voice communications adapter
73nn	3.5″ External floppy disk drive subsystem
74nn	PS/2 Display adapter (VGA card)
76nn	4216 page printer
84nn	Speech adapter
85nn	IBM Expanded Memory Adapter (XMA)
86nn	PS/2 pointing device error
89nn	Musical feature card
100nn	PS/2 Multi-Protocol adapter
101nn	PS/2 Modem adapter
104nn	PS/2 ESDI hard disk subsystem
107nn	PS/2 5.25″ external floppy disk drive or adapter
121nn	PS/2 300/1200/2400 Baud Modem adapter
129nn	PS/2 processor board
149nn	PS/2 Plasma Display adapter
165nn	PS/2 6157 streaming tape
166nn	Primary Token-ring Network adapter
167nn	Secondary Token-ring Network adapter

7

Module Repair

The majority of computer service organizations leave module or component level repair to "fourth-party" maintenance organizations. Component level repairs require expertise that is greater than that of the average technician. Specialized tools and test equipment are also required as well as sources of parts.

The devices that make up a computer system fall into three categories: mechanical, analog, and digital. Mechanical devices include cooling fans, keyboards, floppy disk drives, and hard disk drives. Fans are a throwaway item that can not be repaired. There are companies that sell replacement fans. In some cases it is less expensive to replace (or upgrade) the entire power supply than to replace just the fan.

Keyboards are sometimes repairable by disassembly and cleaning. Some manufacturers, such as Apple, will sell replacement switches. Some keyboards require special tools for reassembly. There are digital components in a keyboard. Cleaning and switch replacement can be performed by a person with limited knowledge, and there is an ultrasonic keyboard cleaner on the market. Keyboard repair services are available.

Floppy disk drives require special equipment for testing and exercising. A special drive tester and a dual trace oscilloscope are required to perform adjustments and head alignment. Special software for testing and alignment is also necessary. This software is made by Dysan and can cost up to $75 per floppy disk. These floppy disks can not be copied, and they are not indestructible. Parts such as heads and track zero sensors may be difficult to obtain. A manufacturer's manual is required for each drive, detailing the specifications for proper alignment and showing the test point locations. An experienced technician is needed to perform proper alignments in an economical manner. There is some software on the market that is supposed to allow alignment and adjustment without special tools and test equipment, but it is not completely reliable. Fourth parties that specialize in floppy drive repair will perform this service for $20.

Hard disk drives require a high level of expertise. A clean room is necessary for disassembly in addition to special test equipment. It is not cost effective to repair hard drives unless your organization can generate income by providing fourth-party services to other organizations. One sure way to destroy a hard drive is to open up the area containing the heads and platters.

Analog devices include video monitors and power supplies. There are plenty of qualified technicians with enough experience to handle the repair of these devices. Anyone who has a background in television repair can fix a monitor. Obtaining parts such as flyback transformers may be an obstacle, but there are several companies who either import or manufacture replacements. Some monitors such as the NEC multisync require special equipment to adjust the synchronizing circuitry. It is probably worth the extra salary to have an analog technician on staff.

Digital devices make up the balance of the system. These include system boards, controllers, and adapters. Repair of digital devices depends on several factors. Schematics are often necessary, but they are difficult or impossible to obtain. Proprietary parts are not available. Generic equivalent parts or functionally equivalent parts may not work properly. A high degree of skill is required. Test equipment used by fourth parties is expensive. The FLUKE system can run upwards of $30,000, with the SCHLUMBERGER system closer to $70,000. Special techniques must be developed for each different type of board. It is necessary for known good boards to be available in order to develop and test programs before attempting to troubleshoot a defective board. Manufacturers will generally not help with board repair problems. A large volume of repairs is necessary to have such an operation be cost effective. The equipment may be able to reverse-engineer a board and even generate schematics, provided the person using the equipment has the necessary expertise. Some low-cost tools such as the R.A.C.E.R. board, CHECK-IT 2.0, and others claim to provide enough information to localize the problem to a chip or group of chips. As most of the chips are soldered (except for the RAM, ROMs, and math coprocessor), experienced people are required in order to prevent damage to boards and components. Many newer boards are multi-layered and utilize surface-mounted components. Surface mount chips require specialized (and costly) tools for removal and replacement. Too much heat on a multi-layer board can be a costly mistake.

POST CARDS

These are cards (or boards) that are inserted into an expansion slot of a "dead" system in order to pinpoint where the trouble is located. There are several variations of these devices with different levels of sophistication. These can be used in systems where there is no video display, as LEDs on the cards themselves produce a visual error code. There are several internal tests performed in a system before the video is activated. Failure of any of these tests will halt testing and the video display will not even be activated. The LEDs on the card indicate whether power is reaching the system board and at what point POST has either halted or in a continuous loop. Some system boards may be repaired by simply replacing a socketed RAM chip or a defective ROM. Other system boards are not that easily repaired and the board must be replaced unless the shop has the capability to perform component level repairs. Several POST cards include a printer port for logging the tests. A few of them also include tests for video, I/O ports, drives, and the keyboard. Depending upon the card, the system type, and the problem, some POST cards include special BIOS ROMs to be installed in place of the regular system ROMs. The manual that is included with the POST card tells how to interpret the LED codes and suggests which components to replace. These cards are also handy for burning in system boards. It should be noted that POST cards test only the system board and associated components (CPU, RAM, and some ROMS) and the video system. They do not test peripheral devices such as drives.

SOPHISTICATED TEST EQUIPMENT

FLUKE produces a nice line of equipment for troubleshooting of printed circuit boards. The model 9100A is a troubleshooting device that works with software that can either be purchased or developed in-house. Existing software is commercially available for about $1,700 to $2,000 per board. To have custom software written, figure on about six months' development time at a cost of roughly $20,000. To develop software, the FLUKE model 9010, at a base cost of $27,000, is required. Also required is a pod to interface the unit under development or test, so add another $1,500 to $3,500. (Pods are required for the 9100A also.) The pod is inserted in place of the microprocessor. The FLUKE unit then becomes the microprocessor. The operator (or software) is then able to send signals to the various components on the board and analyze the results. Once the software is obtained or developed, the testing of the boards is simple. Remove the microprocessor and connect the pod, attach a power supply to the board, and begin testing. The test is automatic, and if the FLUKE encounters a problem, it will stop, and a message will be displayed requesting operator intervention. It may ask for the operator to probe a particular location, move a jumper or switch, or something of that nature depending upon the item under test. If the software is functioning correctly, the problem will be pinpointed. It is then necessary to have a technician perform the actual repair. A skilled person is required to develop the software and test routines. Once the testing routine is perfected, a lower-skilled person can operate the equipment.

SCHLUMBERGER also produces a nice unit for about $60,000, the model 635 Diagnostic Test System. There is also a 635A, a test-only unit that is not capable of developing the suite of diagnostics. This unit works somewhat differently from the FLUKE, but the results are the same. It is necessary to supply a microcomputer system with a minimum of 40Mb of storage to use with the SCHLUMBERGER unit (add another couple of thousand dollars to the cost). The software provided by SCHLUMBERGER runs under the XENIX operating system. This software allows a skilled technician to develop test programs for the boards that will be repaired. The SCHLUMBERGER system is a fully interactive system. The complete characteristics of each chip must be programmed, as well as the expected readings for each pin. The SCHLUMBERGER system comes with a library of over 2,000 devices (ICs). Some chips do not behave as expected (or as the IC book expects) when they are in actual use, so the library is not always useful. This is because the system (and the library) expects to test these devices as individual components and not part of a functional circuit. Many boards are designed with input pins tied to ground, power, or each other. The library must be modified when developing software to account for these deviations. SCHLUMBERGER has an optional piece of software called NETS LEARN that "teaches" the machine how the ICs are connected to the board and to each other. This is important if in-circuit tests are performed on boards with missing, inaccurate, or incomplete schematics. Combining NETS LEARN with another piece of optional software called SCHEMATIC GENERATION can generate schematics through a reverse engineering process. During the development phase, the sequence of the components under test must be selected. Then the component information and the order of testing is programmed. Operator instructions are also programmed, telling him or her which clip to use and which component to clip on to next. The operator moves the clips from one component to another and the machine performs the tests. This system is not as fast as the Fluke, but each unit has its advantages and disadvantages.

If your company invests in either a FLUKE or SCHLUMBERGER, it is necessary to have a person who knows how to program the machine. Both manufacturers provide training on their equipment for a fee. Known good boards are required in order to program either of these machines. This is to provide information about the characteristics of each component on the boards, and how the components behave in actual use, in order to write and debug the test programs. If a technician is programming the machine, how can the boards be tested? Will two machines be needed? A highly skilled technician with knowledge of semiconductors and how they behave is required to develop the test programs. Is such a person on staff at present? Are there backup personnel in case the person with all of the knowledge is not available (ill, vacation, resigns)? How many different boards will be repaired? Will the expense involved in adding another type of board to be repaired, justify the addition? How many boards must be repaired to justify the cost involved? Can the necessary parts be obtained once the faulty component has been identified? How much will be spent for additional tools? A station for the removal of surface mount components can cost from $6,000 to $10,000. Special soldering/desoldering stations are required. It will be necessary to stock some components and provide additional ESD safety equipment. Will component level repairs be offered to competitors in order to offset the costs involved? Could this lead to the company becoming a fourth-party repair facility? What happens when one of the employees destroys a multi-layer system board costing in excess of $3,000?

8

Networks

RELATIONSHIP OF MS-DOS AND NETWORKING

In order to discuss the relationship between DOS and networking, we must first define a network. A network is a group of terminals (or computers) and printers, connected to allow sharing of resources such as printers, storage, software, and data. The heart of the network is the file server (or server). The server has a high-capacity hard disk that is used to store all of the shared files. The hard disk drive on the server is formatted with special software called a Network Operating System. Some servers may contain additional hard disks and controllers for either duplexing or mirroring. Duplexing (duplicate drives and controllers) and mirroring (duplicate drive with a single controller) provide safety procedures for the network in case of a hard drive failure. A network may have more than one file server connected. Because of the special formatting of the hard disk, regular diagnostics will not function with that device. The diagnostics will work with the rest of the system, so floppy disk drives, RAM, and the system board can be tested as well as any other device except the hard disk. Special diagnostics to test the hard disk are available from the company whose network operating system is being used.

Terminals connected to the network can be a regular computer with a network adapter installed. These terminals may or may not have an internal hard disk. All they need to act as a network terminal is the adapter, a floppy disk drive, and a bootable disk with a few files to log on to the network. Terminals called diskless workstations may also be connected to the network. These terminals do not have any disk drives. The network adapter card contains a ROM with the information needed to attach the terminal to the network. In every other respect, these terminals should be treated as normal computers. Each terminal runs on MS-DOS under a network "shell." Normal DOS commands are used on the terminal to access information on either the local (built-in) drive(s) or the network drive(s). Usually, network terminals or work stations are set up to use menus, as the command structure for some of the network functions (selecting a shared printer for instance) are very complicated.

Booting a computer connected to a network with a DOS floppy disk bypasses the software that logs into the network. Testing can then be performed to ascertain where the problem exists. Another method is to RENAME the AUTOEXEC.BAT file and then warm boot the system. When testing a network "NODE" as a standalone system, the software may call for information stored on a shared drive. As the node is not connected to the network, the call to the shared drive will generate an error.

NETWORK TROUBLESHOOTING

The server can be either dedicated (functions only as a file server) or nondedicated (functions as the file server and a terminal). Connected to the file server via coaxial, twisted pair, or fiber-optic cable are one or more terminals or work stations. A printer or printers are connected to the network through a terminal or terminals. A printer may be connected directly to the server. In some cases, a computer will be dedicated as a print server. Some print servers can also be used as terminals. The network server runs under network operating system software such as NETWARE, VINES, or 3+3. The terminals use the MS-DOS operating system, running under the network shell software. First, a few words of caution: *Never touch a file server without the permission of the network supervisor.* Doing so can cause irreparable damage to the information stored on the network.

WIRING TOPOLOGIES

The wiring topology has little effect on the network operating system, nor does the operating system affect the topology used. There are advantages and disadvantages in each of the systems. All kinds and combinations of topologies and operating systems exist. The most important thing to remember is to isolate the problem and then perform the required service. The most common network topologies currently in use are Token-ring, StarLan, ARCnet, and Ethernet. The differences are in the cabling used, number of nodes permitted, the types of interface cards, speed of the network, maximum allowable cable length, and number of nodes that can be connected.

Token-ring uses a twisted pair cable and each device on the network is connected to a Multi-station Access Unit (MSAU). When a node on a Token-ring network is removed, the cable must be disconnected from the MSAU, not at the node end. An unterminated cable connected to a MSAU can lead to problems with the network. When the cable is removed (or the work station is powered down), the MSAU port terminates itself. Sometimes the internal terminating equipment becomes stuck, and the MSAU must be "reset" using a special tool. There are both passive (no external power required) and active (needs an external power source) MSAUs. Connectors on the MSAUs labeled "Ring In" and "Ring Out" are used to expand the network by adding additional MSAUs.

TOKEN-RING

The minimum main ring lengths for Type 1 and Type 3 installations will vary according to the number of MSAUs in the configuration. Adding powered units also affects the main ring length. When running 16-Mbps and 4-Mbps devices on the same network, the network will run at the lower speed. Token-ring on Type 1 uses 22 AWG cable, shielded twisted-pair. An 8-Station Non-Powered MSAU counts as 16 feet (4.9 m) of cable in the main ring. One unbridged main ring will support up to 32 8-Station MSAUs. A maximum of 260 nodes are permitted on the main ring. The maximum lobe length (distance from an 8-Station MSAU to a node) is 330 feet (100 m). Specifications are standardized for speeds of 16/4 Mbps. At speeds of 4 Mbps, a copper repeater can be used to extend ring and lobe distances up to 2460 feet (750 m). With fiber, both distances can be extended up to 2.5 miles (4 km). Token-ring on Type 3 uses 22 AWG cable, unshielded twisted pair. One unbridged main ring will support eight 8-station Type 3 MSAUs. A maximum of 72 nodes is permitted on the main ring. Use a Type 3 Media Filter for each network device. Specifications are standardized for 4 Mbps only. Speeds of 16 Mbps are documented but not widely supported.

STARLAN

StarLan can use either "telephone" type (twisted pair), coaxial, or fiber-optic cabling. Terminals on a StarLan are connected to the network through a "header hub." There can be several smaller hubs (sub-hubs) on the network, feeding into the header hub. To complicate matters even further, terminals can be daisy chained and then connected to a hub. If a terminal must be disconnected from a StarLan and is connected directly to a hub, disconnect the cable from the hub rather than from the terminal. If the terminal is part of a daisy chain, it may be necessary to down several terminals temporarily. The StarLan twisted pair interface cards contain an IN and OUT receptacle for the cables instead of a "T" connector. To disconnect a terminal the chain must be broken. Carry an adapter so that the broken part of the chain can be joined while the trouble is being repaired.

ARCNET

ARCnet is a technology developed by Datapoint Corporation, which is an inexpensive, easy to install, easy to expand, easily modified, 2.5-Mbps token-passing network that operates over RG62 A/U coaxial cable or twisted pair on a distributed star topology. For the star, either a passive or an active hub is required, depending upon the number of terminals and maximum cable lengths. Passive hubs require terminators on any unused ports, while active hubs are self-terminating. Active hubs require an external power source. Fiber-optic, coaxial, or twisted pair cable may be used. Various converters can be located along the network to convert from one type of cabling to another. To isolate a terminal connected directly to a hub, remove the hub end of the cable and terminate the hub if necessary. If the terminal is in a daisy chain, reconnect the broken chain to allow the other terminals on the network to function while the troubled unit is being repaired. In an ARCnet system, nodes may be located up to 2000 feet (609.6 m) from an active hub and up to 100 feet (30.5 m) from a passive hub. A passive hub may be up to 100 feet from an active hub. Nodes may be removed or powered down without affecting other nodes on the network. Active hubs may be daisy-chained for increased connectivity. Passive hubs may not be daisy-chained. The maximum number of nodes that the network can support is 255, but in most applications this number should not exceed 100. Unused passive hub ports must be terminated with RG62 terminators. Unused active hub ports do not require termination.

ETHERNET

Ethernet is a standards-based technology for ensuring compatibility in multi-vendor environments and having a high throughput of 10 Mbps. Ethernet is a bus topology that uses either one of two types of coaxial cable, fiber-optic, or twisted pair cable. The main (or backbone) coaxial cable must be terminated on each end. Thin cable is looped (daisy-chained) from device to device. At each device there is a T connector with the loop connected through the T and the terminal attached to the third side. When disconnecting the device from the network, remove the T connector from the terminal. Do not interrupt the cables that feed through the T or the chain will be broken, causing problems with the network. Thick Ethernet uses a heavy cable as the backbone. Cable taps called transceivers are attached to the backbone, and the transceiver is connected to the terminal by a multi-conductor cable. Disconnect the transceiver end of the cable when removing a terminal from the network.

To permit either type of cabling (thin or thick), the network interface card contains both a DB-15 and a coaxial (BNC type) connector. A jumper must be set to select the type of cabling being used. For Standard Ethernet (10BASE5), the maximum length of a single standard coaxial cable segment is 500 meters (1640 feet). A maximum of 2 IRL (Inter-Repeater Links) is allowed between devices; the maximum length of cable is 4 km (2.5 miles). The maximum length of a transceiver cable is 50 m (165 feet). The minimum distance between transceivers is 2.5 m (8.2 feet). No more than 100 transceiver connections are allowed per segment. Both ends of each segment must be terminated with a 50-ohm resistor. Only transceivers without SQE test (heartbeat) can be used with repeaters.

For Thin-wire Ethernet (10BASE2), the maximum length of a Thin-Net coaxial cable segment is 185 m (607 feet). A maximum of 2 IRL (Inter-Repeater Links) is allowed between devices; the maximum length of cable is 4 km (2.5 miles). Devices are typically connected with T connectors. If a BNC transceiver is used for device connection, then the maximum length of a transceiver cable is 50 m (165 feet). The minimum distance between transceivers is 0.5 m (1.6 feet). No more than 30 device connections are allowed per segment. Both ends of each segment must be terminated with a 50-ohm resistor. Only transceivers without SQE test (heartbeat) should be used with repeaters. A Fiber-optic Inter-Repeater Link (FIRL) consists of a length of fiber between two 802.3 repeaters, connected to the AUI port on the repeaters via a fiber-optic

transceiver. Fiber repeaters are 802.3 repeaters with the fiber transceiver built in. A Fiber-optic Inter-Repeater Link (FIRL) can be up to 2
km (1.2 miles) in length. An 802.3 Ethernet Network can have up to two
Fiber-optic Inter-Repeater Links, for a maximum of up to 4 km (2.5
miles). Twisted-Pair Cable uses 24 AWG, unshielded twisted pair
(standard telephone wire) to connect work stations to a central concentrator. Concentrators can be daisy-chained and can be attached to a
fiber-optic or coaxial backbone. Maximum distance from concentrators
to each node is 100 m (328 feet). Twisted pair is the most economical
cable type and is easiest to work with, but it is not recommended for
installations with abundant EMI/RFI interference (for example, over
fluorescent lights).

PROBLEM ISOLATION

For the purposes of isolating a problem, consider any abnormal situation a network problem until proven otherwise. Problems can be divided into hardware, software, and cabling (including distribution
equipment such as a transceiver, hub, MSAU, and so on). Isolating the
problem is often easy. Repairing the problem may require special tools,
equipment, and knowledge.

Find out from the network supervisor if the problem surfaced as a
result of extending the network (adding or moving equipment). If so, try
to return the network to its original configuration and see if the problem disappears. If one terminal on the network is affected, the problem
may be cabling, the network adapter, the network software on that
terminal (the shell), MS-DOS, or the hardware itself. Notify the supervisor and have him or her assist in disconnecting that terminal from the
network. Remove the network adapter, boot diagnostics, and verify
that the hardware is functional. Reinstall the network adapter, and
reinstall the special software required to log on to the network. Ask the
supervisor to assist with the software installation.

If the same failure is repeated, try connecting the terminal to a
different network connection that is known to be good. This will determine if the cabling is at fault. If the system still fails, test the adapter
using the diagnostics that came with it, or exchange the network
adapter with one that is known to be functioning. Some other adapter
in the terminal may be using the same address as the network adapter.
Remove as many other cards from the system as possible and run the
tests again. Sometimes the conflict will be with a video card using extended video RAM.

If several terminals on the network are affected, the problem is most likely in a cable or distribution device. Determine which terminals are functioning and which terminals are failing. Ask the supervisor for a wiring plan of the network. Determine where the faulty cable is located by following it and using the wiring plan.

If all of the terminals are affected, the problem is either the cabling from the server to the first distribution point, the adapter card in the server, or the server itself. Run diagnostics on the file server. Test all of the installed devices except the hard disk (which requires special diagnostic software). As stated earlier, the network runs under its own operating system and this might affect the hard disk diagnostics. If the server appears to be functioning properly, replace the cable between the server and the first distribution point. An alternative would be to move a work station over to the server and cable them directly. Some cabling topologies will not permit direct connection.

If the file server is nondedicated, see if it can be used as a terminal. Replace the adapter card in the server with a known good adapter. Remember to change the address on the adapter if required. In some topologies, all of the adapters are physically the same. In other topologies, the server requires a special adapter. Terminals may boot from a hard disk drive if one is present, a floppy disk, or, in some cases, there could be a diskless work station. Diskless work stations boot from a ROM.

In cases other than the diskless work station, it may be necessary to reinstall the software needed for the network. Files may be lost or corrupted. If a printer problem is present, disconnect the printer from the network and perform a self-test. If the self-test is normal, reconnect the printer. Boot the work station that the printer is connected to with a DOS floppy disk. This is now a normal standalone system. Try to print using the print screen key or print from locally installed software. If printing is successful, the network software is probably the problem. Network software for a shared printer is located on the terminal to which the printer is connected. In addition, the software on the server and each of the terminals sharing the printer must be configured correctly.

TROUBLESHOOTING SUMMARY

ALL NETWORKS

If the entire network has failed, start at the server and disconnect large segments until the trouble has been isolated. Add smaller segments back until the problem has been localized. Verify the positions of any jumpers or dip switches on the interface cards in the server(s) and terminals. Check for missing jumpers. Check for address conflicts between adapters. Verify that power is being supplied to active equipment—MSAUs, hubs, and so on. Observe diagnostic LEDs on equipment if applicable. Check the network for recently installed equipment.

Depending upon the topology, there are rules governing the number of nodes, length of cables, distance between devices, and so forth. Use the diagnostics that come with the network adapter board whenever possible. Check for cable breaks, bends, or excessive wear. If using a hub, MSAU, or multiple connecting device, try using a different port. Twisted pair cabling may contain media filters. Try replacing these. Test terminators and Baluns for opens, shorts, or incorrect resistance.

Remove the adapter card from the terminal and clean the contacts. Try placing the adapter in a different slot in the terminal. Verify that the correct cable is being used, especially with coax cabling. Confirm that software drivers are installed if necessary, and that the CONFIG.SYS and AUTOEXEC.BAT files are correct. Check for duplicate node addresses. Token-ring adapters have the node address burned into the internal ROM. Other topologies require setting of the addresses manually.

ARCNET

Check for duplicate node addresses. ARCnet interface cards must have their addresses set manually. Make sure that terminators are installed where necessary. This includes passive hubs, T connectors, and cable ends.

TOKEN-RING

If active MSAUs are being used, check the status LEDs to verify the condition of the unit. If passive MSAUs are used, disconnect all cables and reset the ports using the initialization tool that came with the MSAU. Check for shorts between pins 1 & 9 and 5 & 6 on the DB-9 connector of the cable between the MSAU and the interface card. If these pins show a short with BOTH ends of the cable disconnected, the cable is okay.

ETHERNET

Check the adapter for the position of the jumper that selects either the coax connector or the DB-15. Make sure that all T connectors are tight. Check for unterminated cables or connectors.

STARLAN

Try to isolate the trouble to one repeater or hub. Check for unterminated or dangling cables, especially attached to an OUT port. Telephone-type (flat) cables using RJ-45 connectors must have pin-to-pin continuity. Pin 1 connected to pin 1, 2 to 2, and so on.

9

Adding Peripherals and Performing Upgrades

A peripheral is a device that is connected to the system board of the computer. These devices generally require some type of adapter or controller, which is either integrated into the system board or installed into an expansion slot. An upgrade is an enhancement to the system, which may also require installation of an expansion board. Installing additional RAM on a stock PC to increase memory from 256K to 640K is considered an upgrade, while the video display (and associated interface board) is considered a peripheral.

INSTALLING PERIPHERALS AND/OR UPGRADES

These are general guidelines for installing peripherals and performing upgrades. First and foremost, the BIOS must support the upgrade, or there must be a way to modify the system through drivers and the CONFIG.SYS. A classic example deals with adding a hard drive to the original IBM PC. If the hardware installation was performed properly but the system hangs or refuses to recognize the drive, check the ROM BIOS date. If the date is earlier than 10/27/82, a ROM BIOS upgrade is necessary. If the date is 10/27/82 or later, the ROM BIOS is not the problem.[26] It should be noted that this upgrade has been discontinued by IBM. If an upgrade is required, there are two alternatives. One is to purchase a compatible BIOS through a dealer or mail order. The other

---

[26]Routines for determining the BIOS date are detailed in Appendix D.

is to return the system board to an authorized IBM dealer for a replacement. The second suggestion is far more costly than the first.

Different architectures require different methods. Above all else, remember that 8-bit ISA machines contain multiple switches and jumpers. 16-bit and 32-bit ISA machines have switches and jumpers for some items and require a software setup for others. EISA and Microchannel systems have no switches or jumpers. Everything is configured through software. The subject of switch and jumper settings has been discussed in other areas of this book. Before beginning an installation, note all of the current switch and jumper positions. Read the instruction manual for the new equipment, noting any switch or jumper settings. Note any changes that must be made to the existing equipment. Install and test one item at a time. Test the complete system to see if the installation has affected a preexisting device. For systems that store the setup information in CMOS, write down the current settings before making any changes.

Microchannel systems have slightly different requirements. Each MCA machine is delivered with a "reference" floppy disk. This floppy disk contains setup information, user diagnostics, and advanced diagnostics. In addition, there is a DOS patch and disk-caching software.

USING THE IBM REFERENCE DISK

The system must be booted from the reference disk or a backup copy. Copying the reference disk onto a hard disk serves no purpose. Be sure to use the latest revision of the reference disk for the system that is being upgraded. If an upgrade or service is being performed on a previously delivered system, ask the customer for their backup copy of the reference disk. When installing a new system, make a backup of the reference disk for the customer. Tell the customer that this disk must be available if the system requires service.

If the system is to be used as it was delivered from the manufacturer, the reference disk is still necessary to change the time or date, run the configuration setup if the battery is changed, or install or remove passwords. The reference disk also contains information about the installed expansion boards in files called ADFs (Adapter Definition Files). Remember, there aren't any switches or jumpers in these systems. The adapter definition files all follow the same naming convention, conforming to the IBM "registered ID number" for a particular device. The ADFs are named @nnnn.ADF, where nnnn are four hexadecimal digits. Using this scheme, there are more than 61,000 possible combinations. Shipped with each new adapter is a disk containing the correct ADF for that device. The ADF must be copied onto the backup copy of the reference disk before the adapter is installed into the system, using the copy option on the menu. After the adapter is installed, the system must be booted from the updated backup copy of the reference disk. Follow the instructions on the screen to update the configuration.

If an adapter is removed from the system, the configuration must also be updated. When the ADF is read from the backup reference disk and the adapter is not present, a warning may be displayed on the screen. It may be necessary to reconfigure the system manually through the menus provided on the reference disk. If one or more adapters are removed from a system and reinstalled into slots that they were not in originally, the configuration must be run. If the adapters are returned to the same slots, the configuration does not have to be run as long as the battery remained connected to the system board or the CMOS retained sufficient charge to retain the configuration information. If the system board has been removed or replaced, run the configuration. If the battery has been replaced, run the configuration. If an adapter is installed and the system has not been reconfigured with the proper ADFs on the reference disk, errors can be generated that do not have any direct bearing on the actual problem. Collect as many ADFs as possible for use in situations where the backup reference disks are not available or a device must be installed and the ADF for it is either missing or damaged.

The reference disk can be used to change I/O port assignments or disable ports completely. If parallel or serial communication is a problem, boot with the reference disk and verify the port assignments. Even if the ports are disabled, they will test okay using the IBM diagnostics, unless the port being tested is defective. The reference disk has a selection on the main menu to test the computer. This is the user diagnostics. To access the advanced diagnostics, press Ctrl-A at the main menu instead of choosing any of the listed selections.

CONSIDERATIONS REGARDING PERIPHERALS

Generally, peripherals are designed to be generic. Sometimes a particular peripheral can not be installed in a system because the manufacturer did not conform to accepted industry standards. Consider the physical mounting or installation. Is the peripheral device supported by the hardware (BIOS and physical architecture) or the software (applications, DOS)? Can the power supply handle the additional hardware, or is a replacement required? Is it necessary to add or replace a board and/or cables (and are they available)? What is the cost of a new part versus a refurbished part? Should the replacement be an OEM (Original Equipment Manufacturer) or a third-party part? Is this the time for the customer to upgrade the system? Does the customer need more storage or memory? How will the current software (applications and data) be affected?

RECOMMENDING REPLACEMENTS

A technician should be conscious of the present and future needs of his or her customer. While service is being performed, the system should be evaluated and suggestions made to the customer regarding upgrades or enhancements. If a hard disk needs replacing, the technician should make the customer aware of the options available. It may be more cost effective for the customer to upgrade to a higher-capacity drive than to repair (or replace) the defective drive. Would system performance be increased by using two low-capacity drives or one drive with a high capacity? Failure of a memory board or multi-function board may lead to suggestions for an upgrade, rather than a replacement. Perhaps one or more functions on a multi-function board are duplicated or no longer required. A less expensive alternative could serve the purpose. Perhaps different functions may be an improvement to the system. Adding a hard disk or a second hard disk should lead to questions regarding a higher-capacity power supply or a tape backup (or both). Some recently developed applications will perform better on older systems, if the video system (monitor and video board) is upgraded. Considering the cost involved, is this type of upgrade worthwhile? Don't try to upgrade every machine to a supercomputer. Many customers do not need all of the bells and whistles that are available. A customer who makes a purchase based upon a technician's recommendation, only to find out that they do not need or use the equipment, will not consult that technician (or his or her employer) in the future. There are many opportunities to help the customer and increase revenue at the same time, without resorting to overkill.

MEMORY

Random Access Memory (RAM) is included as a peripheral because many systems, especially older PC and XT class machines, have had memory upgrades installed either directly on the system board or an expansion card. Newer systems are having RAM upgrades performed so that they can take advantage of operating environments such as Windows. When installing or replacing RAM chips or SIMMs (Single In-line Memory Modules), remember that the rated speed of the RAM chips must be equal to or greater than the speed of the system clock. There are nine chips in a row, but the number of chips in a bank depend upon the CPU and the bus. A 286 system uses a 16-bit processor, and a bank consists of 18 chips (16 plus 2 parity chips). SIMMs should have either 9 or 18 chips. The 8-chip SIMMs are for Apple equipment, which do not use parity checking. 8- and 9-chip SIMMs are the same size, so count the chips. All of the chips in a bank must be of the same speed (and, preferably, of the same manufacture), but there may be a variation from bank to bank. The speed of floating point math coprocessors must also be equal to or greater than the system clock to prevent damage. Refer to Table 9.1 when selecting RAM chips, math coprocessors, and the clock generation (8284 or 82284) and the bus control (8288 or 82288) chips.

Table 9.1   System chip speeds.

Clock speed	Chip speed
4.77MHz	209ns
6MHz	166ns
8MHz	125ns
10MHz	100ns
12MHz	83ns
16MHz	62ns

The result of installing chips that are too slow for the system may be anything from the system locking up to Parity Check, NMI Interrupt, Stack Overflow, or Divide Overflow error messages. Systems with "wait states" (a method of slowing down the system) can (and usually will) use chips with speeds that are slower than those listed in the table. To be sure that the chips are the correct speed, use the rating stamped on the first bank of RAM chips. These chips were installed by the manufacturer, and RAM of this speed or faster will perform without any problem.

If a math coprocessor that is too slow for the system is used, it will most likely overheat and self-destruct.

VIDEO MONITORS

CAUTION: Video monitors contain high voltages. Improper handling and lack of proper precautions can be fatal. Video monitors (or displays) fail because of several factors. In many cases, there are heavy components, such as transformers and large capacitors, mounted on a vertical board. The combination of gravity (weight on the soldered connections) and high internal heat cause soldered connections to open. Defects often appear in the flyback transformer after prolonged use. Poor contact between the printed circuit boards and components occur due to soldering defects (arcing or cold solder). If a monitor fails, first check that power is present. Look through the vents in the case to see if the heaters in the neck of the CRT (Cathode Ray Tube) are illuminated. If the heaters are not visible, check the power to the monitor. If working inside a monitor, safety precautions are a MUST. Disconnect the monitor from the A.C. power. Use an isolation transformer when working inside a powered up monitor. Discharge the anode of the CRT before disconnecting the high-voltage lead. The CRT may retain a charge even if the monitor has not been used in several weeks. Make sure that a coworker knows what is happening and is checking up regularly. Be sure to have any special tools that may be required, such as a CRT Discharge Tool or a Tamper Torx driver for PS/2 monitors. Try resoldering the heavier components and connectors located on the vertical boards. Flyback transformers (the transformer that provides the high voltage to the anode of the CRT) fail frequently. Most of the components in a monitor can be obtained through electronics suppliers.

Remember that there is a lot of heat generated inside a monitor, and components that are used as replacements must be able to withstand the high temperatures. Tell customers that the vents on monitors must not be blocked. Some replacement CRTs are available through the manufacturer of the monitor, while others need to be obtained from independent suppliers. Generally, cabinet parts are difficult to obtain. The new VGA monitors use a 15-pin connector in a 9-pin housing. The smaller pins are delicate and easily bent. These cables are available from IBM for their PS/2 monitors. Schematics are not usually available from the manufacturers, but Sam's Computerfacts may provide the material that is necessary. The majority of monochrome monitors on the market today (except for the VGA monitors) are so inexpensive that it is often less expensive to sell the customer a new unit than to repair the old one. Be sure that the monitor matches the video board inside the system. Some monitor problems are the result of customers moving monitors from one system to another. Most color monitors will not function with monochrome cards.

MODEMS

There are two types of modems, internal and external. The main differences are that the external modem has status indicator lights on the front panel, and it needs its own power supply. The majority of modems have a small speaker built into them, which will mute when the connection with another modem is completed.

Use communication software that is familiar when testing a modem. If communication with another computer can be established, the hardware is functioning properly (so the problem must be the customer's software, the customer, or an intermittent problem). The instruction manual explains how to perform a communication test between the computer and the modem. This requires communication software and verifies that the modem and the CPU are communicating with each other. The modem does not have to be connected to a telephone line for these tests to function.

If the modem tests normal, perhaps the problem is with the telephone line. The most conclusive test is to communicate with another modem. Use the service that the customer will be using, a bulletin board that is reliable, or a commercial service such as Compuserve. Compuserve allows limited access to its system for demonstration purposes using a special password.[27] This is a great way to test two-way modem communication between the system and a mainframe at a remote location. Compuserve can be reached through a local access number, saving telephone toll charges. If the means to contact another modem is not at hand, dial a telephone number at the current location or a number that will be answered.[28] This way the modem can be tested to see if it dials and connects by listening through the built-in speaker. It is not a conclusive test of the modem's communication capability, but it will rule out several unknowns.

When using a modem, the following sequence of events should occur (the same sequence as using a telephone): a connection is made to the telephone line, the dial tone is heard, and then the modem dials the number of the host.[29] There should be a ringing on the line at the host's

---

[27]Contact Compuserve for specific dealer information.

[28]Use the time or weather telephone number, listed in the telephone directory.

[29]Be sure to select tone or pulse dialing, according to the telephone company service that is being used.

end. If a modem answers, there will be some static and noise followed by the connection, at which time the speaker will mute. At the conclusion of the communication, the modem should hang up and disconnect from the phone line so that another call can be made. Some modems are not very intelligent. They will dial without having a dial tone. Careful listening can determine if the events occur in the proper order.

Is the modem communicating with the computer? A modem is a serial device. Most modems installed in or connected to microcomputers are asynchronous (uses two wires) devices. (Synchronous modems use four wires, but these are found only on mainframes.) Internal modems plug directly into the expansion bus. External modems must connect to an asynchronous serial port. Confirm that the ports are configured correctly. If there is only one serial device or port, it must be configured as COM1. If there is more than one serial device or port, the ports must be configured in sequence as COM1, COM2, and so on. (Some systems may only support a maximum of two serial ports.) A device can not be configured as COM2 unless there is a port or device configured as COM1. Two devices can not be configured to the same address at the same time. An A/B switch may be needed if there is an insufficient number of ports. Most advanced diagnostics will detect the serial port assignments of the various devices. Make sure that the number of assignments is the same as the number of ports or devices.

Be sure that the software that is being used with the modem is configured for the same port assignment as the modem. The software must also be configured for the correct communication parameters such as baud rate, number of data bits, number of stop bits, parity type, duplex, and protocol. Failure to do so will result in garbled communication. Sometimes a host will send characters that can not be handled properly by the video system unless the ANSI.SYS driver is installed in the CONFIG.SYS file. External modems will have to be connected to one of the asynchronous ports. Remember, all serial cables look the same from the outside. It is important to check the pin outs of the cable and compare them to the pin outs that the modem manufacturer requires for proper operation. A Hayes modem requires pins 1 through 8 and pin 20 to be connected straight through. Check the cable using an ohm meter. Check for pins that are jumped together or shorted. If a meter is not available and the cable is not of the molded variety, remove the shells from the connectors and check the colors of the individual wires. It is a good idea to carry a known good cable with you when responding to modem trouble. External modems draw power from an A.C. power supply that is plugged into an A.C. outlet. At least one of the lamps on the front panel will be illuminated if power is connected and the modem is switched on.

Be sure that the customer is using a dedicated telephone line for the modem, terminated in a standard RJ-11 jack. Some multiline telephone systems and private telephone companies use the RJ-11 to connect their instruments. It is not possible to connect a modem to these jacks and expect it to work properly. If the customer wants to use his or her modem with their internal telephone system, they must have their telephone company install a special jack. If the customer's telephone has any special equipment or services connected to it, a special phone line may be required. The first thing to do is to verify that the telephone line is functional. The easiest way to test the telephone line is to connect a telephone to it. If there is a dial tone, and the telephone behaves normally when dialing out or being dialed into, then the line is not the problem. Telephone line problems must be referred to the telephone company.

Verify that the cable connecting the modem to the telephone is working correctly. This cable is usually supplied with the modem. Carry a good spare when responding to a modem problem. Test the customer's cable by substituting it for the cable on their telephone or the spare. Sometimes it is the least expensive item that gives the most headaches. Never overlook the obvious! If the system is fully functional, all of the events are correct, and communication can not be established with a host, the problem may be at the other end. Try another host as a test. Telephone the service that can not be reached by modem and request assistance. Ask them if they have been experiencing problems. Perhaps their system was down due to malfunction or routine maintenance. If communication is established but it is garbled, check the software for correct parameter settings. The host dictates the parameters that must be used.

A word about compatible modems. Almost all of the modems on the market today are Hayes compatible, meaning that they use the command language or command set established by Hayes. The Hayes command set has become the de facto standard of the microcomputer industry. This does not mean that all modems function exactly the same. Most commercial (off-the-shelf) communication software will operate normally with most modems.

There are many companies that write their own communication software, which is distributed as part of a vertical application. The software may not be as tolerant as off-the-shelf applications, and they require strict hardware compatibility as well. Failure to disconnect the phone line, or failure to connect on the first attempt, are little annoyances that can occur. If the customer is using a compatible modem and experiencing problems, especially with noncommercial communications software, try testing with a genuine Hayes modem. Again, a telephone call to the software supplier or publisher should verify the problem, and perhaps supply a solution.

CD-ROM DRIVES

CD-ROM drives (or players) have recently become increasingly popular due to the lowering of prices and the availability of applications published in CD-ROM disk format. The CD-ROM drives are SCSI (Small Computer Systems Interface) devices. Anyone familiar with the Apple product line should have some background in installing SCSI devices, which are relatively new to the PC world. As with all hardware (and software), it is a good idea to read the manual, especially with an unfamiliar product, before attempting a first-time installation. The system into which the CD-ROM drive will be installed must have a minimum of 640K of RAM and must be using MS-DOS 3.1 or higher.

Check the documentation to see if the CD-ROM drive needs to be set to a specific SCSI ID number. All SCSI devices can be set to an ID number between 0 and 6. The higher the number, the higher the priority. Each device must have a unique number (two devices may not use the same ID). The device driver (to be added to the CONFIG.SYS) may require a specific ID number for the drive to operate, so check the software documentation also. Check for proper terminations. SCSI devices are daisy-chained, and the first and last devices on the chain must be terminated. Terminators can be in the form of resistor packs (sometimes as many as three packs), dip switches, or terminating plugs that fit onto a connector on the chassis of the SCSI device. The majority of SCSI devices have two identical connectors. It does not matter which connector is used. Verify that the SCSI host adapter (interface card) does not have an address conflict with any other installed devices or adapters. If there is an address conflict, the SCSI adapter board should be reconfigured. There will be a set of jumpers (or DIP switches) on the board for this purpose.

Install the software that came with the CD-ROM. The driver software must be Microsoft CD-ROM EXTENSIONS VERSION 2.0 or later. This device driver must be added to the CONFIG.SYS file. If the system contains multiple drives, the LASTDRIVE directive may have to be added to the CONFIG.SYS file also. The drive will be assigned a letter and can be accessed by the DIR command. There will be other software included to access the actual data on the CD-ROM disks. The majority of the software has an interactive installation routine. CD-ROM drives have the ability to reproduce sound, including music. CD's can be played through the computer, although the quality of the audio will certainly suffer (as will the listeners). Many of these systems have connectors for attaching external speakers or amplifiers.

There are CD-ROM changers available with capacities of up to six ROMS (or disks). These changers connect through a single SCSI board, the net result being six additional drives with only one expansion slot being used.

BACKUP PROCEDURES

MS-DOS provides a utility called BACKUP for backing up a hard disk. The information is then placed back onto a new or reformatted disk using the RESTORE utility, also included with MS-DOS. It is not safe to mix versions of MS-DOS. When upgrading the operating system, boot the system with the same version of DOS that is being installed on the hard disk, and use this version for the backup. Files backed up with versions of MS-DOS prior to 3.3 can not be restored with DOS 3.3 or higher.

Have a sufficient number of formatted floppy disks available. Early versions of BACKUP require formatted disks. Newer versions allow a switch that tells BACKUP to format the floppy disk prior to backing up. Backing up large hard disks to floppies, especially if the floppies are formatted during the backup procedure, is a time-consuming task. It is necessary for a person to attend this operation, as disks must be changed and the system notified via the keyboard. The backups must be labeled and kept in the order that they are created. An attempt to restore from a set of disks that are out of order will be aborted by the system (MS-DOS). It is good practice to make a second set of backups for safety. Media problems can arise rendering one or more of the backup disks unusable.

Backing up to tape is quicker, easier, and does not require constant supervision by an operator. Prices for both internal and external tape drives have dropped, making them affordable for everyone. As with floppy disk backups, it is necessary to have a sufficient number of formatted tapes available. Formatting (or servo writing) a tape is much more time consuming than performing the actual backup.

Current versions of MS-DOS (version 5.0 as of this writing) do not directly support tape drives. It is therefore necessary to have the proper tape software on a usable floppy disk. For a customer who backs up their system on a regular basis, the tape software can be installed on their hard disk. The problems arise when the drive must be reformatted or replaced. If the tape software is not on a floppy disk, it is not possible to initiate the restore procedure.

When replacing a hard drive, bring a tape backup system to save time. Back up the customer's old drive, perform the replacement, and restore their data. If a tape system is not available, it is possible to use another hard disk. A device such as the Hard Card from Plus Development is perfect for this situation. Using a tape or other hard drive saves the technician and the customer time and negates the need to locate (or bring) and format a quantity of floppy disks.

It is not uncommon in large installations to find one or two external tape backup units being moved from system to system. It is necessary to install a controller card in each system that uses the tape unit, but this is much more cost effective than purchasing a tape drive for each computer. With careful scheduling and coordination, each system can be backed up to tape on a daily basis.

There are several utilities on the market, including FastBack, Norton Backup, and PC Tools, that permit faster backups to disk than the DOS BACKUP utility. Some of these are extremely fast if the system contains two floppy disk drives. As with a tape backup, the software must be available on a floppy disk in order to restore the backed up data to a new or reformatted hard disk. Material that is backed up using any of these methods must be restored by the same method, as the data is handled differently by each of the applications. It is not uncommon for someone in an office to install one of these backup utilities on each system. Customers perform their backups religiously. When a hard drive is replaced or reformatted, it is discovered that the software needed to restore the backups is not to be found.

Whether using tape or floppy disk for a backup method, several options are available. It is possible to make a complete backup of the hard disk or back up individual files, directories, or groups of files. Most backup software can also detect files that have changed since the last backup or backup files based upon the creation (or revision) dates as displayed in the directory. Regardless of the method employed, a minimum of two sets of backups should be made. Alternate the media, using one set of floppies (or tapes) on odd days and the other on even days. By alternating the media, if one set of backups is rendered useless, there is another recent backup available. It is easier to reconstruct one day's worth of work than that of several days (or possibly weeks).

CONFIGURING MULTIPLE DRIVES

Under normal circumstances, one hard drive controller and one floppy drive controller can be installed in a system. Sometimes these are contained on the same expansion board. Each controller can support a maximum of two drives for a total of two hard drives and two floppy drives.

To install multiple drives, verify that the type of drive being added is supported by the controller. Some older controllers will not support high density floppy drives regardless of the revision of the operating system and BIOS that is in the system. Be sure that the drive select jumpers or switches (located on the drives) are set correctly. In MS-DOS machines, the floppy drive select is governed by the twist in the cable leading to the controller. The drive select should not require a change. If the cables are not correct, then the drive select will need to be changed. Remember, hard drive cables are different from floppy drive cables. The twists are in different positions. With some hard drive systems, it is necessary to change the drive select in order to configure the D drive. If in doubt, or if there is a problem, change the drive select and perform some tests. As always, write down the positions of all switches and jumpers before making any changes. Be sure that the power to the system has been turned off before changing any switches, jumpers, or cables.

Mixing the size and density of floppy drives within a system is relatively simple. Hard drives are another story. Because of the great variation in the capacities of hard drives (number of heads and cylinders) it is often difficult to install two drives in the same computer, especially if it is an eight-bit system. The controller must support both drives. In a 286 or higher system, the drives are configured through the BIOS routines, making it simpler for two unlike drives to be installed. IDE drives pose less of a problem, as they use integral controllers. In most cases, it is not possible to install a second controller in a system because of address conflicts. The only exception is in network file servers where disk duplexing is used. Duplexing requires special hard drive controllers and a thorough knowledge of both the hardware and network software for a successful installation.

The last physical drive on the cable requires a termination resistor. When there is only one drive in the system, this is not a problem. When a drive is added, it may be the last logical drive (drive B or D) but not the last physical drive. New drives have the termination resistor installed. In most cases, it is a plug-in device marked with the resistance. Some manufacturers provide DIP switches for removing the resistor from the circuit. Remove termination resistor(s) if necessary. Termination resistors are of different values for different drives. If it becomes necessary to install a termination, be sure to use the correct value.

It may also be necessary to install a device driver or add a DRIVPARM statement to the CONFIG.SYS. This is especially true when adding a 3½" floppy disk drive to an older system. The floppy drive controllers on early systems were not built to support the 3½" drives. When the PS/2 series was introduced, it became necessary to transfer information between machines with 3½" drives and older systems having 5¼" drives. There were several solutions available. IBM made an external 3½" drive available for their XT and AT systems. Because of the BIOS used in these systems and IBM's version of MS-DOS not supporting the DRIVPARM directive, a device driver was packaged with the drive.

MODULE SWAPPING

A module is any item that can be replaced without soldering. These include chips, boards, monitors, cables, cabinet parts, fuses, and so forth. It is important to have a stock of working replacement modules available. This requires that repair or replacement of defective modules be managed properly. It is more cost effective to recycle as many modules as possible than to purchase additional stock, especially since some products have extremely short lifespans.

Frequently, a service manual will suggest the replacement of a system board, controller, or other item. More often, the manual will suggest replacing several parts in a specific order. In cases where the trouble could be caused by one or more items in a chain (floppy disk drive, data or control cable, adapter, system board, power supply), the suggested replacement may not provide the proper fix. Technicians have replaced drives, controllers, and cables, only to discover that the floppy disk media was defective! If the replacement part does not fix the problem, reinstall the old module before proceeding. This eliminates the replacement of a good part with another good part in an effort to find the trouble. Parts must be marked or labeled as to their condition and origin. Technicians must keep track of new parts and parts removed from a system. Defective parts must be marked so that they do not get mixed in with good parts. Mark the part, not the container. Be cost conscious when it comes to parts. Don't shotgun.[30] It is easy for a lazy technician to replace all the parts in a chain in order to solve a

---

[30]Shotgunning refers to replacing parts haphazardly, hoping to cure the problem.

problem. This is not good business practice. It is costly to the customer and to the business.

Several manufacturers have stated that the number of good parts, marked as defective, that are returned to them is close to 40 percent of all parts that they receive. This results in slower turnaround of parts, possible out-of-stock situations, and unnecessary costs. Avoid recalls (return visits). When a board (or any other component) is replaced, the system must be thoroughly tested. First, run several loops of advanced diagnostics. When the system is functioning normally, have the customer attempt to duplicate the problem for which the service was requested. The customer must be satisfied that the trouble has been eliminated.

REMOTE PROCEDURES

Low cost modems and software such as PC Anywhere or Carbon Copy permit remote diagnosis of problems within certain limitations. The system must be bootable, have a modem connected, and have the remote software installed. Most software consultants require the ability to perform remote maintenance as a condition of their employment. Remote maintenance saves traveling time and allows access to the system during nonbusiness hours. In many situations, remote access capability is an intelligent addition to a system.

TECHNICAL SUPPORT FROM MANUFACTURERS

Most manufacturers expect the owners of their products to obtain support from their local dealers. On rare occasions, a customer call will be accepted by a manufacturer. This is the exception, and not the rule. If the customer complains about the service that was provided by an authorized dealer, the manufacturer will intervene. If the dealer is an Authorized Service Provider, then manufacturer support is available to them. It is expected that an authorized dealer has at least one factory-trained technician on staff, as well as a full set of service manuals and documentation. Often, a phone call to technical support will leave the caller on hold for long periods of time. Sometimes, after describing the problem to the support person, they will refer the caller to the manual or document that should have been consulted in the first place. If the problem involves a combination of hardware or software manufactured by several vendors, compatibility issues can arise, and the vendors will blame their competitor's products. Worse yet, they will tell you that it should work when it does not. Every effort should be made to solve the problem by using service manuals and diagnostics before calling the manufacturer. Under no circumstances should technical support be used as a crutch. Do not call technical support for the customer or involve customers in a three-way conference call. It is expensive for manufacturers to maintain support facilities and personnel. Wasting the time of a technical support person means that other technicians are kept waiting. Show some consideration. Technicians should never give a manufacturer's technical support telephone number to a customer!

DISK DRIVES

The material contained in this section pertains to both hard and floppy disks unless a specific mention is made. Disk failures are rather common. The reason that disks (or drives) fail is mostly because they are mechanical devices and they are constantly being accessed by the customer or application software. To understand why disk problems occur, it is important to know something about the workings of disks and disk drives.

When a disk is formatted, a boot record is written at track 0, surface 0, sector 1. If the disk is formatted as a data disk,[31] the boot record identifies the disk as a DOS work disk. On a system disk, the boot record is responsible for continuing to load the operating system that was started by the bootstrap program in ROM. If a track 0 error is encountered during the formatting process, the disk can not be formatted. On a hard disk, sometimes a low-level format can overcome this problem by relocating track 0.

The FAT (File Allocation Table) is written directly after the boot record. In actuality, two identical copies of the FAT are written. If one copy becomes damaged, the second copy can be used to restore the FAT. The FAT contains the status of the space on the disk such as the size and locations of files.

Following the FAT, the (root) directory is written. The directory tells the name and size of files and the date and time that they were created. The root directory on a hard drive can hold a maximum of 512 entries (files and subdirectories). The root directory of a floppy is somewhat more limited. There is no limitation to the number of entries that can be placed in a subdirectory, but the system will appear sluggish after the quantity reaches about 150.

---

[31]Data disks formatted using the FORMAT command without the /S switch and are not bootable. A bootable disk is called a system disk and is prepared with the /S switch, as in FORMAT d:/S.

If the disk is to be bootable, the two hidden system files (IO.SYS and MSDOS.SYS) must reside immediately after the directory. If this area is not reserved for system files by using the /S switch with the FORMAT command, it will be used by data. Once a disk is formatted for data, it can not be made bootable by using the SYS command, as the space reserved for these two files does not exist.

Data (and applications) are arranged sequentially. The data is written at the first available user space, immediately following the directory (or the system files on a bootable disk). Data is written in this manner until the disk is filled.

Fragmentation of files is a normal occurrence, but it can slow down file storage and retrieval. Since data is written sequentially to a disk, each file has a finite space in which it resides. When a file is retrieved, extended, and written back to the disk, MS-DOS tries to replace the file in its original space. Because the file has been extended, DOS must split it into two or more fragments. DOS will write as much of the file as will fit into the original space. It will then fill up any vacant spaces until the complete file has been stored on the disk. Information, called pointers, is then placed in the FAT so that the size and location of the file is available. Otherwise, the file could not be used again. Each time the file is extended, additional fragments are created. Every time the file is retrieved or stored, pointers must be referenced or created. The entire process degrades the speed of the retrieval or storage function. Performing a periodic backup and restore of the hard disk removes all fragmentation. When the files are backed up, they are defragmented by the system and written to the backup media. The restore process places the contiguous files back on the hard disk. If files are large and hard disk space is limited, the fragmentation process will begin again.

As mentioned earlier, hard disk cables and floppy disk cables may look the same, but they are different. Exceptions are IDE and SCSI drive cables which have no resemblance to the cables used on MFM, RLL, or ESDI drives. Be sure to use the correct cables. Hard disk controllers have limitations to the type and size of the drives that they support. When upgrading to a higher-capacity drive, be sure that the controller will support the new configuration. If the configuration is not supported, the controller must be replaced.

There are several encoding techniques used to store data on a hard disk. The two most common methods are MFM and RLL. MFM controllers work with both MFM and RLL drives, but RLL controllers work only with RLL drives. RLL offers 55 percent higher capacity and 55 percent faster access time. All ESDI and SCSI drives use the RLL encoding scheme. MS-DOS version 2.0 supports a maximum of 16Mb per drive; DOS 2.1 supports a maximum of 32Mb. When using a higher-capacity drive, a compatible version of MS-DOS must be employed.

There are general rules for correct drive select setting. Drive manufacturers use one of two numbering systems. Some manufacturers may use 0-3 while others use 1-4 (see Table 9.2). (Floppy drives use these numbering systems, too.) The drive select modifies the drive address so that more than one drive can be attached to a single I/O cable. When there are two drive connectors on the I/O cable and the section between them is split and twisted, both drives use the second drive select. If the cable is straight through between the two drive connectors (no split or twist), use the first drive select for the first drive and the second drive select for the second drive. It should be noted here that the older CP/M systems used straight cables. MS-DOS systems use the split cable system. One of the few variations is found in Compaq Deskpro systems. These have a cable with three connectors and one twist. The third connector is reserved for an internal tape drive, which has its drive select set internally. Using this cable system on another computer is useless, as the controller must also recognize the tape drive.

For hard disks, most XT class systems use the first drive select for the C drive and the second drive select for drive D. AT class machines use the second drive select for both C and D drives. There must be ONE termination resistor in a drive chain, regardless of the number of drives. The drive at the end of the I/O cable (usually drive A or drive C for hard disks) will have the terminating resistor. Remove the resistor from any drive that is being installed as drive B (or drive D).

Some manufacturers, such as Compaq, have slightly different implementations of the terminating resistors when using 3.5″ drives or mixing 3.5″ and 5.25″ drives in the same system. There are different types of termination resistors, and they are not interchangeable. Insure that the correct termination resistor is being used and that it is prop-

Table 9.2   Drive select numbering.

Drive select	Using 0–3	Using 1–4
First	DS0	DS1
Second	DS1	DS2
Third	DS2	DS3
Fourth	DS3	DS4

erly oriented. Improper termination may or may not cause a problem. Be sure that all systems are properly terminated.

Most ribbon cables have a stripe on one side indicating pin 1. Many cables are keyed to prevent improper installation, but sometimes the keys are removed or lost. Pin 1 on the drive must be connected to pin 1 of the controller. The slot for the key is closest to the pin 1 side of the connector. Pin 1 is normally indicated near the chassis connector by the numeral 1 etched on the printed circuit board. If the pins are not marked, look at the solder side of the board. Pin 1 usually has a square solder hole, and the other pins will have round solder holes. If the cable is reversed on a floppy drive, or the large cable on a hard disk, then the drive LED will remain lit when power is applied.

Some drives may be used for several different applications and need to be configured differently. For example, the Seagate ST-225 can be used in an XT class machine as drive C using the first drive select, or in an AT class machine as drive C using the second drive select.

The controller must support (or be configured for) the type of drive with which it is being used. If the controller is configured for a greater capacity drive (more heads and cylinders), partitioning will not be correct, or there may be failure. Attempts to perform a low-level format can permanently damage the drive. If the controller is set for a lower-capacity drive (fewer heads and cylinders), then the full capacity of the drive can not be utilized. Some low-level format routines ask for information to be entered from the keyboard. Some of these require entries in decimal, while others require hexadecimal. (IBM systems containing factory-installed hard disk systems, and all IBM Microchannel machines must use the advanced diagnostics to perform a low-level format.)

Floppy disk drives designed for PC-type machines will not work on AT-type machines unless pin 34 is disconnected. The easiest way to do this without a physical modification is to place a piece of tape over the connector before installing the cable. If the drive must be used on a PC-type machine, remove the tape and clean the contacts. Modification of the drive will void the warranty. A 1.2Mb (high-density) floppy disk drive will read a 360K disk without problems, but it will not write to a 360Kb floppy disk reliably unless the disk has been formatted in a 360Kb drive. This is because the width of the tracks (and read/write heads) are narrower on the high-density drives. With differences in alignment between drives, the tracks can overlap.

If errors are experienced while attempting to write to a floppy disk, make sure that the disk is write-enabled. If the write protect notch on a 5¼" floppy disk is covered, it can not be written to. See Figures 9.1 and 9.2.

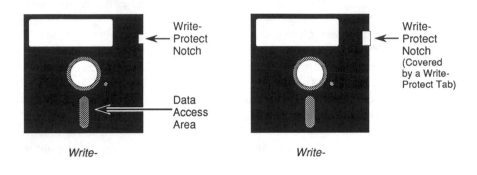

Write-Protect Notch

Data Access Area

Write-

Write-Protect Notch (Covered by a Write-Protect Tab)

Write-

Figure 9.1 5¼" floppy diskette.

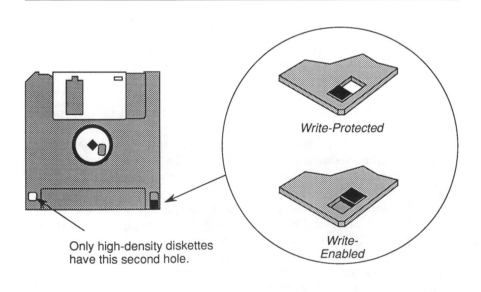

Write-Protected

Write-Enabled

Only high-density diskettes have this second hole.

Figure 9.2 Write-protecting/enabling a 3½" floppy disk.

The 3½" floppy disk is the opposite of the 5¼". When the write-protect opening is covered, the disk is write-enabled. When the opening is exposed, the disk is write-protected. The write-protect/enable cover is a piece of plastic located on the bottom of the disk that slides from the "protect" position to the "enable" position. The 5¼" disks require a piece of tape or a tab to be applied. Do not use transparent tape to write-protect a 5¼" disk. Some drives use an optical device that will see through the tape and not recognize the disk as write-protected.

High-density 3½" floppy disks have a second opening opposite the write-protect/enable hole, but low-density floppy disks do not. The 5¼" high-density floppy disks do not have a reinforcing ring around the center hub, while double-density disks have the hub ring.

REPAIRING FLOPPY DISK DRIVES

Some shops decide to repair their own floppy disk drives, proceed to invest in some equipment, and then abandon the idea altogether. A maintenance manual is necessary for each type of drive. Since there are so many drives on the market, this becomes quite expensive, assuming that the manuals are available. A source of parts is needed. Some parts, especially heads, may be difficult to obtain. The drive manufacturers will probably not sell parts. It is also necessary to invest in some test equipment. An oscilloscope (cost: at least $500) is necessary. A disk drive exerciser is needed for testing and alignment, minimum cost $375. A Dysan Analog Alignment Disk (AAD) for each type of drive, costing from $30 to $75 each, is also required. These disks do wear out, and they can be destroyed by the drive being tested. These disks can not be copied.

Some drives are designed not to be repaired or adjusted. If the drive fails under warranty, the manufacturer will replace it. If the failure is out of warranty, replace the drive. There are companies that will repair a drive for $20.

Before performing any testing or adjustments, verify that the voltage to the drive is within tolerances (+5 VDC and +12 VDC ±5%). Alignment floppy disks are for read-only testing. Use caution to assure that these floppy disks are not written on. The drive to be tested and the alignment floppy disks must be allowed to stabilize at room temperature (65°–75°F, at 40%–60% relative humidity) for at least one hour. There are several tests and adjustments that must be made to a floppy disk drive. They should be performed in a specific order.

Inspect visually for loose connectors, loose or missing screws, dirt, dust, foreign material or objects, obvious physical damage, broken or missing parts, or evidence of misuse or tampering. Remove any glue, nail polish, or sealer that may be on adjustment points or screws.

Cleaning of the heads must be done using a cleaning disk and an approved cleaning solution. Heads should be cleaned for about 15 to 30 seconds. Prolonged use of cleaning disks will increase head wear, as these floppy disks are slightly abrasive.

Speed is adjusted by placing a floppy disk into the drive and changing the setting of a variable resistor until the correct speed is indicated on the drive exerciser. It is important to have the drive running at the correct speed before performing any additional tests or adjustments. Some drives have strobe markings on the spindle. Some drives do not have a speed adjustment. The correct speed for 360K, 48TPI drives is 300RPM ±6RPM; 1.2Mb, 96TPI drives should be set for 360RPM ±7RPM, and 720K or 1.44Mb, 135TPI drives (3½") are 300RPM ±6RPM.

Read/write amplitude and erase current are tested using a formatted scratch disk. It is best to perform these tests before inserting an expensive diagnostic floppy disk. If the read/write/erase circuits and the write protect switch are not functioning properly, the diagnostic disk can be destroyed. The specifications for these tests vary from drive to drive, so the correct maintenance manual is required. It is necessary that all tests are within specifications as published by the drive manufacturer. After verifying that the read/write/erase functions are normal, proceed, using the AAD (Analog Alignment Disk).

The track 0 switch is activated whenever the heads are moved to track 0. If the track 0 switch is not functioning properly or is improperly adjusted, a chattering sound will be heard when the heads attempt to locate track 0. This may result in a hardware failure (601 error) or the inability to locate data on a disk.

A track 0 stop is not found on all drives. The stop (if present) must be adjusted to stop the heads from seeking a negative track.

Radial alignment is performed by adjustment of the stepper motor. An oscilloscope must be used to make this adjustment. The radial alignment adjusts the heads so that they are located at the center of the track that they are supposed to be reading from or writing to.

Hysteresis verifies that the heads can step the proper distance from track to track, and that the stepper motor, associated electronics, and the mechanics are functioning normally.

Azimuth (skew) can not generally be adjusted on head 0. Once head 0 is adjusted, then head 1 can be adjusted with respect to head 0. If head 0 can not be adjusted, the drive mechanism may need to be replaced.

Index to data burst timing sets the timing (distance) between the timing hole on the disk and the start of data.

A system test, using the manufacturer's diagnostic software, should be performed. The tests should include read/write testing. Additional testing should be performed such as formatting a disk, copying files, and reading and rewriting a file.

For practice, use the drive exerciser with a scratch disk. After inserting the scratch disk, step the heads back and forth a few times. Remove the scratch disk and inspect it for abnormal wear before using the AAD. In the shop, this procedure has saved an expensive AAD more than once. Specifications vary from drive to drive. Be sure to use the correct parameters and the proper AAD before attempting to make any adjustments. After completing an adjustment, repeat all of the previous tests again. When making one adjustment, a previous adjustment may have been affected. Seal all screws after the drive has been verified. This will prevent adjustments from changing due to vibration. It may be necessary to build extender cables so that the circuit board can be removed from the drive while mechanical adjustments are made. Replace the circuit board if there are difficulties with the mechanical adjustments.

10

Hard Disk Drives

WHY DO HARD DRIVES FAIL?

A hard disk rotates at 3600 rpm. The heads ride on a cushion of air above the surface of the disk (platters). If the heads should touch the surface of the disk while the disk is rotating at operating speed, serious damage to the heads as well as the disk will occur. A failure of this type is known as a head crash. The damage to both the heads and the surface(s) of the disk is permanent, causing complete data loss. There is another component of the hard drive that is essential to proper operation: the circuit board. The board contains circuitry that controls the speed of the rotation of the disk, movement of the read/write heads, and encoding and decoding of data. A failure on the board can cause the drive to fail. Symptoms of board failure include excessive seek failures and sector not found errors, which become increasingly more frequent until the drive refuses to function. Replacing the board with one from a known good drive of the same manufacturer and model will save the data contained on the "defective" drive.

INTERFACING

The controllers and drives must be matched for drive size and encoding method. The two methods of encoding are MFM (Modified Frequency Modulation) and RLL (Run Length Limited). RLL uses fewer bits on the drive to encode data than MFM, resulting in higher capacities and faster data transfer rates. Most hard disks with a capacity greater than 40Mb use a buffered ESDI (Enhanced Small Device Interface) controller. The ESDI controller has a lookahead buffer that allows the controller to write to memory at the same time that data is read from the drive. This permits the drive to be formatted with a more efficient interleave factor (usually 1:1).

LOW-LEVEL FORMAT

Low-level formatting is accomplished using manufacturer supplied software (Advanced Diagnostics). If software is not supplied by the manufacturer, the low-level format can be performed through a program that is contained in the drive controller ROM. This routine is accessed using the MS-DOS DEBUG utility. (A listing of address locations for various controllers is included in the Appendix.) Sometimes, third-party software is included with the drive to be used for special configurations. The low-level format rewrites address marks internally, including those for track 0. A good set of address marks is all that is needed for the advanced diagnostics to run successfully. Bad tracks are deleted, and their address marks are overwritten (an address mark is at the beginning of each sector). If a bad sector is encountered, the entire track is deleted (17 sectors). Low-level formatting does not check for marginal sectors. A hardware format is performed, mating the drive to the controller. The low-level format does not check the strength of the magnetic signals. It is a go/no-go type of format.

Some manufacturer's advanced diagnostics provide two types of low-level formats, conditional and unconditional. A conditional format retains the old bad sector map and flags any new bad sectors that are found. The unconditional format only flags sectors that are entered manually. It is sometimes necessary to perform an unconditional format followed by a conditional format, depending upon the disk and controller that are being prepared. If a conditional format is being performed and the format is failing, a message will display stating that an unconditional format is required. This is a time-consuming operation but necessary in some cases.

INTERLEAVE FACTOR

In a hard disk system, one sector is read at a time and the contents are transferred to memory. Because the hard disk can transfer data faster than the information can be written to memory, the sectors are not read (or written to) sequentially. The disk continues to spin, and sectors are skipped. The interleave factor refers to the manner in which the disk is read and the number of sectors that are skipped. For instance, a 3:1 interleave factor means that the disk reads every third sector. This requires three rotations of the disk to read an entire track. The ESDI controller contains a lookahead buffer that allows a 1:1 interleave factor. An entire track is read with each revolution of the disk, resulting in higher data transfer rates and an increase in system performance. See Figure 10.1.

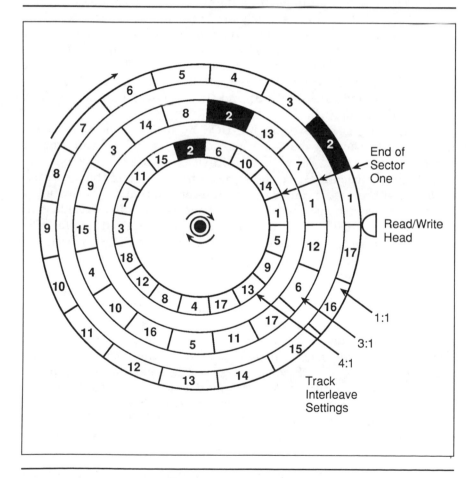

Figure 10.1   Fixed disk interleave factors.

DRIVE PARTITIONING

Partitioning means preparing the drive, or a portion of the drive, to function under a particular operating system. Since the majority of microcomputers currently in use are using MS-DOS, this is the operating system that will be discussed. It should be noted that it is possible for more than one operating system to reside on a drive. In these cases, a portion of the physical hard disk will contain the MS-DOS partition. The remainder may be used for PICK, XENIX, NOVELL, or some other operating system.

It is necessary to discuss the installation of other operating systems with the customer prior to partitioning the drive. Depending upon the version of MS-DOS that is being installed, partitions greater than 32Mb may not be possible. If the drive capacity is less than 32Mb, this is of no concern. If the capacity of the drive is greater than 32Mb, then the options must be discussed with the customer. The customer will have to purchase a current[32] version of MS-DOS to exceed the 32Mb limitation. Compaq MS-DOS 3.31 and IBM PC-DOS 4.0 were the first versions to overcome the 32Mb barrier.

Partitioning is achieved in MS-DOS by use of FDISK, a menu-driven utility. For obvious reasons, FDISK should be run from a bootable floppy disk. As with all MS-DOS utilities, the version of FDISK that is used must be the same as the version of the operating system that booted the computer and the version that will be installed on the hard drive. If more than one operating system will be resident on the disk, use FDISK to create a partition of the required size for MS-DOS, and ignore the balance of the disk space. The FDISK menu permits the customer to select which partition he or she wants to be active. If an additional operating system is to be used, simply activate that partition from the FDISK menu and reboot the system. Other operating systems have a similar utility to reactivate the DOS partition.

If the system contains one drive—called a physical drive—a single DOS partition is adequate. The DOS version and the capacity of the drive determine the maximum partition size. At the request of the customer, or because of DOS constraints, multiple partitions may be required. Multiple partitions are recognized as logical drives. Therefore, one physical drive may contain several logical drives. For example, a system containing one 70Mb drive and using PC-DOS 3.3 will have three logical drives addressed as C:, D:, and E:. If two physical drives

---

[32]As of this writing, MS-DOS 5.0 is the current version and permits partitions of up to 512 Mb.

are installed, they can not be combined into one logical drive. Each drive may be partitioned into one or more logical drives.

The first (or only) MS-DOS partition is called the primary partition, and it needs to be flagged as active in order for the drive to be bootable. The balance of the drive is then set up as the extended DOS partition. Extended partitions are then divided into logical drives.

After the partitions and logical drives are defined, they must be formatted. This operation is called an operating system or high-level format. The operating system format tests for bad sectors. If a bad sector is encountered during the format procedure, an area called a cluster is deallocated. A cluster is composed of the bad sector, the prior sector, and the following sector. When a cluster is deallocated, a notation is written in the FAT stating that the area is defective and can not be used. It is possible that the format process misses a bad sector, or a marginal sector becomes bad after use. This is why the hard disks should be reformatted after a problem arises, or annually as preventative maintenance.

When hard disks are installed in a system, the primary DOS partition of the first physical drive must be bootable. This drive, which is always the logical C drive, must be formatted with the /S switch and contain the hidden system files and the command interpreter. If the drive is not prepared in the proper manner, the system must be booted from a floppy disk in order to access the hard disk. Formatting any other logical drive or partition with the /S switch is of no use, as they will not boot.

11

Techniques, Failures, and General Problems

PROPER TECHNIQUES FOR DISASSEMBLING SYSTEMS

Have a well-lighted area of sufficient size. Do not remove more items than necessary. Arrange parts and mounting hardware in the order that they were removed. Have a sufficient number of grounded outlets available, preferably protected against electrical noise and surges.

Follow ESD (Electro Static Discharge) precautions. ESD is an electrical charge (static electricity) that can damage circuitry and components. Just touching a chip or brushing it with a nylon sleeve can degrade a circuit so that it never again performs to specifications. ESD is a phenomenon produced by contact and separation of unlike materials. Here are some common examples of activities that generate ESD.

coat removal	400 volts
rolling up your sleeves	600 volts
handling a Styrofoam cup	1,500 volts
combing your hair	10,000 volts
walking on a carpet	35,000 volts

Thirty volts of static electricity (about one one-hundredth of what a person can feel) will damage an electronic component!

Use a wrist strap and static mat whenever possible. Do not wear thick-soled (insulated) shoes, polyester, vinyl, plastics, or other static-generating clothing. Boards, chips, and other components must be in static bags when not being used. Technicians must discharge themselves (to the ground of the unit that they are working on) before handling components. Handle boards by the edges. Do not handle chips or other components by their leads or pins; touch only the body. Never let customers handle components or boards. Explain the problems associated with ESD.

Do not put boards or components on any metal surface. Do not wear loose clothing (neckties). Be careful of jewelry, especially bracelets, wristwatches, and rings. Make sure that the power is disconnected before installing any connectors, peripherals, boards, or any other devices.

Verify that all screws and connectors are tight (do not overtighten). Be aware of environmental factors such as high or low temperatures, rapid temperature changes, and excessive humidity. Disconnect all power before opening the machine. Be especially careful with fragile plastic parts that are used in many of the newer IBM computers as well as most portables. Be careful of small parts that may fall into the chassis, get lost on a rug or carpet, or fall on the floor and get stepped on or roll under furniture. Watch for cables being pulled or pinched during reassembly. Be aware of high voltages in display assemblies. Make sure to test the system completely after everything has been reconnected and the cover has been replaced and secured.

WHAT CAUSES A COMPONENT TO FAIL?

Mechanical components, such as floppy disk drives (especially 3½" drives), hard disk drives, keyboards (especially AT&T), and cooling fans, fail quite often. This is because they contain moving parts that are destroyed by heat, friction, dirt, and dust.

Electronic failures are caused by excessive heat and poor air circulation. These include video monitors, power supplies, hard disk drives, and boards that upgrade RAM. Never block any of the vents on a computer or monitor. Proper cooling is necessary for correct functioning. Manufacturing defects such as poor soldering combined with excessive heat will cause a board to fail.

External power problems such as low (or high) line voltage will destroy motors in hard disk drives, fans, floppy disk drives, and printers. Power surges or pulses (rapidly turning the system off and then on) will destroy chips on system boards and adapters, hard disk controllers, and power supply regulators.

Some systems have a feature built into the power supplies to prevent surges or pulses. Once power is lost, time is required for the power supply to reset before it will become active again. This can be as much as 15 seconds in some systems.

Other causes of failure are physical abuse, turning system off and then on again before the hard disk stops spinning, moving the system without parking the hard disk (if required), airborne smoke, dust, chemicals, pet hair, food or beverages (especially for keyboards), or poking foreign objects into floppy disk drives.

Turning the system off while the hard disk is performing a write operation can cause a head crash and ruin the drive. Dropping paper clips or staples into the keyboard, static electricity, normal wear and tear, and manufacturing defects that are not immediately apparent also shorten the life of a system.

SAMPLE SITUATIONS

The following are some of the problems that can occur at a customer location. Before tearing into the system, examine it for obvious problems or failures. Often, the customer will either move the system, add an internal device, or connect an external device and unknowingly cause a problem. Ask the customer if he or she has moved or changed the system before proceeding.

"When I turn on the computer nothing happens."   Make sure the power cord is plugged into a live outlet and is pushed all the way into the AC power connector on the computer. Make sure that the voltage selection switch on the rear of the power supply (if present) is set for the proper voltage.

"The computer is on, but there is no display on the monitor."   Check the monitor cord connection and make sure the monitor is on. Check the video cable connection between the computer and monitor. Adjust the brightness and contrast controls on the monitor. Make sure that any required jumpers or switches are set correctly (on the display, video adapter card, and system board) and that the display adapter is properly installed in the expansion slot (if applicable).

"When I press keys on the keyboard, nothing happens."   Make sure that the keyboard is compatible with the system unit (a PC keyboard will not work with an AT; a PS/2 Model 30 keyboard only works with a Model 30) and is securely plugged into the system unit. If the system

makes use of any hardware or software locking mechanism, or allows for passwords, make sure that the mechanism is deactivated (unlocked) or the correct password has been entered. Verify that the display is functioning properly. If there is an XT/AT switch on the rear of the keyboard, verify that it is set to the correct position.

"The disk drive that I installed doesn't work properly."   Run the setup program and make sure that the drive type is correct. Verify that the correct cabling is used and that the cables are properly connected. Make sure that the drive select pins, switches, or jumpers are set correctly. Be sure that the terminating resistor is installed on the correct drive, usually drive A for floppy drives and drive C for hard drives, and that there are no extra terminating resistors in the system.

"The image on my screen flickers or wavers."   Check for a loose or defective video cable.

"My serial device (printer, modem, etc.) doesn't output anything or is outputing garbled characters"   Make sure that the device is powered up and on line. Check the cable connection between the device and the computer. Verify that the device is plugged into the correct connector on the rear of the computer. Be sure that the cable connecting the device to the computer is configured correctly. All serial cables are not the same. Be sure that the software or operating system sets the correct baud rate, parity, and other communication parameters to match the device. Verify that the communications port is assigned to the correct COM device. This may require changing jumpers or switch settings. If the system has only one serial port, it must be assigned to COM1. There can not be a COM2 unless there is a COM1.

"My parallel printer doesn't respond when I try to print."   Make sure that the power is turned on and that the printer is on line. Check the cable connection between the printer and the computer. Replace the cable if necessary. Verify that the port address is correct. This may require setting jumpers or switches. Be sure that the port to which the printer is connected has not been disabled or bypassed through software.

"The system isn't saving my new setup configuration."   Make sure that the configuration is saved by pressing the "Save Settings" key when exiting the setup program. If the system is still not saving the configuration, the battery may need replacement.

12

Laser Printers

This chapter explains the basic concepts and theory of laser printer technology, and it provides some hints for the service technician. The material is specific to the Hewlett-Packard LaserJet series of printers, as well as other printers using Canon engines,[33] but it applies to all printers using laser technology. The nomenclature of specific parts may be different for other manufacturers. A laser printer is a complex device. It is recommended that the technician use the manufacturer's service manuals until he or she has enough experience to repair a laser printer without one.

The laser printer is comprised of five functional groups. They are image formation, paper handling, machine control, power distribution, and interface. The technician should be familiar with these groups and the functions that they perform.

IMAGE FORMATION

Laser printers and photocopiers use the same xerographic technology. For those who are not familiar with the process, it is based upon two laws of physics: like charges repel and opposite charges attract each other. Electrical fields and forces are composed of protons and electrons. A proton is a positively charged, subatomic particle with a mass of 1836 times that of an electron. A proton holds one unit of positive

---

[33]A cross-reference of laser printers and engines appears in Appendix G.

charge. An electron holds one unit of electrical charge and has a mass of about 1/1836 of a proton, which makes the electron easier to affect with an outside force. Charged particles are referred to as ions.

The EP (Electro-Photographic) cartridge[34] contains an aluminum cylinder, which is coated with a photosensitive material. The photosensitive material is a substance that becomes a conductor when struck by light. Exposure to normal light levels (daylight or room lighting) for more than a few seconds can permanently damage the photosensitive drum.

The surface of the cylinder (also known as the photosensitive drum) is cleaned by a wiper blade, which removes residual toner deposits. A red or orange light provided by a group of LEDs shines on the drum. The photosensitive material is uniformly exposed by the LEDs, effectively erasing any charge that remains from the previous cycle (rotation). Then, the surface of the drum is charged by a negative ion generator called the primary corona, which is located in the EP cartridge.

The semiconductor laser is capable of flashing a finely focused beam of light, on and off, very rapidly. The beam paints information[35] on the drum by striking the surface with a series of dots. The resolution of the information is 300×300 dots per square inch. The beam scans the drum from left to right. After the beam has scanned a single row, the drum rotates a very small distance and the next row of dots are painted. Where the laser strikes the drum, the photosensitive material conducts and neutralizes the negative charge that was placed there by the primary corona. These spots are positively charged relative to the surface of the drum. As the laser beam continues to scan, and the drum rotates, an electrostatic image is formed.

Toner is a mixture of dry ink and epoxy in the form of microscopic particles. The toner particles are charged negatively by the developing cylinder, also located within the EP cartridge. There is an electromagnet in the developing cylinder, controlled by the AC bias. Because this electromagnet is controlled by an AC current, it throws the toner back and forth around the drum. The DC bias controls the AC bias, making the AC bias more positive to darken the image and more negative to lighten the image. In the developing stage, the photosensitive drum passes through

---

[34]The Electro-Photographic cartridge is commonly referred to as a "toner" cartridge. In laser printers using the Canon engine, the cartridge contains several electronic components in addition to the toner supply.

[35]The information is in the form of dots which, when the process is complete, form characters or graphic images.

a cloud of toner particles surrounding the developing drum. The negatively charged toner adheres to the positively charged spots on the photosensitive drum which have been struck with the laser beam.

Located below the EP cartridge is the transfer corona. When paper is fed through the printer, it contacts the rotating photosensitive drum, which contains the latent laser image and the toner that has been attracted to it. After passing through the development stage, the drum transfers the toner to the surface of a piece of paper. The transfer corona applies a positive charge to the back of the paper, which helps to attract the negatively charged toner image.

Since only gravity and a small electrostatic field hold the toner on to the paper, they must be fused together by applying pressure and heat to the paper's surface. The paper is fed through the fusing assembly. The fusing roller is heated to 180°C, through the use of a thermistor and a lamp. The high temperature melts the toner. Pressure from the fusing rollers pushes the toner into the paper. The finished page is sent to the output tray, and the cycle is repeated.

PAPER PICKUP AND FEEDING

The printer must be able to pick up paper from the input tray, deliver it to the image formation system at exactly the right time, move it through the fusing assembly, and pass the finished page into the output tray.

When the machine control system receives a print command, the main drive motor starts. About two seconds later, the paper pickup solenoid is energized. The clutch-driven pickup roller makes one revolution, picking up a sheet of paper from the paper cassette or manual feed. The paper is fed into the registration assembly. The registration rollers, which are also clutch-driven, are not moving at this time. This causes the paper to bow because of pressure against the registration assembly.

The purpose of the registration assembly is to align the front edge of the paper with the leading edge of the photosensitive drum. When the paper is aligned, the registration clutch is energized, the rollers turn, and the paper advances towards the photosensitive drum. After the information is transferred, the paper is fed into the fusing assembly by the feed roller.

Timing for the manual paper feed is the same as the cassette paper feed except that a different input sensor is activated. The manual paper feed has a longer initial warmup time, because it is assumed that envelopes, heavier paper, or transparency material is being used. Heavier paper absorbs more heat, so extra time is allowed for the warmup period to insure that the temperature will be greater than 180°C (or 356°F). The higher temperature is necessary to fuse the toner to the heavy material properly. When the paper is clear of the fusing station, the DC controller is signaled by the paper exit sensor.[36] This sensor is also used to detect paper jams.

Each paper cassette has one or more tabs on the rear, which indicate to the printer (through activation of one or more micro-switches) the size of the paper that is installed. Different cassettes must be used for different-sized paper. When a manual paper feed is required, the software determines the size of the page. The printer knows what size paper to expect and how much time it will take for the page to be printed. The printer will indicate a paper jam in any one three situations. If the print cycle begins, but the paper does not reach the paper exit sensor in the proper amount of time, a paper jam is indicated. If paper reaches but does not clear the paper exit sensor within the correct amount of time, a paper jam exists. If the sensor is active when the printer is powered up (paper was stuck in the printer and it was turned off), a paper jam is indicated.

POWER DISTRIBUTION

Hewlett-Packard Series II and III (except for the P models) printers contain three power supplies. The AC power supply contains a circuit breaker, which can be seen from the left side of the printer. It is a small green button, located beneath the ozone filter. The AC power supply provides line voltage to the fusing lamp and the DC power supply.

The DC power supply has two outputs, called A and B. The DC power supply is protected by a fuse. The fuse is located on the front of the power supply board. The voltages supplied are 5VDC and 24VDC. The 24V A supply powers the main motor, fans, DC controller, interface board, solenoids, erase lamps, photo sensors, and the laser scanner assembly.

There is an interlock switch that disables the 24V B supply when the top cover is open. The 24V B supply provides power to the high-voltage power supply.

The high-voltage power supply generates as much as 6,000 volts during the print cycle. High voltages are used for the primary corona, transfer corona, and functions within the EP cartridge.

---

[36]The paper exit sensor is located on the rear of the fusing assembly.

MACHINE CONTROL

All activities inside the printer are monitored and controlled by the DC controller, a small board that is located in the bottom of the unit. The DC controller is reached by turning the printer over and removing the bottom cover. Connected to the DC controller are the motors, DC power supply, paper size switches, all sensors, solenoids, a fiber-optic cable from the laser scanner assembly, and the fusing assembly. The DC controller monitors the timing of the print cycle, activates the clutch solenoids when necessary, monitors paper movement, and samples the speed and movement of the laser beam.

There is a button on the DC controller that is accessible through a hole in the left side of the printer toward the bottom. This button is used to perform an engine test print. The engine test print generates a page of parallel lines when the mechanical part of the printer (the engine) is functioning normally.

INTERFACE

The interface board is what makes one printer using the Canon engine different from the others. If the covers, control panels, and interfaces were removed from several of these printers, the same engines would remain. This is a subtle way of saying that a technician who can repair a Hewlett-Packard LaserJet should be able to repair many lesser-known brands.

The interface board receives data from a host computer through the parallel, serial, or an optional I/O. An optional unit must be installed through the slot provided on the rear of the printer. Optional units usually permit one printer to be shared by several hosts and are serial devices. There are switches[37] on the I/O board, accessed through the optional I/O cover, that permit selection of RS-232 or RS-422 protocols.

In addition to containing the RAM, ROMS, a CPU, and electronics to translate the digital data from the host to data that the printer needs, the interface board provides for expansion of the printer. There is the capability to add up to 4Mb of RAM[38] through a slot on the left side near

---

[37]Earlier units used switches to change the Serial I/O from RS-232 to RS-422. Newer units incorporated the ability to make this change through the control panel.

[38]The Series II and III are both upgradeable by 4Mb but use different types of RAM cards.

the bottom. The addition of up to two font cartridges is possible through slots on the front of the printer, below the paper cassette.[39]

The operator panel (or control panel) is connected directly to the I/O board. This panel is used to indicate status or errors and for the operator to perform tests and configure the printer. A defective panel will display garbage, but the printer can function normally. Error messages are generated by the DC controller or the interface board.

When servicing the printer, it is often necessary to remove the covers. Be careful not to damage the cable that connects to the panel. Remove the panel from the cover and reconnect it, so that the status can be checked and panel functions can be used. A technician that services these printers frequently will carry an extra panel, saving removal and reinstallation time.

There is an LED that is illuminated when the printer is ON LINE. Control panel functions are inoperable when the printer is in this condition. The printer must be off line for any of the menus to be accessed or a test print to be generated. The engine test is not affected by the control panel.

LIFE EXPECTANCY OF CONSUMABLES

In addition to the EP cartridge and cleaner pad, there are several components within these printers that require periodic replacement. Each situation is different. There are environmental factors to be considered as well as activities and applications. The information that follows is suggested by the manufacturer, assuming that normal conditions are maintained. Under extreme environmental conditions, or unusual applications, these estimates may be shortened.

EP CARTRIDGE

The EP cartridge will last for approximately 4000 pages, dependent upon the application, and the print density setting. When a 16 TONER LOW message is encountered, remove the cartridge, gently rock it from side to side, and reinstall it into the printer. The message is generated through use of a sensor inside the cartridge. It is possible to print several hundred sheets after this message appears without sacrificing quality. Continue this method until the toner is depleted. If the toner

---

[39]Some font cartridges can be used for the Series II and III, while others are machine specific. Some are even slot specific. Check with the cartridge manufacturer.

supply is depleted, large, irregular areas will be either white or contain light characters. This is the time to replace the EP cartridge.

The cartridges have a suggested shelf life of two years, if stored in the original unopened packaging. After the cartridge is removed from the protective packaging, it should be good for six months. Hewlett-Packard boxes have an expiration date printed on the label. The EP cartridge is a customer-replaceable item.

CLEANING PAD

A new cleaning pad is packaged with each EP cartridge. New cleaning pads are impregnated with a silicone lubricant. In addition to cleaning (and prolonging the life of) the fuser roller, the pad dispenses the lubricant. The lubricant prevents the toner from sticking to the Teflon-coated surface of the roller during the fusing process. Customers must be instructed to replace the cleaning pad whenever the EP cartridge is changed. Failure to do so will result in damage to the fusing rollers.

FUSING ASSEMBLY

The manufacturer suggests replacing this unit after approximately 100,000 pages. Because of the possibility of damage outside of normal wear and tear, the fusing assembly may require service before this suggested interval. A physical shock can destroy the fusing lamp. Paper containing staples or the wrong type of paper can ruin the coating on the fuser roller (and the pressure roller beneath). A defective thermistor or overheating will burn out the thermoprotector. The paper exit sensor can develop a problem and require a replacement. If your organization services these printers regularly, keep one or two spare fusing assemblies in stock. There are several companies that can supply parts to repair the fusing assemblies. From an economic standpoint, it is cost effective to repair these assemblies.

PAPER PICKUP/FEED ROLLER

This is a D-shaped, rubber roller. Controlled by a solenoid and clutch mechanism, it makes one rotation each time the print cycle is activated. It is suggested that this roller be replaced after each 100,000 pages, or whenever the separation pad is replaced. When the paper pickup/feed roller begins to wear, paper will be fed late.

Because of the timing involved, and the function of the registration assembly, a worn roller will be difficult to detect. The problem will show up as a decrease in the size of the top margin of a page with an extended bottom margin. The printing is actually higher on the page than it should be. When printing multiple-page documents, this will only happen on the first page. The entire feed roller assembly may be replaced as a unit, or just the roller itself. If replacing only the roller, inspect the clutch mechanism. Clean and lubricate the clutch if necessary.

SEPARATION PAD

The separation pad is made of cork and is attached with a spring-loaded mount. It is located below the paper pickup/feed roller. The purpose of the separation pad is to separate sheets of paper during the feed process so that only one sheet of paper will be picked up and fed. From the rotation of the paper pickup/feed roller, an indentation is worn into the center of the separation pad. When the indentation becomes too deep, the pad can not do its job, and multiple sheets of paper are fed. It is suggested that the separation pad be replaced along with the paper pickup/feed roller, or every 100,000 pages.

OZONE FILTER

The ozone filter is located inside the right side of the printer toward the rear. The top cover must be raised to access the filter. It is suggested that the filter be replaced every 50,000 pages, or whenever the odor of ozone[40] is noticeable.

There are two types of ozone filters used in these printers. The earlier printers had a permanent filter. It is necessary to remove the covers from the printer in order to replace the permanent filter. The later models contain a little flap type of door, and the filter element has a tab attached. It is a simple matter for a customer to raise the cover, open the flap, and remove a used filter by pulling on the tab. Replacement filters are available from some office supply stores. It is possible to convert from the permanent type of filter to the customer replaceable version by the replacement of a few inexpensive parts.

TRANSFER CORONA

The transfer corona should be replaced every 100,000 pages, unless damaged. The corona wire is very fine, and it is protected by a criss-

---

[40]The ozone is produced by the high voltages that are applied to the corona wires. The P series of printers use corona rollers, which require less voltage. Very little ozone is produced in these printers, and a filter is not required.

cross of nylon monofilament fishing line that is wound over the top of the transfer corona assembly. High voltages are sent through the transfer corona wire during printing, which creates the ozone gas. The surface of the wire is prone to oxidation, which reduces is effectiveness. Toner particles manage to create dead spots on the wire, too. In addition to a new cleaning pad, there is a cotton swab packaged with each EP cartridge. The cotton swab is supposed to be used for cleaning the corona wire assembly. Isopropyl alcohol is used on the swab for cleaning the wire. Be extremely careful, and use a bright light. The wire itself is very fine, extremely delicate, and difficult to see. Breaking or kinking the wire will require replacement.

MAINTENANCE CHECKPOINTS

When cleaning the printer, avoid breathing the toner. Remove as much toner as possible with a vacuum cleaner. Toner can be washed from skin, clothing, and other surfaces with cold water. Use a vacuum cleaner to remove toner and paper dust[41] from the interior of the printer. Canned air just blows the debris to another place.

Use extreme caution if it is necessary to clean the beam-to-drum mirror assembly. Obstructions or scratches will degrade the printed image.

There is a green tool with a brush on one end secured by a clip to the inside of the printer. The end opposite the brush is used to clean the primary corona wire, which is inside the EP cartridge. Instructions are included in the users manual and packed with new cartridges. This wire must be cleaned if the print appears to bleed or if dark vertical lines appear on the page.

Table 12.1 contains the information necessary for routine cleaning and maintenance. Do not use cleaning solutions or any liquids on any part of the printer except as indicated.

SERVICE TIPS

There are several different types of screws used in these printers. When an assembly is removed, put the screws back into the holes. Do not put all of the screws together in one container.

Be careful with fragile parts (plastics, connectors, etc.).

---

[41]Fine dust is placed between the sheets of paper when it is manufactured to assist in the separation of the pages during printing.

Table 12.1   Laser printer maintenance.

Service Area	Tool/Solvent	Remarks
Feed Guide Assembly		
Feed guide	Damp cloth	Remove debris
Ozone Filter†		
Fusing Assembly‡		
Fuser roller cleaning pad	Dry cloth or wipe	If dirty, prints will be dirty and paper jams will occur. Replace if necessary.
Separation pawls (claws)	Isopropyl alcohol	Use CAUTION. Tops of pawls are easily damaged.
Paper guides	Isopropyl alcohol	Remove accumulated debris.
Lower delivery guide	Isopropyl alcohol	Remove accumulated debris.
EP-S Cartridge		
Primary corona wire	Brush/wire cleaner	Clean with "pad" end of tool.
Photosensitive drum	Toner on a dry cloth	Unless absolutely required, the drum should NOT be touched or cleaned. Use only a clean, lint-free wipe and toner. Do NOT expose the drum to light.

Table 12.1 (Continued)

Service Area	Tool/Solvent	Remarks
Mirror Assembly		
Mirror	None	Gently blow debris from mirror surface.
Feed Roller Assembly & Separation Pad‡		
Transfer Area		
Registration rollers	Damp, lint-free wipe	
Transfer guide	Damp cloth	
Transfer Corona Assembly‡		
Surface areas	Swab with isopropyl alcohol	Carefully clean all toner around corona wire and filament.
Wire	New swab & isopropyl alcohol	When cleaning wire, be careful not to damage filament.

†Replace every 50,000 pages.
‡Replace every 100,000 pages.

To prevent toner from spilling, remove the EP cartridge before turning the printer sideways or upside down.

There are two shutters on the top of the EP cartridge. These are opened by plastic fingers when the cartridge is inserted into the printer. The top shutter opens to allow the reflected laser beam (from the beam to drum mirror) to strike the drum surface.

The bottom shutter allows the erase lamps, which are mounted in the lid of the printer, to illuminate the surface of the drum, neutralizing any existing electrical charge.

The primary corona wire is located below the black mylar strip, which is between the two shutters. The wire is accessible so that it may be cleaned.

Viewing the EP cartridge from the front, there is a black rectangular plastic tab (possibly two tabs) on the right side, extending out about 2/10". This tab activates the drum sensitivity microswitch inside the printer. The drum sensitivity microswitch (or microswitches) controls the intensity of the laser beam. If neither of the drum sensitivity switches is activated, the printer will display a 14 NO EP CART message.

Always disconnect the AC power before removing the printer covers. If service requires that power be on while the protective covers are removed, proceed with extreme caution and heed all warnings.

When removing the DC power supply, be careful of the paper sensing arm.

The laser-scanner assembly is a single unit. The laser and scanner must not be separated due to a special alignment that is performed at the factory.

Before removing the registration assembly, locate the brass grounding block (transfer corona roller grounding block) on the left side (viewed from the front). When reinstalling the registration assembly, ensure that the transfer corona roller grounding block is positioned correctly.

Use caution when working with or near the fusing assembly. This assembly gets extremely hot. Severe burns can be the result of carelessness.

Do not jar the fusing assembly, or handle it roughly. The lamp is fragile.

Be careful when handling the fusing rollers, heat lamp, and transfer roller. Do NOT get any oil from your fingers on these parts. Use a rag or wear gloves when touching these parts.

There is only one adjustment on these printers, the print density adjustment. The adjusting knob is located inside the printer on top of the high-voltage power supply. Turning this knob changes the DC bias of the developer and so changes the electrostatic attraction of the toner. The smaller the number on the knob, the darker the output (and the shorter the EP cartridge life).

WARNING The laser beam is invisible, but direct or indirect contact to the eye can cause permanent damage. Heed all warnings and <u>DO NOT DISCONNECT</u> the FIBER OPTICS CABLE from the DC controller PCA or the laser/scanner assembly while power is ON.

Push-on connectors require substantial pressure to make proper contact. You will think that you are connected when you are not.

Refilled cartridges can be the cause of additional wear inside the printer.

There are companies that refurbish EP cartridges. Some refurbished cartridges are better than the factory originals.

A loose screw can cause failures, particularly in the high-voltage area.

Paper clips or staples can short out the transfer corona wire.

Often a technician will not replace the exit roller correctly, resulting in paper jams.

Use of the laser power checker[42] is the only way to tell if the drum is being discharged correctly.

Software can have a glitch that will corrupt a file and make the printer appear to be defective when nothing is wrong. Try printing a known good document before chasing after a false hardware problem.

The majority of print quality problems can be traced to bad paper or environmental factors. Use good paper and a known good EP cartridge when testing a laser printer.

50 ERROR indicates a problem with the fusing assembly. The printer must be turned off for a minimum of ten minutes for this error to clear. If the printer is not permitted to cool down for ten minutes, the error message will persist, even if the fusing assembly has been replaced.

WHAT ACTUALLY FAILS?

The EP cartridge contains many components that are subject to wear. The photosensitive drum is easily damaged.

The fusing assembly fails frequently because of the high temperatures generated. Dust and dirt cause problems with the rollers. Excess toner builds up on the surface of the thermoprotector, causing scratches on the Teflon coating of the fusing roller. The paper sepa-

---

[42]A special tool available through Hewlett-Packard for about $130.

ration pawls on the rear of the fusing unit break, or wear out, causing paper jams. The thermistor fails, preventing the fusing assembly from maintaining proper temperature. The lamp burns out.

The scanner motor fails because of mechanical wear, requiring replacement of the laser-scanning assembly. Dust and dirt can accumulate inside this assembly, causing quality problems or laser beam failures.

Paper that is of poor quality can produce paper jams and render poor-quality output.

Recycled EP cartridges that have not been properly refurbished can fail or leak extensive amounts of toner inside the printer.

TROUBLESHOOTING CORRECTLY

Sounds of the motors, high voltages, mechanical movements.

Sight: What moves, lights up, or displays messages? What do the indicators tell you? Examine the printout and analyze it for lack of straight line, areas that are too dark or too light, dots missing, or repeating patterns.

Smell: Ozone filters, burned component

Touch: Too hot or not hot enough.

IMAGE TROUBLESHOOTING

Caused mostly by poor paper quality on the laser printers.

Use a known good EP cartridge.

Check the image on the EP drum.

Could software cause this?

Will a different file or application print properly?

DISPLAY STATUS TROUBLESHOOTING

Error codes are the same for any of the HP LaserJet printers.

A defective high voltage power supply can result in an unreadable control panel display.

PAPER PATH

Determine the principles for correct paper feeding.

Visually examine the problem by powering the machine OFF after paper movement begins, and move the gears by hand until the paper reaches the point where it twists or jams.

Determine if sensors are functioning correctly by checking the cables from the sensor to the connector.

PRINTER MESSAGES

Table 12.2 is a list of all status, attendance, error, and service messages that can display on the operator panel. Some models display different messages for the same code number. All messages are listed. In some cases, the action required refers to the HP service manual.

Table 12.2   Printer messages.

Message	Situation Described—Action Required
(Display is Blank)	Refer to "Blank Display" in HP service manual.
00 READY	Printer is ready for use.
02 WARMING UP	Wait until printer signals 00 READY.
02 WARMING UP (Continuously)	Refer to "02 WARMING UP" (continuous) in HP service manual.
04 SELF TEST	Continuous self-test printing.
05 SELF TEST	Self-test in progress.
06 PRINTING TEST	Self-test printing.
06 FONT PRINTOUT	Printing sample characters from available fonts.
07 RESET	Returns all printer settings to Printer Menu settings, clears buffered pages, temporary soft fonts, and macros.
08 COLD RESET	Returns both configuration and printing menus to factory settings.
09 MENU RESET	Returns all Printing Menu items to factory settings, clears buffered pages, temporary soft fonts, and macros.
10 RESET TO SAVE (HP 33449 Only)	Press and hold RESET until "07 RESET" appears to confirm acceptance of Printing Menu selections, or press CONTINUE or ON LINE to save current settings.11 PAPER OUT (HP 33440 Only)Add media to the input tray. If message persists, refer to "11 PAPER OUT" in the HP service manual.

Table 12.2 (Continued)

Message	Situation Described—Action Required
12 PRINTER OPEN	Close the top cover assembly. If message persists, refer to "12 PRINTER OPEN" in the HP service manual.
13 PAPER JAM	Open printer, clear paper within the printer, and press RESET or ON LINE to reprint the page. If message persists, refer to "13 PAPER JAM" in the HP service manual.
14 NO EP CART	Install an EP cartridge. If message persists, refer to "14 NO EP CART" in the HP service manual.
15 ENGINE TEST	Engine test with printout produced by pressing the Test Print button.
16 TONER LOW	Replace EP cartridge. If problem persists, refer to "16 TONER LOW" in the HP service manual.
17 MEMORY CONFIG (SERIES III Only)	Memory reconfiguration in operation as a result of setting Page Protection ON.
18 SKIP SELFTEST (SERIES III Only)	Skips ROM and RAM portions of the power on self-test. (*Note:* Manufacturing use ONLY!)
20 ERROR 20 MEM OVERFLOW	Memory overflow. Too much data is being sent to the printer, and the printer has run out of memory. Press CONTINUE to print contents of RAM. Additional RAM may be required.
21 ERROR 21 PRINT OVERRUN	Information being sent to the printer is too complex (too many fonts, too many formatting instructions). Simplify the print job.
22 ERROR 22 I/O CONFIG ERROR	Host computer and printer are not communicating properly (BAUD rates different or handshake protocol not compatible). Refer to "Interface Troubleshooting" in the HP service manual.

Table 12.2 (Continued)

Message	Situation Described—Action Required
40 ERROR	An error has occurred during transfer of data from the computer to the printer. Refer to "Interface Troubleshooting" in the HP service manual.
41 ERROR	A temporary error has occurred in the printed page. Press CONTINUE to repeat the page. If the error persists, refer to "41 ERROR Checks" in the HP service manual.
42 ERROR 42 OPT INTERFACE	Indicates a communication problem between the Interface/Formatter PCA and the Optional Interface. Press CONTINUE to resume printing. If the error persists, refer to the documentation for the Optional I/O PCA.
43 ERROR 43 OPT INTERFACE	Indicates a communication problem between the Interface/Formatter PCA and the Optional Interface. If the error persists, refer to the documentation for the Optional I/O PCA.
50 SERVICE	Power OFF the printer for a minimum of 10 minutes. If the problem persists, refer to "50 SERVICE Fuser Malfunction" in the HP service manual.
51 ERROR	Loss of laser beam for over 2 seconds. Refer to "51 ERROR Message" in the HP service manual.
52 ERROR	Scanner motor unable to maintain proper speed. Refer to "52 ERROR Scanner Malfunction" in the HP service manual.
53 ERROR (33440 Only)	Optional memory installed is NOT compatible with the Interface PCA.53-1 ERRORUNIT (SERIES III Only)An error was detected on the optional memory card in the front (right) slot. Verify that correct memory is installed.

Table 12.2 (Continued)

Message	Situation Described—Action Required
53-2 ERRORUNIT (SERIES III Only)	An error was detected on the optional memory card in the rear (left) slot. Verify that correct memory is installed.
54 ERROR (Duplex printers)	An error has been detected in the duplex alignment guide (vertical registration assembly).
55 ERROR	Communications problem between the DC controller and interface/formatter PCA. Perform a 15 engine test print to verify the DC controller. If message persists, refer to the HP service manual.
56 SERVICE (Duplex printers)	Place output selector knob in face-down position.
57-1 ERRORUNIT (SERIES III Only)	The memory card in the front (right) slot can not be configured because it exceeds memory capacity.
57-2 ERRORUNIT (SERIES III Only)	The memory card in the rear (left) slot can not be configured because it exceeds memory capacity.
61 SERVICE	Checksum error detected during self-test in the interface/formatter PCA's program ROM. If the message persists, replace the interface/formatter PCA.
62 SERVICE	Checksum error detected in the interface/formatter PCA's internal font ROM. If the message persists, replace the interface/formatter PCA.
63 SERVICE	An error was detected in either the interface/formatter PCA's dynamic RAM or an optional memory PCA (if present). Remove any memory option and retest. If the message persists, replace the interface/formatter PCA.
64 SERVICE	Laser scan buffer error. If power cycling the printer does not clear the error, replace the interface/formatter PCA.

Table 12.2 (Continued)

Message	Situation Described—Action Required
65 SERVICE	Dynamic RAM controller error. If power cycling the printer does not clear the error, replace the interface/formatter PCA.
67 SERVICE	Miscellaneous hardware or address error on the interface/formatter PCA. Reseat all cables, cartridges, and accessories. If error persists, replace the interface/formatter PCA.
68 ERROR (SERIES III Only)	A *recoverable* error has been detected in Non-Volatile RAM (NVRAM). Press CONTINUE to clear. If the condition persists, replace the interface/formatter PCA.
68 SERVICE (33440 AND 33449) 68 READY/SERVICE (SERIES III Only)	NVRAM *failure* has occurred. Replace the interface/formatter PCA. (Printer may be operated temporarily.)
69 SERVICE	A timeout error has occurred between the interface/formatter PCA and the optional I/O PCA. Refer to the Optional Interface documentation.
70 ERROR (SERIES III Only)	The firmware cartridge was not designed for this printer. Turn the printer OFF and then back ON. If the error persists, consult the cartridge vendor.
71 ERROR (SERIES III Only)	The firmware cartridge was not designed for this printer. Turn the printer OFF and then back ON. If the error persists, consult the cartridge vendor.
72 SERVICE (SERIES III Only)	A font cartridge was removed too quickly after it was inserted. Turn the printer OFF and then back ON. Font cartridge or connectors on printer may be defective.
79 SERVICE (SERIES III Only)	Unexpected error has been encountered. Turn the printer OFF and then back ON. If error persists after accessories have been removed, replace the interface/formatter PCA.

Table 12.2 (Continued)

Message	Situation Described—Action Required
CONFIG LANGUAGE (SERIES III Only)	Result of holding the ENTER key while powering on the printer. User requested to select desired display language using the +, −, and ENTER keys.
EC LOAD [envelope size]	User request for envelope size not currently installed, or tray is out of envelopes. Load or press CONTINUE to override. If message persists, refer to "11 PAPER OUT Message" in the HP service manual.
PC LOAD [paper size]	User request for a paper size not currently installed, or paper tray is out of media. Load or press CONTINUE to override. If message persists, refer to "11 PAPER OUT Message" in the HP service manual.
PE FEED [envelope size] or PE FEED ENVELOPE	User request to feed an envelope manually. Feed through manual feed slot or press CONTINUE to feed from tray. If manual feed fails, perform "Manual Feed Sensor (PS302) Functional Check" described in the HP service manual.
PF FEED [paper size]	User request to feed paper manually. Feed through manual feed slot or press CONTINUE to feed from tray. If manual feed fails, perform "Manual Feed Sensor (PS302) Functional Check" described in the HP service manual.
ENVELOPE=[env. size] (SERIES II Only) PE TRAY=[envelope size] (SERIES III Only)	This message is displayed when an envelope tray is installed. User must tell printer which size envelopes are being used by scrolling through choices (use + and − keys) and pressing ENTER. If message persists or envelope tray is not installed, see "Tray Size Switches Functional Check" in the HP service manual.

Table 12.2   (Continued)

Message	Situation Described—Action Required
FC [LEFT/RIGHT/BOTH]	Font cartridge(s) were removed or replaced while printer was off line and contained buffered data. Reinsert cartridge(s) and press CONTINUE. If the problem continues replace the cartridge before replacing the interface/formatter PCA.
FC [LEFT/RIGHT/BOTH] FONT (SERIES III Only)	Font cartridge(s) could not be read by the NO printer. Reinsert the cartridge(s) and press CONTINUE. If the problem continues, replace the cartridge before replacing the interface formatter PCA.
FE CARTRIDGE	A cartridge has been removed while the printer was on line. Turn the printer OFF, reinsert the cartridge, and turn the printer ON. If the problem continues, replace the cartridge before replacing the interface/formatter PCA.
UC or LC EMPTY (DUPLEX Models)	Load paper into the upper or lower paper tray.

Post Error Codes

All error codes for the diagnostic and advanced diagnostic packages are represented with the device number followed by two digits other than 00. The device number plus 00 represents a successful completion of the test. For example: a 301 would indicate a keyboard failure, while a 300 means that the keyboard test has completed successfully.

Error Codes	Indication of failure	Corrective action
Power On Self-Test (POST) system board failures		
01X	Undetermined problem	
02X	Power supply error	
101	8259 interrupt failure	
102	Timer failure (BIOS EPROM)	Replace system board
103	Timer interrupt failure	Replace system board
104	Protected mode failure	Replace system board
105	Last 8042 command not accepted	Replace system board
106	Converting logic test	Replace system board
107	Hot non-maskable interrupt	Replace system board

Error Codes	Indication of failure	Corrective action
108	Timer bus test failure 8253/8254	Replace system board
109	Memory select error (DMA) 8237	Replace system board
110	PS/2 parity check error	Replace system board
111	PS/2 memory adapter error	Adapter memory/adapt.
112	PS/2 MCA arbitration error	Any adapter/sys bd.
113	PS/2 MCA arbitration error	Any adapter/sys bd.
114	PS/2 external ROM checksum error	
115	PS/2 test 80386 protect mode	
121	Unexpected hardware interrupt	Replace system board
131	PC system board cassette port	
132	PS/2 test DMA extended registers	
133	PS/2 test DMA verify logic	
151	Battery defective or new battery	Replace old battery
152	PS/2 real time clock or CMOS err.	Replace system board & (run Set-UP)
160	PS/2 planar ID not recognized	
161	System options not set	Run setup (dead batt)
162	System option error	Run setup-CMOS ck sum
163	Date and time not set	Clock not updating
164	Memory size error	(CMOS does not match memory—Run setup)
165	PS/2 options not set	Run setup
166	PS/2 MCA time out error	Any adapter
167	PS/2 clock not updating	
199	User indicated configuration not correct.	

Error Codes	Indication of failure	Corrective action
Power On Self-Test (POST) system memory		
201	Memory test failed	Replace defective memory module.
202	PS/2 memory address error	
203	PS/2 memory address or refresh	
204	PS/2 relocated memory	Run diagnostics again
205	PS/2 CMOS error	
207	PS/2 ROM failure	
211	PS/2 base 64K on I/O channel failure	
215	PS/2 base 64K on daughter card 2	System board memory card failed, or system board.
216	PS/2 base 64K on daughter card 1	System board memory card failed, or system board.
225	Memory failure—incorrect SIMMs	Replace SIMMs
Power On Self-Test (POST) keyboard		
301	Software reset failed, or stuck key	Replace keyboard. If stuck key, scan code displayed. Correct/ replace key, replace keyboard cable
302	System key lock is engaged	Keyboard or cable
303	Keyboard or system board	
304	Keyboard or system board	
305	PS/2 keyboard fuse (on system board)	Replace fuse
341	Keyboard failure	

Error Codes	Indication of failure	Corrective action
342	Keyboard cable failure	
343	Interface cable or enhancement card failure	
365	Keyboard failure	
366	Keyboard cable failure	
367	Interface cable or enhancement card failure	

Power On Self-Test (POST) Monochrome Display Adapter (MDA) and PS/2 system board parallel port

401	Monochrome memory or horizontal sync frequency test or video test or PS/2 parallel port (system board)	Replace system board
408	User indicated display attributes	
416	User indicated character set error	
424	User indicated 80×25 mode failure	
432	Parallel port failure on monochrome display card	

Power On Self-Test (POST) Color Graphics Adapter (CGA)

501	CGA memory test or horizontal sync test or video test failure
508	User indicated attribute failure
516	User indicated character set failure
524	User indicated 80×25 mode failure
532	User indicated 40×25 mode failure
540	User indicated 320×200 graphics mode failure
548	User indicated 640×200 graphics mode failure

Error Codes	Indication of failure	Corrective action
556	Light pen test failed	
564	User indicated screen paging test failure	

Power On Self-Test (POST) diskette drive

601	Drive /adapter POST failure	Replace drive/adapter (check for missing jumper P3 on IBM PC/ XT adapter).
602	Drive test failure (boot record)	Replace media
603	Incorrect diskette installed	Replace media
606	Disk change line function failure	Replace drive
607	Diskette is write protected	
608	Bad command or replace diagnostic disk	Replace media
610	Disk initialization failure	Replace media
611	Time out	Replace drive
612	Bad controller chip	Replace adapter
613	DMA access error (drive error)	Replace drive
614	DMA access error (boundary overrun)	Replace media
615	Bad index timing (drive error)	Replace drive
616	Drive speed error	Correct-replace drive
621	Seek error (drive error)	Replace drive
622	Cyclic redundancy check error	Replace drive
623	Record not found (drive error)	Replace drive
624	Address mark error (drive error)	Replace drive
625	Bad controller chip (seek error)	Replace adapter
626	Data compare error	Replace media/drive

Error Codes	Indication of failure	Corrective action
627	Bad index	
628	Diskette removed	
630	PS/2 index stuck HI (drive A)	
631	PS/2 index stuck LO (drive A)	
632	PS/2 track 0 stuck off (drive A)	
633	PS/2 track 0 stuck on (drive A)	
640	PS/2 index stuck HI (drive B)	
641	PS/2 index stuck LO (drive B)	
642	PS/2 track 0 stuck off (drive B)	
643	PS/2 track 0 stuck on (drive B)	
650	PS/2 drive speed error	
651	PS/2 format failure	
652	PS/2 verify failure	
653	PS/2 read failure	
654	PS/2 write failure	
655	PS/2 controller error	
656	PS/2 drive failure	
657	PS/2 write protect stuck (protected)	
658	PS/2 change line stuck (changed)	
659	PS/2 write protect stuck (unprotected)	
660	PS/2 change line stuck (unchanged)	

Power On Self-Test (POST) math coprocessor

7nn	8087 math coprocessor or system board	
7nn	PS/2 80287 math coprocessor or system board	

Error Codes	Indication of failure	Corrective action
701	Math coprocessor failed test	
702	Math coprocessor exception errors test	
703	PS/2 80387 math coprocessor rounding test	
704	PS/2 80387 math coprocessor arithmetic test 1	
705	PS/2 80387 math coprocessor arithmetic test 2	
706	PS/2 80387 math coprocessor arithmetic test 3	
707	PS/2 80387 math coprocessor combination test	
708	PS/2 80387 math coprocessor integer/store test	
709	PS/2 80387 math coprocessor equivalent expressions	
710	PS/2 80387 math coprocessor exceptions (interrupts)	
711	PS/2 80387 math coprocessor save state (FSAVE)	
712	PS/2 80387 math coprocessor protected mode test	
713	PS/2 80387 math coprocessor voltage/temp test	

Power On Self-Test (POST) parallel printer adapter

9nn	Parallel printer adapter test failed	
901	Printer adapter data register latch error	
902	Printer adapter control register latch error	

Error Codes	Indication of failure	Corrective action
903	Printer adapter register address decode error	
904	Printer adapter address decode error	
910	Status line(s) wrap connector error	
911	Status line bit 7 wrap error	
912	Status line bit 7 wrap error	
913	Status line bit 6 wrap error	
914	Status line bit 5 wrap error	
915	Status line bit 4 wrap error	
916	Printer adapter interrupt wrap failed	
917	Unexpected printer adapter interrupt	

Power On Self-Test (POST) alternate parallel printer adapter

10nn	Alternate parallel printer adapter	
1001	Printer adapter failure	

Power On Self-Test (POST) Asynchronous communications adapter

1101	Asynchronous communications adapter test failed	
1101	PS/2 16550 ASYNC chip error	
1101	PS/2 POST error	
1102	PS/2 card selected feedback error	
1103	PS/2 port 102H register test failed	
1106	PS/2 serial option can not be put to sleep	
1107	PS/2 cable error or system board	
1108	PS/2 ASYNC IRQ3 error—system board or serial device	

Error Codes	Indication of failure	Corrective action
1109	PS/2 ASYNC IRQ4 error—system board or serial device	
1110	PS/2 16550 ASYNC chip register failure	
1111	PS/2 internal wrap test of 16550 MODEM control line failure	
1112	PS/2 external wrap test of 16550 MODEM control line failure	
1113	PS/2 16550 transmit error	
1114	PS/2 16550 receive error	
1115	PS/2 16550 receive error data not equal to transmit data	
1116	PS/2 16550 interrupt function error	
1117	PS/2 16550 fails baud rate test	
1118	PS/2 16550 interrupt driven receive external data wrap test failure	
1119	PS/2 16550 FIFO	
1120	Interrupt enable failure—all bits can not be set	
1121	Interrupt enable failure—all bits can not be reset	
1122	Interrupt pending stuck on	
1123	Interrupt ID register stuck on	
1124	MODEM control register—all bits can not be set	
1125	MODEM control register—all bits can not be reset	
1126	MODEM status register—all bits can not be reset	

Error Codes	Indication of failure	Corrective action
1127	MODEM status register—all bits can not be set	
1128	Interrupt ID failure	
1129	Can not force overrun failure	
1130	No MODEM status interrupt	
1131	Invalid interrupt pending	
1132	No data ready	
1133	No data available interrupt	
1134	No transmit holding interrupt	
1135	No interrupt	
1136	No received line status interrupt	
1137	No received data available	
1138	Transmit holding register not empty	
1139	No MODEM status interrupt	
1140	Transmit holding register not empty	
1141	No interrupts	
1142	No IRQ4 interrupt (possible bad interrupt controller)	
1143	No IRQ3 interrupt (possible bad interrupt controller)	
1144	No data transferred	
1145	Maximum baud rate failure	
1146	Maximum baud rate failure	
1148	Timeout error	
1149	Invalid data returned	
1150	MODEM status register failure	
1151	No DSR and delta DSR	
1152	No DCR	

Error Codes	Indication of failure	Corrective action
1153	No delta DSR	
1154	MODEM status register not clear	
1155	No CTS and delta CTS	
1156	No CTS	
1157	No delta CTS	

Power On Self-Test (POST) alternate asynchronous communications

1201	Alternate ASYNC adapter test failed	
1201	PS/2 can not detect presence of dual ASYNC adapter	
1202	PS/2 dual ASYNC adapter card selected feedback error	
1203	PS/2 dual ASYNC adapter port 102H register test failed	
1206	PS/2 dual ASYNC adapter serial option can not be put to sleep	
1207	PS/2 dual ASYNC adapter or adapter cable error	
1208	PS/2 dual ASYNC adapter ASYNC IRQ3 error or device error	
1209	PS/2 dual ASYNC adapter ASYNC IRQ4 error or device error	
1210	PS/2 16550 ASYNC chip register failure	
1211	PS/2 internal wrap test of 16550 MODEM control line failure	
1212	PS/2 external wrap test of 16550 MODEM control line failure	
1213	PS/2 16550 transmit error	
1214	PS/2 16550 receive error	

Error Codes	Indication of failure	Corrective action
1215	PS/2 16550 receive error data not equal to transmit data	
1216	PS/2 16550 interrupt function error	
1217	PS/2 16550 fails baud rate test	
1218	PS/2 16550 interrupt driven receive external data wrap test failure	
1219	PS/2 16550 FIFO	
1225	PS/2 16550 ASYNC chip register failure	
1226	PS/2 internal wrap test of 16550 MODEM control line failure	
1227	PS/2 external wrap test of 16550 MODEM control line failure	
1228	PS/2 16550 transmit error	
1229	PS/2 16550 receive error	
1230	PS/2 16550 receive error data not equal to transmit data	
1231	PS/2 16550 interrupt function error	
1232	PS/2 16550 fails baud rate test	
1233	PS/2 16550 interrupt driven receive external data wrap test failure	
1234	PS/2 16550 FIFO	
1235	No interrupt	
1236	No received line status interrupt	
1237	No received data available	
1238	Transmit holding register not empty	
1239	No MODEM status interrupt	

Error Codes	Indication of failure	Corrective action
1240	Transmit holding register not empty	
1241	No interrupts	
1242	No IRQ4 interrupt (possible bad interrupt controller)	
1243	No IRQ3 interrupt (possible bad interrupt controller)	
1244	No data transferred	
1245	Maximum baud rate failure	
1246	Maximum baud rate failure	
1248	Timeout error	
1249	Invalid data returned	
1250	MODEM status register failure	
1251	No DSR and delta DSR	
1252	No DSR	
1253	No delta DSR	
1254	MODEM status register not clear	
1255	No CTS and delta CTS	
1256	No CTS	
1257	No delta CTS	

Power On Self-Test (POST) game control/joy stick

1301	Game control adapter test failed	
1302	Joy stick test failed	

Power On Self-Test (POST) parallel printer

14nn	Printer test failed	
1401	PS/2 printer failure	
1402	Printer not ready error	

Error Codes	Indication of failure	Corrective action
1402	PS/2 out of paper	
1403	Printer no paper error	
1403	PS/2 interrupt failure	
1404	Matrix printer failed	
1404	PS/2 system board time out	
1405	PS/2 parallel adapter failure	
1406	PS/2 presence test failed	

Power On Self-Test (POST) SDLC communications adapter

15nn	SDLC communications adapter errors	
1501	Adapter test failed—must use wrap plug to test	
1510	8255 port B failure	
1511	8255 port A failure	
1512	8255 port C failure	
1513	8253 timer 1 did not reach terminal count	
1514	8253 timer 1 stuck on	
1515	8253 timer 0 did not reach terminal count	
1516	8253 timer 0 stuck on	
1517	8253 timer 2 did not reach terminal count	
1518	8253 timer 2 stuck on	
1519	8273 port B error	
1520	8273 port A error	
1521	8273 command/read timeout	
1522	Interrupt level 4 failure	

Error Codes	Indication of failure	Corrective action
1523	Ring indicate stuck on	
1524	Receive clock stuck on	
1525	Transmit clock stuck on	
1526	Test indicate stuck on	
1527	Ring indicate not on	
1528	Receive clock not on	
1529	Transmit clock not on	
1530	Test indicate not on	
1531	Data set ready not on	
1532	Carrier detect not on	
1533	Clear to send not on	
1534	Data set ready stuck on	
1536	Clear to send stuck on	
1537	Level 3 interrupt failure	
1538	Receive interrupt results error	
1539	Wrap data miscompare	
1540	DMA channel 1 error	
1541	DMA channel 1 error	
1542	Error in 8273 error checking or status reporting	
1547	Stray interrupt level 4	
1548	Stray interrupt level 3	
1549	Interrupt presentation sequence timeout	

Power On Self-Test (POST) display emulation (327X, 5520, 525X)

16nn	Display emulation adapter	
1604	Adapter failure or system twinaxial network problem	

Error Codes	Indication of failure	Corrective action
1608	Adapter failure or system twinaxial network problem	
1624	Adapter failure	
1634	Adapter failure	
1644	Adapter failure	
1652	Adapter failure	
1654	Adapter failure	
1658	Adapter failure	
1662	Interrupt switches set wrong or adapter failure	
1664	Adapter failure	
1668	Interrupt switches set wrong or adapter failure	
1669	Bug in early version of diagnostics	
1674	Bug in early version of diagnostics	
1684	Feature not installed or address switches set wrong	
1688	Feature not installed or address switches set wrong	

Power On Self-Test (POST) hard disk drive subsystem

1701	Disk drive not ready, nonfatal drive 0 error, hard file/adapter test failed	Check drive motor (spin), check that +12VDC reaches spec within 1 second
1702	Timeout (hard file/adapter)	Check cables/adapter
1703	Seek failed (hard file/drive)	Check low level format
	ECC error	Check controller
1704	Disk adapter error	Check drive select

Error Codes	Indication of failure	Corrective action
1705	No record found	Check drive
1706	Write fault	Check drive, DC voltages
1707	Track 0 error	Check drive format
1708	Bad select error	Check drive format
1709	Bad block check character (BCC)	Check drive interface
1710	Read buffer overrun	Check interface and interleave
1711	Hard file bad address mark	Check low level format or interface
1712	Bad address mark	Check interface
1713	Data compare error	
1714	Drive select error	Check cables/jumpers
1715	No record found (can be caused by a bug in the diagnostics)	
1726	Data compare error	Check format/other HD errors
1730	Adapter failure	
1732	Time out error	
1750	PS/2 drive "X" verify failure	
1751	PS/2 drive "X" read failure	
1752	PS/2 drive "X" write failure	
1753	PS/2 drive "X" random read test error	
1754	PS/2 drive "X" seek test error	
1755	PS/2 controller failure	
1756	PS/2 controller ECC test failure	
1757	PS/2 controller head select fail	
1770	Surfaces error	Check for other HD error

Error Codes	Indication of failure	Corrective action
1780	Drive 0 error	Check data cable & setup
1781	Drive 1 error	Check cables, jumpers, setup
1782	Fixed disk controller error	Check interface
1790	Drive 0 error	Check drive, adapter, setup
1791	Drive 1 error	

Power On Self-Test (POST) expansion unit

18nn	I/O expansion unit errors
1801	I/O expansion unit POST error
1810	Enable/disable failure
1811	Extender card wrap test failed (disabled)
1812	High order address lines failure (disabled)
1813	Wait state failure (disabled)
1814	Enable/disable could not be set
1815	Wait state failure (enabled)
1816	Extender card wrap test failed (enabled)
1817	High order address lines failure (enabled)
1818	Disable not functioning
1819	Wait request switch not set correctly
1820	Receiver card wrap test failure
1821	Receiver high order address lines failure

Error Codes	Indication of failure	Corrective action

Power On Self-Test (POST) fixed disk drive backup (tape)

19nn	Tape backup failure	

Power On Self-Test (POST) Binary Sync Communications (BSC) errors

20nn	BISYNC communications adapter	
2001	Adapter test failed—wrap plug must be installed for testing	
2010	8255 port A failure	
2011	8255 port B failure	
2012	8255 port C failure	
2013	8253 timer 1 did not reach terminal count	
2014	8253 timer 1 stuck on	
2015	8253 timer 2 did not reach terminal count	
2016	8253 timer 2 did not reach terminal count or timer 2 stuck on	
2017	8251 data set ready failed to come on	
2018	8251 clear to send not sensed	
2019	8251 data set ready stuck on	
2020	8251 clear to send stuck on	
2021	8251 hardware reset failed	
2022	8251 software reset failed	
2023	8251 software "error reset" failed	
2024	8251 transmit ready did not come on	
2025	8251 receive ready did not come on	
2026	8251 could not force "overrun" error status	

Error Codes	Indication of failure	Corrective action
2027	Interrupt failure-no timer interrupt	
2028	Interrupt failure-transmit	Replace card/planar
2029	Interrupt failure-transmit	Replace card
2030	Interrupt failure-receive	Replace card/planar
2031	Interrupt failure-receive	Replace card
2033	Ring indicate stuck on	
2034	Receive clock stuck on	
2035	Transmit clock stuck on	
2036	Test indicate stuck on	
2037	Ring indicate stuck on	
2038	Receive clock not on	
2039	Transmit clock not on	
2040	Test indicate not on	
2041	Data set ready not on	
2042	Carrier detect not on	
2043	Clear to send not on	
2044	Data set ready stuck on	
2045	Carrier detect stuck on	
2046	Clear to send stuck on	
2047	Unexpected transmit interrupt	
2048	Unexpected receive interrupt	
2049	Transmit data did not equal receive data	
2050	8251 detected overrun error	
2051	Lost data set ready during data wrap	
2052	Receive timeout during data wrap	

Error Codes	Indication of failure	Corrective action

Power On Self-Test (POST) alternate BISYNC communications adapter

21nn	Alternate BISYNC adapter errors	
2101	Adapter test failed—wrap plug must be installed for testing	
2110	8255 port A failure	
2111	8255 port B failure	
2112	8255 port C failure	
2113	8253 timer 1 did not reach terminal count	
2114	8253 timer 1 stuck on	
2115	8253 timer 2 did not reach terminal count	
2116	8253 timer 2 did not reach terminal count or timer 2 stuck on	
2117	8251 data set ready failed to come on	
2118	8251 clear to send not sensed	
2119	8251 data set ready stuck on	
2120	8251 clear to send stuck on	
2121	8251 hardware reset failed	
2122	8251 software reset failed	
2123	8251 software "error reset" failed	
2124	8251 transmit ready did not come on	
2125	8251 receive ready did not come on	
2126	8251 could not force "overrun" error status	
2127	Interrupt failure-no timer interrupt	

Error Codes	Indication of failure	Corrective action
2128	Interrupt failure-transmit	Replace card/planar
2129	Interrupt failure-transmit	Replace card
2130	Interrupt failure-receive	Replace card/planar
2131	Interrupt failure-receive	Replace card
2133	Ring indicate stuck on	
2134	Receive clock stuck on	
2135	Transmit clock stuck on	
2136	Test indicate stuck on	
2137	Ring indicate stuck on	
2138	Receive clock not on	
2139	Transmit clock not on	
2140	Test indicate not on	
2141	Data set ready not on	
2142	Carrier detect not on	
2143	Clear to send not on	
2144	Data set ready stuck on	
2145	Carrier detect stuck on	
2146	Clear to send stuck on	
2147	Unexpected transmit interrupt	
2148	Unexpected receive interrupt	
2149	Transmit data did not equal receive data	
2150	8251 detected overrun error	
2151	Lost data set ready during data wrap	
2152	Receive timeout during data wrap	

Error Codes	Indication of failure	Corrective action

Power On Self-Test (POST) cluster adapter errors

22nn	Cluster adapter	
2201	Adapter test failed—need 75 ohm BNC terminator to test	

Power On Self-Test (POST) plasma monitor adapter

23nn	Plasma monitor adapter	

Power On Self-Test (POST) enhanced graphics adapter

24nn	Enhanced graphics adapter	
2401	PS/2 planar video error	
2402	PS/2 diagnostic video error	
2408	User indicated display attributes failure	
2416	User indicated character set failure	
2424	User indicated 80 × 25 mode failure	
2432	User indicated 40 × 25 mode failure	
2440	User indicated 320 × 200 graphics mode failure	
2448	User indicated 640 × 200 graphics mode failure	
2456	Light pen test	
2464	User indicated screen paging test failure	

Power On Self-Test (POST) alternate EGA or VGA adapter

25nn	Enhanced graphics adapter	
2501	PS/2 planar video error	
2502	PS/2 diagnostic video error	

Error Codes	Indication of failure	Corrective action
2508	User indicated display attributes failure	
2516	User indicated character set failure	
2524	User indicated 80 × 25 mode failure	
2532	User indicated 40 × 25 mode failure	
2540	User indicated 320 × 200 graphics mode failure	
2548	User indicated 640 × 200 graphics mode failure	
2556	Light pen test	
2564	User indicated screen paging test failure	

Power On Self-Test (POST) XT/370 processor or memory card

26nn	XT/370 error codes
2601–55	XT/370 memory card
2657–68	XT/370 memory card
2672	XT/370 memory card
2673–74	XT/370 processor card
2677–80	XT/370 processor card
2681	XT/370 memory card
2682–94	XT/370 processor card
2697	XT/370 processor card
2698	XT/370 diagnostic diskette error

Power On Self-Test (POST) XT/370 emulator card

2701–03	XT/370 emulator card

Error Codes	Indication of failure	Corrective action
Power On Self-Test (POST) 3278/79 emulation card		
28nn	3278/9 emulation	NOTE: run diags with coax unplugged
Power On Self-Test (POST) color printer errors		
29nn	Color printer	
2901	Printer test failed	
2902	Printer test failed	
2904	Printer test failed	
Power On Self-Test (POST) PC network errors		
3001	Processor error	Replace network adapter
3002	ROM	Replace network adapter
3003	ID	Replace network adapter
3004	RAM	Replace network adapter
3005	Host interrupt	Replace network adapter
3006	+ or −12VDC	Replace network adapter
3007	Digital wrap	Replace network adapter
3008	Host interrupt	Replace network adapter
3009	Sync	Replace network adapter
3010	Time out	Replace network adapter
3011	Time out	Replace network adapter

Error Codes	Indication of failure	Corrective action
3012	Digital	Replace network adapter
3013	Digital	Replace network adapter
3014	Digital	Replace network adapter
3015	Analog	
3020	Rom BIOS	
3041	Continuous RF signal detected	
3042	Continuous RF signal sent-replace alternate PC network adapter	
Note:	If 3041 or 3042 error occurs with the cover removed, install the cover and rerun the test. If the error remains, take action as indicated in the table.	

Power On Self-Test (POST) secondary network adapter

31nn	Secondary network adapter failed
3101	CPU failure
3102	ROM failure
3103	ID failure
3104	RAM failure
3105	HIC failure
3106	+/− 12VDC failure
3107	Digital loop back failure
3108	Host detected HIC failure
3109	Sync fail & no go bit
3110	HIC test OK & no go bit
3111	Go bit & no CMD 41
3112	Card not present

Error Codes	Indication of failure	Corrective action
3113	Digital failure (fall thru)	
3115	Analog failure	
3141	Hot carrier (not this card)	
3142	Hot carrier (this card)	

Power On Self-Test (POST) display adapter (3270 PC or AT)

32nn	Display adapter	

Power On Self-Test (POST) compact printer adapter

33nn	Compact printer adapter	
3301	Printer test failed	

Power On Self-Test (POST) enhanced display station emulation

35nn	Enhanced display station emulation adapter	
3504	Adapter connected on the twin-axial cable during off-line test	
3508	Work station address in use by another work-station. Diagnostic diskette from another PC was used	
3509	Diagnostic program failing (recreate Adapter Integrated Diagnostic diskette on a blank diskette).	
3540	Work station address invalid, not configured at the controller. Twin-axial cable not connected or is failing	
3588	Enhanced display station emulation adapter feature not installed	

Error Codes	Indication of failure	Corrective action
3599	Diagnostic program failing (recreate Adapter Integrated Diagnostic diskette on a blank diskette)	

Power On Self-Test (POST) GPIB adapter (IEEE 488 interface)

36nn	GPIB adapter	
3601	Adapter test failed	
3602	Write to serial poll mode register failed	
3603	Write to address failure	
3610	Adapter can not be programmed to listen	
3611	Adapter can not be programmed to talk	
3612	Adapter can not take control of IFC	
3613	Adapter card can not go to standby	
3614	Adapter card can not take control asynchronously	
3615	Adapter card can not take control asynchronously	
3616	Adapter can not pass control	
3617	Adapter can not be addressed to listen	
3618	Adapter can not be unaddressed to listen	
3619	Adapter can not be addressed to talk	
3620	Adapter can not be unaddressed to talk	
3621	Can not be addressed to listen with extended addressing	

Error Codes	Indication of failure	Corrective action
3622	Can not be unaddressed to listen with extended address.	
3623	Can not be addressed to talk with extended addressing	
3624	Can not be unaddressed to talk with extended addressing	
3625	Adapter can not write to self	
3626	Adapter can not generate handshake error	
3627	Adapter can not detect device clear message	
3628	Adapter can not detect selected device clear message	
3629	Adapter can not detect end with end of identity	
3630	Adapter can not detect end of xmit with end of identity	
3631	Adapter can not detect end with 0-bit EOS	
3632	Adapter can not detect end with 7-bit EOS	
3633	Adapter can not detect group executive trigger	
3634	Mode 3 addressing not functioning	
3635	Adapter can not recognize undefined command	
3636	Adapter can not detect remote, remote changed, lockout or lockout changed	
3637	Adapter can not clear remote or lockout	

Error Codes	Indication of failure	Corrective action
3638	Adapter can not clear service request	
3639	Adapter can not conduct serial poll	
3640	Adapter can not conduct parallel poll	
3650	Adapter can not DMA to 7210	
3651	Data error on DMA to 7210	
3652	Adapter can not DMA from 7210	
3653	Data error on DMA from 7210	
3658	Uninvoked interrupt received	
3659	Adapter can not interrupt on address status changed	
3660	Adapter can not interrupt on address status changed	
3661	Adapter can not interrupt on convert output	
3662	Adapter can not interrupt on data out	
3663	Adapter can not interrupt on data in	
3664	Adapter can not interrupt on error	
3665	Adapter can not interrupt on device clear	
3666	Adapter can not interrupt on end	
3667	Adapter can not interrupt on device executive trigger	
3668	Adapter can not interrupt on address pass through	
3669	Adapter can not interrupt on command pass through	

Error Codes	Indication of failure	Corrective action
3670	Adapter can not interrupt on remote changed	
3671	Adapter can not interrupt on lockout changed	
3672	Adapter can not interrupt on service request in	
3673	Can not interrupt on terminal count on DMA to 7210	
3674	Can not interrupt on terminal count on DMA from 7210	
3675	Spurious DMA terminal count interrupt	
3697	Illegal DMA configuration setting detected	
3698	Illegal interrupt level configuration setting detected	

Power On Self-Test (POST) data acquisition and control adapter

38nn	Data acquisition & control adapter	
3801	Adapter test failed—wrap plug must be used for test	
3810	Timer read test failed	
3811	Timer interrupt test failed	
3812	Delay, binary input 13 test failed	
3813	Rate, binary input 13 test failed	
3814	Binary output 14, interrupt status interrupt request test failed	
3815	Binary output 0, count-in test failed	
3816	Binary input strobe, count-out test failed	

Error Codes	Indication of failure	Corrective action
3817	Binary output 1, binary output CTS test failed	
3818	Binary output 1, binary input 0 test failed	
3819	Binary output 2, binary input 1 test failed	
3820	Binary output 3, binary input 2 test failed	
3821	Binary output 4, binary input 3 test failed	
3822	Binary output 5, binary input 4 test failed	
3823	Binary output 6, binary input 5 test failed	
3824	Binary output 7, binary input 6 test failed	
3825	Binary output 8, binary input 7 test failed	
3826	Binary output 9, binary input 8 test failed	
3827	Binary output 10, binary input 9 test failed	
3828	Binary output 11, binary input 10 test failed	
3829	Binary output 12, binary input 11 test failed	
3830	Binary output 13, binary input 12 test failed	
3831	Binary output 15, binary input convert enable test failed	
3832	Binary output strobe, binary output gate failed	

Error Codes	Indication of failure	Corrective action
3833	Binary input CTS, binary input hold test failed	
3834	Analog input converter output, binary input test 15 failed	
3835	Counter interrupt test failed	
3836	Counter read test	
3837	Analog output 0 ranges test failed	
3838	Analog output 1 ranges test failed	
3839	Analog input 0 values test failed	
3840	Analog input 1 values test failed	
3841	Analog input 2 values test failed	
3842	Analog input 3 values test failed	
3843	Analog input interrupt test failed	
3844	Analog input 23 address or value test failed	

Power On Self-Test (POST) Professional Graphics Adapter (PGA)

39nn	Professional graphics adapter	
3901	Adapter test failed	
3902	ROM 1 self-test failed	
3903	ROM 2 self-test failed	
3904	RAM self-test failed	
3905	Cold start cycle power failed	
3906	Data error in communications RAM	
3907	Address error in communications RAM	
3908	Bad data detected while read/write to 6845	

Error Codes	Indication of failure	Corrective action
3909	Bad data detected in lower HEX— EO while attempting read/write to 6845	
3910	Adapter display bank output latches failed	
3911	Basic clock failure	
3912	Command control failure	
3913	Vertical sync scanner failure	
3914	Horizontal sync scanner failure	
3915	Intech failure	
3916	Look-up table address error	
3917	Look-up table red RAM chip error	
3918	Look-up table green RAM chip error	
3919	Look-up table blue RAM chip error	
3920	Look-up table data latch error	
3921	Horizontal display error	
3922	Vertical display error	
3923	Light pen error	
3924	Unexpected error	
3925	Emulator addressing error	
3926	Emulator data latch	
3927	Base for error codes 3928—3930 (emulator RAM)	
3928	Emulator RAM	
3929	Emulator RAM	
3930	Emulator RAM	
3931	Emulator horizontal vertical display problem	

Error Codes	Indication of failure	Corrective action
3932	Emulator cursor position	
3933	Emulator attribute display problem	
3934	Emulator cursor display error	
3935	Fundamental emulation RAM error	
3936	Emulation character set problem	
3937	Emulation graphics display	
3938	Emulation character display problem	
3939	Emulation bank select error	
3940	Display RAM U2	
3941	Display RAM U4	
3942	Display RAM U6	
3943	Display RAM U8	
3944	Display RAM U10	
3945	Display RAM U1	
3946	Display RAM U3	
3947	Display RAM U5	
3948	Display RAM U7	
3949	Display RAM U9	
3950	Display RAM U12	
3951	Display RAM U14	
3952	Display RAM U16	
3953	Display RAM U18	
3954	Display RAM U20	
3955	Display RAM U11	
3956	Display RAM U13	
3957	Display RAM U15	

Error Codes	Indication of failure	Corrective action
3958	Display RAM U17	
3959	Display RAM U19	
3960	Display RAM U22	
3961	Display RAM U24	
3962	Display RAM U26	
3963	Display RAM U28	
3964	Display RAM U30	
3965	Display RAM U21	
3966	Display RAM U23	
3967	Display RAM U25	
3968	Display RAM U27	
3969	Display RAM U29	
3970	Display RAM U32	
3971	Display RAM U34	
3972	Display RAM U36	
3973	Display RAM U38	
3974	Display RAM U40	
3975	Display RAM U31	
3976	Display RAM U33	
3977	Display RAM U35	
3978	Display RAM U37	
3979	Display RAM U39	
3980	Adapter RAM timing error	
3981	Adapter read/write latch failed	
3982	Shift register bus output latches failed	
3983	Addressing error (vertical column memory, U2 at top)	

Error Codes	Indication of failure	Corrective action
3984	Addressing error (vertical column memory; U4 at top)	
3985	Addressing error (vertical column memory; U6 at top)	
3986	Addressing error (vertical column memory; U8 at top)	
3987	Addressing error (vertical column memory; U10 at top)	
3988	Horizontal bank latch error	
3989	Horizontal bank latch error	
3990	Horizontal bank latch error	
3991	Horizontal bank latch error	
3992	Row address generator/column address generator failure	
3993	Multiple write modes, nibble mask error	
3994	Row nibble (display RAM)	
3995	Adapter addressing error	

Power On Self-Test (POST) display attachment unit and display

44nn   Display attachment unit & display

Power On Self-Test (POST) IEEE-488 interface adapter card

45nn   IEEE-488 interface adapter card

Power On Self-Test (POST) PS/2 multiport interface board

46nn   Multiport interface adapter

Power On Self-Test (POST) internal MODEM

48nn   Internal MODEM

Error Codes	Indication of failure	Corrective action

Power On Self-Test (POST) alternate internal MODEM

49nn	Alternate internal MODEM	

Power On Self-Test (POST) financial communications system

56nn	Financial communications system	

Power On Self-Test (POST) voice communications adapter

71nn	Voice communications adapter	
7101	I/O control register	
7102	Instruction or external data memory	
7103	PC to VCA interrupt	
7104	Internal data memory	
7105	DMA	
7106	Internal registers	
7107	Interactive shared memory	
7108	VCA to PC interrupt	
7109	DC wrap	
7111	External analog wrap/tone output	
7112	Mic to speaker wrap	
7114	Telephone attach test	

Power On Self-Test (POST) 3.5" external diskette drive & adapter

7301	Diskette drive or adapter test failed	
7306	Disk line change function failure	Replace drive
7307	Disk is write protected	Check media/drive
7308	Bad command (drive error)	Check media/drive
7310	Disk initialization failure	Track 0 bad
7311	Time out (drive error)	Replace drive
7012	Bad controller chip	Replace adapter

Error Codes	Indication of failure	Corrective action
7313	DMA access error (drive error)	Replace drive
7314	DMA access error (boundary overrun)	Replace media
7315	Bad index timing (drive error)	Replace drive
7316	Drive speed error	Correct or replace
7321	Seek error (drive error)	Replace drive
7322	Cyclic redundancy check error	Replace drive
7323	Record not found (drive error)	Replace drive
7324	Address mark error (drive error)	Replace drive
7325	Bad controller chip (seek error)	Replace adapter
7326	Data compare error	Replace media/drive

Power On Self-Test (POST) PS/2 display adapter (VGA cards)

74nn	VGA display adapter

Power On Self-Test (POST) 4216 page printer

76nn	4217 page printer
7601	Printer adapter card error
7602	Printer adapter card error
7603	Printer error
7604	Printer cable error

Power On Self-Test (POST) speech adapter

84nn	Speech adapter

Power On Self-Test (POST) iBM expanded memory adapter (XMA)

85nn	Expanded memory adapter

Power On Self-Test (POST) pointing device (mouse)

86nn	PS/2 mouse related error	
8601	PS/2 system board or mouse error	Pointing device

Error Codes	Indication of failure	Corrective action
8602	PS/2 user indicated mouse error	Pointing device
8603	PS/2 system board or mouse error	System board
8604	PS/2 system board or mouse error	System board or device

Power On Self-Test (POST) musical feature card

89nn	Musical feature card

Power On Self-Test (POST) multi-protocol communications adapter

100nn	PS/2 multi-protocol adapter
10001	PS/2 can not detect presence of multi-protocol adapter
10002	PS/2 card selected feedback error
10003	PS/2 port 102H register test failure
10004	PS/2 port 103H register test failure
10006	PS/2 serial option can not be put to sleep
10007	PS/2 cable error
10008	PS/2 ASYNC IRQ3 error
10009	PS/2 ASYNC IRQ4 error
10010	PS/2 16550 ASYNC chip register failure
10011	PS/2 internal wrap test of 16550 MODEM control line failure
10012	PS/2 external wrap test of 16550 MODEM control line failure
10013	PS/2 16550 transmit error
10014	PS/2 16550 receive error
10015	PS/2 16550 receive error data not equal transmit data
10016	PS/2 16550 interrupt function error

Error Codes	Indication of failure	Corrective action
10017	PS/2 16550 fails baud rate test	
10018	PS/2 16550 interrupt driven receive external data wrap test failure	
10019	PS/2 16550 FIFO	
10026	PS/2 8255 port A error	
10027	PS/2 8255 port B error	
10028	PS/2 8255 port C error	
10029	PS/2 8254 timer 0 error	
10030	PS/2 8254 timer 1 error	
10031	PS/2 8254 timer 2 error	
10032	PS/2 BISYNC DSR response to DTR error	
10033	PS/2 BISYNC CTS response to RTS error	
10034	PS/2 8251 hardware reset test failed	
10035	PS/2 8251 function error	
10035	PS/2 8251 internal software retest failed	
10035	PS/2 8251 error reset command failed	
10035	PS/2 8251 can not detect overrun error	
10036	PS/2 8251 status error	
10036	PS/2 8251 Tx ready error	
10037	PS/2 8251 Rx ready error	
10037	PS/2 BISYNC timer interrupt error	
10038	PS/2 BISYNC transmit interrupt error	

Error Codes	Indication of failure	Corrective action
10039	PS/2 BISYNC receive interrupt error	
10040	PS/2 stray IRQ3 error	
10041	PS/2 stray IRQ4 error	
10042	PS/2 BISYNC external wrap error	
10044	PS/2 BISYNC data wrap error	
10045	PS/2 BISYNC line status/condition error	
10046	PS/2 BISYNC time out error during data wrap test	
10050	PS/2 8273 command acceptance or results ready time out error	
10051	PS/2 8273 port A error	
10052	PS/2 8273 port B error	
10053	PS/2 SDLC modem status change logic error	
10054	PS/2 SDLC timer interrupt (IRQ4) error	
10055	PS/2 SDLC modem status change interrupt (IRQ4) error	
10056	PS/2 SDLC external wrap error	
10057	PS/2 SDLC interrupt results error	
10058	PS/2 SDLC data wrap error	
10059	PS/2 SDLC transmit interrupt error	
10060	PS/2 SDLC receive interrupt error	
10061	PS/2 DMA channel 1 error (transmit)	
10062	PS/2 DMA channel 1 error (receive)	
10063	PS/2 8273 status detect failure	

Error Codes	Indication of failure	Corrective action
10064	PS/2 8273 error detect failure	

Power *On self-test (POST) PS/2 MODEM adapter*

101nn	PS/2 modem adapter	
10101–24	PS/2 modem adapter/A	Adapter or device
10125	PS/2 modem reset result code error	
10126	PS/2 modem general result code error	
10127	PS/2 modem S registers write/read error	
10128	PS/2 modem turn echo on/off error	
10129	PS/2 modem enable/disable result codes error	
10130	PS/2 modem enable number/word result codes error	
10133	PS/2 connect results for 300 baud not received	
10134	PS/2 connect results for 1200 baud not received	
10135	PS/2 modem fails local analog loop back test at 300 baud	
10136	PS/2 modem fails local analog loop back test at 1200 baud	
10137	PS/2 modem does not respond to escape/reset sequence	
10138	PS/2 s reg 13 does not show correct parity or number of data bits	
10139	PS/2 s reg 15 does not reflect correct bit rate	

Error Codes	Indication of failure	Corrective action
Power On Self-Test (POST) PS/2 ESDI		
104nn	PS/2 ESDI drive/controller error	
10450	PS/2 read write test failed	Replace drive
10451	PS/2 read verify test failed	Replace drive
10452	PS/2 seek test failed	Replace drive
10453	PS/2 wrong device type indicated	Replace drive
10454	PS/2 controller test failed sector buffer test	Replace controller
10455	PS/2 controller failure	
10456	PS/2 controller diagnostic command failure	
10460	PS/2 unknown failure	
10461	PS/2 format error	Replace drive
10462	PS/2 head select error	Replace controller
10463	PS/2 read/write sector error	Replace drive
10464	PS/2 primary map unreadable	Replace drive
10465	PS/2 ECC 8-bit error	Replace controller
10466	PS/2 ECC 9-bit error	Replace controller
10467	PS/2 soft seek error	Replace drive
10468	PS/2 hard seek error	Replace drive
10469	PS/2 soft seek error count exceeded	Replace drive
10470	PS/2 attachment diagnostic error	Replace controller
10471	PS/2 wrap mode interface error	Replace controller
10472	PS/2 wrap mode drive select error	Replace controller
10473	PS/2 unknown	
10474	PS/2 unknown	
10475	PS/2 unknown	

Error Codes	Indication of failure	Corrective action
10476	PS/2 unknown	
10477	PS/2 unknown	
10478	PS/2 unknown	
10479	PS/2 unknown	
10480	PS/2 drive 0 seek failure	Drive/adapter/system board
10480	PS/2 com/data attention bad	Replace controller
10481	PS/2 drive 1 seek failure	Drive/adapter/system board
10481	PS/2 xfer request-ready bad	Replace controller
10482	PS/2 controller test failure	Replace controller
10482	PS/2 drive select 1 transfer acknowledge bad	Replace controller
10483	PS/2 controller reset failure	Adapter or system board
10483	PS/2 drive select 0 config. or status bad	Replace controller
10484	PS/2 head select 3 selected bad	Replace controller
10485	PS/2 head select 2 selected bad	Replace controller
10486	PS/2 head select 1 selected bad	Replace controller
10487	PS/2 head select 0 selected bad	Replace controller
10488	PS/2 rg command complete 2	Replace controller
10489	PS/2 wg command complete 1	Replace controller
10490	PS/2 drive 0 read failure	Disk or adapter
10490	PS/2 drive connected-no test done	Replace controller
10491	PS/2 drive 1 read failure	Disk or adapter
10499	PS/2 controller failure	

Error Codes	Indication of failure	Corrective action

Power On Self-Test (POST) 5.25 inch external diskette drive

107nn	5.25 inch external diskette drive or adapter	

Power On Self-Test (POST) PS/2 300/1200/2400 modem adapter

121nn	PS/2 300/1200/2400 modem adapter	

Power On Self-Test (POST) processor board (8570)

129nn	8570 processor or system board	

Power On Self-Test (POST) PS/2 plasma display adapter

149nn	PS/2 plasma display adapter	

Power On Self-Test (POST) PS/2 6157 streaming tape

165nn	6157 streaming tape	
16500	6157 tape attachment adapter	
16520	6157 streaming tape drive	
16540	6157 streaming tape drive or adapter	

Power On Self-Test (POST) primary token-ring network adapter

166nn	Primary token-ring adapter	

Power On Self-Test (POST) alternate token-ring network adapter

167nn	Alternate token-ring adapter	

NOTES

1. All personal computer error codes for the diagnostic and advanced diagnostic package are represented with the device number followed by two digits other than 00. The device number plus 00 represents successful completion of the test.

2. The personal computer has a habit of displaying error codes that are sometimes not documented or otherwise unexplained. This list may be of some use in problem determination.
3. This is not a complete or definitive list of codes. The information contained herein is combined from information received from Compaq and IBM.
4. Some of the codes may appear to be redundant. There are new codes for Microchannel and EISA adapters and devices. Therefore, a device such as a video port may have several codes depending on whether it is ISA, EISA, microchannel or an integral part of the system board.

Disk Drive Tables

IBM FIXED-DISK SPECIFICATIONS

Type	Cyl	HD	WPC	LZ	S/T	MB	Notes
1	306	4	128	305	17	10.65	
2	615	4	300	615	17	21.41	
3	615	6	300	615	17	32.12	
4	940	8	512	940	17	65.45	
5	940	6	512	940	17	49.09	
6	615	4	NONE	615	17	21.41	
7	462	8	256	511	17	32.17	
8	733	5	NONE	733	17	31.90	
9	900	15	0	901	17	117.50	
10	820	3	0	820	17	21.41	
11	855	5	NONE	855	17	37.21	
12	855	7	NONE	855	17	52.09	
13	306	8	128	319	17	21.31	
14	733	7	NONE	733	17	44.66	

Type	Cyl	HD	WPC	LZ	S/T	MB	Notes
15	Reserved EOT 1/10/84 AT						
16	612	4	0	66	17	21.31	
17	977	5	300	97	17	42.52	
18	977	7	NONE	99	17	59.53	
19	1024	7	512	102	17	62.39	
20	733	5	300	73	17	31.90	
21	733	7	300	73	17	44.66	
22	733	5	300	73	17	31.90	EOT
23	306	4	0	33	17	10.65	EOT 6/10/85 AT
24	612	4	305	66	17	21.31	EOT 11/15/85 AT
25	306	4		34	17	10.65	EOT 4/21/86 XT286
26	612	4		67	17	21.31	EOT 12/12/86 PS/2×0
27	698	7	300	732	17	42.53	Defect Map Cyl+1
28	976	5	488	977	17	42.48	Defect Map Cyl+1
29	306	4	0	340	17	10.65	
30	611	4	306	663	17	21.27	Defect Map Cyl+1
31	732	7	300	732	17	44.60	Defect Map Cyl+1
32	1023	5		1023	17	44.52	Defect Map Cyl+1 EOT 10/7/87 PS/2
33	749	8	NONE	749	33	100.0	
34	NONE						
35	1024	9	1024	1024	17		
36	1024	5	512	1024	17		
37	830	10	NONE	830	17	70.0	
38	823	10	256	824	17		
39	615	4	128	664	17	20.0	

Type	Cyl	HD	WPC	LZ	S/T	MB	Notes
40	615	8	128	664	17	40.0	
41	917	15	NONE	918	17		
42	1023	15	NONE	1024	17		
43	823	10	512	823	17		
44	820	6	NONE	820	17	40.0	
45	1024	8	NONE	1024	17	67.0	
46	925	9	NONE	925	17		
47	699	7	256	700	17		EOT Defect Map Cyl+1

COMPAQ HARD DISK DRIVE TYPES

Type	Cyl	HD	WPC	LZ	S/T	MB
1	306	4	128	305	17	10.65
2	615	4	128	638	17	21.41
3	615	6	128	615	17	32.12
4	1024	8	512	1023	17	71.30
5	940	6	−1	805	17	49.09
6	967	5	128	696	17	30.33
7	462	8	256	511	17	32.17
8	925	5	128	924	17	40.26
9	900	15	−1	899	17	117.50
10	980	5	−1	980	17	42.65
11	925	7	128	924	17	56.36
12	925	9	125	924	17	72.46
13	612	8	256	611	17	42.61
14	980	4	128	980	17	34.12
15	Reserved					
16	612	4	0	612	17	21.31
17	980	5	128	980	17	42.65

Type	Cyl	HD	WPC	LZ	S/T	MB
18	966	6	128	966	17	50.45
19	1023	8	−1	753	17	71.23
20	733	5	256	732	17	31.90
21	733	7	256	732	17	44.66
22	805	6	−1	524	40	42.04
23	924	8	−1	924	17	64.34
24	966	14	−1	966	17	117.71
25	966	16	−1	966	17	134.53
26	1023	14	−1	1023	17	124.66
27	966	10	−1	832	33	84.08
28	748	16	−1	1222	34	104.17
29	805	6	−1	1240	34	64.30
30	615	4	128	615	25	31.49
31	615	8	128	615	25	62.98
32	905	9	128	905	25	104.26
33	748	8	−1	832	33	104.17
34	966	7	−1	966	34	117.71
35	966	8	−1	966	34	134.53
36	966	9	−1	966	34	151.35
37	966	5	−1	966	3	84.08
38	611	16	−1	611	63	315.33
39	1023	11	−1	1023	33	190.13
40	1023	15	−1	1023	34	267.13
41	Unused					
42	Unused					
43	805	4	−1	805	26	42.86
44	805	2	−1	805	26	21.43
45	748	8	−1	748	33	101.11
46	748	6	−1	748	33	75.83
47	966	5	128	966	25	61.82

DRIVE TYPES FOR VARIOUS BIOS MANUFACTURERS

ROM BIOS Manufacturer

Heads	Cyls	IBM	Compaq	DTK	Award	Phoenix	American Megatrends
0	0	15	15	15	15	15	15
0	0	15	15	15	15	24	15
0	0	15	15	15	41	33	15
0	0	15	15	15	41	34	15
2	612						34
2	615					30	
2	756		44				
2	768		46				
2	1024				37		
3	771		28				
3	820	10		10	10	10	10
3	966		32				
3	987						38
4	306	1	1	1	1	1	1
4	306	23	1	1	1	1	23
4	306	25	1	23	23	23	
4	306	29	13	32	33	32	
4	578		29				
4	611	30		30		30	
4	612	16	16	16	16	16	16
4	612	24	16	16	16	16	
4	612	26	16	16	16	16	
4	615	2	2	2	2	2	2
4	615	2	30	25	6	25	6
4	615	2	30	39	6	39	

Heads	Cyls	ROM BIOS Manufacturer					
		IBM	Compaq	DTK	Award	Phoenix	American Megatrends
4	615	6	30	6	6	6	
4	756		43				
4	768		45				
4	980		14				
4	1024			26		26	
5	697		6				
5	733	8	20		22		8
5	733	8	20	8	8	8	20
5	733	8	20	20	20	20	22
5	733	20	20	20	20	20	
5	855	11		11	11	11	11
5	925		8				
5	966		33				
5	966		37				
5	966		47				
5	976	28		34			
5	977	17		17	17	17	17
5	977	17		17	24	17	41
5	980		10				
5	980		17				
5	981						42
5	989					31	
5	1023	32		32			
5	1024			27		27	33
5	1024			36		36	
6	615	3	3	3	3	3	3
6	768		22				

ROM BIOS Manufacturer

Heads	Cyls	IBM	Compaq	DTK	Award	Phoenix	American Megatrends
6	771		23				
6	820			44	40	44	40
6	940	5	5	5	5	5	5
6	966		18				
7	698	27		24		24	
7	699			47		47	28
7	732	31		31			
7	733	14	21	14	14	14	14
7	733	21	21	21	21	21	21
7	733	22	22	22	22	22	
7	754						26
7	830						43
7	855	12		12	12	12	12
7	918						30
7	925		11				24
7	966		34				
7	977	18		18	18	18	18
7	987						39
7	1024	19		19	19	19	19
7	1224				26		
8	306	13		13	13	13	13
8	462	7	7	7	7	7	7
8	512			29		29	
8	612		13				
8	615		31	40		40	37
8	940	4		4	4	4	4
8	966		35				

ROM BIOS Manufacturer

Heads	Cyls	IBM	Compaq	DTK	Award	Phoenix	American Megatrends
8	1023		19				
8	1024		4	28	29	28	36
8	1024		4	45	29	45	36
9	925		12	46	32	46	25
9	966		36				
9	1023		38				
9	1024			35	25	35	35
10	823			38		38	29
10	823			43		43	
10	830			37		37	44
10	966		27				
10	1024				33		
11	732					31	
11	754						27
11	918				31		
11	1023		39				
11	1024				30		31
11	1224				27		
12	1024				34		
13	1023		40				
13	1024				35		
14	966		24				
14	1023		26				
14	1024				36		
15	900	9	9	9	9	9	9
15	917			41		41	45
15	918				39		

ROM BIOS Manufacturer

Heads	Cyls	IBM	Compaq	DTK	Award	Phoenix	American Megatrends
15	1020					32	
15	1023		41	42		42	
15	1024				38		32
15	1224				28		46
16	966		25				
16	1023		42				

Most BIOS manufacturers reserve Type 47 for drives that are not directly supported by the drive table. When Type 47 is selected in SETUP, a screen appears requesting that the drive parameters be entered manually.

If Type 47 is not available, choose the Type from the table that is the closest match to the drive. The number of heads for the Type must match the number of heads in the drive. The number of cylinders listed under the Type must be equal to, or smaller than, the number of cylinders in the drive. The result will be a working drive with a formatted capacity that is slightly lower than specified by the manufacturer. Choosing a Type that has a different number of heads or more cylinders than the drive will result in damage to the drive.

AMERICAN MEGATRENDS (AMI) HARD DISK BIOS TABLE

Type	Cylinders	Heads	W/Precomp	L/Zone	Sectors	Size in MB
1	306	4	128	305	17	10
2	615	4	300	615	17	20
3	615	6	300	615	17	31
4	940	8	512	940	17	62
5	940	6	512	940	17	47
6	615	4	65535	615	17	20
7	462	8	256	511	17	31
8	733	5	65535	733	17	30

Type	Cylinders	Heads	W/Precomp	L/Zone	Sectors	Size in MB
9	900	15	65535	981	17	112
10	820	3	65535	828	17	20
11	855	5	65535	855	17	35
12	855	7	65535	855	17	50
13	306	8	128	319	17	28
14	733	7	65535	733	17	43
15	Reserved					
16	612	4	0	663	17	20
17	977	5	300	977	17	41
18	977	7	65535	977	17	57
19	1024	7	512	1024	17	60
20	733	5	300	732	17	30
21	733	7	300	732	17	43
22	733	5	300	733	17	30
23	306	4	0	336	17	10
24	925	7	0	925	17	54
25	925	9	65535	925	17	69
26	754	7	754	754	17	44
27	754	11	65535	754	17	69
28	699	7	256	699	17	41
29	823	10	65535	823	17	68
30	918	7	918	918	17	53
31	1024	11	65535	1024	17	94
32	1024	15	65535	1024	17	128
33	1024	5	1024	1024	17	43
34	612	2	128	612	17	10
35	1024	9	65535	1024	17	77
36	1024	8	512	1024	17	68

Type	Cylinders	Heads	W/Precomp	L/Zone	Sectors	Size in MB
37	615	8	128	615	17	41
38	987	3	987	987	17	25
39	987	7	987	987	17	57
40	820	6	820	820	17	41
41	977	5	977	977	17	41
42	981	5	981	981	17	41
43	830	7	512	830	17	48
44	830	10	65535	830	17	69
45	917	15	65535	918	17	114
46	1224	15	65535	1223	17	152

HARD DRIVE SPECIFICATIONS BY MANUFACTURER

Manufacturer	MB	Cyl	Head	R/W	W/P	C/B	LZ	S/T
AMPEX								
7	7.0	320	2		0			
13	13.0	320	4		0			
20	20.0	320	6		0			
27	27.0	320	8		0			
ATASI								
3020		645	3		NONE			
3033		645	5		NONE			
3046	38.3	645	7	323	323	13	644	17
3051	41.8	704	7	352	352	13	703	17
3051+	43.6	733	7	352	368	13	732	17
3058	69.6	1024	8	0	0	13	1023	17
3085		1024	8		NONE			
CDC (CONTROL DATA CORP.)								
9415-20	20.0							

Manufacturer	MB	Cyl	Head	R/W	W/P	C/B	LZ	S/T
9415-36	36.0							
9415-48	48.0							
9415-86	86.0							
9415-519	17.7	697	3	0	128	5	0	17
9415-521	18.0	697	3		256			
9415-525AT	20.0	612	4		128			
9415-528	24.0	697	4		256			
9415-536	29.6	697	5	0	128	5	0	17
9415-538	31.1	733	5	0	128	5	0	17
94151-44	40.0	925	5					
94151-80	80.0	925	9					
94155-29	24.0	925	3		256			
94155-37	32.0	925	4					
94155-48	39.3	925	5	0	128	13	0	17
94155-57	47.1	925	6	0	128	13	0	17
94155-67	55.0	925	7	0	128	13	0	17
94155-77	62.9	925	8	0	128	13	0	17
94155-85	69.6	1024	8	0	65535	13	0	17
94155-86	70.7	925	9	0	128	13	0	17
94155-96	78.3	1024	9	0	128	13	0	17
94156-48	39.3	925	5	0	128	13	0	17
94156-67	55.0	925	7	0	128	13	0	17
94156-86	70.7	925	9	0	128	13	0	17
94161-155	145.0	969	7					
94166-101	82.3	969	5	0	128	13	0	34
94166-101X	82.3	969	10	0	128	13	0	17
94166-141	115.3	969	7	0	128	13	0	34
94166-141X	115.3	969	14	0	128	13	0	17

Manufacturer	MB	Cyl	Head	R/W	W/P	C/B	LZ	S/T
94166-161	135.0	969	8					
94166-182	148.2	969	9	0	128	13	0	34
94166-182X	131.7	969	16	0	128	13	0	17
94171-300	300.0	1549	9					
94205-30	26.0	989	3		256			
94205-41	34.0	989	4		256			
94205-51	42.0	989	5	0	128	5	0	17
94208-51	42.0	989	5	0	128	5	0	17
94208-75	63.0	989	7					
94211-91	80.0	1024	5					

CMI - (COMPUTER MEMORIES INTERNATIONAL)

CM-3212		612	2		128			
CM-3426	26.0	612	4		128			
CM-5206	5.0	306	2		128			
CM-5410	9.0	256	4		128			
CM-5412	11.0	306	4		128			
CM-5616	13.0	256	6		128			
CM-5619	15.6	306	6	256	128	13	0	17
CM-6426S	21.7	615	4	0	256	13	0	17
CM-6426	22.0	640	4	0	256	13	0	17
CM-6626	21.7	640	4	0	256	13	615	17
CM-6640	32.6	612	6	0	613	11	615	17
CM-8425	21.0	612	4	0	613	11		

DATA-TECH MEMORIES

DTM-553	43.5	1024	5	0	850	13	0	17
DTM-853	43.5	640	8	0	256	13	0	17
DTM-885	69.6	1024	8	0	850	13	0	17

Manufacturer	MB	Cyl	Head	R/W	W/P	C/B	LZ	S/T
DISCTRON								
D514	10.4	306	4	128	128	13	0	17
D518	14.6	215	8	128	128	13	0	17
D519	15.6	306	6	128	128	13	0	17
D526	20.8	306	8	128	128	13	0	17
DMA								
360	10.4	612	2	0	0	13	0	17
EVOTEK								
5820	24.0	375	8		0			
FUJITSU								
2235 AS	21.7	320	8	128	128	13	0	17
2241 AS	25.6	754	4	498	498	13	0	17
M2225D	20.9	615	4	0	65535	13	615	17
M2227D	41.8	615	8	0	65535	13	615	17
M2233	10.0	306	4		0			
M2234	15.0	306	6		256			
M2241AS	25.6	754	4	0	128	13	0	17
M2242AS	44.8	754	7	0	128	13	0	17
M2243AS	70.4	754	11	0	128	13	0	17
HITACHI								
3033	27.4	645	5	0	320	13	0	17
DK511-3	29.7	699	5	0	300	13	699	17
DK511-5	41.5	699	7	0	300	13	699	17
DK511-8	69.9	823	10	0	256	13	823	17
DK512-8	34.9	823	5	0	256	13	823	17
IBM								
WD12	10.0	306	4		128			

Manufacturer	MB	Cyl	Head	R/W	W/P	C/B	LZ	S/T
WD25	20.0							
665-38	30.0							
665-30	20.0							
20 MB (2)	20.0	615	4		128			
20 MB (13)	20.0	306	8		128			
30 MB (22)	30.0	733	5		300			

IMI (INTERNATIONAL MEMORIES, INC.)

5012	10.0	306	4		214			
5018H	18.0							

LAPINE

TITAN20	20.9	615	4	0	0	13	615	17
LT200	21.0	612	4	0	128	11	5	
3065	10.0	306	4		0			
3512	10.0	306	4		0			
3522	10.0	306	4		0			

MAXTOR

XT1050	40.0	918	5					
XT1065	54.6	918	7	0	65535	13	0	17
XT1085	69.6	1024	8	1024	1024	11	7	17
XT1105	85.8	918	11	0	65535	13	0	17
XT1140	117.0	918	15	0	65535	13	0	17
XT2085	72.8	1224	7	0	65535	13	0	17
XT2140	117.0	1224	11					
XT2190	156.0	1224	15	0	65535	13	0	17

MICROPOLIS

1302	21.1	830	3	831	400	13	830	17
1303	36.0	830	5					

Manufacturer	MB	Cyl	Head	R/W	W/P	C/B	LZ	S/T
1304	56.4	830	8	831	400	13	830	17
1323	34.8	1024	4	1024	65535	13	1024	17
1323A	45.0	1024	5					
1324	52.2	1024	6	1024	65535	13	1024	17
1324A	62.0	1024	7					
1325	69.6	1024	8	1024	65535	13	1024	17
1333	36.0	1024	4					
1333A	45.0	1024	5					
1334	54.0	1024	6					
1334A	62.0	1024	7					
1335	71.0	1024	8					
1355	170.0	1024	8					

MICROSCIENCE

HH-312	10.0	306	4		0			
HH-325	20.9	612	4	0	613	13	615	17
HH-612	10.4	306	4	306	0	13	306	17
HH-725	20.9	612	4	0	613	13	615	17
HH-1050	43.5	1024	5	1024		13	1023	17
HH-2085	87.0	1024	5	1024		13	1023	34

MINISCRIBE The letter "E" after the Model Number = ESDI

1006	5.0	306	2		128			
1012	10.0	306	4		128			
2006	5.0	306	2		128			
2012	10.4	306	4	306	128	5	0	17
3012	10.4	612	2	613	128	5	0	17
3053	44.6	1024	5		512			
3085	71.3	1170	7		512			
3130E	112.0	1250	5		512			

Manufacturer	MB	Cyl	Head	R/W	W/P	C/B	LZ	S/T
3180E	152.0	1250	7		512			
3212	10.4	612	2	613	128	5	0	17
3412	10.4	306	4	307	128	5	0	17
3425	20.9	612	4	613	300	11	656	17
3438	31.9	612	4	613	300	11	656	26
3650	42.2	809	6	809	128	5	852	17
3675								
4010	8.0	480	2		128			
4020	16.3	480	4	480	128	5		17
6032	26.1	1024	3	1025	512	5	0	17
6036	30.0							
6053	43.5	1024	5	1025	512	5	0	17
6053II								
6074	60.9	1024	7	1024	512	5	0	17
6079	66.5	1024	5	1024	512	5	0	26
6085	69.6	1024	8	1025	512	5	0	17
6128	106.4	1024	8	1025	512	5	0	26
7426	20.8	612	4	613	613	5	0	17
8051A								
8212	10.0	615	2		128			
8225	20.3	771	2		128			
8412	10.0	306	4		308			
8425	21.4	615	4	615	128	5	663	17
8425F	21.4	615	4		1128			
8438	32.7	615	4	615	128	5	663	26
8450	40.6	771	4		128			
9230								
9380E	329.0	1224	15		512			

Manufacturer	MB	Cyl	Head	R/W	W/P	C/B	LZ	S/T
MMI								
M125	20.0	612	4		128			
M212	10.6	306	4	0	128	11		
M225	20.0	612	4		128			
M325	20.0	612	4		128			
MITSUBISHI								
MR522	20.8	612	4	300	300	13	612	17
MR533	24.7	971	3	0	0	13	971	17
NEC								
3126	20.0	615	4					
5124	10.0	310	4					
5126	20.0	615	4					
5144	20.0	310	8					
5146	41.8	615	8	615	256	0	664	17
NEWBURY								
NDR320	20.9	615	4	0	65535	13	615	17
NDR340	41.8	615	8	0	65535	13	615	17
NDR1065	54.6	918	7	0	65535	5	0	17
NDR1085	69.6	1024	8	1024	65535	13	0	17
NDR1105	85.8	918	11	0	65535	13	0	17
NDR1140	117.0	918	15	918	65535	13	0	17
NDR2190	156.0	1224	15	0	65535	13	0	17
OLIVETTI								
5210	10.0	306	4		128			
5220	20.0	612	4		128			
5221	21.0	612	4					
512/3		430	5					

Manufacturer	MB	Cyl	Head	R/W	W/P	C/B	LZ	S/T
562/13		180	6					
562/12		180	4					
563/11		306	2					
563/12		306	4					
661/11		306	2		128			
661/12		306	4		128			
662/11		612	2					
662/12		612	4					
OTARI								
C256	20.8	306	8	128	128	13	0	17
PANASONIC								
JU116-12	20.0	615	4					
PRIAM								
502	44.9	755	7	0	65535	13	0	17
504	44.9	755	7	0	65535	13	0	17
514	144.4	1224	11	0	65535	13	0	17
519	156.0	1224	15	0	65535	13	0	17
617	140.6	752	11	0	65535	13	0	34
623	191.7	752	15	0	65535	13	0	34
6650		2242	2					
V130	25.1	987	3	0	128	13	0	17
V150	41.9	987	5	0	128	13	0	17
V160	50.0	1166	6					
V170	58.7	1166	7	0	128	13	0	17
V185	69.3	1166	7	0	128	13	0	17
QUANTUM								
Q250	20.0							

Manufacturer	MB	Cyl	Head	R/W	W/P	C/B	LZ	S/T
Q280	40.0	815	6					
Q520	17.4	512	4	256	256	13	512	17
Q530	26.1	512	6	256	256	13	512	17
Q540	34.8	512	8	256	256	13	512	17
2020	20.0	512	4					
2030	30.0	512	6					
2040	40.0	512	8					

RODIME   The letter "R" after the Model Number = RLL
The letter "S" or "T" after the Model Number = SCSI

	MB	Cyl	Head	R/W	W/P	C/B	LZ	S/T
201	6.0	320	2		0			
201E	10.8	640	2	210	0	13	640	17
202	11.0	320	4					
202E	21.7	640	4	641	300	11	5	17
203	15.9	321	6	132	132	13	321	17
203E	32.6	640	6	641	300	11	5	17
204	21.8	321	8	132	132	13	321	17
204E	43.5	640	8	641	128	11	6	17
251	5.0	306	2		0			
252	10.0	306	4	307	128	11	5	
350	11.0	306	4					
351	5.0	306	4		0			
352	10.0	306	4		0			
652	21.0	306	4					
3045	38.0	872	5					
3055	46.0	872	6					
3055T	52.0	1053	3					
3057S	45.0	680	6					
3065	53.0	872	7					

Manufacturer	MB	Cyl	Head	R/W	W/P	C/B	LZ	S/T
3075R	58.0	750	6					
3085R	67.0	750	7					
3085S	70.0	750	7					
3095T	82.0	1053	7					
3130	98.0	1047	7					
3130T	121.0	1053	7					

SEAGATE NOTE: See SEAGATE in APPENDIX D for additional information.

ST124	21.4	615						
ST125	21.4	615	4	615	65535	5	0	17
ST125-1	20.0							
ST125A	21.5							
ST125N	21.5							
ST138	32.1	615	6	615	65535	5	0	17
ST138A	32.1							
ST138-1	30.0							
ST138R-1	31.9	615	4	615	65535	5	0	26
ST138N	32.2							
ST138R	32.7	615	4	615	65535	5	0	26
ST151	42.5	977						
ST157A	44.7	NA						
ST157N	48.6	NA						
ST157R	47.1	615	6	615	65535	5	0	26
ST157R-1	49.0							
ST1096N	83.9	NA						
ST1100	83.9	1072						
ST1102A	89.1	NA						
ST1111E	98.7	1072						
ST1126A	111.0							

Manufacturer	MB	Cyl	Head	R/W	W/P	C/B	LZ	S/T
ST1126N	107.0							
ST1144A	130.7	NA						
ST1150R	128.4							
ST1162A	143.0							
ST1186A	163.8	NA						
ST1186N	158.8	NA						
ST1201E	177.8	1072						
ST1201N	171.9	NA						
ST1201A	177.0	NA						
ST1239A	211.0	NA						
ST1239N	204.2	NA						
ST1400A	331	1475	7					
ST1400N	331	1476	7					
ST1401A	340	1121	9					
ST1401N	390	1100	9					
ST1480A	426	1474	9					
ST1480N	426	1476	9					
ST1480NV	426	1476	9					
ST1481N	426	1476	9					
ST1481ND	426	1476	9					
ST1581N	525	1476	9					
ST1581ND	525	1476	9					
ST1980N	860	1717	13					
ST1980ND	860	1717	13					
ST11200N	1050	1877	15					
ST11200ND	1050	1877	15					
ST212	10.4	306	4	307	128	11	5	17
ST213	10.7	612	2	613	300	11	5	17
ST225	21.4	615	4	613	300	11	5	17

Manufacturer	MB	Cyl	Head	R/W	W/P	C/B	LZ	S/T
ST225N	21.0							
ST225R	20.0							
ST238R	32.7	615	4	613	300	11	5	26
ST250R	40.0							
ST251	42.8	820	6	821	300	11	6	17
ST251N	43.0							
ST251-1	42.0	820	6					
ST251R	42.6	820	4	820	65535	5	0	26
ST277N	64.9	NA						
ST277R-1	65.0							
ST277R	65.5	820	6	820	65535	5	0	26
ST296N	84.9	NA						
ST2106N Wren-3	91.0	1024	5					
ST2106NM Wren-3	91.0	1024	5					
ST2106E Wren-3	94.0	1024	5					
ST2125N Wren-5	107.0	1544	3					
ST2125NM Wren-5	107.0	1544	3					
ST2182E Wren-6	160.0	1453	4					
ST2209N Wren-5	179.0	1544	5					
ST2209NM Wren-5	179.0	1544	5					
ST2209NV Wren-5	179.0	1544	5					
ST2274A Wren-6	241.0	1747	5					

Manufacturer	MB	Cyl	Head	R/W	W/P	C/B	LZ	S/T
ST2383A Wren-6	338.0	1747	7					
ST2383E Wren-6	338.0	1747	7					
ST2383N Wren-6	332.0	1261	7					
ST2383NM Wren-6	332.0	1261	7					
ST2383ND Wren-6	332.0	1261	7					
ST2502N Wren-6	435.0	1756	7					
ST2502NM Wren-6	435.0	1756	7					
ST2502ND Wren-6	435.0	1756	7					
ST2502NV Wren-6	435.0	1756	7					
ST351A/X	42.8	820						
ST3051A	43.1	820						
ST3096A	89.1	1024						
ST3120A	106.9	1024						
ST3144A	130.7	1001						
ST3283A	245.3	1024						
ST3283N	248.6	NA						
ST3500A	426	1546						
ST3500N	426	1546						
ST3500ND	426	1546						
ST3600A	525	1877						
ST3600N	525	1877						
ST3600ND	525	1877						

Manufacturer	MB	Cyl	Head	R/W	W/P	C/B	LZ	S/T
ST406	5.0	306	2		128			
ST412	10.4	306	4	307	128	11	5	17
ST419	15.0	306	6		256			
ST425	20.8	306	8	0	128	11	5	17
ST4026	21.4	612	4	613	300	11	6	17
ST4038	31.9	733	5	734	300	11	6	17
ST4051	42.5	977	5	978	300	11	6	17
ST4053	43.5	1024	5	1024	65535	13	0	17
ST4077R	66.5	1024	8	1024	65535	13	0	26
ST4096	80.2	1024	9	1023	65535	13	0	17
ST4097	80.0							
ST4144	122.7							
ST4144R	122.7	1024	9	1024	65535	13	0	26
ST4182E Wren-3	160.0	969	9					
ST4182N Wren-3	155.0	969	9					
ST4182NM Wren-3	155.0	969	9					
ST4350N Wren-4	300.0	1412	9					
ST4350NM Wren-4	300.0	1412	9					
ST4376N Wren-4	323.0	1549	9					
ST4376NM Wren-4	323.0	1549	9					
ST4376NV Wren-4	323.0	1549	9					
ST4383E Wren-5	338.0	1412	13					

Manufacturer	MB	Cyl	Head	R/W	W/P	C/B	LZ	S/T
ST4384E Wren-5	338.0	1224	15					
ST4442E Wren-5	380.0	1412	15					
ST4702N Wren-5	601.0	1546	15					
ST4702NM Wren-5	601.0	1546	15					
ST4385N W-runner 1	330.0	NA	15					
ST4385NM W-runner 1	330.0	NA	15					
ST4385NV W-runner 1	330.0	NA	15					
ST4766E Wren-6	676.0	1632	15					
ST4766N Wren-6	663.0	1632	15					
ST4766NM Wren-6	663.0	1632	15					
ST4766NV Wren-6	663.0	1632	15					
ST4767N W-runner 2	665.0	1356	15					
ST4767NM W-runner 2	665.0	1356	15					
ST4767ND W-runner 2	665.0	1356	15					
ST4767NV W-runner 2	665.0	1356	15					
ST4767E W-runner 2	676.0	1399	15					
ST4769E W-runner 2	691.0	1552	15					

Manufacturer	MB	Cyl	Head	R/W	W/P	C/B	LZ	S/T
ST41097J Elite-1	1,097.0	2101	17					
ST41200N Wren-7	1,037.0	1931	15					
ST41200NM Wren-7	1,037.0	1931	15					
ST41200ND Wren-7	1,037.0	1931	15					
ST41200NV Wren-7	1,037.0	1931	15					
ST41201J Elite-1	1,200.0	2101	17					
ST41201K Elite-1	1,200.0	2101	17					
ST41520N Elite-1	1,352.0	2101	17					
ST41520ND Elite-1	1,352.0	2101	17					
ST41600N Elite-1	1,352.0	2101	17					
ST41600ND Elite-1	1,352.0	2101	17					
ST41601N Elite-1	1,352.0	2101	17					
ST41601ND Elite-1	1,352.0	2101	17					
ST41650N Wren-8	1,415.0	2107	15					
ST41650ND Wren-8	1,415.0	2107	15					
ST41651N Wren-8	1,415.0	2107	15					
ST41651ND Wren-8	1,415.0	2107	15					

Manufacturer	MB	Cyl	Head	R/W	W/P	C/B	LZ	S/T
ST41800K Elite-2	1,986.0	2627	18					
ST42100N Wren-9	1,900.0	2574	15					
ST42100ND Wren-9	1,900.0	2574	15					
ST42101N Wren-9	1,900.0	2574	15					
ST42101ND Wren-9	1,900.0	2574	15					
ST42400N Elite-2	2,129.0	2627	19					
ST42400ND Elite-2	2,129.0	2627	19					
ST43400N Elite-3	2,846.0	2627	21					
ST43400ND Elite-3	2,846.0	2627	21					
ST43401N Elite-3	2,846.0	2627	21					
ST43401ND Elite-3	2,846.0	2627	21					
ST43200K Elite-3, 2HP	3,388.0	2627	20					
ST506	5.0	153	4	128	64	11	0	
ST9051A	42.8	1024						
ST9052A	42.6	1024						
ST9077A	64.0	1024						
ST9096A	85.3	1024						
ST9096N	85.3	NA						
ST9144A	127.9	1024						
ST9144N	127.9	NA						

Manufacturer	MB	Cyl	Head	R/W	W/P	C/B	LZ	S/T
SHUGART								
SA612	10.0							
SA706	5.0	320	2		128			
SA712	10.4	306	4	0	128	11	5	17
SA1004	12.0							
SYQUEST								
SQ306	5.2	306	2	0	0	13	0	17
SQ312RD	10.4	612	2	0	0	13	615	17
SQ315F	20.8	612	4	0	0	13	615	17
SQ338F	31.2	612	6	0	0	13	615	17
TANDON								
TM251	5.0	306	2		128			
TM252	10.4	306	4	0	128	13	0	17
TM262	20.9	612	4	0	613	13	615	17
TM362	20.9	612	4	0	613	11	615	17
TM501	5.0	306	2		128			
TM502	10.6	306	4	0	128	11		
TM503	15.9	306	6	0	256	13	306	26
TM503S	19.0							
TM602S		153	4		NONE			
TM603	S9.0	153	6		NONE			
TM603SE		230	6		NONE			
TM702	31.0							
TM702AT	21.0	615	4		256			
TM703	30.0	695	5	0	0	13	615	17
TM703AT	32.0	733	5	0	0	13	733	17
TM705	40.8	962	5	0	0	13	962	17
TM755	43.0	981	5	980	128	13	981	17

Manufacturer	MB	Cyl	Head	R/W	W/P	C/B	LZ	S/T
TASI								
3046	38.3	645	7	323	323	13	644	17
3051	41.8	704	7	352	352	13	703	17
3051+	43.6	733	7	352	368	13	732	17
3058	69.6	1024	8	0	0	13	1023	17
TEAC								
SD-308H	86.02	1050	4					
SD-3105	105.02	1282	4					
TEXAS INSTRUMENTS								
525/62		153	4		NONE			
525/122		306	4		128			
TOSHIBA								
MK-53F	35.2	830	5	831	65535	5	831	17
MK-53F-R	53.9	830	5	831	65535	5	831	26
MK-54F	49.3	830	7	831	65535	5	831	17
MK-54F-R	75.5	830	7	831	65535	5	831	26
MK-56F	70.5	830	10	831	65535	13	831	17
MK-56F-R	107.9	830	10	831	65535	13	831	26
MK-130	43.6	733	7	734	65535	5	734	17
MK-153FA	70.5	830	5	831	65535	5	831	34
MK-153FAX	70.5	830	10	831	65535	5	831	17
MK-154	98.7	830	7	831	65535	5	831	34
MK-154FAX	98.7	830	14	831	65535	5	831	17
MK-156FA	141.1	830	10	831	65535	13	831	34
TULIN								
TL213	10.8	640	2	656	65535	13	640	17
TL226	21.7	640	4	0	65535	13	640	17

Manufacturer	MB	Cyl	Head	R/W	W/P	C/B	LZ	S/T
TL238	22.0	640	4					
TL240	32.6	640	6	0	65535	13	640	17
TL258	33.0	640	6					
TL326	22.0	640	4					
TL340	33.0	640	6					
UPL								
1085	71.0	918	8					
1105	88.0	918	11					
1140	120.0	918	15					
2190	117.0	1224	11					
VERTEX								
V130	25.1	987	3	0	128	13	0	17
V150	41.9	987	5	0	128	13	0	17
V170	58.7	987	7	0	128	13	0	17
V185	69.3	1166	7	0	128	13	0	17

Notes: Capacities listed in the above charts may be for FORMATTED or UNFORMATTED drives and will vary depending upon the controller that is used.

For additional information on the above-mentioned drives, or specifications for drives that are not listed, try calling the Western Digital Bulletin Board Service (BBS). Set your modem for 1200 BAUD, NO PARITY, 8 DATA BITS, and 1 STOP BIT. The Western Digital BBS number is (714) 756-8176.

FLOPPY DRIVE SPECIFICATIONS BY MANUFACTURER

In addition to information on density and capacity, the following charts indicate the proper Analog Alignment Diskette (AAD) and/or Digital Diagnostic Diskette (DDD) to be used when testing or aligning a floppy diskette drive. The information in these charts is as accurate as possible, but drive specifications are frequently changed by manufacturers during production.

Mfr. & Model	DDD Sd/DD	AAD	TPI	# of Sides	Density '1	PAT '4	Notes:
ALPS ELECTRIC							
FDM 2000	508-1/200	224A	48.0	1	D	Y	1/2 Ht.
FDD 2111	N/A *3	208-10	48.0	1	—	N	Commodore 1541
FDD 2115	508-100	224A	48.0	1	S	Y	1/2 Ht.
FDD 2125	508-1/200	224A	48.0	1	D	Y	1/2 Ht.
FDD 2225	508-3/400	224/2A	48.0	2	D	Y	1/2 Ht.
FDD 2745	506-1/200	206-11	96.0	1	D	Y	0' Azimuth, 1/2 Ht.
FDD 2845	506-3/400	206-31	96.0	2	D	Y	0' Azimuth, 1/2 Ht.
FDD 7364	305-200	350A	135.0	1	D	Y	3.5" Micro
FDD 7368	305-200	350A	135.0	1	D	Y	3.5", 600 RPM
FDD 7374	N/A	N/A	67.5	1	D	Y	3.5" Micro
FDD 7464	305-400	350/2A	135.0	2	D	Y	3.5" Micro
FDD 7468	305-400	350/2A	135.0	2	D	?	3.5", 600 RPM
FDD 7474	N/A	N/A	67.5	2	D	Y	3.5" Micro
DFL 13A							3.5", 1.44Mb
DFL 130							3.5", 700K
DFL 313	305-200	350A	135.0	1	D	Y	3.5"
DFL 413	305-400	350/2A	135.0	2	D	?	3.5"
DFC 122	508-200	224A	48.0	1	D	Y	
DFC 222	508-400	224/2A	48.0	2	D	Y	
DFC 422	506-400	206-3?	96.0	2	D	Y	
DFC 642	516-400	206-34	96.0	2	D	Y	1.6Mb
DFC 682	516-400	206-34	96.0	2	D	Y	1.6Mb
AMDEK							
Amdisk	N/A *3	N/A	100.0	1	D	E	3.0" Micro

Mfr. & Model	DDD Sd/DD	AAD	TPI	# of Sides	Density *1	PAT *4	Notes:
AMLYN							
ALL	N/A *3	N/A	170.0	2	D	E *5	Servo
APPLE							
IIe, IIc	N/A *3	208-10	48.0	1	—	A *4	GCR
III	N/A *3	208-10	48.0	1	—	A *4	GCR
Macintosh	N/A *3	350A	135.0	2	—	N	3.5" Variable speed
Lisa—all	N/A *3	350A	135.0	2	—	N	3.5" Variable speed
AT&T *6							
AT&T	N/A	N/A	?	?	?	?	1/2 Ht.
ATARI							
810/1050	N/A *3	208-10	48.0	1	—	N	GCR
BASF SYSTEMS							
6106	508-1/200	224A	48.0	1	D	Y	2/3 Ht.
6108	508-3/400	224A/2A	48.0	2	D	Y	2/3 Ht.
6116	506-1/200	206-1?	96.0	1	D	Y	Ejector
6118	506-3/400	206-3?	96.0	2	D	Y	2/3 Ht.
6128	508-3/400	224/2A	48.0	2	D	Y	1/2 Ht.
6138	506-3/400	206-31	96.0	2	D	Y	0' Azimouth, 1/2 Ht.
6238	506-3/400	206-3?	96.0	2	D	Y	2/3 Ht.
C. ITOH							
See YE Data							
CAL DISK							
14M	508-3/400	224/2A	48.0	2	D	?	
CANON							
MDD110	508-1/200	224A	48.0	1	D	Y	

Mfr. & Model	DDD Sd/DD	AAD	TPI	# of Sides	Density ˙1	PAT ˙4	Notes:
MDD210	508-3/400	224/2A	48.0	2	D	Y	
MDD211	508-3/400	224/2A	48.0	2	D	Y	1/3 Ht.
MDD220	506-3/400	206-31	96.0	2	D	Y	0′ Azimuth
MDD221	506-3/400	206-31	96.0	2	D	Y	0′ Azimuth, 1/3 Ht.
MDD221-04	506-3/400	206-31	96.0	2	D	Y	0′ Azimuth
MDD413	508-3/400	224/2A	48.0	2	D	Y	
MDD422	506-3/400	206-31	96.0	2	D	Y	0′ Azimuth, 1/3 Ht.
MDD423	506-3/400	206-31	96.0	2	D	Y	0′ Azimuth, 1/3 Ht.
MDD6106	508-1/200	224A	48.0	1	D	Y	1/2 Ht.
MDD6108	508-3/400	224A	48.0	2	D	Y	1/2 Ht.
MD350	305-400	350/2A	135.0	2	D	Y	3.5″
MD351	305-200	350A	135.0	1	D	Y	3.5″
MD352	N/A	N/A	67.5	2	D	Y	3.5″
MD353	N/A	N/A	67.5	2	D	Y	3.5″
C. ITOH							
YD620/625	N/A	N/A	67.5	2	D	Y	3.5″
YD640/645	305-400	350/2A	135.0	2	D	Y	3.5″
YD380	516-400	206-34	96.0	2	D	Y	1.6Mb
YD380/1714	N/A	N/A					
CITIZEN							
OMDT00A	305-200	350A	135.0	1	D	Y	3.5″
OMDT10A	305-400	350/2A	135.0	2	D	Y	3.5″
OMDT40A	305-200	350A	135.0	1	D	Y	3.5″
OMDT50A	305-400	350/2A	135.0	2	D	Y	3.5″
COMMODORE							
20/64	N/A ˙3	208-10	48.0	1	—	N	Vic 20, Commodore 64

Mfr. & Model	DDD Sd/DD	AAD	TPI	# of Sides	Density *1	PAT *4	Notes:
1541	N/A *3	208-10	48.0	1	—	N	Vic 20, Commodore 64
2031	N/A *3	208-10	48.0	1	—	N	35 Track
4040	N/A *3	224/2A	48.0	2	—	N	35 Track
8050	N/A *3	206-10	96.0	1	—	N	33' Azimuth
8250	N/A *3	206-30	96.0	2	—	N	33' Azimuth
CONTROL DATA							
9408	508-1/200	224A	48	1	D	Y	
9409	508-3/400	224/2A	48	2	D	Y	Standard in IBM PC and XT
9409-T	506-3/400	206-31	96	2	D	Y	0' Azimuth
9428	508-3/400	224/2A	48	2	D	Y	1/2 Ht.
9429	506-3/400	206-31	96	2	D	Y	0' Azimuth, 1/2 Ht.
DATA TRACK							
1.0	506-1/200	206-1?	96	1	D	Y	Dual Disk
2.0	506-3/400	206-3?	96	2	D	Y	Dual Disk
DEC							
RX-50	506-1/200	206-10	96	1	D	Y	33' Azimuth, Rainbow PC
DRIVETEC							
320	N/A *3	N/A	192	2	—	N	Servo Floppy
EASTMAN KODAK							
3.3	See DRIVETEC 320						
EPSON							
TF-20	508-3/400	224/2A	48.0	2	D	Y	Dual Disc
SMD 110	N/A	N/A	67.5	1	D	Y	3.5" Micro
SMD 120	N/A	N/A	67.5	2	D	Y	3.5" Micro

Mfr. & Model	DDD Sd/DD	AAD	TPI	# of Sides	Density *1	PAT *4	Notes:
SMD 130	305-200	350A	135.0	1	D	Y	3.5″ Micro
SMD 140	305-400	350/2A	135.0	2	D	Y	3.5″ Micro
SMD 150	N/A	N/A	67.5	1	D	Y	3.5″ Battery
SMD 160	N/A	N/A	67.5	2	D	Y	3.5″ Battery
SMD 170	305-200	350A	135.0	1	D	Y	3.5″ Battery
SMD 180	305-400	350/2A	135.0	2	D	Y	3.5″ Battery
SD 310	508-1/200	224A	48.0	1	D	Y	1/3 Ht. w/ Head Load
SD 311	508-1/200	224A	48.0	1	D	Y	1/3 Ht.
SD 320	508-3/400	224/2A	48.0	2	D	Y	1/3 Ht. w/ Head Load
SD 321	508-3/400	224/2A	48.0	2	D	Y	1/3 Ht.
FDD 521	508-3/400	224/2A	48.0	2	D	Y	1/2 Ht.
FDD 540	506-3/400	206-31	96.0	2	D	Y	0′ Azimuth, 1/2 Ht.
FDD 560	506-3/400	206-31	96.0	2	D	Y	0′ Azimuth, 1/2 Ht.
SD-580S	516-400	206-34	96.0	2	D	Y	1.6Mb
SD-580D	516-400	206-34	96.0	2	D	Y	1.6Mb

EX-CELL-O

See REMEX

EXXON

QYX	N/A	*5	48.0	1	—	N	Spins in reverse

FORMAT

48 DS	508-3/400	224/2A	48.0	2	D	Y	1/2 Ht.
96 DS	506-3/400	206-3?	96.0	2	D	Y	1/2 Ht.
96 DS 360	516-400	206-34	96.0	2	D	Y	1.6Mb

FRANKLIN

ACE 1000	N/A *3	208-10	48.0	1	—	A *4	GCR-Apple

Mfr. & Model	DDD Sd/DD	AAD	TPI	# of Sides	Density '1	PAT '4	Notes:
FUJITSU							
M220A	N/A	N/A	?	?	?	?	
223A	N/A	N/A	?	?	?	?	
M224A	N/A	N/A	?	?	?	?	
M2531A							3.5"
M2532A							3.5"
M2533A							3.5"
M2534A							3.5"
M2536A							3.5"
M2551A	N/A	N/A	?	?	?	?	1/2 Ht.
M2552A	N/A	N/A	?	?	?	?	1/2 Ht.
M2553A	N/A	N/A	?	?	?	?	1/2 Ht.
M2553K	N/A	N/A	?	?	?	?	1/2 Ht.
M2554A	N/A	N/A	?	?	?	?	1/2 Ht.
GOLD STAR							
See FORMAT							
HEWLETT PACKARD							
9121S	305-200	350A	135.0	1	D	A *4	3.5" Micro
9121D	305-200	350A	135.0	1	D	A *4	3.5" Dual
HITACHI							
HFD 305S	N/A	N/A	100.0	1	D	E	3.0" Micro
HFD 305D	N/A	N/A	100.0	2	D	E	3.0" Micro
HFD 505	508-3/400	224/2A	48.0	2	D	Y	1/2 Ht.
HFD 510	506-3/400	206-3?	96.0	2	D	Y	1/2 Ht.
HFD 516	516-400	206-34	96.0	2	D	Y	1.6Mb
HI-TECH							
H548-25	508-1/200	224A	48.0	1	D	Y	1/2 Ht.
H548-50	508-3/400	224/2A	48.0	2	D	Y	1/2 Ht.

Mfr. & Model	DDD Sd/DD	AAD	TPI	# of Sides	Density '1	PAT '4	Notes:
H596-05	506-1/200	206-10	96.0	1	D	Y	33' Azimuth, 1/2 Ht.
H596-08	516-200	206-34	96.0	1	D	Y	1.6Mb
H596-10	506-3/400	206-30	96.0	2	D	Y	33' Azimuth, 1/2 Ht.
H596-16	516-400	206-34	96.0	2	D	Y	1.6Mb

IOMEGA

BETA-5	N/A	N/A	394.0	1	—	N	Servo Drive

MAGNETIC PERIPHERALS INC.

See CONTROL DATA CORP.

MAGNUM

See TANDON

MATSUSHITA

EME-101	N/A	N/A	100.0	1	D	E	3.0" Micro
EME-112	N/A	N/A	100.0	2	D	E	3.0" Micro
JA-200	508-1/200	224A	48.0	1	D	Y	
JU-311	N/A	N/A	100.0	1	D	E	3.0" Micro
JU-323	N/A	N/A	?	?	?	?	3.5"
JU-363	305-400	350/2A	135.0	2	D	Y	3.5", 300 RPM
JU-455-5	N/A	N/A	48.0	2	D	Y	1/2 Ht.
JU-475-2	N/A	N/A	?	?	?	?	1/2 Ht.
JA-551	508-3/400	224/2A	48.0	2	D	Y	1/2 Ht.
JA-551-105	N/A	N/A	48.0	2	D	Y	1/2 Ht.
JA-551-2	N/A	N/A	48.0	2	D	Y	1/2 Ht.
JA-551-3	N/A	N/A	48.0	2	D	Y	1/2 Ht.
JA-561	506-3/400	206-31	96.0	2	D	Y	1/2 Ht.
JU-581	516-400	206-34	96.0	2	D	Y	1.6Mb
JU-595-10	N/A	N/A	?	?	?	?	1/2 Ht.

Mfr. & Model	DDD Sd/DD	AAD	TPI	# of Sides	Density '1	PAT '4	Notes:
JU-595-13	N/A	N/A	?	?	?	?	1/2 Ht.
JK-873/4	508-1/200	208-10	48.0	1	D	Y	SA400 Copy
JK-875	508-3/400	224/2A	48.0	2	D	Y	SA450 Copy
JU-455	508-400	224/2A	48.0	2	D	Y	
JU-475	516-400	206-34	96.0	2	D	Y	1.6Mb

METRONEX

MCD-1	N/A	N/A	100.0	1	D	E	3.0″ Micro

MICRO PERIPHERALS, INC.

51	508-1/200	224A	48.0	1	D	Y	
52	508-3/400	224/2A	48.0	2	D	Y	Standard in IBM PC
91SH	506-1/200	206-10	96.0	1	D	Y	33′ Azimuth
91SZ	506-1/200	206-11	96.0	1	D	Y	0′ Azimuth
91MH	506-1/200	206-10	96.0	1	D	Y	33′ Azimuth
91MZ	506-1/200	206-11	96.0	1	D	Y	0′ Azimuth
92SH	506-3/400	206-30	96.0	2	D	Y	33′ Azimuth
92SZ	506-3/400	206-31	96.0	2	D	Y	0′ Azimuth
92MH	506-3/400	206-30	96.0	2	D	Y	33′ Azimuth
92MZ	506-3/400	206-31	96.0	2	D	Y	0′ Azimuth
101	500-1/200	206-10[2]	100.0	1	D	Y	0′ Azimuth [2]
102	500-3/400	206-30[2]	100.0	2	D	Y	0′ Azimuth [2]
301	N/A	N/A	100.0	1	D	E	3.0″ Micro
501	508-1/200	224A	48.0	1	D	Y	1/2 Ht.
502	508-3/400	224/2A	48.0	2	D	Y	1/2 Ht.
901	506-1/200	206-11	96.0	1	D	Y	0′ Azimuth, 1/2 Ht.
902	506-3/400	206-31	96.0	2	D	Y	0′ Azinuth, 1/2 Ht.

MICROPOLIS

1006	500-3/400	206-30	100.0	2	D	Y	33′ Azimuth
1006-1	N/A[3]	206-10	100.0	1	–	N	GCR

Mfr. & Model	DDD Sd/DD	AAD	TPI	# of Sides	Density '1	PAT '4	Notes:
1006-2	N/A*3	206-30	100.0	2	–	N	GCR
1015-1	508-1/200	224A	48.0	1	D	Y	
1015-2	500-1/200	206-10	100.0	1	D	Y	33'Azimuth
1015-4	500-3/400	206-30	100.0	2	D	Y	33'Azimuth
1015-5	506-1/200	206-10	96.0	1	D	Y	33'Azimuth
1015-6	506-3/400	206-30	96.0	2	Y	3	3'Azimuth
1016-2	N/A*3	206-10	100.0	1	–	E	33'Azimuth, GCR
1016-4	N/A*3	206-30	100.0	2	–	E	33'Azimuth, GCR
1023-1	508-1/200	224A	48.0	1	D	Y	
1023-2	500-1/200	206-10	100.0	1	D	Y	33'Azimuth
1023-4	500-3/400	206-30	100.0	2	D	Y	33'Azimuth
1023-5	506-1/200	206-10	96.0	1	D	Y	33'Azimuth
1023-6	506-3/400	206-30	96.0	2	D	Y	33'Azimuth
1027-1	508-1/200	224A	48.0	1	D	Y	For TANDY
1027-2	500-1/200	206-10	100.0	1	D	Y	For TANDY
1033-2	500-1/200	206-10	100.0	1	D	Y	33'Azimuth
1033-4	500-3/400	206-30	100.0	2	D	Y	33'Azimuth
1035-2	N/A*3	206-10	100.0	1	–	E	33'Azimuth, GCR
1035-4	N/A*3	206-30	100.0	2	–	E	33'Azimuth, GCR
1043-2	500-1/200	206-10	100.0	1	D	Y	33'Azimuth
1043-4	500-3/400	206-30	100.0	2	D	Y	33'azimuth
1055-2	N/A*3	206-10	100.0	1	–	N	33'Azimuth, GCR
1055-4	N/A*3	206-30	100.0	2	–	N	33'Azimuth, GCR
1115-1	508-1/200	224A	48.0	1	D	Y	
1115-2	500-1/200	206-10	100.0	1	D	Y	33'Azimuth
1115-4	500-3/400	206-30	100.0	2	D	Y	33'Azimuth
1115-5	506-1/200	206-10	96.0	1	D	Y	33'Azimuth

Mfr. & Model	DDD Sd/DD	AAD	TPI	# of Sides	Density '1	PAT '4	Notes:
1115-6	506-3/400	206-30	96.0	2	D	Y	33' Azimuth
1117-6	516-400	206-34	96.0	2	D	Y	1.6Mb
MICROSCIENCE							
A2	N/A	208-10	48.0	1	GCR	N	APPLE IIe
MITSUBISHI							
MF351	305-200	350A	135.0	1	D	Y	3.5", 300 RPM
MF353	305-400	350/2A	135.0	2	D	Y	3.5", 300 RPM
M501B	N/A	N/A	48.0	2	D	Y	1/2 Ht.
MF501A	N/A	N/A	48.0	2	D	Y	1/2 Ht.
MF501B	N/A	N/A	48.0	2	D	Y	1/2 Ht.
MF504	N/A	N/A	48.0	2	D	Y	1/2 Ht.
M4851	508-3/400	224/2A	48.0	2	D	Y	1/2 Ht.
M4852	506-3/400	206-31	96.0	2	D	Y	0' Azimuth
M4853	506-3/400	206-31	96.0	2	D	Y	0' Azimuth, 1/2 Ht.
M4854	516-400	206-34	96.0	2	D	Y	1.6Mb
M4855	506-3/400	206-31	96.0	2	D	Y	0' Azimuth, 1/2 Ht.
NEC							
FD1035	305-400	350/2A	135.0	2	Y		3.5"
FD1053	506-400	206-3?	96.0	2	D	Y	
FD1055	516-400	206-34	96.0	2	D	Y	1.6Mb
FD1155	516-400	206-34	96.0	2	D	Y	1.6Mb
NISSEI SANGYO							
FB501	508-1/200	224A	48.0	1	D	Y	1/2 Ht.
FB502	506-1/200	206-1?	96.0	1	D	Y	1/2 Ht.
FB503	508-3/400	224/2A	48.0	2	D	Y	1/2 Ht.
FB504	506-3/400	206-3?	96.0	2	D	Y	1/2 Ht.

Mfr. & Model	DDD Sd/DD	AAD	TPI	# of Sides	Density *1	PAT *4	Notes:
OKIDATA							
GM 3505H	508-3/400	224/2A	48.0	2	D	Y	1/2 Ht.
GM 3315B	508-3/400	224/2A	48.0	2	D	Y	1/3 Ht.
GM 3405H	506-3/400	206-31	96.0	2	D	Y	0' Azimuth, 1/2 Ht.
GM 3415B	506-3/400	206-3?	96.0	2	D	Y	1/3 Ht.
OLIVETTI OPE							
FD501	508-1/200	224A	48.0	1	D	Y	3/4 Ht.
FD502	508-3/400	224/2A	48.0	2	D	Y	3/4 Ht.
FD591	506-1/200	206-1?	96.0	1	D	Y	
FD592	506-3/400	206-3?	96.0	2	D	Y	
FD595	516-400	206-34	96.0	2	D	Y	1.6Mb
XM4311	N/A	N/A	48.0	2	D	Y	1/2 Ht.
OMEK							
OM55	508-3/400	224/2A	48.0	2	D	Y	1/2 Ht.
OM55AT	508-3/400	224/2A	48.0	2	D	Y	1/2 Ht.
OM56	506-3/400	206-31	96.0	2	D	Y	0' Azimuth
OM57	516-400	206-34	96.0	2	D	Y	1.6Mb
OM57AT	516-400	206-34	96.0	2	D	Y	1.6Mb
OSBORNE*6							
One SD	508-100	224A	48.0	1	S	A*4	5" Screen
One DD	508-200	224A	48.0	1	D	A*4	5" Screen
Executive	508-400	224/2A	48.0	2	D	Y	9" Screen
Vixen	508-400	224/2A	48.0	2	D	Y	9" Screen
PANASONIC							
See MATSUSHITA							
PERKIN-ELMER							
82	508-1/200	224A	48.0	1	D	Y	SIEMENS-WANGCO Drive

Mfr. & Model	DDD Sd/DD	AAD	TPI	# of Sides	Density '1	PAT '4	Notes:
282	508-3/400	224/2A	48.0	2	D	Y	SIEMENS-WANGCO Drive
PERTEC							
FD200	508-1/200	224A	48.0	1	D	Y	Flippy Drive
FD250	508-3/400	224/2A	48.0	2	D	Y	
PHILLIPS							
H1100	508-?/?00	224/?	48.0	?	?	?	2/3 Ht.
X3111	508-1/200	224A	48.0	1	D	Y	2/3 Ht.
X3112	508-3/400	224/2A	48.0	2	D	Y	2/3 Ht.
X3113	506-1/200	206-10	96.0	1	D	Y	33' Azimuth, 2/3 Ht.
X3114	506-3/400	206-30	96.0	2	D	Y	33' Azimuth, 2/3 Ht.
X3116	506-3/400	206-30	96.0	2	D	Y	33' Azimuth
X3118	516-400	206-34	96.0	2	D	Y	1.6Mb
X3131	508-1/200	224A	48.0	1	D	Y	1/2 Ht.
X3132	508-3/400	224/2A	48.0	2	D	Y	1/2 Ht.
X3133	506-1/200	206-10	96.0	1	D	Y	33' Azimuth, 1/2 Ht.
X3134	506-3/400	206-30	96.0	2	D	Y	33' Azimuth, 1/2 Ht.
QUME							
Datatrack 5	508-3/400	224/2A	48.0	2	D	Y	
142	508-3/400	224/2A	48.0	2	D	Y	1/2 Ht.
192	506-3/400	206-30	96.0	2	D	Y	33' Azimuth, 1/2 Ht.
542	508-3/400	224/2A	48.0	2	D	Y	
592	506-3/400	206-31	96.0	2	D	Y	0' Azimuth

Mfr. & Model	DDD Sd/DD	AAD	TPI	# of Sides	Density '1	PAT '4	Notes:
RADIO SHACK							
III/4	508-1/200	224A	48.0	1	D	Y	TRS Modified
REMEX							
RFD480	508-3/400	224/2A	48.0	2	D	Y	2/3 Ht.
RFD481	508-1/200	224A	48.0	1	D	Y	2/3 Ht.
RFD485	508-3/400	224/2A	48.0	2	D	Y	1/2 Ht.
RFD486	508-1/200	224A	48.0	1	D	Y	1/2 Ht.
RFD960	506-3/400	206-30	96.0	2	D	Y	33′ Azimuth, 2/3 Ht.
RFD961	506-1/200	206-10	96.0	1	D	Y	33′ Azimuth, 2/3 Ht.
RFD965	506-3/400	206-30	96.0	2	D	Y	33′ Azimuth, 2/3 Ht.
RFD966	506-1/200	206-10	96.0	1	D	Y	33′ Azimuth, 2/3 H\T.
RFD1600	N/A	N/A	170.0	1	D	N	Amlyn Type
RFD3200	N/A	N/A	170.0	2	D	N	Amlyn Type
SANKYO SEIKI							
FDU300S	N/A	N/A	100.0	1	D	E	3.0″ Micro
FDU300D	N/A	N/A	100.0	2	D	E	3.0″ Micro
FDU355	305-400	350/2A	135.0	2	D		3.5″
SHUGART							
SA200	508-1/200	224A	48.0	1	D	Y	2/3 Ht.
SA210	508-1/200	224A	48.0	1	D	Y	2/3 Ht.
SA215	508-1/200	224A	48.0	1	D	Y	2/3 Ht.
SA300	305-200	350A	135.0	1	D	Y	3.5″ Micro
SA350	305-400	350/2A	135.0	2	D	Y	3.5″ Micro
SA390A	N/A'3	208-10	48.0	1	S	A'4	APPLE Compatible

Mfr. & Model	DDD Sd/DD	AAD	TPI	# of Sides	Density '1	PAT '4	Notes:
SA400	508-1/200	224A	48.0	1	D	Y	
SA400L	508-1/200	224A	48.0	1	D	Y	
SA405	508-1/200	224A	48.0	1	D	Y	
SA410	506-1/200	206-11	96.0	1	D	Y	0' Azimuth
SA450	508-3/400	224/2A	48.0	2	D	Y	
SA455	508-3/400	224/2A	48.0	2	D	Y	1/2 Ht.
SA460	506-3/400	206-31	96.0	2	D	Y	0' Azimuth
SA465	506-3/400	206-31	96.0	2	D	Y	0' Azimuth, 1/2 Ht.
SA475	516-400	206-34	96.0	2	D	Y	1.6MB

SIEMENS

See WORLD STORAGE TECHNOLOGY

SONY

Mfr. & Model	DDD Sd/DD	AAD	TPI	# of Sides	Density '1	PAT '4	Notes:
OA-D30V	305-200	350A	135.0	1	D	A*4	3.5", 600 RPM
OA-D31V	305-200	350A	135.0	1	D	A*4	3.5", 300 RPM
OA-D32V	305-200	350A	135.0	1	D	A*4	3.5", 600 RPM
OA-D32W	305-400	350/2A	135.0	2	D	A*4	3.5", 600 RPM
OA-D33V	305-200	350A	135.0	1	D	Y	3.5", 300 RPM
OA-D33W	305-400	350/2A	135.0	2	D	Y	3.5", 300 RPM
OA-D34V	N/A*3	350A	135.0	1	–	N	Macintosh

TANDON

Mfr. & Model	DDD Sd/DD	AAD	TPI	# of Sides	Density '1	PAT '4	Notes:
TM50-1	508-1/200	224A	48.0	1	D	Y	1/2 Ht.
TM50-2(S)	508-3/400	224/2A	48.0	2	D	Y	1/2 Ht.
TM55-2	508-3/400	224/2A	48.0	2	D	Y	1/2 Ht.

Mfr. & Model	DDD Sd/DD	AAD	TPI	# of Sides	Density '1	PAT '4	Notes:
TM55-4	506-3/400	206-30	96.0	2	D	Y	1/2 Ht.
TM65-1	508-1/200	224A	48.0	1	D	Y	1/2 Ht.
TM65-1L	508-1/200	224A	48.0	1	D	Y	1/2 Ht.
TM65	N/A	N/A	?	?	?	?	1/2 Ht.
TM65-2L	508-3/400	224/2A	48.0	2	D	Y	1/2 Ht.
TM65-4	506-3/400	206-30	96.0	2	D	Y	1/2 Ht.
TM65-8	516-400	206-34	96.0	2	D	Y	1.6Mb
TM100-1	508-1/200	224A	48.0	1	D	Y	Most common
TM100-2	508-3/400	224/2A	48.0	2	D	Y	Standard in IBM PC
TM100-2A	508-3/400	224/2A	48.0	2	D	Y	
TM100-3	506-1/200	206-10	96.0	1	D	Y	33' Azimuth
TM100-3M	500-1/200	206-10	100.0	1	D	Y	33' Azimuth
TM100-4	506-3/400	206-30	96.0	2	D	Y	33' Azimuth
TM100-4M	500-3/400	206-30	100.0	2	D	Y	33' Azimuth
TM101-2	506-1/200	206-10	96.0	1	D	Y	33' Azimuth
TM101-4	506-3/400	206-30	96.0	2	D	Y	33' Azimuth
TM102-2	506-3/400	206-30	96.0	2	D	Y	33' Azimuth

TEAC

Mfr. & Model	DDD Sd/DD	AAD	TPI	# of Sides	Density '1	PAT '4	Notes:
FD30A	N/A	N/A	100.0	1	D	E	3.0" Micro
FD35A	N/A	N/A	67.5	1	D	Y	3.5" Micro
FD35B	N/A	N/A	67.5	2	D	Y	3.5" Micro
FD35E	305-200	350A	135.0	1	D	Y	3.5" Micro
FD35F	305-400	350/2A	135.0	2	D	Y	3.5" Micro
FD35F-20	305-400	350/2A	135.0	2	D	N	3.5", 600 RPM
FD50A	508-1/200	224A	48.0	1	D	Y	
FD50B	508-3/400	224/2A	48.0	2	D	Y	
FD50C	500-1/200	206-10	100.0	1	D	Y	0' Azimuth
FD50E	506-1/200	206-10	96.0	1	D	Y	33' Azimuth

Mfr. & Model	DDD Sd/DD	AAD	TPI	# of Sides	Density '1	PAT '4	Notes:
FD50F	506-3/400	206-30	96.0	2	D	Y	33' Azimuth
FD55A	508-1/200	224A	48.0	1	D	Y	1/2 Ht.
FD55B	508-3/400	224/2A	48.0	2	D	Y	1/2 Ht.
FD55BV	508-3/400	224/2A	48.0	2	D	Y	1/2 Ht.
FD55E	506-1/200	206-11	96.0	1	D	Y	0' Azimuth, 1/2 Ht.
FD55F	506-3/400	206-31	96.0	2	D	Y	0' Azimuth, 1/2 Ht.
FD55G	516-400	206-34	96.0	2	D	Y	1.6Mb
FD55GV	N/A	N/A	?	?	?	?	1/2 Ht.

TOKYO ELECTRIC COMPANY (TEC)

Mfr. & Model	DDD Sd/DD	AAD	TPI	# of Sides	Density '1	PAT '4	Notes:
MC-108	N/A	N/A	33.0	1	–	N	1 Track Spiral
MC-116	N/A	N/A	33.0	2	–	N	1 Track Spiral
FB-201	508-1/200	224A	48.0	1	D	Y	35 Track
FB-202	508-1/200	224A	48.0	2	D	Y	
FB-501	508-1/200	224A	48.0	1	D	Y	1/2 Ht.
FB-502	506-1/200	206-10	96.0	1	D	Y	33' Azimuth, 1/2 Ht.
FB-503	508-3/400	224/2A	48.0	2	D	Y	1/2 Ht.
FB-504	506-3/400	206-30	96.0	2	D	Y	33' Azimuth, 1/2 Ht.

TEXAS INSTRUMENTS[6]

Mfr. & Model	DDD Sd/DD	AAD	TPI	# of Sides	Density '1	PAT '4	Notes:
99/4	508-1/200	224A	48.0	1	D	Y[5]	TI-99 Expansion System

TEXAS PERIPHERALS

Mfr. & Model	DDD Sd/DD	AAD	TPI	# of Sides	Density '1	PAT '4	Notes:
01-0053	508-1/200	224A	48.0	1	D	Y	Made for TANDY

Mfr. & Model	DDD Sd/DD	AAD	TPI	# of Sides	Density '1	PAT '4	Notes:
TRAK							
AT-D2	N/A*3	208-10	48.0	1	–	N	ATARI Compatible
TOSHIBA							
ND-01	508-3/400	224/2A	48.0	2	D	Y	
ND-02D	508-3/400	224/2A	48.0	2	D	Y	35 Track
ND-04D	508-3/400	224/2A	48.0	2	D	Y	1/2 Ht.
ND-06D	506-3/400	206-30	96.0	2	D	Y	33' Azimuth, 1/2 Ht.
ND-08D	516-400	206-34	96.0	2	D	Y	1.6Mb
ND-08DE	5?6-400	206-3?	96.0	2	D	Y*5	Variable Data Rate
ND-301D	N/A	N/A	100.0	1	D	E	3.0" Micro
ND-353A	305-200	350A	135.0	1	D	Y	3.5", 300 RPM
ND-353S	305-200	350A	135.0	1	D	Y	3.5", 300 RPM
ND-354A	305-400	350/2A	135.0	2	D	Y	3.5", 300 RPM
ND-354S	305-400	350/2A	135.0	2	D	Y	3.5", 300 RPM
5401	N/A	N/A	?	?	?	?	5.25", 360Kb, 1/2 Ht.
5451	N/A	N/A	?	?	?	?	5.25", 720Kb, 1/2 Ht.
5655D2T	N/A	N/A	?	?	?	?	5.25", 1.2Mb, 1/2 Ht.
5861	N/A	N/A	?	?	?	?	5.25". 1.2Mb, 1/2 Ht.
VICTOR							
9000	N/A*3	N/A	96.0	2	–	Y	Variable Speed

Mfr. & Model	DDD Sd/DD	AAD	TPI	# of Sides	Density *1	PAT *4	Notes:
WORLD STORAGE TECHNOLOGY (WST)							
FDD100-5	506-1/200	224A	48.0	1	D	Y	Flippy Drive
FDD111-5	508-3/400	224/2A	48.0	2	D	Y	
FDD112-5	508-1/200	224A	48.0	1	D	Y	1/2 Ht.
FDD121-5	506-1/200	206-10	96.0	1	D	Y	33′ Azimuth
FDD196-5	506-1/200	206-10	96.0	1	D	Y	33′ Azimuth
FDD200-5	508-3/400	224/2A	48.0	2	D	Y	
FDD211-5	508-3/400	224/2A	48.0	2	D	Y	
FDD212-5	508-3/400	224/2A	48.0	2	D	Y	1/2 Ht.
FDD221-5	506-3/400	206-30	96.0	2	D	Y	33′ Azimuth
FDD222-5	506-3/400	206-30	96.0	2	D	Y	33′ Azimuth
FDD296-5	506-3/400	206-30	96.0	2	D	Y	33′ Azimuth
YE DATA							
YD180	516-400	206-34	96.0	2	D	Y	1.6Mb
YD274	508-3/400	224/2A	48.0	2	D	Y	
YD280	506-3/400	206-31	96.0	2	D	Y	0′ Azimuth
YD380	N/A	N/A	96.0	2	D	Y	1/2 Ht.
YD380T	516-400	206-34	96.0	2	D	Y	1.6Mb
YD480	506-3/400	206-31	96.0	2	D	Y	0′ Azimuth, 1/2 Ht.
YD560	N/A	N/A	48.0	2	D	Y	1/2 Ht.
YD580	508-3/400	224/2A	48.0	2	D	Y	1/2 Ht.
YD620	N/A	N/A	67.5	2	D	Y	
YD640	305-400	350/2A	135.0	2	D	Y	
YD1355	N/A	N/A	?	?	?	?	720Kb, 3.5″
ZENITH*6							
Z-37	506-3/400	206-30	96.0	2	D	Y	Usually TANDON Drives
Z-87	508-3/400	224/2A	48.0	2	D	Y	Usually TANDON Drives

* NOTES to 3.5″ and 5.25″ applications:

*1 Highest density mode known to be supported by the drive.

    S = Single Density (FM)

    D = Double Density (MFM)

    − = Other

*2 100 TPI drives with heads @ 0′ Azimuth can use 206-10/30 AAD's for radial alignment. However, azimuth tests are not available for these drives.

*3 Group Code Recording (GCR) format or other recording format used is not compatible with the DDD's format.

*4 PAT compatibility: Y = Yes, N = No, A = Special Adaptor Required and E = Exerciser mode only. Exerciser mode includes formatting and read/write testing ability.

*5 Consult manufacturer's technical staff directly.

*6 System manufacturer, not drive manufacturer.

Part Numbers

The part numbers contained in this appendix are for some older systems. With new machines and models being introduced so frequently, it is impossible to keep information such as this current. Hopefully, these listings will be of some assistance.

AT&T PC-6300

403319064	Motherboard, 640K
403319064	Motherboard, 128K
403319072	Motherboard, 256K
403350928	Display Controller
403350952	Hard Disk Unit Controller
403350986	Bus Converter Module
403351240	Power Supply
403351281	Keyboard
403351299	Memory Expansion Board
403351331	Color Display
403351349	Monochrome Display
403351356	Color Display

COMPAQ DESKPRO

101062-001	Speaker Assembly
101339-001	256K System Board, Version 1

101340-001	Color Graphics Adapter (LP)
101341-001	Diskette/Printer Board
101397-001	83 Key Keyboard w/Cable
101437-001	10Mb Hard Drive
101438-001	10Mb Tape Backup
101439-001	Dual Mode Monitor—Green
101439-002	Dual Mode Monitor—Amber
101440-001	Async./Clock Card
101664-001	30Mb Hard Drive
101672-001	Hard Drive Controller Card
102710-001	System Board, 256K, 8MHz, Version 1
102777-001	20Mb Hard Drive
102927-001	Power Supply (8MHz)
102928-001	360K Half Height Floppy Drive
105191-001	256K System Board, Version 2
106373-001	Enhanced Color Graphics Adapter
106374-001	256K System Board, Version 3
106568-001	Color Monitor (EGA)
106886-001	Async./Parallel Printer Board
108067-001	101 Key Keyboard w/Cable
109196-001	Enhanced Color Graphics Adapter, Version 2

COMPAQ DESKPRO 286

000179-001	Magnum Memory (Old Style)
101340-001	Color Graphics Adapter (LP)
101438-001	10Mb Tape Backup
101439-001	Dual Mode Monitor—Green
101439-002	Dual Mode Monitor—Amber
101664-001	30Mb Hard Drive
102705-001	Multipurpose Controller Card
102710-001	System Board, 256K, 8MHz, Version 1
102774-001	System Board, 8MHz, w/No Memory
102775-001	1.2Mb Floppy Disk Drive
102776-001	84 Key Keyboard w/Cable
102777-001	20Mb Hard Drive
102778-001	Hard Drive Controller, 20Mb–70Mb

102927-001	Power Supply (8MHz)
102928-001	360K Half Height Floppy Drive
102932-001	70Mb Hard Drive
104174-001	Multipurpose Hard Drive Controller
105033-001	512/2048Kb Memory Expansion Board
106373-001	Enhanced Color Graphics Adapter
106434-001	256K System Board, Version 2
106558-001	8MHz 80287 Math Coprocessor
106568-001	Color Monitor (EGA)
106707-001	System Board, Version 1 (12MHz)
106886-001	Async./Parallel Printer Board
108058-001	40Mb Hard Drive
108065-001	Power Supply, 120V
108067-001	101 Key Keyboard w/Cable
108081-001	40Mb Tape Backup
108140-001	ESDI Fixed Disk Controller
109196-001	Enhanced Color Graphics Adapter, Version 2
109253-001	Video Graphics Controller Board
113016-001	20Mb Hard Drive (12MHz)

COMPAQ DESKPRO 286e

106886-001	Async./Parallel Printer Board
112570-001	Power Supply
113225-001	1Mb Memory Module
113226-001	4Mb Memory Module
117469-001	System Board
117470-001	4Mb, 16 Bit Memory Expansion Board
117471-001	1Mb, 16 Bit Memory Expansion Board

COMPAQ DESKPRO 386/16

101439-001	Dual Mode Monitor—Green
101439-002	Dual Mode Monitor—Amber
102776-001	84 Key Keyboard w/Cable
102778-001	Hard Drive Controller, 20Mb–70Mb
104174-001	Multipurpose Hard Drive Controller
104174-002	Multipurpose Hard Drive Controller

106373-001	Enhanced Color Graphics Adapter
106568-001	Color Monitor (EGA)
106886-001	Async./Parallel Printer Board
108059-001	32 Bit System Memory Board
108060-001	System Board, 16Mhz, Ver. 1
108065-001	Power Supply, 120V
108067-001	101 Key Keyboard w/Cable
108080-001	130Mb Hard Disk Drive
108082-001	32-Bit Memory Board (1–2Mb)
108083-001	32-Bit Memory Board (4–8Mb)
108138-001	32-Bit Memory Board (.5 2Mb)
108407-001	System Board, 16Mhz, Ver. 2, w/387 Socket
112565-001	3.5″, 1.44Mb Disk Drive
112566-001	5-1/4″, 1.2Mb Disk Drive
112567-001	5-1/4″, 360K Disk Drive

COMPAQ DESKPRO 386/s

106886-001	Async./Parallel Printer Board
112519-001	1Mb Memory Module
112520-001	4Mb Memory Module
112521-001	4Mb, 16MHz Memory Expansion Board
112522-001	1Mb, 16MHz Memory Expansion Board
112570-001	Power Supply
112572-001	System Board
113526-001	40Mb Hard Disk Drive
113527-001	20Mb Hard Disk Drive

COMPAQ DESKPRO 386/20

101340-001	Color Graphics Adapter (LP)
106373-001	Enhanced Color Graphics Adapter
106886-001	Async./Parallel Printer Board
108065-001	Power Supply, 120V
109196-001	Enhanced Color Graphics Adapter, Version 2
109253-001	Video Graphics Controller Board
113222-001	4Mb System Memory Board
113223-001	System Board (20Mhz)

113224-001	1Mb System Memory Board
113225-001	1Mb Memory Module
113226-001	4Mb Memory Module
113446-001	Multipurpose Controller
113625-001	ESDI Hard Drive Controller (130–300Mb)

COMPAQ DESKPRO 386/20e

106886-001	Async./Parallel Printer Board
112517-001	4Mb, 32 Bit Memory Expansion Board
112518-001	1Mb, 32 Bit Memory Expansion Board
112570-001	Power Supply
112571-001	System Board (20Mhz)
113225-001	1Mb Memory Module
113226-001	4Mb Memory Module

COMPAQ DESKPRO 386/25

113265-001	ESDI Fixed Disk Controller
115519-001	ESDI Multipurpose Controller
115526-001	System Board

COMPAQ PORTABLE AND PLUS

100478-002	256K System Board
100643-001	10Mb Hard Drive
100644-001	Hard Drive Controller
100041-001	Power Switch/Filter Assembly
100421-001	360K Disk Drive
100475-001	Power Supply
100478-001	256K System Board
100479-001	Color Graphics Adapter (HP)
100480-001	Diskette/Printer Board
100482-001	Fan Assembly, 120V
100487-001	Keyboard w/Cable
101095-001	Async. Board
101340-001	Color Graphics Adapter (LP)
101341-001	Diskette/Printer Board
101421-001	360K Full Height Floppy Drive

101440-001	Async./Clock Card
102710-001	System Board, 256K, 8MHz, Version 1
105034-001	Monochrome Monitor
106373-001	Enhanced Color Graphics Adapter
106568-001	Color Monitor (EGA)
106886-001	Async./Parallel Printer Board
109196-001	Enhanced Color Graphics Adapter, Version 2

COMPAQ PORTABLE 286

101340-001	Color Graphics Adapter (LP)
101790-001	Keyboard w/Cable
101795-001	256K System Board, Version 1
101798-001	Power Switch/Filter
102705-001	Multipurpose Controller Card
102706-001	20Mb Hard Drive
102775-001	1.2Mb Floppy Disk Drive
102777-001	20Mb Hard Drive
102778-001	Hard Drive Controller, 20Mb–70Mb
102818-001	Power Supply, 120V
102928-001	360K Half Height Floppy Drive
104174-001	Multipurpose Hard Drive Controller
105033-001	512/2048Kb Memory Expansion Board
105034-001	Monochrome Monitor
106373-001	Enhanced Color Graphics Adapter
106568-001	Color Monitor (EGA)
106886-001	Async./Parallel Printer Board
109196-001	Enhanced Color Graphics Adapter, Version 2

COMPAQ PORTABLE 386

107357-001	40Mb Hard Drive
107359-001	1.2Mb Disk Drive

COMPAQ PORTABLE II

101340-001	Color Graphics Adapter (LP)
102705-001	Multipurpose Controller Card
104174-001	Multipurpose Hard Drive Controller

104175-001	System Board, 256K, Version 1
104176-001	512/2048K Memory Expansion
104179-001	Keyboard
104180-001	Power Supply w/Line Filter
104182-001	Monitor
104184-001	360K Disk Drive
104407-001	Hard Drive w/Integrated Controller
104444-001	System Board, 256K, Version 2
104479-001	1.2Mb Disk Drive, 1/3 Ht.
106373-001	Enhanced Color Graphics Adapter
106568-001	Color Monitor (EGA)
106886-001	Async./Parallel Printer Board
107357-001	40Mb Hard Drive

COMPAQ PORTABLE III

106373-001	Enhanced Color Graphics Adapter
106886-001	Async./Parallel Printer Board
107358-001	20Mb Hard Drive
107359-001	1.2Mb Disk Drive
107360-001	360K Disk Drive
107362-001	Keyboard
107372-001	System Board
107373-001	Power Supply
107374-001	Plasma Controller
107375-001	Modem/Memory Board
107378-001	Memory Expansion Board
107381-001	Plasma Display
108067-001	101 Key Keyboard w/Cable

IBM 5153 COLOR DISPLAY

8529291	Color Monitor Power Supply
8529323	Color Monitor Analog Board

IBM 5154 ENHANCED COLOR DISPLAY

6321052	Enhanced Color Display Analog Board
6321053	Enhanced Color Display Power Supply
6321054	Enhanced Color Display Video Driver Board

IBM AT

1504910	Color Graphics Adapter
6278099	20Mb Fixed Disk
6321035	5154 Enhanced Color Display
6447033	101 Key Keyboard (w/o Cable)
6447039	Enhanced Keyboard Assembly
6450210	30Mb Hard Drive
6450215	Serial/Parallel Adapter
6450357	3.5", 720K Disk Drive
6480072	System Board, 512K, 6MHz (Type 2)
6480170	System Board, 256K, 8MHz (Type 1)
6489922	System Board, 512K, 8MHz (Type 3)
8286097	CGA Adapter
8286098	Binary Synchronous Adapter
8286099	SDLC Adapter
8286112	256K System Board
8286113	512K System Board
8286115	512K Memory Card
8286116	128K Memory Card
8286117	Key Switch Assembly w/Keys
8286121	System Battery
8286122	192 Watt Power Supply
8286124	Floppy Drive Signal Cable
8286125	Fixed Disk Adapter
8286127	80287 Math Coprocessor Option
8286128	20Mb Hard Drive
8286129	Fixed Disk Data Cable
8286130	1.2Mb Floppy Drive
8286131	360K Floppy Drive
8286139	RAM Module IC, 128K
8286140	Keyboard
8286141	Keyboard Foot
8286146	External Keyboard Cable
8286147	Serial/Parallel Card
8286165	Keyboard w/Cover
8286171	PC Network Adapter

8286216	30Mb Hard Disk
83X9144	Token-Ring Adapter
8520171	Monochrome Display
8529143	Speaker Assembly
8529146	Color Video Adapter
8529148	Monochrome/Printer Adapter
8529149	Printer Adapter
8529150	Async. Comm. Adapter
8529151	Game Adapter
8529171	5151 Monochrome Display
8529227	5153 Color Display
8529251	Receiver Card
8529252	Extender Card
8529295	SDLC Adapter
8529296	Bisync. Adapter
8654215	EGA Adapter

IBM PC 5150

1390290	Keyboard, 101 Key
4584656	Keyboard CSA
5154001	EGA Color Monitor
6321035	5154 Enhanced Color Display
6450215	Serial/Parallel Adapter
8286096	64/256Kb Memory Expansion Board
8286097	CGA Adapter
8286098	Binary Synchronous Adapter
8286099	SDLC Adapter
8286171	PC Network Adapter
83X9144	Token-Ring Adapter
8520171	Monochrome Display
8529143	Speaker and Cable Assembly
8529144	32K Expansion Memory Adapter
8529145	64K Expansion Memory Adapter
8529146	Color Graphics Video Adapter
8529147	8087 Math Coprocessor
8529148	Monochrome/Printer Adapter

8529149	Printer Adapter
8529150	Async. Comm. Adapter
8529151	Game Adapter
8529152	Floppy Drive Adapter
8529153	160K Floppy Disk Drive
8529155	63.5 Watt Power Supply
8529158	A. C. Power Cord, 120V
8529159	Diskette Drive Signal Cable
8529166	Keyboard
8529168	Keyboard Cable
8529171	5151 Monochrome Display
8529205	16/64K System Board
8529206	360K Floppy Diskette Drive (Double Sided)
8529211	64K RAM Modules (RAM Chips)
8529212	64/256K Memory Expansion
8529227	5153 Color Display
8529238	16/64K System Board w/64K
8529247	Power Supply, 130 Watt (Optional)
8529251	Receiver Card
8529252	Extender Card
8529295	SDLC Adapter
8529296	Bisync. Adapter
8529297	Keyboard
8586096	64/256K Expansion Memory Adapter
8654213	64/256K System Board
8654215	EGA Adapter

IBM PC 5271

2683110	Keyboard Adapter
2683549	256K Memory Expansion
6110344	Keyboard Assembly
6931932	Monitor
8529247	130 Watt Power Supply
8529254	System Board w/128K
8529269	10Mb Fixed Disk Adapter
8654378	Emulation Board (56X4927, 8665792)

8654381	Programmed Symbols Adapter
8654386	Color Display Card (6320986)
8654390	All Points Address Adapter
8654395	128K Printer Adapter

IBM PORTABLE 5155

8268097	CGA Adapter
8529152	Floppy Drive Adapter
8529254	System Board w/128K
8654417	114 Watt Power Supply
8654419	Monitor Assembly
8654422	Keyboard

IBM PC/XT EXPANSION CHASSIS MODEL 5161

8529158	Power Cord, 120V
8529247	Power Supply, 120V, 130 Watt
8529250	Expansion Chassis System Board
8529251	Expansion Chassis Receiver Board
8529253	Expansion Chassis Interface Cable
8529269	Hard Drive Adapter

IBM PS/2 DISPLAYS

61X8924	8512, 14″ VGA Color Monitor
61X8925	Tilt/Swivel Stand for 8512 Monitor
68X3045	8503, 12″ VGA Monochrome Monitor
68X3061	Tilt/Swivel Stand for 8503 & 8513 Monitor
68X3088	8513, 12″ VGA Color Monitor
75X5907	Tilt/Swivel Stand for 8514 Monitor
75X5945	8514, 16″ VGA Color Monitor

IBM PS/2 MODEL 25

00F2052	Monochrome Monitor
00F2053	Color Monitor
00F2100	System Board
00F2101	Bus Adapter
00F2109	Diskette Drive, Cable, 1/2 Ht.

00F2112	Diskette Drive, Bezel, 1/2 Ht.
00F2120	Memory Module ZM1 and ZM2
00F2121	Memory Module U16, U22, U34, U35
1391401	Keyboard
1391987	Space Saving Keyboard (84/85 Key)
1392090	Keyboard, 101/102 Key
1393082	Cable for Space Saving Keyboard
1497250	2Mb Expanded Memory Adapter
15F8511	Speech Viewer Adapter
27F4119	Diskette Drive, 720K, 1/3 Ht.
27F4130	Fixed Disk Drive (with Adapter Only)
33F4094	Diskette Drive, Shield, 1/2 Ht.
33F4947	Diskette Drive, Bezel, 1/3 Ht.
33F4948	Diskette Drive, Spacer, 1/3 Ht.
33F4949	Diskette Drive, Cable, 1/3 Ht.
33F8471	Fixed Disk Drive Adapter Cables
6181768	Data Acquisition Adapter (DAD)
6181770	GPIB Adapter
61X8898	Keyboard Cable
61X8906	256K Memory Module
61X8921	Speech Adapter
61X8922	8087 Math Coprocessor
61X8929	20Mb Fixed Disk Drive
62X1045	Power Cord
6820821	Diskette Drive, 720K, 1/2 Ht.
72X6757	External Drive Adapter
72X8101	PC Network Baseband Adapter
72X8105	PC Network Adapter II
78X9088	Fixed Disk Bezel and Keylock
78X9089	Fixed Disk Drive Cable
81X8620	PC Music Adapter
81X8624	MIDI Adapter
8286098	Binary Synchronous Communications Adapter
8286099	SDLC Adapter
8286147	Serial/Parallel Adapter
8286171	PC Network Adapter

8529151   Game Control Adapter

IBM PS/2 MODEL 30

11F8126	30Mb Fixed Disk Drive
11F8696	System Board
1391401	Keyboard
1391987	Space Saving Keyboard (84/85 Key)
1392090	Keyboard, 101/102 Key
1393082	Cable for Space Saving Keyboard
1497250	2Mb Expanded Memory Adapter
15F8511	Speech Viewer Adapter
1887743	Display Adapter
27F4119	Diskette Drive, 720K, 1/3 Ht.
27F4178	Fixed Disk Drive Cable
27F4230	Diskette Drive, Cable, 1/3 Ht.
27F4964	Bus Adapter
33F8472	5.25″ External Diskette Drive Adapter Cable
33F8474	System Board
34F0002	Diskette Drive, Spacer, 1/3 Ht.
6128285	20Mb Fixed Disk Drive
6181768	Data Acquisition Adapter (DAD)
6181770	GPIB Adapter
61X8898	External Keyboard Cable
61X8899	Diskette Drive, 720K, 1/2 Ht.
61X8900	Diskette Drive, Cable, 1/2 Ht.
61X8901	Diskette Drive, Bezel, 1/2 Ht.
61X8903	Fixed Disk Drive Cable
61X8904	Fixed Disk Drive Bezel
61X8905	70 Watt Power Supply
61X8906	256K Memory Module
61X8907	System Board, 128K
61X8910	Bus Card Assembly
61X8912	Keylock Assembly
61X8921	Speech Adapter
61X8922	8087 Math Coprocessor
61X8923	Mouse

61X8929	20Mb Fixed Disk Drive
72X6757	External Drive Adapter
72X6759	5-1/4" External Drive
72X7568	20Mb Fixed Disk Drive
72X8101	PC Network Baseband Adapter
72X8105	PC Network Adapter II
72X8523	1.44Mb Diskette Drive
81X8620	PC Music Adapter
81X8624	MIDI Adapter
8286098	Binary Synchronous Communications Adapter
8286099	SDLC Adapter
8286147	Serial/Parallel Adapter
8286171	PC Network Adapter
8529151	Game Control Adapter

IBM PS/2 MODEL 30-286

1392090	Keyboard, 101/102 Key
1497256	Memory Pack—256K
27F4069	System Board
27F4164	Bus Adapter
27F4166	Power Supply
27F4169	Cover Lock
27F4178	Fixed Disk Drive Cable
27F4228	1.44Mb Diskette Drive
27F4236	30Mb Fixed Disk Drive
27F4912	Diskette 1 Drive Cable (1/3 Ht.)
27F4916	Diskette 1 Drive Cable (1/2 Ht.)
27F4984	Keyboard Cable
33F8211	Diskette Drive, 1.44Mb, 1/3 Ht.
34F0000	Diskette 2 Drive Cable (1/3 Ht.)
34F0001	Diskette Drive 2 Cable (1/2 Ht.)
34F0046	System Board
6128279	30Mb Fixed Disk Drive
6128285	20Mb Fixed Disk Drive
6181768	Data Acquisition Adapter (DAD)
6181770	GPIB Adapter

61X8921	Speech Adapter
61X8923	Mouse
72X6757	External Drive Adapter
72X6759	5-1/4" External 360K Drive
72X6768	5-1/4" External 360K Drive
72X8101	PC Network Baseband Adapter
72X8105	PC Network Adapter II
72X8523	1.44Mb Diskette Drive
72X8528	80287 Math Coprocessor
74X8637	Memory Pack—1Mb
81X8620	PC Music Adapter
81X8624	MIDI Adapter
8286147	Serial/Parallel Adapter
8286171	PC Network Adapter
8509237	Clock Module
8529151	Game Control Adapter

IBM PS/2 MODEL 50

1391401	Keyboard
1392090	Keyboard
1497253	Expanded Memory Adapter
1497256	Expanded Memory Module
15F7472	Battery/Speaker Assembly w/Attached Cable
15F7570	1.44Mb Floppy Diskette Drive
1887708	Video Memory Expansion Module
1887971	8514 Display Adapter
34F0006	300/1200 Baud Internal Modem
34F0008	Dual Async. Adapter
61X8906	80286 Memory Expansion Module
61X8923	Mouse
72X6758	5-1/4" External Drive Adapter
72X6759	5.25" External Diskette Drive
72X8498	Battery
72X8499	Power Supply
72X8505	Fixed Disk Adapter, Type 1 (20Mb)
72X8511	Battery/Speaker Assembly

72X8515	Fan Assembly
72X8516	System Board (Type 1)
72X8517	512K Memory Module
72X8522	20Mb Fixed Disk
72X8523	1.44Mb Diskette Drive
72X8524	Diskette Drive Bus Adapter
72X8528	80287 Math Coprocessor
72X8529	Dual Async. Adapter
72X8532	80286 Memory Expansion Adapter
72X8537	Keyboard Cable
72X8558	Battery/Speaker Cable
72X8561	Fuse
83X7488	Token-Ring Adapter
90X6806	20Mb Fixed Disk Drive
90X8624	1Mb Memory Module
90X8625	2Mb Memory Module
90X8627	60Mb Fixed Disk Drive
90X8995	Multiprotocol Adapter
90X9366	Power Supply
90X9403	30Mb Fixed Disk Drive
90X9441	Fixed Disk Bus Adapter, Type 2 (30/60Mb)
90X9533	System Board (Type 2)
92X1459	6157 Tape Adapter

IBM PS/2 MODEL 50Z

61X8923	Mouse
90X8625	2Mb Memory Kit
90X9441	HF Buss Card
90X9533	System Board

IBM PS/2 MODEL 55SX

1392090	Keyboard
1497253	0–8Mb Expanded Memory Adapter
1497256	256K Memory Module Kit (for 1497253)
15F8292	2–8Mb 80286 Memory Expansion
1887708	Video Memory Module (for 1887971)

1887971	8514 Display Adapter
27F4166	Power Supply/Fan Assembly
27F4667	System Board, 16MHz
27F4672	Speaker
33F8160	80387SX Math Coprocessor, 16MHz
33F8211	1.44Mb Diskette Drive
34F0006	300/1200 Internal Modem
34F0008	Dual Async. Adapter
6128272	60Mb Fixed Disk Drive
6128277	30Mb Fixed Disk Drive
61X8898	Keyboard Cable
61X8923	Mouse
74X8637	1Mb Memory Module Kit (for 1497253)
83X7488	Token-Ring Adapter
8509237	Real-Time Clock Module
90X8624	1Mb Memory Module (for 15F8292)
90X8624	1Mb Memory Module Kit
90X8625	2Mb Memory Module (for 15F8292)
90X8625	2MB Memory Module Kit
90X8995	Multiprotocol Adapter
92X1459	6157 Tape Adapter

IBM PS/2 MODEL 60

1391401	Keyboard
1392090	Keyboard
1497253	Expanded Memory Adapter
1497256	Expanded Memory Adapter Module
15F6551	Power Supply, 225 Watt
15F6865	ESDI Fixed Disk Adapter
1887708	Video Memory Expansion Module
1887971	8514 Display Adapter
34F0006	300/1200 Baud Internal Modem
34F0008	Dual Async. Adapter
61X8906	256K Memory Module
61X8923	Mouse
62X0407	Fixed Disk Adapter

62X0415	44Mb Hard Drive Adapter
6373507	44Mb Hard Drive Adapter
68X8825	Optical Disk Assembly
72X6669	Power Supply, 225 Watt
72X6758	5-1/4" External Drive Adapter
72X6759	5.25" External Diskette Drive
72X8498	Battery
72X8500	Power Supply, 207 Watt
72X8511	Battery/Speaker Assembly
72X8519	70Mb ESDI Fixed Disk Drive
72X8521	Fixed Disk Power Cable
72X8523	1.44Mb Diskette Drive
72X8528	80287 Math Coprocessor
72X8529	Dual Async. Adapter
72X8530	80286 Memory Module Adapter
72X8532	80286 Memory Expansion Adapter
72X8533	256K Memory Module
72X8537	External Keyboard Cable
72X8538	System Board
72X8540	Fixed Disk Adapter
72X8541	44Mb Fixed Disk Drive
72X8542	Fixed Disk Controller Cable
72X8543	Disk Drive Cable
72X8545	Fixed Disk C Signal Cable
72X8561	Fuse
72X8567	Fixed Disk D Signal Cable
72X8581	ESDI Fixed Disk Drive Adapter
83X7488	Token-Ring Adapter
90X7392	115Mb ESDI Fixed Disk Drive
90X8643	Fixed Disk Drive Adapter
90X8995	Multiprotocol Adapter
90X9063	ESDI Fixed Disk Drive Adapter
92X1459	6157 Tape Adapter

IBM PS/2 MODEL 70

1391401	Keyboard

1392090	Keyboard
15F7570	1.44Mb Floppy Diskette Drive
15F7657	System Board, 25MHz
15F7658	2Mb Memory Module, 25MHz
15F7659	System Board, 25MHz
15F7661	80387 Math Coprocessor, 25MHz
1887708	Video Memory Module (for 1887971)
1887971	8514 Video Display Adapter
33F5834	System Board, 16MHz
33F5835	System Board, 20MHz
33F5950	Battery/Speaker Assembly w/Attached Cable
34F0006	300/1200 Baud Internal Modem
34F0008	Dual Async Adapter
61X8923	Mouse
72X6671	80386 Memory Expansion Adapter
72X6672	Memory Expansion Kit (for 72X6671)
72X6673	80387 Math Coprocessor, 16MHz
72X6758	5.25″ Ext. Diskette Dr. Feature Group w/Adapter
72X6759	5.25″ External Diskette Drive
72X8498	Battery
72X8511	Battery/Speaker Assembly
72X8523	1.44Mb Diskette Drive
72X8537	Keyboard Cable
72X8558	Battery/Speaker Assembly Cable
90X7393	80387 Math Coprocessor, 20MHz
90X8623	System Board, 20MHz
90X8624	1Mb Memory Module, 16MHz and 20MHz
90X8625	2Mb Memory Module, 16MHz and 20MHz
90X8626	Power Supply/Fan Assembly
90X8627	60Mb Fixed Disk Drive (Includes ESDI Controller)
90X8995	Multiprotocol Adapter
90X9286	120Mb Fixed Disk Drive (Includes ESDI Controller)
90X9287	Fixed Disk and Diskette Drive Bus Adapter
90X9355	System Board, 16MHz
90X9556	2–8Mb 80386 Memory Expansion Option
92X1459	6157 Tape Adapter

IBM PS/2 MODEL 80

1391401	Keyboard
1392090	Keyboard
15F6551	Power Supply, 225 Watt
15F6865	ESDI Fixed Disk Adapter
1887708	Video Memory Expansion Module
1887971	8514 Display Adapter
33F8415	System Board, 20Mhz
34F0006	300/1200 Baud Internal Modem
34F0008	Dual Async. Adapter
61X8923	Mouse
62X0407	Fixed Disk Adapter
68X8825	Optical Disk Assembly
72X6668	System Board, 16MHz
72X6669	Power Supply, 225 Watt
72X6670	1Mb System Board Memory
72X6671	80386 Memory Expansion Adapter
72X6672	Memory Expansion Kit
72X6673	80387 Math Coprocessor, 16MHz
72X6758	Ext. Diskette Drive Adapter w/Feature Group
72X6759	5.25" External Diskette Drive
72X8498	Battery
72X8511	Battery/Speaker Assembly
72X8519	70Mb ESDI Fixed Disk Drive
72X8521	Fixed Disk Power Cable
72X8523	1.44Mb Diskette Drive
72X8529	Dual Async. Adapter
72X8537	External Keyboard Cable
72X8540	Fixed Disk Adapter
72X8541	44Mb Fixed Disk Drive
72X8542	Fixed Disk Controller Cable
72X8543	Diskette Drive Cable
72X8545	Fixed Disk C Signal Cable
72X8567	Fixed Disk D Signal Cable
72X8581	ESDI Fixed Disk Drive Adapter
83X7488	Token-Ring Adapter

90X6766	1.44Mb Floppy Disk Drive
90X7390	System Board, 20MHz
90X7391	2Mb System Board Memory Kit
90X7392	115Mb ESDI Fixed Disk Drive
90X7393	80387 Math Coprocessor, 20MHz
90X8643	Fixed Disk Drive Adapter
90X8745	314Mb ESDI Fixed Disk Drive
90X8995	Multiprotocol Adapter
90X9063	ESDI Fixed Disk Drive Adapter
92X1459	6157 Tape Adapter

IBM PS/2 MODEL P70

23F3230	External Storage Device Cable
34F0008	Dual Async Adapter
38F4686	Plasma Display Adapter
38F4734	Power Supply
38F4737	Plasma Display Assembly
38F5936	1.44Mb Diskette Drive
38F5939	Cable, Plasma Display Power
61X8923	Mouse
65X1253	300/1200/2400 Internal Modem
65X1319	Speaker
65X1537	Keyboard
65X1564	System Board, 20MHz
65X1576	Keyboard Cable
72X6759	5.25″ External Diskette Drive
72X8498	Battery
90X7393	80387 Coprocessor, 20MHz
90X8624	1Mb Memory Module Kit
90X8625	2Mb Memory Module Kit
90X8627	60Mb ESDI Fixed Disk (includes Controller)
90X8995	Multiprotocol Adapter
90X9286	120Mb ESDI Fixed Disk (includes Controller)
90X9566	2–8Mb 80386 Memory Expansion Option
92X1459	6157 Tape Adapter
94X1540	Modem Cable

IBM XT

1390290	Keyboard, 101 Key
4584656	Keyboard CSA
5154001	EGA Color Monitor
6134316	256K Memory Expansion
6321035	5154 Enhanced Color Display
6323445	Expansion Board
6450210	30Mb Fixed Disk Drive
6450215	Serial/Parallel Adapter
6489907	20Mb Fixed Disk Drive
6489910	Diskette Drive
6489914	20Mb Fixed Disk Adapter
8286096	64/256K Memory Expansion Board
8286097	CGA Adapter
8286098	Binary Synchronous Adapter
8286099	SDLC Adapter
8286124	Diskette/Fixed-Disk Cable
8286128	20Mb Fixed Disk Drive
8286147	Serial/Parallel Adapter
8286171	PC Network Adapter
83X1520	256/640K System Board
83X9144	Token-Ring Adapter
8520171	Monochrome Display
8520247	130 Watt Power Supply
8520254	640K System Board
8520275	XEBEC Fixed Disk Adapter
8529143	Speaker and Cable Assembly
8529144	32K Expansion Memory Adapter
8529145	64K Expansion Memory Adapter
8529146	Color Video Adapter
8529147	8087 Math Coprocessor
8529148	Monochrome/Printer Adapter
8529149	Printer Adapter
8529150	Async. Comm. Adapter
8529151	Game Adapter
8529152	Floppy Drive Adapter

8529153	Diskette Drive, Single Sided
8529158	Power Cord, 120V
8529159	Diskette Drive Signal Cable
8529166	Keyboard
8529168	Keyboard Cable
8529171	5151 Monochrome Display
8529206	360K Floppy Diskette Drive (Double Sided)
8529211	64K RAM Modules (RAM Chips)
8529212	64/256K Memory Expansion
8529227	5153 Color Display
8529247	130 Watt Power Supply
8529250	Expansion Board
8529251	Receiver Card
8529252	Extender Card
8529254	System Board w/128K
8529269	10Mb Fixed Disk Adapter
8529271	Fixed Disk Data/Control Cable
8529275	10Mb Fixed Disk Drive
8529295	SDLC Adapter
8529296	Bisync. Adapter
8529297	Keyboard
8586096	64/256K Expansion Memory Adapter
8654215	EGA Adapter

IBM XT 286

1390131	Enhanced Keyboard
62X1025	6MHz, 640K System Board
62X1028	1.2Mb Floppy Disk Drive
62X1031	20Mb Hard Drive Adapter
62X1032	Floppy Disk Drive Adapter
62X1034	157 Watt Power Supply
62X1036	360K Floppy Disk Drive
6447033	101 Key Keyboard (w/o Cable)
8286147	Serial/Parallel Card

Technical Tips and Information

The following pages contain technical information pertaining to various hardware and software. Much of this information was gathered as a result of situations encountered in the field. The solutions to these problems required research, telephone calls, call backs, trial-and-error troubleshooting, and perseverance. Some of the information is found in bulletins issued by the manufacturers after publication of the service manuals.

Often, a customer complaint leads to the discovery of a condition that has not been documented. This is especially true with systems that are new to the market. Solutions for undocumented problems are then released in a bulletin from the manufacturer. These bulletins are distributed to authorized dealers and service providers. Occasionally, the information is printed in industry-related publications or consumer magazines. Sometimes, a hardware or software revision (such as a ROM upgrade or installation of a device driver) is required to cure the problem. This is the type of information that should be collected and put in the notebook that is carried with your tools.

COMPAQ

CACHE.EXE

Compaq has identified a problem with CACHE.EXE Version 1.40 (comes with Compaq User Programs Versions 5.08 and 5.09) which may cause data loss under certain circumstances. Use CACHE.EXE Version 1.41 or later.

TAPE.EXE

The TAPE.EXE Version 3.01 is required to support all Compaq 10 Mb and 40 Mb tape drives operating under MS-DOS Version 4.01.

LTE—LTE/286

A special tool (Compaq P/N 119186-001) is required for removal of the math coprocessor or the system ROMs in either of these two units. These components and their sockets can be damaged by improper removal.

COMPAQ MS-DOS VERSION 4.01

There is a potential problem using Compaq MS-DOS Version 4.01 revision A and B on fixed-disks with partitions greater than 32 Mb which may result in data corruption. It is necessary to use the 401FILEFIX patch, or Revision C (or later) of MS-DOS.

PORTABLE

Before installing a fixed disk drive, make sure that the power supply can handle it.

PORTABLE

To upgrade the memory above 256K, it is necessary to replace the decoder ROM and the BIOS ROM. Switch 2 becomes inoperative.

PORTABLE

If the system appears to boot properly but there is no video, connect an external monitor to the video port. CTRL-ALT-> or CTRL-ALT-< is used to switch video modes.

PORTABLE

When video problems occur, do not discount the internal cable from the video assembly to the video adapter board. Use CAUTION when working in the video area.

PORTABLE

The ROM revision can be found by using DEBUG to dump address F0000:FFE6.

PORTABLE

When installing third-party, fixed-disk drives, be sure that the power supply will not be taxed, and that the mechanical shock and vibration will not hurt the drive.

PORTABLE

For 0000 201 through 1080 201 memory errors on system boards using 256K chips, replace the system board.

PORTABLE

There was a chassis design change starting with serial number 1524020B0001. The monitor, power switch, fuse value, and fan are affected.

PORTABLE

The plastic board retainers on the inside of the card cage can be installed in either of two positions. They come from the factory set for standard height boards. They must be rotated 180 degrees for low profile boards.

PORTABLE

There are two versions of the system board. Version 2 requires setting a jumper when configuring memory.

COMPAQ (ALL)

Generally, the top of the drive cage inside the computer has a map of the switch and jumper settings and the power connectors for storage devices.

COMPAQ (ALL)

Verify the proper BIOS ROM is installed before performing memory upgrades or installing fixed disk drives.

SLT/286

Uses either of two interchangeable system boards. One of these has a piggyback board, the other does not.

SLT/286

There is a potential problem with the fixed-disk drive not spinning up quickly enough from the "standby" mode. To remedy this problem, it is necessary to use the CACHE.EXE on Compaq User Programs Version 6.04 or later (if you are using CACHE), and replace the ROMs with Part # 110091-012 and 110092-012 in locations U56 and U57.

SLT/286

Compaq suggests using CAUTION when installing either the 2400 BAUD internal modem or the Asynchronous Communications Board in the SLT/286, in order to avoid bent or broken pins on the system board connector J114.

SLT/286

The 20Mb type 2 fixed disk has a 1:1 interleave factor.

SLT/286

The 40Mb tape backup unit in the external storage module requires a 220 Ohm terminating resistor, not the 1K Ohm found on some units.

SLT/286 WITH EXPANSION UNIT

Power on all external devices before powering up the system unit.

SLT/286

Some system boards lock up when using expanded memory configured through the CEMMP driver.

SLT/286

CACHE.EXE prior to version 6.02 may cause data corruption due to fixed-disk spinup problems. It is necessary to use ROM Revision 286B H.7 or later.

DESKPRO

All Compaq fixed-disk drives (EXCEPT the full height 30Mb) are self-parking. The 30Mb full height has a mechanical lock which must be engaged before shipping.

DESKPRO (ALL)

When installing storage devices, make sure that the power cables are connected to the proper places on the system board. Otherwise, power supply problems may result.

DESKPRO (ALL)

If the fixed-disk drive whines or squeals, remove the grounding spring (static discharge spring).

DESKPRO 386

Some systems lock up or display PARITY errors if configured with more than 2Mb of RAM and are running operating systems other than MS-DOS (MS-OS/2, UNIX, XENIX or WINDOWS 386).

DESKPRO 386

Remove the system board when installing a math coprocessor to prevent damage to the board.

DESKPRO 386

Uses either of two types of multipurpose controllers.

DESKPRO 386

The power supply can NOT accommodate a Tape Backup unit if there are two fixed-disk drives present.

DESKPRO 386

When using a fixed-disk drive of 60Mb or larger, an ESDI controller is required. The multipurpose controller must be disabled.

DESKPRO 386

The front bezel may need adjustment when installing the 135Mb tape backup.

DESKPRO 386

A 3.5" diskette drive may be used as the "A" drive with ROM revision J.2 or later.

DESKPRO 386

Use FASTART only if configuring the entire fixed disk for MS-DOS.

DESKPRO 386

Uses either of 2 system boards. One version has sockets for either 80287 or 80387 math coprocessors. Do NOT use BOTH coprocessors. Either one by itself is okay.

DESKPRO 386

There have been some problems with the 80386 processor. Use Advanced Diagnostics Version 5.04 or later to test.

DESKPRO 386

Do not use CACHE.EXE Version 1.00 or 1.10 with extended memory. There is a possibility that fixed-disk data may be corrupted.

DESKPRO 386

A software patch may be needed with early versions of the Microsoft Mouse Driver on systems using the VGC adapter.

DESKPRO 386/25

Deskpro 386/25 systems with revision "L" or earlier system boards, using an Intel 25-MHz 80387 coprocessor, have the potential of producing random calculation errors if the software is using the coprocessor. This can be verified using Compaq Advanced Diagnostics Version 6.07 or greater.

EPSON

EQUITY SERIES

Dusty or dirty circuit boards give more problems than the average PC. Clean them often, even if they don't need it. (*Note:* Dust can block air circulation in any computer. The air circulation is necessary to cool the components. Chips do generate heat.)

EQUITY SERIES

Do not use IBM diagnostics on the EQUITY series of computers. The IBM diagnostics will give totally unpredictable and unreliable results.

Use the EPSON diagnostics, and make sure that the version of diagnostics matches the machine. There are separate diagnostics for each of the EQUITY models.

EQUITY I+

To upgrade an EQUITY I+ to a fixed disk, do not use any of the standard upgrade kits (drive, controller, cables). Instead, keep both diskette drives and use a low-power device such as the Hard card from Plus Development. Do not use the Miniscribe 8425 or 8438.

IBM

MODELS   8550-021
             8560 (ALL)
             8580 (ALL)

The file DASDDRVR.SYS located on the Reference Diskettes (version 1.2 and higher) for the above-mentioned machines must be installed in order to eliminate some problems with these systems when they are using IBM PC-DOS versions 3.3 or 4.0.

Insure that the file DASDDRVR.SYS is either 698 or 734 bytes. The 648 byte version should be replaced with either the 698 or 734 byte version.

The statement DEVICE=DASDDRVR.SYS must be inserted in the CONFIG.SYS file.

Problems eliminated:

Intermittent read failures on 720Kb program diskettes.

Highly intermittent problem with either a diskette drive "Not Ready" or a fixed-disk "General Failure" message.

FORMAT fails on multiple 3.5 in diskettes.

301 and 8602 messages.

Intermittent 162 (configuration) or 163 (time/date) errors reported during system initialization.

MODEL 8550

Right Alternate Key Not Functional with DOS 3.30:
Test the system by performing a warm boot using the CTRL-(LEFT)

ALT-DELETE key combination. If this is successful, try using the RIGHT ALT key.

If the system does not boot, then the right ALT key is not responding. Check the AUTOEXEC.BAT file for the following statement:

KEYB US 437

This file will appear if the initial installation of PC-DOS was performed using the SELECT command.

Using the DOS Line Editor, remove this statement from the file.

MODEL 8570

Diagnostics may hang with a Token-Ring Adapter installed and set to interrupt level 3. Either remove the Token-Ring Adapter or set it to another level.

MODEL 8570

Under some conditions, using Advanced Diagnostics Version 1.03 will cause false 401 Parallel Port Errors. Use Version 1.04 or later.

MODEL 8570

In some circumstances, the Planar Board diagnostics will hang when using Version 1.03 of the Advanced Diagnostics. Use Version 1.04 or later.

MODEL 8573 (PORTABLE 370)

The PS/2 Model P70 386 reference diskette (and Advanced Diagnostics) can NOT be used to diagnose failures on any other PS/2 models.

MODEL 8580

The Reference diskette must be version 1.01 or greater to be used with the Model 111 or 311 (or other Model 80's with an ESDI adapter and ESDI fixed disk). Failure to recognize the ESDI adapter or memory errors will result with the use of version 1.00.

MODEL 8580-111

A false "10463" error code may occur while running fixed disk diagnostics on a 115Mb drive, telling the user to "Replace Fixed Disk C". If this occurs during the ESDI Read Write Test portion of the diagnostics, and the customer is not experiencing fixed-disk related problems, the error should be ignored. This error only occurs on drives manufactured prior to 12/21/87.

MODEL 8580-111
MODEL 8580-115

The installed RAM is 2048Kb, but usable RAM is only 1920Kb. The remaining 128Kb of RAM is used by the system in order to load ROM BIOS code which enhanced system performance.

PS/2 MICROCHANNEL

Adapter Definition Files (ADF's) must be added to a backup copy of the reference diskette, when adding expansion boards, for the system to be set up properly.

PS/2 MICROCHANNEL

Be sure that boards are seated properly in their sockets. It is very easy to tighten the retaining nut that holds the boards, with the board skewed in the socket.

MODEL 8530

Plastic covers on rear must be broken off to access expansion boards or adapters having connectors or switches on them.

AT

This system has two types of system boards. They use different types of RAM chips.

AT

System will appear dead if the switch on the rear of the power supply is set for the wrong line voltage.

AT

The only switch on the system board is SW1. It is monochrome (switch towards back of system) or color video (switch towards front).

AT

J18 is the RAM jumper (jump pins 1 & 2 for 512K system board RAM, pins 2 & 3 for 256K RAM).

PS/2

Check for bent pins on monitor cable if screen is not functional or off color.

PS/2

Most of these machines have fragile plastic parts. Use caution.

PS/2

Make sure that the battery is connected before powering up these systems.

PS/2

In case of a communications failure (parallel or serial port), check the SET-UP program and make sure that the port is enabled.

ALL KEYBOARDS

Do NOT remove the space bar when disassembling the keyboard. There are two plastic tabs that are easily broken. You can disassemble the entire keyboard for cleaning without removing the space bar.

ALL KEYBOARDS

Use a puller or your fingers to remove the key caps. Prying may break the plastic retaining tabs.

MODEL 8530

The Model 30 keyboard uses different scancodes. If you encounter a scancode error, make sure that you are using the correct keyboard.

PC AND PC-2 SYSTEMS

Jumper P4 is to select the function of the "Cassette" jack; Cassette, Microphone, or Auxiliary (this jack is seldom used).

PC AND PC-2 SYSTEMS

The PC power supply (63.5 watt) and the XT power supply (135 watt) are physically identical. When installing a hard drive in a PC, the power supply should be upgraded.

PC, PC-2, AND OLDER XT'S

Older systems may contain a 160Kb, 8-sector, single-sided, full-height drive or a 320Kb 8-sector, double-sided, full-height drive. The standard is 360Kb 9-sector, double-sided drives, either full height or half height (half-height drives will not be original IBM drives).

PC/XT AND IBM ASYNC BOARD

If the IBM ASYNCHRONOUS board is installed in slot 8 of an IBM XT, jumper J13 must be installed. If this board is installed in any other slot, or a different machine, J13 must be removed.

SEAGATE

MODEL NUMBERS

Seagate model numbers are coded to indicate the form-factor, capacity, and interface type. For example: ST 9 096 A

ST = Seagate Technology

9   = Form-Factor   1xx = 3.5 inch, half-height
                                   2xx = 5.25 inch, half-height
                                   3xx = 3.5 inch, 1 inch high
                                   4xx = 5.25 inch, full-height
                                   6xx = 9 inch
                                   8xx = 8 inch
                                   9xx = 2.5 inch

096 = Unformatted capacity in megabytes (approx.)

A   = Interface   (None) = ST412/MFM
                                    N = SCSI
                                    R = ST412/RLL
                                    A = AT (IDE)
                                    X = XT Bus
                                    E = ESDI
                                    J = SMD/SMD-E
                                    K = IPI-2
                               ND = Differential SCSI
                              NM = Apple Macintosh Compatible SCSI
                              NS = Synchronized Spindle
                              NV = Novell NetWare Ready

The example is a 2.5 inch, 96Mb IDE drive.

SEAGATE XT AND AT CONTROLLERS AND XT, AT AND SCSI HOST ADAPTERS

Model	Host Bus	Interface	Drives Supported	Cylinders	Data Encoding	Heads	Floppy Drives Supported
ST11M	XT	ST412	2	up to 1024	MFM		NA
ST11R	XT	ST412	2	up to 1024	RLL		NA
ST21M	AT	ST412	2	up to 1024	MFM		NA
ST21R	AT	ST412	2	up to 1024	RLL		NA
ST22M	AT	ST412	2	up to 1024	MFM		2-3.5/5.25
ST22R	AT	ST412	2	up to 1024	RLL		2-3.5/5.25
ST05X	XT	XT	2	up to 1024		up to 16	NA
ST07A	AT	AT	2	up to 1024		up to 16	NA
ST08A	AT	AT	2	up to 1024		up to 16	2-3.5/5.25
ST01	XT/AT	SCSI	2	up to 1024		up to 16	NA
ST02	XT/AT	SCSI	2	up to 1024		up to 16	2-3.5/5.25

TECHNICAL SUPPORT SERVICES

Telephone	408-438-8222
Automated FAX	408-438-2620
Technical Support FAX	408-438-8137
Bulletin Board	408-438-8771

Communication settings for the Bulletin Board are 300 - 9600 BAUD, 8 DATA BITS, 1 STOP BIT, NO PARITY.

WYSE

Bad batteries cause a multitude of problems.

1. The clock loses time (same on most systems).
2. On power up, the system appears to have a blown system board. (The system can not read the CMOS configuration and will not respond correctly.)
3. Some systems will not boot at all. No error message displayed.

When in doubt, replace the battery before replacing the system board.

Beware of ever-changing BIOS ROM versions. Servers and work stations running under NOVELL Advanced Netware/286 version 2.0A need a BIOS upgrade. The upgrade does not support the 101 key keyboard, so the keyboard scanner must also be replaced.

Bent or shorting of phone-plug type keyboard connectors will result in the following:

1. "SCROLL LOCK," "CAPS LOCK," and "NUM LOCK" lights either flashing or dim all at the same time during system boot.
2. "Keyboard data line" error message.

Make sure that you are using the correct (latest version) diagnostic disk.

MS-DOS version 3.3, as published by WYSE, supports fixed disk partitions up to 512Mb. Use only WYSE's DISKPACK utility to defragment the MS-DOS file system. Some third-party software utilities may not work or damage the contents of the fixed disk.

ALL SYSTEMS

List the existing switch and jumper settings before making any changes.

Remove math coprocessors before sending board back to manufacturer (or anyone else) for repair. You may not get the same board returned to you.

Do NOT mix speed or size of RAM chips within the same bank.

You can use 256K chips instead of 64K chips provided that all of the chips in the bank are the same.

Watch address conflicts when installing boards or performing upgrades.

You can use a math coprocessor that is rated at a faster speed than the system clock with no problem, but a slower coprocessor will burn out.

Get a list of installed devices and their locations before removing, replacing, or adding adapters. This is especially necessary on CMOS type systems.

If the clock in a system begins losing time, replace the battery.

If there are two or more identical connectors in a system, verify what they do and how they are configured before connecting a device to them.

The hidden MS-DOS system files can get corrupted just like any other file.

Prevent fixed-disk problems by backing them up, reformatting them, and reinstalling software every 6 to 12 months, depending upon usage.

Mixed versions of MS-DOS can cause problems. There should be only one version of MS-DOS on a fixed disk. Erase any extra copies of COMMAND.COM also.

All serial cables are not the same, even though they may look that way. If you have problems with a serial device, or replace a serial peripheral, check the pin outs.

Some older software may not run on a CPU with a clock speed faster than 4.77MHz (especially if it is copy protected). Fixed disks should not be formatted (low-level or MS-DOS) until their temperature and speed have stabilized. The drive should run for about 20 to 30 minutes before formatting.

Power problems may result from a blown fuse or circuit breaker on a surge protector, or the surge protector being switched off.

Internal cables do fail. Before replacing a drive, adapter card, and so forth, verify that the cables connecting them inside the system unit are not faulty.

Chips (RAM, ROM-BIOS) sometimes will vibrate loose. Observing ESD precautions, reseat the chips by pressing down on them. Sometimes this will bring a system back to life.

If you have a problem with a machine where the customer replaced a chip (or chips), or upgraded the RAM, check for correct orientation. Some people don't know that the chips must face in a certain direction.

A problem of "No video" may just be that the brightness control is turned down.

Check for address conflicts when installing boards:

Parallel Port	LPT1	IRQ 7
Primary Serial Port	COM1	IRQ 4
Secondary Serial Port	COM2	IRQ 3

Did you leave your diagnostics or some other diskette in the customer's machine?

Some systems do not fully conform to the addressing standards of MS-DOS-based systems. ROM address conflicts may appear and cause some irregularities. An example of this is a BIOS incompatibility between the AT&T 6300 and the ROM(s) on Western Digital Fixed Disk Controllers.

Do not power up a system that has been turned off until you have waited at least one minute.

The hard disk can be damaged.

The RAM in some machines does not clear immediately. Some residual information may remain.

Some machines need time for the power supply to reset itself. If you power down these machines and then power them up again, the machine will appear to be stalled or dead.

Rapid exercising of the switch on the power supply may damage the switch, not to mention creating surges that can damage components.

Intermittent characters may appear if the keyboard is not properly grounded. Check the ground strap inside the keyboard unit.

FINDING THE ROM-BIOS DATE

In all of the IBM products, and many other brands, the ROM-BIOS includes a date indicating when the BIOS was completed. This BASIC program will display the date on the screen.

```
10 REM THIS PROGRAM DISPLAYS THE ROM-BIOS DATE
20 DEF SEG = &HFFFF
30 DATE.$ = ""
40 FOR I = 5 TO 12
50 DATE.$ = DATE.$ + CHR$(PEEK(I))
60 NEXT
70 IF PEEK (7) <> ASC("/") THEN DATE.$ = "missing"
80 PRINT "The ROM-BIOS date is ";DATE.$
```

You can use DEBUG to read the ROM-BIOS date.

At the DEBUG prompt (-), type: D=F000:FFF5 FFFC <enter>

INTERRUPT LEVELS (IRQ)

Level 0 (IRQ0) has the highest level.

IBM PC AND XT

Level #	Description
0	System Timer
1	Keyboard
2	Reserved for INT line from slave interrupt controller on systems with dual interrupt controllers (286, 386, 486)
3	Serial port COM2 (and COM4)
4	Serial port COM1 (and COM3)
5	Hard Disk controller
6	Floppy Disk controller
7	Parallel port LPT1

IBM AT

Level #	Description
0	System Timer
1	Keyboard
2	Interrupt line to slave interrupt controller
3	Serial port COM2 (and COM4)
4	Serial port COM1 (and COM3)
5	LPT2
6	Floppy Disk controller
7	Parallel port LPT1
8	Clock/Calendar
9	Tied to IRQ2
10	Reserved
11	Reserved
12	Mouse
13	Math Coprocessor
14	Hard Disk controller
15	Reserved

IBM MICROCHANNEL

Level #	Description
0	System Board Timer
1	Keyboard
2	Cascade Interrupt Control
3	Secondary Async. Port (COM2–COM8)
4	Primary Async. Port (COM1)
5	Reserved
6	Floppy Disk controller
7	Parallel Printer Port
8	Real Time Clock
9	Redirect Cascade
10	Reserved
11	Reserved
12	Mouse
13	Math Coprocessor
14	Fixed Disk
15	Reserved

DIRECT MEMORY ACCESS (DMA)

A Direct Memory Address (DMA) Channel allows a peripheral device to control the bus in order to speed up data transfer within the system.

IBM PC AND XT

Level #	Description
0	RAM Refresh
1	Spare
2	Floppy Disk
3	Hard Disk

IBM AT

Level #	Description
0	Reserved
1	SDLC controller
2	Floppy Disk
3	Hard Disk
4	Intercontroller Interface
5	Reserved
6	Reserved
7	Reserved

I/O ADDRESSES

Hex address	Description
000-01F	DMA controller 1
020-021	Interrupt controller 1
040-047	System timers
060-064	Programmable Peripheral Interface (PPI) controller and keyboard
080-087	DMA page registers
089-08F	DMA page registers
090	Central Arbitration Control Point (PS/2's)
0A0-0A1	Interrupt controller 2 (286, 386, 486 and PS/2's)
0C0-0DF	DMA controller 2 (286, 386, 486 and PS/2's)

Hex address	Description
0F0-0FF	Math coprocessor
100-107	Programmable Option Select (PS/2's)
200-20F	Game port
278-27B	Parallel port LPT3
2E8-2EF	Serial port COM4 (shares IRQ4, address may vary)
2F8-2FF	Serial port COM2
320-32F	Hard disk drive controller
378-37B	Parallel port LPT2
3B0-3BF	Monochrome display
3B4-3DA	Ega or VGA video adapter
3BC-3BF	Parallel port LPT1
3D0-3DF	CGA video adapter
3F0-3F7	Floppy disk drive adapter
3E8-3EF	Serial port COM3 (shares IRQ3, address may vary)
3F8-3FF	Serial port COM1

LOW-LEVEL FORMAT USING DEBUG

Low-level formatting must be performed whenever a fixed disk (other than SCSI or IDE) or controller are replaced.
The procedure is as follows:

1. Boot with a copy of MS-DOS from the diskette (A) drive.
2. At the A> prompt, type DEBUG, and press enter.
3. At the DEBUG prompt (a dash or minus sign, "-"), type G and the address of the read-only memory Basic Input/Output System (ROM BIOS) on the controller; then press enter.
4. Follow the instructions displayed on the screen.

Note: IBM and Compaq drives can be low-leveled through their respective advanced diagnostics.

Here are some common ROM BIOS controller addresses.

Manufacturer	Address
ADAPTEC	G=C800:CCC
DATA TECHNOLOGY (DTC)	G=C800:5
NCL	G=C800:5
OMTI	G=C800:6
SEAGATE	G=CA00:5
SMS/OMTI	G=C800:6
STIO	G=C800:5
WESTERN DIGITAL	G=C800:5 or G=C800:800 or G=C800:6 (some older WD controllers)
XEBEC	G=C800:13C

COMPAQ PORTABLE DIP SWITCHES AND JUMPERS

Function	1	2	3	4	5	6	7	8
Always OFF	OFF							
Math Coprocessor installed		OFF						
Math Coprocessor NOT inst.		ON						
128K memory installed			OFF	ON				
192K memory installed			ON	OFF				
256K memory installed			OFF	OFF				
VDU adapter 40 × 25					OFF	ON		
VDU adapter 80 × 25					ON	OFF		
One 5-1/4" diskette drive							ON	ON
Two 5-1/4" diskette drives							OFF	ON

COMPAQ PORTABLE JUMPER SETTINGS

J3	1-2	External Composite Video and RGB Sync disabled. (Can be enabled by CTRL-ALT-< keys.)
	2-3	External Composite Video and RGB Sync enabled.
J5	1-2	RGB Video disabled. (Can be enabled by CTRL-ALT-< keys.)
	2-3	RGB Video Enabled.

COMPAQ PORTABLE RAM FAILURES

When a RAM failure occurs, a numeric code will be displayed on the monitor. This code will be four characters followed by 201. The first bank indicates which bank has the bad chip. The third and fourth numbers indicate which chip in the bank is defective.

3rd & 4th # 00	80	40	20	10	08	04	02	01
Defective IC Parity	7	6	5	4	3	2	1	0

For Example: 3004 201 would be Bank 3, Chip 2

COMPAQ DESKPRO 386 SWITCHES

Function	1	2	3	4	5	6	7	8
Always ON	ON							
Math Coprocessor installed		ON						
Math Coprocessor NOT inst.		OFF						
80287 (coprocessor) at 4MHz			ON					
80287 (coprocessor) at 8MHz			OFF					
Power-on clock speed AUTO				ON				
Power-on clock speed HIGH				OFF				
Reserved—always OFF					OFF			
Monitor Power-On—Compaq mon.						ON		
Monitor Power-On—3rd party						OFF		
Co-processor type 80287							ON	
Co-processor type 80387							OFF	
Reserved—always ON								ON

COMPAQ 386 32-BIT SYSTEM MEMORY BOARD JUMPERS

Jumper	Function	Memory
E1-E2, E4-E5, E7-E8	256K base memory no extended memory	1MB
E2-E3, E4-E5, E7-E8	512K base memory no extended memory	1MB
E2-E3, E5-E6, E7-E8 (Default)	640K base memory no extended memory	
E1-E2, E4-E5, E8-E9	256K base memory 1024K extended memory	2MB or above
E2-E3, E4-E5, E8-E9	512K base memory 1024K extended memory	2MB or above
E2-E3, E5-E6, E8-E9	640K base memory 1024K extended memory	2MB or above

Note: Do NOT connect E3-E4 or E6-E7. Damage to the 32-Bit System Memory Board will occur.

COMPAQ MULTIPURPOSE CONTROLLER

DIP SWITCH SETTINGS AND JUMPERS

Jumper or Switch Position	Function	Setting
J1 (Shunt Jumper)	Asynchronous Communications	Open on LEFT COM1
		Open on RIGHT COM2 IRQ3
J2 (Shunt Jumper)	Controller address select	Open on LEFT Primary Addr.
		Open on RIGHT Secondary Add.
Switch 1-1	Fixed disk drive	ON = enable OFF = disable
Switch 1-2	Parallel printer port	ON = enable OFF = disable
Switch 1-3	Serial port Reserved on assy. 000336-001	ON = enable OFF = disable
Switch 1-4	Reserved	OFF

IBM PS/2 MODEL 50 & 60 MEMORY FAILURE CODES

ERROR 110   SYSTEM BOARD PARITY CHECK

ERROR 111   MEMORY ADAPTER BOARD PARITY CHECK

ERROR 201   MEMORY MODULE PACKAGE OR SYSTEM BOARD (SEE BELOW)

Memory failure error messages will appear in the following format (where n = any number):

nnnnnn nnnn 201

For the Model 50:

Note: There are TWO banks of memory (SIMMs) on the Model 50. EACH bank has a Position 1 and a Position 2.

Middle four characters	Position
00nn	ONE
nn00	TWO
nnnn	BOTH
0000	Replace the SYSTEM BOARD

For the Model 60:

First six characters	Bank
Up to 080000	ONE
080000 and above	TWO

The MIDDLE FOUR characters are the same as for the Model 50.

IBM PC/XT/AT SYSTEM BOARD COMPONENT LOCATIONS

The illustrations on the following pages will assist in identifying the differences between the IBM PC, XT, and AT system boards. Locations of the various connectors and memory chips are indicated.

Information regarding the settings of the switches and jumpers can be found in other parts of this manual.

The following charts show how to identify faulty RAM chips based upon error codes generated through the POST or use of the manufacturer supplied diagnostics:

IBM PC/XT 64K—256K SYSTEM BOARD

First character of error code	Bank #	Last two characters of error code	Chip #
0	0	00	P
1	1	01	0
2	2	02	1
3	3	04	2
		08	3
		10	4
		20	5
		40	6
		80	7

IBM PC/XT 256K—640K SYSTEM BOARD

First character of error code	Bank #	Last two characters of error code	Chip #
0, 1, 2, or 3	0	00	P
4, 5, 6, or 7	1	01	0
8	2	02	1
9	3	04	2
		08	3
		10	4
		20	5
		40	6
		80	7

IBM AT TYPE 2 SYSTEM BOARD

Last four characters of error code	Chip #
0000	P
0001	0
0002	1
0004	2
0008	3
0010	4
0020	5
0040	6
0080	7
0100	8
0200	9
0400	10
0800	11
1000	12
2000	13
4000	14
8000	15

Note: If an 0000 Error Code is generated, replace both parity chips.

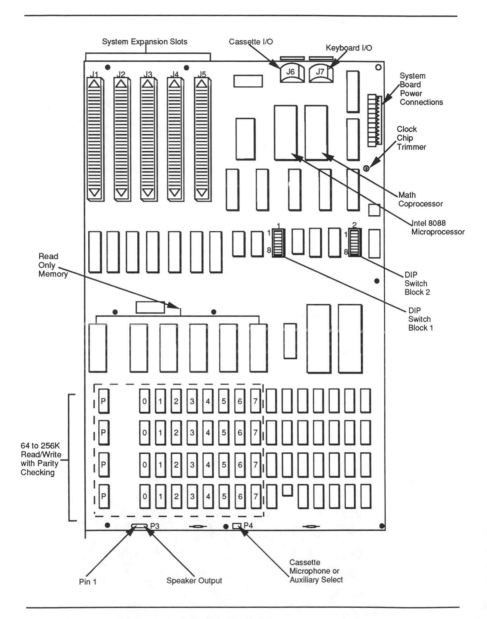

IBM PC system board component locations.

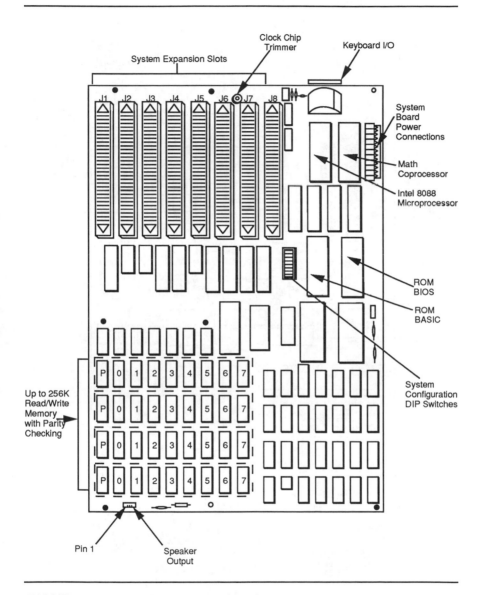

IBM XT system board component locations.

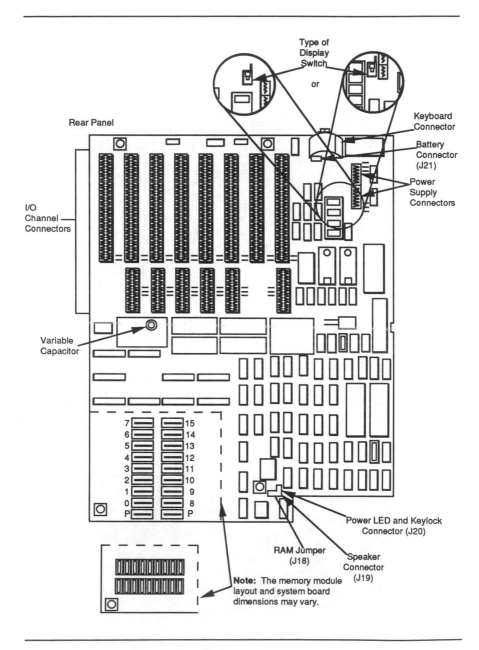

AT system board component locations.

IBM PC 16K-64K SWITCH SETTINGS

Function	Switch block 1								Switch block 2							
	1-1	1-2	1-3	1-4	1-5	1-6	1-7	1-8	2-1	2-2	2-3	2-4	2-5	2-6	2-7	2-8
# of Floppy Drives:																
0 drives	ON						ON	ON								
1 drive	OFF						ON	ON								
2 drives	OFF						OFF	ON								
Display Monitor Type:																
No display					ON	ON										
EGA Display					ON	ON										
CGA 40 × 25					OFF	ON										
CGA 80 × 25					ON	OFF										
Monochrome					OFF	OFF										
8087 Coprocessor:																
Installed		OFF														
Not Installed		ON														
Total System RAM:																
16K			ON	ON					ON	ON	ON	ON	ON	OFF	OFF	OFF
32K			OFF	ON					ON	ON	ON	ON	ON	OFF	OFF	OFF

IBM PC 16K-64K SWITCH SETTINGS (Continued)

Function	Switch block 1								Switch block 2							
	1-1	1-2	1-3	1-4	1-5	1-6	1-7	1-8	2-1	2-2	2-3	2-4	2-5	2-6	2-7	2-8
48K			ON	OFF					ON	ON	ON	ON	ON	OFF	OFF	OFF
64K			OFF	OFF					ON	ON	ON	ON	ON	OFF	OFF	OFF
96K			OFF	OFF					OFF	ON	ON	ON	ON	OFF	OFF	OFF
128K			OFF	OFF					ON	OFF	ON	ON	ON	OFF	OFF	OFF
160K			OFF	OFF					OFF	OFF	ON	ON	ON	OFF	OFF	OFF
192K			OFF	OFF					ON	ON	OFF	ON	ON	OFF	OFF	OFF
224K			OFF	OFF					OFF	ON	OFF	ON	ON	OFF	OFF	OFF
256K			OFF	OFF					ON	OFF	OFF	ON	ON	OFF	OFF	OFF
288K			OFF	OFF					OFF	OFF	OFF	ON	ON	OFF	OFF	OFF
320K			OFF	OFF					ON	ON	ON	OFF	ON	OFF	OFF	OFF
352K			OFF	OFF					OFF	ON	ON	OFF	ON	OFF	OFF	OFF
384K			OFF	OFF					ON	OFF	ON	OFF	ON	OFF	OFF	OFF
416K			OFF	OFF					OFF	OFF	ON	OFF	ON	OFF	OFF	OFF
448K			OFF	OFF					ON	ON	OFF	OFF	ON	OFF	OFF	OFF
480K			OFF	OFF					OFF	ON	OFF	OFF	ON	OFF	OFF	OFF
512K			OFF	OFF					ON	OFF	OFF	OFF	ON	OFF	OFF	OFF
544K			OFF	OFF					OFF	OFF	OFF	OFF	ON	OFF	OFF	OFF
576K			OFF	OFF					ON	ON	ON	ON	OFF	OFF	OFF	OFF
608K			OFF	OFF					OFF	ON	ON	ON	OFF	OFF	OFF	OFF
640K			OFF	OFF					ON	OFF	ON	ON	OFF	OFF	OFF	OFF

Note: PC-1 (16K–64K) must have a BIOS dated 10/27/82 or later to support RAM greater than 544K.

IBM PC 64K-256K SWITCH SETTINGS

Function	Switch block 1								Switch block 2							
	1-1	1-2	1-3	1-4	1-5	1-6	1-7	1-8	2-1	2-2	2-3	2-4	2-5	2-6	2-7	2-8
# of Floppy Drives:																
0 drives	ON						ON	ON					OFF	OFF	OFF	OFF
1 drive	OFF						ON	ON					OFF	OFF	OFF	OFF
2 drives	OFF						OFF	ON					OFF	OFF	OFF	OFF
Display Monitor Type:																
No display					ON	ON							OFF	OFF	OFF	OFF
EGA Display					ON	ON							OFF	OFF	OFF	OFF
CGA 40 × 25					OFF	ON							OFF	OFF	OFF	OFF
CGA 80 × 25					ON	OFF							OFF	OFF	OFF	OFF
Monochrome					OFF	OFF							OFF	OFF	OFF	OFF
8087 Coprocessor:																
Installed		OFF											OFF	OFF	OFF	OFF
Not Installed		ON											OFF	OFF	OFF	OFF

317

IBM PC 64K-256K SWITCH SETTINGS (Continued)

Function	Switch block 1								Switch block 2							
	1-1	1-2	1-3	1-4	1-5	1-6	1-7	1-8	2-1	2-2	2-3	2-4	2-5	2-6	2-7	2-8
Total System RAM:																
64K			OFF	OFF					ON	ON	ON	ON	ON	OFF	OFF	OFF
128K			OFF	OFF					ON	OFF	ON	ON	ON	OFF	OFF	OFF
192K			OFF	OFF					ON	ON	OFF	ON	ON	OFF	OFF	OFF
256K			OFF	OFF					ON	OFF	OFF	ON	ON	OFF	OFF	OFF
320K			OFF	OFF					ON	ON	ON	OFF	ON	OFF	OFF	OFF
384K			OFF	OFF					ON	OFF	ON	OFF	ON	OFF	OFF	OFF
448K			OFF	OFF					ON	ON	OFF	OFF	ON	OFF	OFF	OFF
512K			OFF	OFF					ON	OFF	OFF	OFF	ON	OFF	OFF	OFF
576K			OFF	OFF					ON	ON	ON	ON	OFF	OFF	OFF	OFF
640K			OFF	OFF					ON	OFF	ON	ON	OFF	OFF	OFF	OFF

IBM EXPANSION UNIT EXTENDER CARD SWITCH SETTINGS

If an IBM expansion unit is installed, the extender card (the card that installs in one of the slots in the PC) must be configured for total system memory by setting four switches on the switch block.

		Switch settings			
Total system memory	Memory Segment	SW-1	SW-2	SW-3	SW-4
16K to 64K	1	ON	ON	ON	OFF
96K to 128K	2	ON	ON	OFF	ON
160K to 192K	3	ON	ON	OFF	OFF
224K to 256K	4	ON	OFF	ON	ON
288K to 320K	5	ON	OFF	ON	OFF
352K to 384K	6	ON	OFF	OFF	ON
416K to 448K	7	ON	OFF	OFF	OFF
480K to 512K	8	OFF	ON	ON	ON
544K to 576K	9	OFF	ON	ON	OFF
608K to 644K	A	OFF	ON	OFF	ON

IBM XT SWITCH SETTINGS

	Switch block							
Function	**SW-1**	**SW-2**	**SW-3**	**SW-4**	**SW-5**	**SW-6**	**SW-7**	**SW-8**
Run P.O.S.T. continuously								
Loop	ON							
Do Not Loop	OFF							
# of Diskette Drives:								
1 Drive							ON	ON
2 Drives							OFF	ON
3 Drives							ON	OFF
4 Drives							OFF	OFF
Display Monitor Type:								
No display					ON	ON		
EGA Display					ON	ON		
CGA 40 × 25					OFF	ON		
CGA 80 × 25					ON	OFF		
Monochrome					OFF	OFF		
8087 Coprocessor:								
Installed		OFF						
Not Installed		ON						
Total System RAM:								
128K			OFF	ON				
192K			ON	OFF				
256K and Greater			OFF	OFF				

IBM EGA CARD SWITCHES & JUMPERS

Jumpers P1 and P3 control the type of display being used.

Type of display	P1	P3
Color or Mono	2 & 3	1 & 2
Enhanced Color	1 & 2	1 & 2

If the EGA card is the only adapter installed, or if it is installed with a monochrome adapter, use the following chart to determine the correct switch settings:

Type of display on EGA card	EGA Primary				EGA Secondary			
	SW1	SW2	SW3	SW4	SW1	SW2	SW3	SW4
No Display					OFF	ON	ON	ON
Monochrome Display	OFF	OFF	ON	OFF				
Color Display 40 × 25 Mode	ON	OFF	OFF	ON	ON	ON	ON	ON
Color Display 80 × 25 Mode	OFF	OFF	OFF	ON	OFF	ON	ON	ON
Enhanced - Normal Mode	ON	ON	ON	OFF	ON	OFF	ON	ON
Enhanced - Enhanced Mode	OFF	ON	ON	OFF	OFF	OFF	ON	ON

If the EGA board is installed along with a Color/Graphics board, use the following chart:

Type of display on EGA card	EGA Primary				EGA Secondary			
	SW1	SW2	SW3	SW4	SW1	SW2	SW3	SW4
Color Display - 40 × 25 Mode	ON	OFF	ON	OFF	ON	ON	OFF	ON
Color Display - 80 × 25 Mode	OFF	OFF	ON	OFF	OFF	ON	OFF	ON
No Display - 80 × 25 Mode	OFF	OFF	ON	OFF				

LOOP BACK PLUG (WRAP PLUG) PIN OUTS

These are the pinouts for a set of loop back plugs to use with the Advanced Diagnostics for Compaq and IBM systems. These plugs may not work with diagnostics from other sources.

There is a 25-pin male for testing the parallel port, a 25-pin female for testing the 25-pin serial port, and a 9-pin female for testing the 9-pin serial port found on the AT and some portables. You will also need hoods to protect the wiring and simplify handling.

Connectors are available from Radio Shack. The cost of the parts will be under $10.

The jumpering of the pins are as follows:

PARALLEL PORT (25-PIN MALE)

1 - 13
2 - 15
10 - 16
11 - 17
12 - 14

SERIAL PORT (25-PIN FEMALE)

1 - 7
2 - 3
4 - 5 - 8
6 - 20*
11 - 22*
15 - 17 - 23
18 - 25

* *Note:* Connect a 3.9K OHM resistor from pins 6 & 20 to pins 11 & 22.

SERIAL PORT (9-PIN FEMALE)

1 - 7 - 8
2 - 3
4 - 6 - 9

I/O PORT CONNECTOR PIN ASSIGNMENTS

PARALLEL PORT PIN ASSIGNMENTS (25 PIN)

Pin	Signal name	
1	– Strobe	→
2	+ Data Bit 0	→
3	+ Data Bit 1	→
4	+ Data Bit 2	→
5	+ Data Bit 3	→
6	+ Data Bit 4	→
7	+ Data Bit 5	→
8	+ Data Bit 6	→
9	+ Data Bit 7	→
10	– Acknowledge	←
11	+ Busy	←
12	+ Paper Out	←
13	+ Select	←
14	– Auto Feed	←
15	– Error	←
16	– Initialize Printer	→
17	– Select Input	→
18-25	Ground	

SERIAL PORT PIN ASSIGNMENTS (9 PIN)

Pin	Signal name	
1	Carrier Detect (DCD)	←
2	Receive Data (RX)	←
3	Transmit Data (TX)	→
4	Data Terminal Ready (DTR)	→
5	Signal Ground (SG)	
6	Data Set Ready (DSR)	←
7	Request to Send (RTS)	→
8	Clear to Send (CTS)	←
9	Ring Indicator (RI)	←

SERIAL PORT PIN ASSIGNMENTS (25 PIN)

Pin	Signal name	
1	Frame Ground (FG)	
2	Transmit Data (TXD)	→
3	Receive Data (RXD)	←
4	Request to Send (RTS)	→
5	Clear to Send (CTS)	←
6	Data Set Ready (DSR)	←
7	Signal Ground (SG)	
8	Carrier Detect (CD)	←
9	Reserved	
10	Reserved	
11	Unassigned	
12	Secondary Carrier Detect (SCD)	←
13	Secondary Clear to Send (SCTS)	←
14	Secondary Transmit Data (STXD)	→
15	Transmitter Clock (TC)	←
16	Secondary Receive Data (SRXD)	←
17	Receiver Clock (RC)	→
18	Unassigned	
19	Secondary Request to Send (SRTS)	→
20	Data Terminal Ready (DTR)	→
21	Signal Quality Detector (SO)	←
22	Ring Indicator (RI)	←
23	Data Rate Selector	→
24	External Transmitter Clock (ETC)	→
25	Unassigned	

PARALLEL PORT PIN ASSIGNMENTS (36 PIN)

Pin	Signal name
1	Strobe
2	Data Bit 0
3	Data Bit 1
4	Data Bit 2
5	Data Bit 3
6	Data Bit 4
7	Data Bit 5
8	Data Blt 6
9	Data Bit 7
10	Acknowledge
11	Busy
12	Paper Out
13	Select
14	Auto Feed
15	No Connection
16	Logic Ground
17	Chassis Ground
18	No Connection
19	Strobe Return (Ground)
20	Data Bit 0 Return (Ground)
21	Data Bit 1 Return (Ground)
22	Data Bit 2 Return (Ground)
23	Data Bit 3 Return (Ground)
24	Data Bit 4 Return (Ground)
25	Data Bit 5 Return (Ground)
26	Data Bit 6 Return (Ground)
27	Data Bit 7 Return (Ground)
28	Acknowledge Return (Ground)
29	Busy Return (Ground)
30	Paper Out Return (Ground)
31	Initialize Printer
32–36	No Connection

AST SIX PAK PLUS SWITCH AND JUMPER SETTINGS

Starting address of card	Switches 1	2	3	Maximum RAM on card	Banks installed on card	Switches 4	5	6	Total RAM on card
64KB (:10000)	OFF	OFF	OFF	384KB	NONE	OFF	OFF	OFF	0KB
128KB (:20000)	OFF	OFF	ON	384KB	1	OFF	OFF	ON	64KB
192KB (:30000)	OFF	ON	OFF	384KB	2 (1 & 2)	OFF	ON	OFF	128KB
256KB (:40000)	OFF	ON	ON	384KB	3 (1 - 3)	OFF	ON	ON	192KB
320KB (:50000)	ON	OFF	OFF	320KB	4 (1 - 4)	ON	OFF	OFF	256KB
384KB (:60000)	ON	OFF	ON	256KB	5 (1 - 5)	ON	OFF	ON	320KB
448KB (:70000)	ON	ON	OFF	192KB	6 (1 - 6)	ON	ON	OFF	384KB
512KB (:80000)	ON	ON	ON	128KB					

JUMPERS:

IRQ4 must be enabled for COM1 to be active

IRQ3 must be enabled for COM2 to be active

IRQ7 must be enabled for LPT1 to be active

SWITCHES:

Switches 1, 2, and 3 control the starting address of the RAM on the SixPak Plus board.

Switches 4, 5, and 6 allow configuration for the number of banks of RAM installed on the board.

Switch 7 is not used.

Switch 8 is used for parity checking: OFF = Parity Check Disabled, ON = Parity Check Enabled.

VGA CARD PINOUTS

Pin	Function
1	Red Video
2	Green Video
3	Blue Video
4	Monitor ID Bit 2
5	Ground
6	Red Return (Ground)
7	Green Return (Ground)
8	Blue Return (Ground)
9	Key
10	Sync Return (Ground)
11	Monitor ID Bit 0
12	Monitor ID Bit 1
13	Horizontal Sync
14	Vertical Sync
15	Not Used

Note: Monochrome-type monitors use Green Video for all video input and ignore Red and Blue Video signals.

PRACTICAL MODEM 1200 DIP SWITCH SETTINGS

Port/Function	SW-1	SW-2	SW-3	SW-4	SW-5	SW-6
COM1	ON	ON	ON	OFF		
COM2	OFF	ON	OFF	ON		
COM3	ON	OFF	ON	OFF		
COM4	OFF	OFF	OFF	ON		
Ignore DTR					ON	
Support DTR					OFF	
DCD always true						ON
DCD true if connected						OFF

HEXADECIMAL NUMBERS

HEXADECIMAL or "HEX" is a computer-oriented numbering system that allows the representation of a BYTE (8 BITS) to be shortened from 8 binary characters to 2 hex characters. The decimal numbering system uses 10 characters (0–9) to represent the 10 digit values. Decimal is a base 10 system. The BINARY system uses 2 characters (0–1) to represent the 2 digit values. This is called a base 2 numbering system. HEX is a base 16 system. The characters 0–9, and A–F represent the values of 0–15.

HEX, DECIMAL, AND BINARY RELATIONSHIPS.

Hex digit	decimal	binary	value
0	0	0000	Zero
1	1	0001	One
2	2	0010	Two
3	3	0011	Three
4	4	0100	Four
5	5	0101	Five
6	6	0110	Six
7	7	0111	Seven
8	8	1000	Eight
9	9	1001	Nine
A	10	1010	Ten
B	11	1011	Eleven
C	12	1100	Twelve
D	13	1101	Thirteen
E	14	1110	Fourteen
F	15	1111	Fifteen

The conversion is performed by starting with the right-most character and working to the left. To convert the hex number CA7FB to decimal, look up B in the first column (11), F0 in the second column (240), 700 in the third column (1,792), A000 in the fourth column (40,960), and C0000 in the fifth column (786,432). Add the five numbers together to get the decimal equivalent of CA7FB, which is 829,435.

To convert the decimal number 846,523 to hex, look up the largest number in the table that is not greater than our decimal number (786,432). Subtract the number in the table from our decimal number and write down the hex equivalent (C0000). The remainder is 60,091. Repeat the subtraction until the remainder is zero. The hex equivalent for 846,523 is CEABB.

DECIMAL, HEXADECIMAL, AND CHARACTER (ASCII) CODES

The ASCII (American Standard Code for Information Interchange) character set is a decimal representation of all of the characters that can be entered from the keyboard, plus a group of special nonkeyboard characters. The ASCII code is used for programming, mostly because it is easier to use than HEX. The ASCII characters 0 through 31 are control characters, and are different from the way that they appear on the screen.

HEX TO DECIMAL CONVERSION TABLE

Hex	Dec	Hex	Dec	Hex	Dec	Hex	Dec	Hex	Dec
1	1	10	16	100	256	1000	4,096	10000	65,536
2	2	20	32	200	512	2000	8,192	20000	131,072
3	3	30	48	300	768	3000	12,288	30000	196,608
4	4	40	64	400	1,024	4000	16,384	40000	262,144
5	5	50	80	500	1,280	5000	20,480	50000	327,680
6	6	60	96	600	1,536	6000	24,576	60000	393,216
7	7	70	112	700	1,792	7000	28,672	70000	458,752
8	8	80	128	800	2,048	8000	32,768	80000	524,288
9	9	90	144	900	2,304	9000	36,864	90000	589,824
A	10	A0	160	A00	2,560	A000	40,960	A0000	655,360
B	11	B0	176	B00	2,816	B000	45,056	B0000	720,896
C	12	C0	192	C00	3,072	C000	49,152	C0000	786,432
D	13	D0	208	D00	3,328	D000	53,248	D0000	851,968
E	14	E0	224	E00	3,584	E000	57,344	E0000	917,504
F	15	F0	240	F00	3,840	F000	61,440	F0000	983,040

Dec	Hex	Cha	Dec	Hex	Cha	Dec	Hex	Cha	Dec	Hex	Cha
0	00	^@	32	20		64	40	@	96	60	`
1	01	^A	33	21	!	65	41	A	97	61	a
2	02	^B	34	22	"	66	42	B	98	62	b
3	03	^C	35	23	#	67	43	C	99	63	c
4	04	^D	36	24	$	68	44	D	100	64	d
5	05	^E	37	25	%	69	45	E	101	65	e
6	06	^F	38	26	&	70	46	F	102	66	f
7	07	^G	39	27	~	71	47	G	103	67	g
8	08	^H	40	28	(	72	48	H	104	68	h
9	09	^I	41	29	)	73	49	I	105	69	i
10	0A	^J	42	2A	*	74	4A	J	106	6A	j
11	0B	^K	43	2B	+	75	4B	K	107	6B	k
12	0C	^L	44	2C	'	76	4C	L	108	6C	l
13	0D	^M	45	2D	-	77	4D	M	109	6D	m
14	0E	^N	46	2E	.	78	4E	N	110	6E	n
15	F0	^O	47	2F	/	79	4F	O	111	6F	o

Dec	Hex	Cha	Dec	Hex	Cha	Dec	Hex	Cha	Dec	Hex	Cha
16	10	^P	48	30	0	80	50	P	112	70	p
17	11	^Q	49	31	1	81	51	Q	113	71	q
18	12	^R	50	32	2	82	52	R	114	72	r
19	13	^S	51	33	3	83	53	S	115	73	s
20	14	^T	52	34	4	84	54	T	116	74	t
21	15	^U	53	35	5	85	55	U	117	75	u
22	16	^V	54	36	6	86	56	V	118	76	v
23	17	^W	55	37	7	87	57	W	119	77	w
24	18	^X	56	38	8	88	58	X	120	78	x
25	19	^Y	57	39	9	89	59	Y	121	79	y
26	1A	^Z	58	3A	:	90	5A	Z	123	7A	z
27	1B	^[	59	3B	;	91	5B	[	124	7B	{
28	1C	^\	60	3C	<	92	5C	\	125	7C	|
29	1D	^]	61	3D	=	93	5D	]	126	7D	}
30	1E	^^	62	3E	>	94	5E	^	127	7E	~
31	1F	^_	63	3F	?	95	5F	_	128	7F	

Resource List

The following list of resources is for reference only. Neither the publisher nor the author endorse any of the vendors mentioned or their products or services. If you are interested in any information about these products or services, contact the vendor directly. Resources are listed in alphabetical order by product or service. Some of the companies listed may have moved, merged, changed their telephone numbers, or discontinued their business since this list was published. Some of the resources provide BBS (bulletin-board-services) for downloading information or utility software. Some manufacturers provide technical support for their authorized dealers. There may be an access charge for some of the bulletin-boards.

BATTERIES

Computer Component Source, Inc., 135 Eileen Way, Syosset, NY 11791, 800-356-1227 or 516-496-8727

ELS, 2420 Park Central Blvd., Decatur, GA 30035, 800-334-5066

Fedco Electronics, Inc., P.O. Box 1403, Fond du Lac, WI 54936, 414-922-6490 or 800-542-9761, FAX 414-922-6750

Lamp Technology, Inc., Bohemia, NY 11716, 516-567-1800 or 800-533-7548, FAX 516-567-1806

Micro Power Electronics, Beaverton, OR, 800-642-7612, FAX 503-643-1556

Plainview Batteries, Inc., 23 Newtown Rd., Plainview, NY 11803, 516-249-2873, FAX 516-249-2876

Tadiran, 21303 Sherman Way, Canoga Park, CA 91303, 818-887-3337 or 800-234-2444, FAX 818-887-1686

BIOS (ROM BIOS) MANUFACTURERS

American Megatrends, Inc. (AMI), 1346 Oakbrook Drive, Suite 120, Norcross, GA 30093, 404-263-8181

Award Software, Inc., 130 Knowles Drive, Los Gatos, CA 95030, 408-370-7979

Phoenix Technologies Ltd., 846 University Ave., Norwood, MA 02062, 617-551-4000

BOARD (EXPANSION) MANUFACTURERS

Aamazing Technologies Corp., 5980 Lakeshore Drive, Cypress, CA 90630, 714-826-9680 or 800-821-2711, FAX 714-826-9681

Apricorn, 10670 Treena Street, San Diego, CA 92131, 800-458-5448

Artisoft, 691 East River Road, Tucson, AZ 85704, 602-293-4000, Technical Support 602-293-6363, FAX 602-293-8065

AST Research, 2121 Alton Ave., Irvine, CA 92714, 714-863-1333

ATI Technologies, Inc., 3761 Victoria Park Avenue, Scarborough, Ontario Canada M1W 3S2, 416-756-0718, User Support 416-756-0711,

BlueLynx, 800-832-4526

Boca Research, Inc., 6413 Congress Avenue, Boca Raton, FL 33487, 407-997-6227, FAX 407-997-0918

Creative Labs, Inc., Santa Clara, CA, 408-986-1461

Cumulus Corp., 216-247-2236

DCA, 1000 Alderman Dr., Alpharetta, GA 30201, 404-442-4416 or 800-322-0058 (IRMA BOARDS)

Emulex Corp., 3545 Harbor Blvd., Costa Mesa, CA 92626, 800-368-5393

Everex Systems, Inc., 48431 Milmont Dr., Fremont, CA 94538, 800-356-4283 FAX 416-756-0720

Future Domain, 2801 McGaw Avenue, Irvine, CA 92714, 800-879-7599

Hercules, 2550 Ninth Street, Berkeley, CA 94710, 415-540-6000

IDEASSOCIATES, Inc., 29 Dunham Road, Billerica, MA 01821, 617-663-6878 or 800-257-5027

Intel Corp., 5200 N. E. Elam Young Pkwy., Hillsboro, OR 97124, 503-629-7354 or 800-548-4725

Kingston Technology Corporation, 17600 Newhope St., Fountain Valley, CA 92708, 714-435-2600 or 800-835-6575, FAX 714-435-2699

Microsoft, 206-454-2030

NSI Logic, Inc., 257-B Cedar Hill Rd., Marlboro, MA 01752, 617-460-0717

Orchid, 45365 Northport Loop West, Fremont, CA 94538, 415-683-0300

Paradise Systems, 217 East Grand Ave., South San Francisco, CA 94080, 415-588-6000

Persyst, 3545 Harbor Gateway, Suite 101, Costa Mesa, CA 92626, 714-662-5600 or 800-854-7112

Quadram, 1 Quad Way, Norcross, GA 30093, 404-923-6666, FAX 404-564-5528

Quickpath Systems, 44053 S. Grimmer Blvd., Fremont, CA 94538, 510-651-8848

Sigma Designs, Inc., 46501 Landing Pkwy., Fremont, CA 94538, 415-770-0100

Stac Electronics, 5993 Avenida Encinas, Carlsbad, CA 92008, 619-431-7474

STB Systems, 1651 N. Glenville - Suite 210, Richardson, TX 75081, 214-234-8750

Tecmar, 6225 Cochran Rd., Solon, OH 44139, 216-349-0600 or 800-624-8560

Video Seven, Inc., 46335 Landing Pkwy., Fremont, CA 94538, 415-656-7800

Vu-tek Systems, 10855 Sorrento Valley Rd., San Diego, CA 92121, 619-587-2800

Western Digital Imaging/Paradise, 800 E. Middlefield Rd., Mountain View, CA 94043, 415-960-3360 or 800-356-5787

BOARD REPAIR

A. I. C., Inc., 1003 Bayview Overlook, Stafford, VA 22554, 703-659-0031

Accu-tek Service, Inc., 25365 Dequindre, Madison Heights, MI 48071, 313-542-9960

Advanced Video Technology, Inc., 1310 S. Dixie Hwy., Ste. 18W, Pompano Beach, FL 33060, 305-785-2490

Albany Microcomputer Services, 12553 San Pablo Ave., Richmond, CA 94805, 415-253-5935

Alchemitron, Inc., 1435 Holmes Rd., Elgin, IL 60123, 312-697-2024

Amcom Corp., 6205 Bury Dr., Eden Prairie, MN 55346, 612-949-9400 or 800-328-7723 (IBM parts)

American Digital, 82 Winchester St., Newton, MA 02161, 617-964-5270

American Computer Repair, Inc., RD6 Farm Bureau Rd., Allentown, PA 18106, 215-391-0100

American Computer Engineers, 11175 Flintkote Ave., Ste. F, San Diego, CA 92121, 619-587-9002

American Computer Hardware, 2205 S. Wright St., Santa Ana, CA 92705, 714-549-2688 or 800-447-1237

Amtec Computer Systems, 8515 Douglas, #17, Des Moines, IA 50322, 515-270-2480

Area TV & Computers, 561 E. 12 St., Erie, PA 16503, 814-453-4200

Avnet Computer Technologies, Inc., 10000 W. 76th St., Eden Prairie, MN 55344, 800-877-2285

BBS, 10649 Haddington #180, Houston, TX 77043, 800-683-2044

Broder Enterprises, 2648-A Brenner Dr., Dallas, TX 75220, 214-350-0501

C. Hoelzle Associates, Inc., 2632 S. Croddy Way, Santa Ana, CA 92704

C.N. Services of Florida, 504 S. Federal Hwy., Deerfield Beach, FL 33441, 305-481-3683

C3, Inc., 460 Herndon Pkwy., Herndon, VA 22070, 703-471-6000

Century Data Systems, 506 N. Harrington St., Raleigh, NC 27603, 919-821-5696

Century Computer Marketing Service Div., 4755 Alla Rd., Marina Del Rey, CA 90292, 213-827-0999

Circuit Test, Inc., 12749 W. Hillsborough Ave., Tampa, FL 33635, 813-855-6685

Cirvis, Inc., 5082 Bolsa Ave., Ste. 112, Huntington Beach, CA 92649, 714-891-2000

CJF Enterprises, Inc., 4834 NE 12 Ave., Ft. Lauderdale, FL 33334, 305-491-1850

CNS, 21 Pine St., Rockaway, NJ 07866, 201-625-4056

Coastal Electronics, 8 Mall Ct., Savannah, GA 31406, 912-352-1444

Communications Test Design, Inc., 1373 Enterprise Dr., West Chester, PA 19380, 215-436-5203 or 800-223-3910

Compufix, Inc., 4 W. Chimney Rock Rd., Bound Brook, NJ 08805, 201-271-0020

Compupair, Inc., 7808 Cherry Creek So. Dr., #102, Denver, CO 80231, 303-368-4541

Computer Maintenance Service, 7930 Alabama Ave., Canoga Park, CA 91304, 818-347-3588

Computer Maintenance Co., 1636 Wilshire Blvd., Los Angeles, CA 90017, 213-483-2400

Computer Technology Services, Inc., 15801 Rockfield Blvd., Ste. L, Irvine, CA 92718, 714-855-8667

Computer Service Supply Corp., P.O. Box 673, Londonderry, NH 03053, 603-437-0634 or 800-255-7815

Computer Care, Inc., 1116 Smith St., Room 213, Charleston, WV 25301, 304-340-4283

Computer Commodities, 7573 Golden Triangle Dr., Minneapolis, MN 55344, 612-942-0992

Computer Labs, Inc., 14 River St., Baldwinsville, NY 13027, 315-635-7236

Computer Doctor, 4801A Burnet Rd., Austin, TX 78756, 512-467-9355

Computer Exchange Repair, Inc., 42 Donald St., Clifton, NJ 07011, 201-340-2662

Comstar, Inc., 5250 W. 74th St., Minneapolis, MN 55435, 800-735-5502

Cosmic Enterprises, Inc., 84 South St., Hopkinton, MA 01748, 508-435-6967

Cosmic Services, Inc., 3750 Hacienda Blvd., Ste. F, Ft. Lauderdale, FL 33314, 305-797-0143

CPR, 641 E. Walnut St., Carson, CA 90746, 213-538-1900

Crisis Computer Corp., 2298 Quimby Rd., San Jose, CA 95122, 800-729-0729

CRT Systems, Inc., 3071 Research Dr., Richmond, CA 94806, 415-262-1730

Daisy Disc Corp., P.O. Box 5150, Salisbury, MA 01952, 508-462-3475

Data Products Corp., 6219 DeSoto Ave., Woodland Hills, CA 91367, 818-887-3909

Data Systems Maintenance, 4551 Ponce de Leon Blvd., Coral Gables, FL 33146, 305-665-3626

Data Exchange Corp., 708 Via Alondra, Camarillo, CA 93010, 805-388-1711

Datagate, Inc., 1971 Tarob Ct., Milpitas, CA 95035, 408-946-6222

Dataserv, 12125 Technology Dr., Eden Prairie, MN 55344, 612-829-6000 or 800-245-7378

Datatech Depot, Inc., 1081 N. Shepard St., Anaheim, CA 92806, 714-632-1800

Digital Repair Corp., 8918 Tesoro Dr., Suite 108, San Antonio, TX 78217, 512-828-2256

Digital Computer Service, 624 Krona Dr., Ste. 195, Plano, TX 75074, 214-422-1864

Digitronix, Inc., 9005 F St., Omaha, NE 68127, 402-339-5340

DJS Electronics, Inc., 589 Bethlehem Pike, Ste. 700, Montgomeryville, PA 18936, 215-822-5515

DMA, Inc., 611 Development Blvd., Amery, WI 54001, 715-268-8106

EDP Research & Development Co., 118 W. Pond Meadow, Westbrook, CT 06498, 203-399-5018

Efficient Field Service Corp., 11 School St., N. Chelmsford, MA 01863, 508-251-7800

Electronic Products Service, Inc., 6500 McDonough Dr., Ste. E-4, Norcross, GA 30093, 404-448-0748

Electroservice Laboratories, 6085 Sikorsky St., Ventura, CA 93003, 805-644-2944

ETI, Electro-Tech Industries, 101 State Pl., Bldg. B, Escondido, CA 92029, 619-745-3575

Federated Consultants, Inc., 2306 Country Valley Rd., Garland, TX 75041, 800-443-6400

FRS, Inc., 1101 National Dr., Sacramento, CA 95834, 916-928-1107

GE Computer Service, 6875 Jimmy Carter Blvd., Norcross, GA 30071, 800-GESERVE

General Diagnostics, Inc., 1515 W. 190th St., Ste. 20, Gardena, CA 90248, 213-715-1222

Genicom Corp., Genicom Dr., Turner #3, Waynesboro, VA 22980, 703-949-1000

Hanson Data Systems, Inc., 734 Forest St., Marlboro, MA 01752, 617-481-3901

Hard Drive Associates, 3323 SE 17th Ave., Portland, OR 97202

Hayes Instruments Service, 530 Boston Rd., Billerica, MA 01821, 508-663-4800

Headmaster Repair, Inc., 1330 Memorex Dr., Santa Clara, CA 95050, 408-988-7600

Hi-Tek Services, Inc., 32970 Alvarado-Niles Rd., #720, Union City, CA 94587, 415-489-8909

Hyland/Rice Business Systems, 112 River St., Valley W. Plaza, Fitchburg, MA 01420, 617-342-9707

ICSS, 400 Devon Park Dr., Wayne, PA 19087, 215-687-0900

Iicon Corp., 16040 Caputo Dr., Morgan Hill, CA 95037, 408-779-7466

Images-Ink, 14180 E. Firestone Blvd., Santa Fe Springs, CA 90670, 213-926-6842

Independent Computer Support Services, Inc., 400 Devon Park Dr., Wayne, PA 19087, 215-687-0900

Independent Technology Service, 9146 Jordan Ave., Chatsworth, CA 91311, 818-882-7747

INTEC, 1008 Astoria Blvd., Cherry Hill, NJ 08003, 800-225-1187

Integrated Computer Services, Inc., 14180 Live Oak Blvd., Ste. B, Baldwin Park, CA 91706, 818-960-1921

Intelogic Trace, Turtle Creek Tower I, P.O. Box 400044, San Antonio, TX 78229, 800-531-7186

JC Enterprises, P.O. Box 4172, Dept. 363, Woodland Hills, CA 91364, 818-773-0296

Lasersource Dept., 18 Corporate Circle, East Syracuse, NY 13057, 315-463-6090

Lupac Computer Parts & Services USA, Inc., 21345 Lassen St., Chatsworth, CA 91311, 818-709-2621

Magnetic Data, Inc., 6978 Shady Oak Rd., Eden Prairie, MN 55344, 612-944-0842

Manufacturers Equipment Repair Group, 3860 Trade Center Dr., Ann Arbor, MI 48104, 313-429-4028

Micro Medics, 7041 Jackson, Warren, MI 48091, 313-759-0231

Micro Products Repair Center, Inc., 405 Murray Hill Pkwy., E. Rutherford, NJ 07073, 201-896-1810

Micro Medic, Inc., 22515 Aspan, Ste. G, El Toro, CA 92630, 714-581-3651

Microlife Corp., 537 Olathe, Ste. F, Aurora, CO 80011, 303-367-8333

Midwest Service Management, 26 N. Park Pl., Newark, OH 43055, 614-345-9843

Modumend, Inc., 30961 Agoura Rd. #311, Westlake Village, CA 91361, 818-889-5550

Morrow Microcomputer Service, Inc., 1232-D Village Way, Santa Ana, CA 92705, 714-834-1351

NBSS, 8639 Loch Raven Blvd., Baltimore, MD 21204, 301-665-8870

Nordisk Systems, Inc., 11807 E. Smith St., Santa Fe, CA 90670, 213-942-1797

Northeast Technical Services, 146 Londonderry Tpke., Hooksett, NH 03106, 800-537-0359

Northstar MatrixServ, 8055 Ranchers Rd., Minneapolis, MN 55432, 800-537-0359

Nova Technology Services, 7509 Connelle Dr., Hanover, MD 21076, 800-523-2773

Novadyne Computer Systems, Inc., 1775 E. St. Andrews Pl., Santa Ana, CA 92705, 714-566-4965

On Board Electronics, 250 Main St., Beacon Falls, CT 06403, 203-729-4503

P.C.S., 6782 Sunnybrook Dr., Frederick, MD 21701, 301-695-9577

PC Repair Corporation, 2010 State St., Harrisburg, PA 17103, 717-232-7272 or 800-727-3724

Peripheral Solutions, Inc., 151 Harvey West Blvd., 8-B, Santa Cruz, CA 95060, 408-425-8280

Peripheral Parts Support, Inc., 219 Bear Hill Rd., Waltham, MA 02154, 617-890-9101

Peripheral Maintenance, Inc., 16 Passaic St., Fairfield, NJ 07006, 201-227-8411

Peripheral Computer Support, 1629 S. Main St., Milpitas, CA 95035, 408-263-4043

Princeton Computer Support, P.O. Box 7063, Princeton, NJ 08540, 609-921-8889

QIC Technology, Inc., 499 Salmar Ave., Ste. G, Campbell, CA 95008, 408-378-8330

Quality Repair Services, 45973 Warm Springs Blvd., Ste. 1, Fremont, CA 94539, 415-651-8486

R&M Associates, 330 Phillips Ave., S. Hackensack, NJ 07606, 201-440-8585

Raynet, 16810 Barker Springs Rd., Ste. 200, Houston, TX 77084, 713-578-3802

RBB Systems, Inc., 8767 T.R. 513, Shreve, OH 44676, 216-567-2906

React Computer Services, Inc., 865 N. Ellsworth, Villa Park, IL 60181, 708-832-1181

Repair Pro/D.S. Walker, 11210 Steeplecrest Dr., Houston, TX 77065, 800-262-7339

Restorr Magnetics, 1455 McCandless Dr., Milpitas, CA 95035, 408-946-9207

Rodax, Inc., 12366 Northup Way, Bellevue, WA 98005, 206-885-9999

Rotating Memory Repair, Inc., 23382 Madero, Mission Viejo, CA 92692, 714-472-0159

S.A.I.D., Inc., 417 West Broad St., Falls Church, VA 22046, 703-532-9190

Seagate, 12701 Whitewater Dr., Minnetonka, MN 55343, 800-382-6060

Sequel, Inc., 2300 Central Expwy., Santa Clara, CA 95054, 408-987-1401

Service 2000, Inc., 5301 E. River Rd., Suite 108, Minneapolis, MN 55421, 800-338-6824

Servitech, Inc., 1509 Brook Dr., Downers Grove, IL 60515, 708-620-8750

Servonics Corp., 14 Kendrick Rd., Wareham, MA 02571, 508-295-9089

SMH Electronics Co., 16 Kendrick Rd., Wareham, MA 02571, 508-291-7447

Solutronix, 7255 Flying Cloud Dr., Eden Prairie, MN 55344, 800-875-2580

Sprague Magnetics, Inc., 15720 Stagg St., Van Nuys, CA 91406, 800-325-4243

SRM, Inc., 2231 S. Oneida, Green Bay, WI 54304, 414-497-7863

Synergy Computer Services, Inc., 755 Queesnway E., Unit 26, Mississauga, ONT, CN L4 4C5, 416-273-9565

Systems Diagnosis, Inc., 3 Richmond Sq., Providence, RI 02906, 401-331-8980

Technical Sales & Service, 2820 Dorr Ave., Fairfax, VA 22031, 703-698-0347

Telford Technical Service, Inc., 9213 Fairview, Boise, ID 83704, 208-322-1434

Test Point Enterprise, 405 Unit F, River St., Warwick, RI 02886, 401-739-7900

The Repair Co., 1585 McCandless Dr., Milpitas, CA 95035, 408-946-5015

Total Maintenance Concepts, 746 Industrial Dr., Elmhurst, IL 60126

Trans Datacorp, 1200 O'Brien Dr., Menlo Park, CA 94025, 415-327-2692

Unicomp System, 11362 Westminster Ave., Ste. U, Garden Grove, CA 92643, 714-534-5092

Uptime Computer Support, 26366 Via Primero, Valencia, CA 91355, 805-254-3384

Valtron Technologies, Inc., 26074 Avenue Hall, Bldg. 23, Valencia, CA 91355, 805-257-0333

Victor Computer Service, Inc., 8125 Westglen Drive, Houston, TX 77063, 713-789-1888 or 800-999-1827

Welling Electronics, 529 No. 33, Omaha, NE 68131, 402-342-6564

Wisk Computer Services, Inc., 1605 Watt Dr., Santa Clara, CA 95054, 408-748-9891 or 800-688-9701

Yaltronics, Inc., 650 W. Smith Rd., Medina, OH 44256, 216-723-HELP

CABLES AND CONNECTORS

Basic Cable, 2023 N. Gateway #107, Fresno, CA 93727, 209-251-6402 or 800-227-9225

Communication Cable Co., P.O. Box 600, Wayne, PA 19087, 215-644-1900

CTI, 14792 Franklin Ave., Tustin, CA 92680, 714-669-1899

CTI, 300 McGraw Dr., Edison, NJ 08837, 201-225-1166

Data Spec, 9410 Owensmouth Ave., Chatsworth, CA 91313, 818-772-9177 or 800-431-8124

Greatlink Electronics USA, Inc., 1506 Centre Pointe Dr., Milpitas, CA 95035, 408-562-4133 or 800 326-4193 ($100 minimum order)

Jameco Electronics, 1355 Shoreway Rd., Belmont, CA 94002, 415-592-8097

MCM Electronics, 650 Congress Park Dr., Centerville, OH 45459, 513-434-0031 or 800-543-4330

MOD-TAP System, 285 Ayer Road, P.O. Box 706, Harvard, MA 01451-0706, 508-772-5630

Mouser Electronics, P.O. Box 699, Mansfield, TX 76063, 800-346-6873

Quality Computer Accessories, 800-766-3678 ($100 minimum order)

South Hills Electronics, 1936 W. Liberty Ave., Pittsburgh, PA 15226, 412-341-6200 or 800-245-6215

CATHODE RAY TUBES

Richardson Electronics, Ltd., 40W267 Keslinger Rd., LaFox, IL 60147, 708-208-2200 or 800-348-5580

Video Display Corporation (VDC), 1868 Tucker Industrial Dr., Tucker GA, 30084, 404-938-2080 or 800-241-5005

CD-ROM DRIVES

Chinon America, Inc., 660 Maple Avenue, Torrance, CA 90503, 213-533-0274 or 800-441-0222, FAX 213-533-1727

NEC, 800-632-4636

CHEMICALS

Chemtronics, Inc., 8125 Cobb Centre Drive, Kennesaw, GA 30144, 404-424-4888 or 800-645-5244

L&M Computer Products, 380 N.E. 191st St., Miami, FL 33179, 305-651-3885 or 800-544-2910

Rite Off, 1545 5th Industrial Court, Bay Shore, NY 11706, 516-665-6868 or 800-645-5853

COMPONENTS, SEMICONDUCTORS, FLYBACK TRANSFORMERS

All Electronics Corp., P.O. Box 567, Van Nuys, CA 91408-0567, 800-826-5432

B. G. Micro, P.O. Box 280298, Dallas, TX 75228, 214-271-5546

C.R.C. Components, 15308 East Valley Blvd., City of Industry, CA 91746, 818-330-1266 or 800-366-1272

Computer Component Source, Inc., 135 Eileen Way, Syosset, NY 11791, 516-496-8727 or 800-356-1227

Consolidated Electronics, Inc., 705 Watervliet Ave., Dayton, OH 45420, 513-252-5662 or 800-543-3568

International Components Marketing, 310-826-3116 or 800-748-6232, FAX 310-826-3395

Jameco Electronic Components, 1355 Shoreway Rd., Belmont, CA 94002, 415-592-8097

Lead Electronics, Inc., 5858 East Molloy Rd., Syracuse, NY 13211, 315-454-4544

MCM Electronics, 650 Congress Park Dr., Centerville, OH 45459, 513-434-0031 or 800-543-4330

Mouser Electronics, P.O. Box 699, Mansfield, TX 76063, 800-346-6873

Parts Express International, Inc., 340 East First St., Dayton, OH 45402, 513-222-0173 or 800-338-0531

Prelco Electronics, 605 Chestnut St., Union, NJ 07083, 201-851-8600

Syracuse Semiconductors, Inc., 4357 Jordan Rd., P.O. Box 746, Skaneateles, NY 13152, 315-685-0014

Video Display Corporation (VDC), 1868 Tucker Industrial Dr., Tucker GA, 30084, 404-938-2080 or 800-241-5005 (FLYBACKS)

DATA RECOVERY

American Computer Repair, Inc., 6330 Farm Bureau Rd., Allentown, PA 18106, 215-391-0100

Data Retrieval Services, Inc., 1250 Rogers St., Suite C, Clearwater, FL 34616, 813-461-5900

Data Retrieval Services, Inc., 11600 Washington Pl., Suite 112, Los Angeles, CA 90066, 213-398-2764

Magnetic Data, Inc., 6754 Shady Oak Rd., Eden Prairie, MN 55344, 612-942-4500 or 800-634-8355

Ontrack Data Recovery, Inc., 6321 Bury Dr., Eden Prairie, MN 55346, 612-937-1107 or 800-872-2599

Peripheral Repair Corp., 9233 Eton Ave., Chatsworth, CA 91311, 818-700-8482 or 800-627-3475

Valtron Technologies, Inc., 26074 Avenue Hall, Bldg. 23, Valencia, CA 91355, 805-257-0333

DIAGNOSTIC HARDWARE & SOFTWARE

Accurite Technologies, Inc., 231 Charcot Ave., San Jose, CA 95131, 408-433-1980

DiagSoft, Inc., 6001 Butler Ln., Scotts Valley, CA 95066, 408-438-8247 (QA-PLUS)

Dysan Corporation, 1244 Reamwood Ave., Sunnyvale, CA 94086, 408-734-1624

International Debug Tools, 6830 Champions Plaza Dr., Houston, TX 77069, 800-84DEBUG

Landmark, 703 Grand Central St., Clearwater, FL 34616, 813-443-1331

Micro 2000, Inc., 1100 East Broadway, Suite 300, Glendale, CA 91205-1316, 818-547-0125 (Micro-Scope)

PCS Diagnostics, Inc., 3825 Gilbert St., Suite 207, Shreveport, LA 71104, 318-861-5979 or 800-258-8283

Print Products International Inc., 8931 Brookville Rd., Silver Spring, MD 20910, 301-587-7824 or 800-638-2020

Techpro Corporation, P.O. Box 5294, Springfield, VA 22150, 703-550-8898 (PC TESTER)

Touchstone, 813-822-5646 (CHECKIT)

Ultra-X, 2005 De La Cruz Blvd., Suite 115, Santa Clara, CA 95050, 408-988-4721 or 800-722-3789, FAX 408-988-4849

Vista Microsystems, Inc., 6 Whipple St., North Attleboro, MA 02760, 508-695-8459

Windsor Technologies, Inc., 130 Alto Street, San Rafael, CA 94901, 415-456-2200 (PC-TECHNICIAN)

DISK DRIVE REPAIR

A. I. C., Inc., 1003 Bayview Overlook, Stafford, VA 22554, 703-659-0031

Abex Data Systems Inc., 1 Barnida Dr., East Hanover, NJ 07936, 201-887-2600

Accram, Inc., Computer Repair Center, 2901 W. Clarendon, Phoenix, AZ 85017, 602-264-0288

ACT Disk Drive Service, 800-626-2117

Adahk, Inc., 7260 Collamer Rd., East Syracuse, NY 13057, 315-656-3988 (FLOPPY DRIVES)

Albany Microcomputer Services, 12553 San Pablo Ave., Richmond, CA 94805, 415-253-5935 (FLOPPY DRIVES)

All Systems Go., 2441 Cheshire Bridge Rd., Suite 200, Atlanta, GA 30324, 404-329-4564 (HARD DRIVES)

Amcom Corp., 6205 Bury Dr., Eden Prairie, MN 55346, 612-949-9400 or 800-328-7723 (FLOPPY DRIVES)

American Digital, 82 Winchester St., Newton, MA 02161, 617-964-5270 (FLOP-PY DRIVES)

American Computer Repair, Inc., RD6 Farm Bureau Rd., Allentown, PA 18106, 215-391-0100

American Computer Engineers, 11175 Flintkote Ave., Ste. F, San Diego, CA 92121, 619-587-9002

Amtec Computer Systems, 8515 Douglas, #17, Des Moines, IA 50322, 515-270-2480

Area TV & Computers, 561 E. 12 St., Erie, PA 16503, 814-453-4200

Avnet Computer Technologies, Inc., 10000 W. 76th St., Eden Prairie, MN 55344, 800-877-2285

BBS, 10649 Haddington #180, Houston, TX 77043, 800-683-2044 (FLOPPY DRIVES)

BRC Electronics, 3361 Boyington, Ste. 160, Carrolton, TX 75006, 214-385-3561

Broder Enterprises, 2648-A Brenner Dr., Dallas, TX 75220, 214-350-0501 (FLOPPY DRIVES)

C. Hoelzle Associates, Inc., 2632 S. Croddy Way, Santa Ana, CA 92704

C3, Inc., 460 Herndon Pkwy., Herndon, VA 22070, 703-471-6000

Century Computer Marketing Service Div., 4755 Alla Rd., Marina Del Rey, CA 90292, 213-827-0999

Century Data Systems, 506 N. Harrington St., Raleigh, NC 27603, 919-821-5696

CNS, 21 Pine St., Rockaway, NJ 07866, 201-625-4056

Coastal Electronics, 8 Mall Ct., Savannah, GA 31406, 912-352-1444 (FLOPPY DRIVES)

Communications Test Design, Inc., 1373 Enterprise Drive, West Chester, PA 19380, 215-436-5203 or 800-223-3910

Compupair, Inc., 7808 Cherry Creek So. Dr., #102, Denver, CO 80231, 303-368-4541

Computer Maintenance Co., 1636 Wilshire Blvd., Los Angeles, CA 90017, 213-483-2400 (FLOPPY DRIVES)

Computer Care, Inc., 1116 Smith St., Room 213, Charleston, WV 25301, 304-340-4283

Computer Service Supply Corp., P.O. Box 673, Londonderry, NH 03053, 800-255-7815

Computer Field Services, Inc., 197 Main St., N. Reading, MA 01864, 508-664-2828 (HARD DRIVES)

Computer Exchange Repair, Inc., 42 Donald St., Clifton, NJ 07011, 201-340-2662

Computer Commodities International, 7573 Golden Triangle Dr., Minneapolis, MN 55344, 612-942-0992

Computer Doctor, 4801A Burnet Rd., Austin, TX 78756, 512-467-9355

Cosmic Services, Inc., 3750 Hacienda Blvd., Ste. F, Ft. Lauderdale, FL 33314, 305-797-0143 (FLOPPY DRIVES)

Cosmic Enterprises, Inc., 84 South St., Hopkinton, MA 01748, 508-435-6967 (HARD DRIVES)

Crisis Computer Corp., 2298 Quimby Rd., San Jose, CA 95122, 800-729-0729 (FLOPPY DRIVES)

CRT Systems, Inc., 3071 Research Dr., Richmond, CA 94806, 415-262-1730 (FLOPPY DRIVES)

Daisy Disc Corp., P.O. Box 5150, Salisbury, MA 01952, 508-462-3475 (HARD DRIVES)

Damomics Computer System, 111 N. Main St., Elmira, NY 14901, 607-732-5122

Data Systems Maintenance, 4551 Ponce de Leon Blvd., Coral Gables, FL 33146, 305-665-3626 (FLOPPY DRIVES)

Data Exchange Corp., 708 Via Alondra, Camarillo, CA 93010, 805-388-1711

Dataserv, 12125 Technology Dr., Eden Prairie, MN 55344, 612-829-6000

Datatech Depot, Inc., 1081 N. Shepard St., Anaheim, CA 92806, 714-632-1800

Digitronix, Inc., 9005 F. St., Omaha, NE 68127, 402-339-5340 (FLOPPY DRIVES)

Disk Drive Repair, Inc., 863 Industry Dr., Seattle, WA 98188, 206-575-3181

DMA, Inc., 611 Development Blvd., Amery, WI 54001, 715-268-8106

Drive Service Company, 3505 Cadillac Ave, Costa Mesa, CA 92626, 714-549-3475

Drive Service Company, 2122 Adams Ave., San Leandro, CA 94577, 415-430-0595

EDP Research & Development, 118 W. Pond Meadow, Westbrook, CT 06498, 203-399-5018 (FLOPPY DRIVES)

Efficient Field Service Corp., 11 School St., N. Chelmsford, MA 01863, 508-251-7800 (FLOPPY DRIVES)

Electronic Products Service, Inc., 6500 McDonough Dr. Ste. E-4, Norcross, GA 30093 (FLOPPY DRIVES)

ETI, Electro-Tech Industries, 101 State Pl., Bldg. B, Escondido, CA 92029, 619-745-3575

F-P Electronics, 6030 Ambler Dr., Mississauga, ONT, CN L4W 2PI, 416-624-3025

Federal Computer Service, Inc., 15338 Jordans Journey Dr., Centreville, VA 22020, 703-968-9444

Federated Consultants, Inc., 2306 Country Valley Rd., Garland, TX 75041, 800-443-6400 (FLOPPY DRIVES)

Fessenden Computers, 116 North 3rd St., Ozark, MO 65721, 417-485-2501 (HARD DRIVES)

FRS, Inc., 1101 National Dr., Sacramento, CA 95834, 916-928-1107

GE Computer Service, 6875 Jimmy Carter Blvd., Norcross, GA 30071, 800-GESERVE

General Disk Corp., 1530 Montague Expwy., San Jose, CA 95131, 408-432-0505 (HARD DRIVES)

General Diagnostics, Inc., 1515 W. 190th St., Ste 20, Gardena, CA 90248, 213-715-1222 (FLOPPY DRIVES)

Golden Coast Electronics, Inc., 4343 Viewridge Ave., San Diego, CA 92123, 619-268-8447 (FLOPPY DRIVES)

Hanson Data Systems, Inc., 734 Forest St., Marlboro, MA 01752, 617-481-3901

Hard Drive Associates, 3323 SE 17th Ave., Portland, OR 97202

Headmaster Repair, Inc., 1330 Memorex Dr., Santa Clara, CA 95050, 408-988-7600 (HARD DRIVES)

Hi-Tek Services, Inc., 32970 Alvarado-Niles Rd., #720, Union City, CA 94587, 415-489-8909 (FLOPPY DRIVES)

Hyland/Rice Business Systems, 112 River St., Valley W. Plaza, Fitchburg, MA 01420, 617-342-9707 (HARD DRIVE)

Images-Ink, 14180 E. Firestone Blvd., Santa Fe Springs, CA 90670, 213-926-6842 (FLOPPY DRIVES)

Independent Technology Service, 9146 Jordan Ave., Chatsworth, CA 91311, 818-882-7747

Independent Computer Support Services, Inc., 400 Devon Park Dr., Wayne, PA 19087, 215-687-0900 (FLOPPY DRIVES)

INTEC, 1008 Astoria Blvd. Cherry Hill, NJ 08003, 800-225-1187

Intelogic Trace, Turtle Creek Tower I, P.O. Box 400044, San Antonio, TX 78229, 800-531-7186

jb Technologies, Inc., 5105 Maureen La., Moorpark, CA 93021, 805-519-0908

JC Enterprises, P.O. Box 4172, Dept., 363, Woodland Hills, CA 91364, 818-773-0296

KCS Computer Service, Inc., 7462 Talbert Ave., Huntington Beach, CA 92647, 714-848-7971

Lupac Computer Parts & Services USA, Inc., 21345 Lassen St., Chatsworth, CA 91311, 818-709-2641

Magnetic Recovery Technologists, Inc., 25431 Rye Canyon Rd., Valencia, CA 91355, 805-257-2262

Magnetic Data, Inc., 6978 Shady Oak Rd., Eden Prairie, MN 55344, 612-944-0842

Manufacturers Equipment Repair Group, 3860 Trade Center Dr., Ann Arbor, MI 48104, 313-429-4028

Micro Clinic, 105 State St., Schenectady, NY 12305, 518-370-8092 (HARD DRIVES)

Micro Medics, 7041 Jackson, Warren, MI 48091, 313-759-0231

Micro Products Repair Center, Inc., 405 Murray Hill Pkwy., E. Rutherford, NJ 07073, 201-896-1810

Micro Medic, Inc., 22515 Aspan, Ste. G, El Toro, CA 92630, 714-581-3651

Monterey Computer Consulting, 149 Bonafacio Pl., Monterey, CA 93940, 408-394-5980 (FLOPPY DRIVES)

Morrow Microcomputer Service, Inc., 1232-D Village Way, Santa Ana, CA 92705, 714-834-1351

NBSS, 8639 Loch Raven Blvd., Baltimore, MD 21204, 301-665-8870

Nordisk Systems, Inc., 11807 E. Smith St., Santa Fe, CA 90670, 213-942-1797 (HARD DRIVES)

Northeast Technical Services, 146 Londonderry Tpke., Hooksett, NH 03106, 800-537-0359 (FLOPPY DRIVES)

Northstar MatrixServ, 8055 Ranchers Rd., Minneapolis, MN 55432, 800-969-0009 (FLOPPY DRIVES)

Nova Technology Services, 7509 Connelle Dr., Hanover, MD 21076, 800-523-2773 (FLOPPY DRIVES)

Novadyne Computer Systems, Inc., 1775 E. St. Andrews Pl., Santa Ana, CA 92705, 714-566-4965

On Board Electronics, 250 Main St., Beacon Falls, CT 06403, 203-729-4503 (FLOPPY DRIVES)

P.C.S., 6782 Sunnybrook Dr., Frederick, MD 21701, 301-695-9577 (HARD DRIVES)

PC Repair Corporation, 2010 State St., Harrisburg, PA 17103, 717-232-7272 or 800-727-3724

PCSI, 104 E. 23rd St., New York, NY 10010. 212-475-5575

Peripheral Solutions, Inc., 151 Harvey West Blvd., 8-B, Santa Cruz, CA 95060, 408-425-8280 (HARD DRIVES)

Peripheral Repair Corp., 9233 Eton Ave., Chatsworth, CA 91311, 800-627-DISK

Peripheral Computer Support, 1629 S. Main St., Milpitas, CA 95035, 408-263-4043 (HARD DRIVES)

Peripheral Parts Support, Inc., 219 Bear Hill Rd., Waltham, MA 02154, 617-890-9101

Peripherals, 1363 Logan Ave., Costa Mesa, CA 92626, 714-540-4925 (HARD DRIVES)

Precision Methods, Inc., 112 Juliad Ct., P.O. Box 5546, Fredericksburg, VA 22403, 703-339-7050 (HARD DRIVES)

Premier Computer Corp., 8200 Normandale Blvd., Minneapolis, MN 55437, 612-835-2586

Princeton Computer Support, P.O. Box 7063, Princeton, NJ 08540, 609-921-8889

Print-Com Services Co., 440 Kirkwood Ave., Iowa City, IA 52240, 319-337-3845 (FLOPPY DRIVES)

Quality Repair Services, 45973 Warm Springs Blvd., Ste. 1, Fremont, CA 94539, 415-651-8486

R&M Associates, 330 Phillips Ave., S. Hackensack, NJ 07606, 201-440-8585 (FLOPPY DRIVES)

RBB Systems, Inc., 8767 T.R. 513, Shreve, OH 44676, 216-567-2906 (FLOPPY DRIVES)

React Computer Services, Inc., 865 N. Ellsworth, Villa Park, IL 60181, 708-832-1181 (HARD DRIVES)

Repair Pro/D.S. Walker, 11210 Steeplecrest Dr., Houston, TX 77065, 800-262-7339

Resource Dynamics, Inc., 17304 N. Preston Rd. #800, Dallas, TX 75252, 214-733-6886

Restorr Magnetics, 1455 McCandless Dr., Milpitas, CA 95035, 408-946-9207

Rodax, Inc., 12366 Northup Way, Bellevue, WA 98005, 206-885-9999

Rotating Memory Repair, Inc., 23382 Madero, Mission Viejo, CA 92692, 714-472-0159

Seagate, 12701 Whitewater Dr., Minnetonka, MN 55343, 800-382-6060 (HARD DRIVES)

Sequel, Inc., 2300 Central Expwy., Santa Clara, CA 95054, 408-987-1401 (HARD DRIVES)

Service 2000, Inc., 5301 E. River Rd., Ste. 108, Minneapolis, MN 55421, 800-338-6824 (FLOPPY DRIVES)

Serviceland of Upstate NY, Inc., 3259 Winton Rd., S. Rochester, NY 14623, 716-427-0880 (HARD DRIVES)

Servitech, Inc., 1509 Brook Dr., Downers Grove, IL 60515, 708-620-8750 (FLOPPY DRIVES)

Servo Labs, Inc., 21040 Victor Blvd., Woodland Hills, CA 91367, 818-884-7300 (HARD DRIVES)

Sim-Trade Co., 8040 Remmet Ave., Canoga Park, CA 91304, 818-703-5155

SMH Electronics Co., 16 Kendrick Rd., Wareham, MA 02571, 508-291-7447

Spectrum Computer Service, 10832 Capital Ave., Garden Grove, CA 992643, 714-554-2029

Sprague Magnetics, Inc., 15720 Stagg St., Van Nuys, CA 91406, 800-325-4243

Synergy Computer Services, Inc., 755 Queensway E., Unit 26, Mississauga, ONT, CN L4 4C5, 416-273-9565

Systems Diagnosis, Inc., 3 Richmond Sq., Providence, RI, 02906, 401-331-8980 (FLOPPY DRIVES)

TCE Co., 63 Douglas Ave., Elgin, IL 60120, 312-741-7200

Telford Technical Service, Inc., 9213 Fairview, Boise, ID 83704, 208-322-1434 (FLOPPY DRIVES)

The Main Source, 9260 Owensmouth, Chatsworth, CA 91311, 818-882-7500

The Repair Co., 1585 McCandless Dr., Milpitas, CA 95035, 408-946-5015 (FLOPPY DRIVES)

The Eighth Bit, Inc., 19701 Detroit Rd., Rock River, OH 44116, 216-333-5010 (FLOPPY DRIVES)

The Datasat Co., Inc., 10072 Willow Creek Rd., San Diego, CA 92131, 619-566-3371 (HARD DRIVES)

Total Maintenance Concepts, 746 Industrial Dr., Elmhurst, IL 60126, (FLOPPY DRIVES)

Trans Datacorp, 1200 O'Brien Dr., Menlo Park, CA 94025, 415-327-2692

Uptime Computer Support Services, 23633 Via Primero, Valencia, CA 91355, 805-254-3384 (FLOPPY DRIVES)

Valtron Technologies, Inc., 26074 Avenue Hall, Bldg. 23, Valencia, CA 91355, 805-257-0333

Victor Computer Service, Inc., 8125 Westglen Dr., Houston, TX 77063, 800-999-1827 (FLOPPY DRIVES)

Westor, Inc., 667 S. Pierce Ave., Louisville, CO 80027, 800-548-1606 (HARD DRIVES)

Wisk Computer Services, Inc., 1605 Watt Dr., Santa Clara, CA 95054, 408-748-9891 or 800-688-9701

Yaltronics, Inc., 650 W. Smith Rd., Medina, OH 44256, 216-723-HELP

FAX

JetFax, Inc., 978 Hamilton Court, Menlo Park, CA 94025, 415-324-0600 or 800-753-8329, FAX 415-326-6003

Sharp Electronics, Sharp Plaza, Mahwah, NJ 07430

FLOPPY DRIVE MANUFACTURERS

Chinon America, Inc., 660 Maple Ave., Torrance, CA 90503, 310-533-0274 or 800-441-0222, FAX 310-533-1727

Citizen America Corp., 2425 Colorado Ave. - Suite 300, Santa Monica, CA 90404, 213-453-0614

Cumulus Corp., 216-247-2236

Mitsubishi Electronics America, Inc., Information Systems Division, 991 Knox St., Torrance, CA 90502, 213-217-5732

Qume Corp., 2350 Qume Dr., San Jose, CA 95131, 408-942-4000 or 800-223-2479

Sony Corp. of America, Sony Dr., Park Ridge, NJ 07656, 201-930-6034

Tandon, 49 Strathearn Place, Simi Valley, CA 93065, 805-581-2995

Teac Computer Products Div., 7733 Telegraph Rd., Montebello, CA 90640, 213-726-0303 or 213-727-7609, FAX 213-727-7652

Toshiba, 9740 Irvine Blvd., Irvine, CA 92718, 714-380-3000 or 714-583-3961 or 800-624-5932

HARD DRIVE CONTROLLERS

Acumen Computer Systems, 12116 Severn Way, Riverside, CA 92503, 714-371-2992

Adaptec, 565 Sinclair Rd., Milpitas, CA 95035-5470, 408-945-8600

Boca Research, 6413 Congress Ave., Boca Raton, FL 33487, 407-997-0918

Data Technology Corp (DTC), 617-275-4044

Distributed Processing Technology, 140 Candace Dr., Maitland, FL 32751, 407-830-5522, FAX 407-260-5366

OMTI, 408-374-1381

Perceptive Solutions, Inc., 2700 Flora St., Dallas, TX 75201, 214-954-1774

Seagate Technology, Inc., 920 Disc Dr., Scotts Valley, CA 95066, 408-438-8222 or 800-468-DISC, FAX 408-438-2620 or 408-438-8137, BBS 408-438-8771

Western Digital, 8105 Irvine Center Dr., Irvine, CA 92718, 714-932-5000 or 800-777-4787, BBS 714-756-8176

Xebec, 3579 Hwy. 50 E., Carson City, NV 89701, 702-883-4000 or 800-982-3232

HARD DRIVES AND MASS STORAGE

Alliance Peripheral Systems, 2900 South 291 Hwy., Independence, MO 64057, 800-233-7550

BSE, 14701 Candeda Dr., Tustin, CA 92680, 714-832-4316

Chinon America, Inc., 660 Maple Ave., Torrance, CA 90503, 800-441-0222

CMI, 9216 Eton Ave., Chatsworth, CA 91311, 818-709-6445

CMS Enhancements, 1372 Valencia Ave., Tustin, CA 92680, 714-259-9555

Conner Peripherals, Inc., 3881 Zanker Road, San Jose, CA 95134, 408-433-3340

Core International, 7171 N. Federal Hwy., Boca Raton, FL 33487, 407-997-6055, FAX 407-997-6009

Iomega, 5725 Harold Gatty Dr., Salt Lake City, UT 84116, 801-778-1000 or 800-777-4123 (BERNOULI BOX)

Kyocera, 100 Randolph Rd. , CN 6700, Somerset, NJ 08875, 201-563-4333

Liberty Systems, 160 Saratoga Ave., Suite 38, Santa Clara, CA 95051, 408-983-1127, FAX 408-243-2885

Maxtor Corp., 211 River Oaks Pkwy., San Jose, CA 95134, 408-432-1700

MicroNet Technology, Inc., 20 Mason, Irvine, CA, 714-837-6033

Micropĺlis Corp., 21211 Nordhoff Street, Chatsworth, CA 91311, 818-709-3300 or 800 872-8893

MicroSolutions Computer Products, 132 W. Lincoln Hwy., DeKalb, IL 60115, 815-756-3411, FAX 815-756-2928

Miniscribe Corp., 1861 Lefthand Circle, Longmont, CO 80501, 800-356-5333

Mitsubishi Electronics America, Inc., Information Systems Division, 991 Knox St., Torrance, CA 90502, 213-217-5732

Mountain Computer, 360 El Pueblo Road, Scotts Valley, CA 95066, 408-438-7897

Plus Development Corp., 1778 McCarthy Blvd., Milpitas, CA 95035, 408-946-3700 or 800-826-8022 (HARDCARD)

Priam Systems, 1140 Ringwood Ct., San Jose, CA 95131, 408-954-8680

Procom Technology, 200 McCormick Ave., Costa Mesa, CA 92626, 714-549-9449

Quantum Corp., 1804 McCarthy Blvd., Milpitas, CA 95033, 408-432-1100 or 800-624-5545

Rodime Systems, Inc., 901 Broken Sound Pkwy. NW, Boca Raton, FL 33484, 407-994-5585

Seagate Technology, Inc., 920 Disc Dr., Scotts Valley, CA 95066, 408-438-6550 or 800-468-3472, FAX 408-438-2620 or 408-438-8137, BBS 408-438-8771

Simplicity Computing, Inc., 415 Madison Ave., 22nd Fl., New York, NY 10017, 800-275-6525, FAX 212-678-6143

Storage Dimensions, 2145 Hamilton Ave., San Jose, CA 95125, 408-879-0300

Tallgrass Technology, 11100 W. 82nd St., Overland Park, KS 66214, 913-492-1496

Tandberg Data, 2649 Townsgate Rd., Ste. 600, Westlake Village, CA 91362, 805-495-8384

Tandon, 49 Strathearn Place, Simi Valley, CA 93065, 805-581-2995

Teac America, Inc., 7733 Telegraph Road, Montebello, CA 90640, 213-726-0303 or 213-726-7609, FAX 213-727-7652

Tempustech, 295 Airport Rd., Naples, FL 33942, 800-634-0701

Toshiba, 9740 Irvine Blvd., Irvine, CA 92718, 714-380-3000 or 714-583-3961 or 800-624-5932

Valitek, Inc., Mountain Farms Mall, Hadley, MA 01035, 800-825-4835

HARD DRIVE UTILITY SOFTWARE

1st Aid Software, 42 Radnor Rd., Boston, MA 02135, 800-343-3497 or 617-783-7118 (Deluxe 1st Aid Kit)

Central Point Software, Inc., 15220 Northwest Greenbrier Pkwy., Suite 200, Beaverton, OR 97006, 503-690-8090 (PC Tools Deluxe)

DiagSoft, Inc., 5615 Scotts Valley Drive, Suite 140, Scotts Valley, CA 95066, 408-438-8247 (DiagSoft)

Fifth Generation Systems, 10049 North Reiger Rd., Baton Rouge, LA 70809, 800-873-4384 or 504-291-7221 (Mace Utilities)

Gazelle Systems, 42 North University Ave., Suite 10, Provo, UT 84601, 800-233-0383 or 801-377-1288 (OPTune)

Gibson Research Corp., 22991 La Cadena, Laguna Hills, CA 92653, 714-830-2200 (SpinRite)

Ontrack Computer Systems, 6321 Bury Dr., Suite 16-19, Eden Prairie, MN 55346, 800-752-1333 or 612-937-1107 (Disk Manager)

Peter Norton Computing, Inc., 2210 Wilshire Blvd., Suite 186, Santa Monica, CA 90403, 213-319-2000 (Norton Utilities)

Prime Solutions, Inc., 1940 Garnet Ave., San Diego, CA 92109, 800-847-5000 or 619-274-5000 (Disk Technician)

SoftLogic Solutions, 1 Perimeter Rd., Manchester, NH 03101, 800-272-9900 or 603-627-9900 (Disk Optimizer)

Storage Dimensions, 2145 Hamilton Ave., San Jose, CA 95125, 408-879-0300 (SpeedStor)

Symantec Corp., 10201 Torre Ave., Cupertino, CA 95014, 408-253-9600 (SUM II)

Timeworks, Inc., 444 Lake Cook Rd., Deerfield, IL 60015, 312-948-9202 (DOS Rx)

INPUT/OUTPUT DEVICES (MICE, LIGHTPENS, ETC.)

Appoint, 1332 Vendels Circle, Paso Robles, CA 93446, 805-239-8976 or 800-448-1184

Boxlight Corp., 17771 Fjord Dr. N.E., Poulsbo, WA 98370, 800-736-6955

Chinon America, Inc., 660 Maple Ave., Torrance, CA 90503, 800-441-0222

DFI, 2544 Port St., West Sacramento, CA 95691, 916-373-1234 (HANDY SCANNER 3000 Plus)

FTG Data Systems, 10801 Dale St., Stanton, CA 90680, 800-962-3900

Hewlett-Packard, 1131 Chinden Blvd., Boise, ID 83714, 800-367-4772

Kensington, 800-535-4242

Logitech, Inc., 805 Veterans Blvd., Redwood City, CA 94063, 415-365-9852 or 800-231-7717

Microsoft Corp., One Microsoft Way, Redmond, WA 98052, 206-882-8080

Pentax Technologies, 100 Technology Dr., Broomfield, CO 80021, 303-460-1600 or 800-543-6098

Suncom Technologies, 6400 W. Gross Point Road, Niles, IL 60648, 708-647-4040

UMAX Technologies, 2352 Walsh Ave., Santa Clara, CA 95051, 408-982-0771

KEYBOARDS

Genovation, Inc., 17741 Mitchell North, Irvine, CA 92714, 714-833-3355, FAX 714-833-0322

Key Tronic, 13717 Omiga Rd., Dallas, TX 75234, 509-927-5515 or 800-262-6006

U.S. Keyboards, 509-927-5207

KEYBOARD REPAIR

7-Sigma, Inc., 2843 26th Ave., S. Minneapolis, MN 55406, 612-722-5358

A. I. C., Inc., 1003 Bayview Overlook, Stafford, VA 22554, 703-659-0031

Abex Data Systems Inc., 1 Barnida Dr., East Hanover, NJ 07936, 201-887-2600

Accram, Inc., Computer Repair Center, 2901 W. Clarendon, Phoenix, AZ 85017, 602-264-0288

Advanced Video Technology, Inc., 1310 S. Dixie Hwy., Ste. 18W, Pompano Beach, FL 33060, 305-785-2490

Albany Microcomputer Services, 12553 San Pablo Ave., Richmond, CA 94805, 415-253-5935

Amcom Corp., 6205 Bury Dr., Eden Prairie, MN 55346, 612-949-9400 or 800-328-7723

American Computer Repair, Inc., RD6 Farm Bureau Rd., Allentown, PA 18106, 215-391-0100

American Computer Engineers, 11175 Flintkote Ave., Ste. F, San Diego, CA 92121, 619-587-9002

American Digital, 82 Winchester St., Newton, MA 02161, 617-964-5270

Amtec Computer Systems, 8515 Douglas, #17, Des Moines, IA 50322, 515-270-2480

Analog Technology Center, 62B Route 101-A, Amherst, NH 03031, 603-673-0404

Area TV & Computers, 561 E. 12 St., Erie, PA 16503, 814-453-4200

Avnet Computer Technologies, Inc., 10000 W. 76th St., Eden Prairie, MN 55344, 800-877-2285

BBS, 10649 Haddington #180, Houston, TX 77043, 800-683-2044

C3, Inc., 460 Herndon Pkwy., Herndon, VA 22070, 703-471-6000

Century Data Systems, 506 N. Harrington St., Raleigh, NC 27603, 919-821-5696

Century Computer Marketing Service Div., 4755 Alla Rd., Marina Del Rey, CA 90292, 213-827-0999

Circuit Test, Inc., 12749 W. Hillsborough Ave., Tampa, FL 33635, 813-855-6685

Cirdata Corp., 1175 Tourmaline Dr., Newbury Park, CA 91320, 800-829-4379

CJF Enterprises, Inc., 4834 NE 12 Ave., Ft. Lauderdale, FL 33334, 305-491-1850

CNS, 21 Pine St., Rockaway, NJ 07866, 201-625-4056

Coastal Electronics, 8 Mall Ct., Savannah, GA 31406, 912-352-1444

Compufix, Inc., 4 W. Chimney Rock Rd., Bound Brook, NJ 08805, 201-271-0020

Compupair, Inc., 7808 Cherry Creek So. Dr., #102, Denver, CO 80231, 303-368-4541

Computer Services Group., 22 West 38th St., New York, NY 10018, 212-819-0122

Computer Service Supply Corp., P.O. Box 673, Londonderry, NH 03053, 800-255-7815

Computer Care, Inc., 1116 Smith St., Room 213, Charleston, WV 25301, 304-340-4283

Computer Doctor, 4801A Burnet Rd., Austin, TX 78756, 512-467-9355

Computer Repair Co., 225 Water St., Quincy, MA 02169, 617-786-7405

Computer Parts Interchange, 5272 Fulton Dr. NW, Canton, OH 44718, 216-494-4074

Computer Maintenance Co., 1636 Wilshire Blvd., Los Angeles, CA 90017, 213-483-2400

Comstar, Inc., 5250 W. 74th St., Minneapolis, MN 55435, 800-735-5502

Cosmic Enterprises, Inc., 84 South St., Hopkinton, MA 01748, 508-435-6967

Cosmic Services, Inc., 3750 Hacienda Blvd., Ste. F, Ft. Lauderdale, FL 33314, 305-797-0143

CPE, Inc., 220 Mavis, Irving, TX 75061, 214-259-6010

CPR, 641 E. Walnut St., Carson, CA 90746, 213-538-1900

Crisis Computer Corp., 2298 Quimby Rd., San Jose, CA 95122, 800-729-0729

CRT Systems, Inc., 3071 Research Dr., Richmond, CA 94806, 415-262-1730

CRT Corp., 15822 Arminta St., Bldg. A, Van Nuys, CA 91406, 818-786-8967

Damomics Computer System, 111 N. Main St., Elmira, NY 14901, 607-732-5122

Data Exchange Corp., 708 Via Alondra, Camarillo, CA 93010, 805-388-1711

Data Systems Maintenance, 4551 Ponce de Leon Blvd., Coral Gables, FL 33146, 305-665-3626

Dataserv, 12125 Technology Dr., Eden Prairie, MN 55344, 612-829-6000

Datatech Depot, Inc., 1081 N. Shepard St., Anaheim, CA 92806, 714-632-1800

DATEC, Inc., 364 Upland Dr., Seattle, WA 98188, 206-575-1470

Digital Computer Service, 624 Krona Dr., Ste. 195, Plano, TX 75074, 214-422-1864

Digitronix, Inc., 9005 F St., Omaha, NE 68127, 402-339-5340

DMA, Inc., 611 Development Blvd., Amery, WI 54001, 715-268-8106

EDP Research & Development Co., 118 W. Pond Meadow, Westbrook, CT 06498, 203-399-5018

Efficient Field Service Corp., 11 School St., N. Chelmsford, MA 01863, 508-251-7800

Electronic Products Service, Inc., 6500 McDonough Dr., Ste. E-4, Norcross, GA 30093, 404-448-0748

ETI, Electro-Tech Industries, 101 State Pl., Bldg. B, Escondido, CA 92029, 619-745-3575

Federated Consultants, Inc., 2306 Country Valley Rd., Garland, TX 75041, 800-443-6400

GE Computer Service, 6875 Jimmy Carter Blvd., Norcross, GA 30071, 800-GESERVE

General Diagnostics, Inc., 1515 W. 190th St., Ste. 20, Gardena, CA 90248, 213-715-1222

Genicom Corp., Genicom Dr., Turner #3, Waynesboro, VA 22980, 703-949-1000

Hanson Data Systems, Inc., 734 Forest St., Marlboro, MA 01752, 617-481-3901

HB Computer Tech. Co., 12704 Yukon Ave., Hawthorne, CA 90250, 213-644-2602

Hi-Tek Services, Inc., 32970 Alvarado-Niles Rd., #720, Union City, CA 94587, 415-489-8909

Hyland/Rice Business Systems, 112 River St., Valley W. Plaza, Fitchburg, MA 01420, 617-342-9707

Images-Ink, 14180 E. Firestone Blvd., Santa Fe Springs, CA 90670, 213-926-6842

Independent Computer Support Services, Inc., 400 Devon Park Dr., Wayne, PA 19087, 215-687-0900

Instrument Repair Labs., Inc., 2100 W. 6th Ave., Broomfield, CO 80020, 303-469-5375

INTEC, 1008 Astoria Blvd., Cherry Hill, NJ 08003, 800-225-1187

Integrated Computer Services, Inc., 14180 Live Oak Blvd., Ste. B, Baldwin Park, CA 91706, 818-960-1921

Jadtec Computer Group, 546 W. Katella Ave., Orange, CA 92667, 714-997-8927

JC Enterprises, P.O. Box 4172, Dept. 363, Woodland Hills, CA 91364, 818-773-0296

Lupac Computer Parts & Services USA, Inc., 21345 Lassen St., Chatsworth, CA 91311, 818-709-2681

Magnetic Data, Inc., 6978 Shady Oak Rd., Eden Prairie, MN 55344, 612-944-0842

Manufacturers Equipment Repair Group, 3860 Trade Center Dr., Ann Arbor, MI 48104, 313-429-4028

Micro Medic, Inc., 22515 Aspan, Ste. G, El Toro, CA 92630, 714-581-3651

Micro Products Repair Center, Inc., 405 Murray Hill Pkwy., E. Rutherford, NJ 07073, 201-896-1810

Micro Clinic, 105 State St., Schenectady, NY 12305, 518-370-8092

Micro Medics, 7041 Jackson, Warren, MI 48091, 313-759-0231

Midwest Service Management, 26 N. Park Pl., Newark, OH 43055, 614-345-9843

Miller Services, 100 E. Park Ave., Charlotte, NC 28203, 704-372-3320

Monterey Computer Consulting, 149 Bonifacio Pl., Monterey, CA 93940, 408-394-5980

Morrow Microcomputer Service, INc., 1232-D Village Way, Santa Ana, CA 92705, 714-834-1351

NBSS, 8639 Loch Raven Blvd., Baltimore, MD 21204, 301-665-8870

Northeast Technical Services, 146 Londonderry Tpke, Hooksett, NH 03106, 800-537-0359

Northstar MatrixServ, 8055 Ranchers Rd., Minneapolis, MN 55432, 800-969-0009

Nova Technology Services, 7509 Connelle Dr., Hanover, MD 21076, 800-523-2773

Novadyne Computer Systems, 1775 E. St. Andrew Pl., Santa Ana, CA 92705, 714-566-4965

On Board Electronics, 250 Main St., Beacon Falls, CT 06403, 203-729-4503

PC Repair Corporation, 2010 State St., Harrisburg, PA 17103, 717-232-7272 or 800-727-3724

PCSI, 104 E. 23rd St., New York, NY 10010, 212-475-4475

Peripheral Maintenance, Inc., 16 Passaic St., Fairfield, NJ 07006, 201-227-8411

Peripheral Parts Support, Inc., 219 Bear Hill Rd., Waltham, MA 02154, 617-890-9101

Princeton Computer Support, P.O. Box 7063, Princeton, NJ 08540, 609-921-8889

Print-Com Services Co, 440 Kirkwood Ave., Iowa City, IA 52240, 319-337-3845

Quality Repair Services, 45973 Warm Springs Blvd., Ste. 1, Fremont, CA 94539, 415-651-8486

R&M Associates, 330 Phillips Ave., S. Hackensack, NJ 07606, 201-440-8585

Raynet, 16810 Barker Springs Rd., Ste. 200, Houston, TX 77084, 713-578-3802

React Computer Services, Inc., 865 N. Ellsworth, Villa Park, IL 60181, 708-832-1181

Repair Pro/D.S. Walker, 11210 Steeplecrest Dr., Houston, TX 77065, 800-262-7339

Rodax, Inc., 12366 Northup Way, Bellevue, WA 98005, 206-885-9999

Rotating Memory Repair, Inc., 23382 Madero, Mission Viejo, CA 92692, 714-472-0159

S.A.I.D., Inc., 417 West Broad St., Falls Church, VA 22046, 703-532-9190

Service 2000, Inc., 5301 E. River Rd., Ste. 108, Minneapolis, MN 55421, 800-338-6824

Servitech, Inc., 1509 Brook Dr., Downers Grove, IL 60515, 708-620-8750

SMH Electronics Co., 16 Kendrick Rd., Wareham, MA 02571, 508-291-7447

Sprague Magnetics, Inc., 15720 Stagg St., Van Nuys, CA 91406, 800-325-4243

SRM, Inc., 2231 S. Oneida, Green Bay, WI 54304, 414-497-7863

Synergy Computer Services, Inc., 755 Queensway E., Unit 26, Mississauga, ONT, CN L4 4C5, 416-273-9565

Systems Support, Inc., 5879 W. 34th St., Houston, TX 77092, 713-683-6824

Systems Diagnosis, Inc., 3 Richmond Sq., Providence, RI 02906, 401-331-8980

Telford Technical Service, Inc., 9213 Fairview, Boise, ID 83704, 208-322-1434

The Repair Co., 1585 McCandless Dr., Milpitas, CA 95035, 408-946-5015

The Eighth Bit, Inc., 19701 Detroit Rd., Rock River, OH 44116, 216-333-5010

Total Maintenance Concepts, 746 Industrial Dr., Elmhurst, IL 60126

Unicomp System, 11362 Westminster Ave., Ste. U, Garden Grove, CA 92643, 714-534-5092

Victor Computer Service, Inc., 8125 Westglen Dr., Houston, TX 77063, 800-999-1827

Wisk Computer Services, Inc., 1605 Watt Dr., Santa Clara, CA 95054, 408-748-9891 or 800-688-9701

Yaltronics, Inc., 650 W. Smith Rd., Medina, OH 44256, 216-723-HELP

LASER CARTRIDGE REMANUFACTURERS

Advantage Laser Products, 2216 University Blvd., Tuscaloosa, AL 35401, 800-239-4047

American Ribbon Co., 2890 Northwest 55th Ct., Ft. Lauderdale, FL 33309, 800-327-1013

BeeDee Enterprises, 100 Hurricane Shores, Scottsville, KY 42164, 502-622-4129

Black Lightning, RR 1, Box 87, Depot Rd., Hartland, VT 05048, 800-252-2599

Chenesco Products, 62 N. Coleman Rd., Centereach, NY 11720, 800-221-3516

Environmental Computer Supplies, 1001 Louisiana Ave., Suite 407, Corpus Christi, TX 78404, 800-521-3289

Heartland Laser, 1716 Murray Hill, Manly, IA 50456, 515-454-2576

Laser Group, 115 Crabtree Dr., Suite 100, Westmont, IL 60559, 800-527-3712

Laser Research, 8334-L Arrowridge Blvd., Charlotte, NC 28273, 800-462-7143

Laser's Edge, 201 S. 23rd St., Fairfield, IA 52556, 800-635-8088

LASERQuipt, 7615 Washington Ave. S., Edina, MN 55435, 800-777-8444

Omega Computer Services, 4825 E. Indianapolis Ave., Fresno, CA 93726, 800-736-6342

Printworx, 3322 S. Memorial Pkwy., Huntsville, AL 35801, 800-777-9679

LASER PRINTER PARTS AND SUPPLIES

Atlantis Laser Center, Alpharetta, GA, 800-733-9155 - repair I/O boards and Fusing Assemblies

Brother International, Piscataway, NJ, 908-356-8880

Crisis Computer, CA, 408-270-1100

Hewlett Packard, 800-227-8164

LaserCharge, Austin, TX, 800-299-8134, HP Laser Printer Parts

LaserSource, 315-463-6090

Parts Now, Inc., Madison, WI, 800-421-0967 or 608-244-8040

PC Parts Express, 800-727-8669

QMS, Mobile, AL, 205-633-4300

Quality Laser Charge, Scottsdale, AZ, 800-828-6649 - stocks Canon Laser Printer Parts, rebuilds Fusing Assemblies

MATH CO-PROCESSORS

Advanced Micro Devices, Inc., 9020-11 Capital of Texas Hwy. North, Suite 400, Austin, TX 78759, 800-888-5590

Chips and Technologies, 2099 Gateway Place, Suite 260, San Jose, CA 95110, 800-323-4477

Cyrix Corp., 703 North Central Expwy., Richardson, TX 75080, 214-234-8387 or 800-327-6284

Integrated Information Technologies, 2445 Mission College Blvd., Santa Clara, CA 95054, 408-727-1885 or 800-832-0770

Intel Corp., 3065 Bowers Ave., Santa Clara, CA 95052, 800-538-3373

Weitek Corp., 1060 East Arques Ave., Sunnyvale, CA 94086, 408-738-8400

MODEMS AND FAX MODEMS

Advanced Microcomputer Systems, Inc., 1321 NW 65th Pl., Fort Lauderdale, FL 33309, 305-970-9097

American Data Technology, Inc., 44 W. Bellevue Dr., Suite #6, Pasadena, CA 91105, 818-578-1339

Anchor Automation, Inc., 20675 Bahama St., Chatsworth, CA 91311, 818-998-6100

ATI Technologies, Inc., 3761 Victoria Park Ave., Scarborough, ONT, CN M1W 3S2, 416-756-0711, BBS 416-756-4591

Calpak Corp., 22825 Lockness Ave., Torrance, CA 90501, 213-539-4734

Cardinal Technologies, 1827 Freedom Rd., Lancaster, PA 17601, 717-293-3124

Citifax Corp., 28427 N. Ballard Dr., Lake Forest, IL 60045-4510, 800-248-4329

Compucom Corp., 1180-J Miraloma Way, Sunnyvale, CA 94086, 619-283-1136

Computer Peripherals, Inc., 667 Rancho Conejo Blvd., Newbury Park, CA 91320, 805-499-5751 or 800-854-7600

Data Race, Inc., 11550 Interstate Hwy 10 West, Suite #395, San Antonio, TX 78230, 512-558-1910

Elite High Technology, Inc., 383 Del Amo Blvd., Torrance, CA 90503, 213-370-2762 or 800-874-6698

Forval America, Inc., 6985 Union Park Circle, Suite 425, Midvale, UT 84047, 800-367-8251

GVC Technologies, Inc., 99 Demarest Rd., Sparta, NJ 07871, 201-579-3630 or 800-289-4821, BBS 201-579-2380

Hayes Microcomputer Products, Inc., P.O. Box 105203, Atlanta, GA 30348, 404-441-1617, BBS 900-884-2937

Holmes Microsystems, 2620 S. 900 West, Salt Lake City, UT 84119, 801-975-9929, BBS 801-975-0431

Image Communications, 6 Caesar Pl., Moonachie, NJ 07074, 201-935-8882

Intel Corp., PC Enhancements Div., 5200 NE Elam Young Pkwy, MS C03-80, Hillsboro, OR 97124, 503-629-7000 or 800-538-3373, FAX

800-525-3019, BBS 503-645-6275

Logicode Technology, Inc., 1817 DeHavilland Drive, Newbury Park, CA 91320, 805-499-4443 or 800-735-6442, FAX 805-499-8588

Macronix, Inc., 1348 Ridder Park Dr., San Jose, CA 95131, 408-453-8088 or 800-468-4629

Megahertz Corp., 4505 S. Wasatch Blvd., Salt Lake City, UT 84124, 801-272-6000 or 800-527-8677

MICC (Micro Integrated Communications Corp.), 3255-3 Scott Blvd., Suite #102, Santa Clara, CA 95054, 800-289-6422

Micronet Computer Systems, Inc., 6970 Aragon Circle, Bldg. #3, Buena Park, CA 90620, 714-739-8832

Mitsuba, 650 Terrace Dr., San Dimas, CA 91773, 800-648-7822

Multi-Tech Systems, Inc., 2205 Woodale Dr., Mounds View, MN 55112, 800-328-9717

OAZ Communications, 44920 Osgood Rd., Fremont, CA 94539, 415-226-0171 or 800-638-3295

Practical Peripherals, 31245 La Baya Dr., Westlake Village, CA 91362, 818-991-8200

Product R&D Corp., 1194 Pacific St., Suite #201, San Luis Obispo, CA 93401, 805-546-9713 or 800-321-9713

Racal-Vadic, 1525 McCarthy Blvd., Milpitas, CA 95035, 800-4-VADICS

Shiva, One Cambridge Center, Cambridge, MA 02142, 617-252-6300 or 800-458-3550, FAX 617-252-4852

Star Logic, Inc., 238 E. Caribbean Dr., Sunnyvale, CA 94089, 408-747-0903 or 800-800-5632

Trans PC Systems, 11849 E. Firestone, Norwalk, CA 90701

U.S. Robotics, 8100 McCormick Blvd., Skokie, IL 60076, 708-982-6000 or 800-982-5151

Universal Data Systems, 5000 Bradford Dr., Huntsville, AL 35805, 205-721-8000

Ven-Tel, Inc., 2121 Zanker Rd., San Jose, CA 95131, 800-538-5121

Vital Communications, 3366 Hillside Ave., New Hyde Park, NY 11040, 516-294-5424

MONITORS

ADI, 2121 Ringwood Ave., San Jose, CA 95131, 408-944-0100 or 800-228-0530 or 800-232-8282, FAX 408-944-0300, BBS 408-944-0100

Altos Computer Systems, 2641 Orchard Pkwy., San Jose, CA 95134, 800-258-6787, FAX 408-432-6221

Amdek, 3741 N. First St., San Jose, CA 95134, 800-800-9973, FAX 800-800-9973, BBS 408-922-4400 or 408-473-2260

American Mitac Corp., 410 E. Plumeria Dr., San Jose, CA 95134, 408-435-1958 or 800-648-2287

AOC International (USA) Ltd., 10991 NW Airworld Dr., Kansas City, MO 64154, 800-343-5777

Cordata Technologies, Inc., 1055 W. Victoria St., Compton, CA 90220, 213-603-2901 or 800-255-8216

Dell Computer Corp., 9505 Arboretum Blvd., Austin, TX 78759, 512-338-4400 or 800-624-9896, FAX 800-950-1239, BBS 512-338-8528

Digiview Technology, Inc., 300 McGraw Dr., Edison, NJ 08837, 908-225-8899

Falco Data Products, 440 Potrero Ave., Sunnyvale, CA 94086, 408-745-7123 or 800-325-2648

Fora, Inc., 3096 Orchard Dr., San Jose, CA 95134, 408-894-8382 or 800-336-3962, BBS 408-943-0416

Fujikama U.S.A., Inc., 865 N. Ellsworth Ave., Villa Park, IL 60181, 800-883-8830

Goldstar Technology, 3003 N. First St., san Jose, CA 95134-2004, 408-432-1331

Hewlett-Packard, 800-752-0900

Hitachi America, Ltd., 950 Elm Ave., Ste., 100, San Bruno, CA 94066, 415-872-1902

Hyundai Electronics America, 166 Baypointe Pkwy., san Jose, CA 95134

Image Systems Corp., 11543 K-Tel Dr., Hopkins, MN 55343, 612-935-1171 or 800-462-4370

KFC USA, Inc., 1585 Sunland La., Costa Mesa, CA 92626

Leading Technology, Inc., 10430 Fifth Ave., SW, Beaverton, OR 97005-3447, 503-343-3424 or 800-999-5323

MAG Innovision, 4392 Corporate Center Dr., Los Alamitos, CA 90720, 714-827-3998 or 800-827-3998

Magnavox Consumer, 178 Manor Road, E. Rutherford, NJ 07073, 201-935-0600

Microvitec, Inc., 1943 Providence Ct., College Park, GA 30307, 404-991-2246

Mitsuba Corp., 1925 Wright Ave., La Verne, CA 91750

Mitsubishi Electronics America, Inc., 5665 Plaza Dr., P.O. Box 6007, Cypress, CA 90630-0007, 714-220-2550 or 800-344-6352, BBS 714-236-6286

Modgraph, Inc., 83 Second Ave., Burlington, MA 01803, 800-327-9962

Nanao USA Corp., 23535 Teld Ave., Torrance, CA 90505, 213-325-5202 or 800-800-5202

NEC Technologies, Inc., 1255 Michael Dr., Wood Dale, IL 60191, 800-366-3632, FAX 800-336-0476, BBS 708-860-2602

Nissei Sangyo/Hitachi, 800 South St., Waltham, MA 02164, 617-893-5700

Panasonic, 800-742-8086

PC Craft, Inc., 640 Puente St., Brea, CA 92621, 714-256-5000, BBS 714-256-5033

Princeton Graphic Systems, 1125 Northmeadow Pkwy., Suite #120, Roswell, GA 30076, 404-664-1010 or 800-221-1490

Quadram, 1 Quad Way, Norcross, GA 30093, 404-923-6666

Qume Corp., 500 Yosemite Dr., Milpitas, CA 95035, 408-942-4000 or 800-457-4447

Radius, Inc., 1710 Fortune Dr., San Jose, CA 95131, 408-434-1010

Sampo America, 5550 Peachtree Industrial Boulevard, Norcross, GA 30071, 404-449-6220, FAX 404-447-1109

Samsung Information Systems America, Inc., 3655 North First St., San Jose, CA 95134, 800-624-8999

Seiko Instruments, Inc., 1144 Ringwood Ct., San Jose, CA 95131, 408-922-5900

Sony Corp. of America, Sony Dr., Park Ridge, NJ 07656, 201-930-6034

Supercom Industries, Inc., 4710 S. Eastern Ave., Los Angeles, CA 90040, 213-721-6699

SuperMac Technology, 485 Potrero Ave., Sunnyvale, CA 94086, 408-245-2202

Swan Technologies, 3075 Research Dr., State College, PA 16801, 814-234-2236 or 800-468-7926, BBS 814-237-6145

Tatung Company of America, Inc., 2850 El Presidio St., Long Beach, CA 90810, 213-979-7055 or 800-827-2850, BBS 213-635-9090

Taxan America, Inc., 161 Nortech Parkway, San Jose, CA 95134, 408-263-4900

TTX Computer Products, 8515 Parkline Blvd., Orlando, FL 32809

Viewsonic, 12130 Mora Dr., Santa Fe Springs, CA 90670, 213-946-0711 or 800-888-8583

Wyse Technology, 3471 N. First St., San Jose, CA 95134, 800-800-9973, FAX 800-800-9973, BBS 408-922-4400 or 408-473-2260

XTRON, 19 Rector St., 19th Flr., New York, NY 10016, 212-344-6583 or 800-854-4450

Zenith Data Systems, 1000 Milwaukee Ave., Glenview, IL 60025, 312-391-8744

MONITOR AND TERMINAL REPAIR

7-Sigma, Inc., 2843 26th Ave., S. Minneapolis, MN 55406, 612-722-5358

A. I. C., Inc., 1003 Bayview Overlook, Stafford, VA 22554, 703-659-0031

Accram, Inc., Computer Repair Center, 2901 W. Clarendon, Phoenix, AZ 85017, 602-264-0288

Accu-tek Service, Inc., 25365 Dequindre, Madison Heights, MI 48071, 313-542-9960

Acetron Data Products, Inc., 16518 Arminta St., Van Nuys, CA 91406, 818-786-9789

Adahk, Inc., 7260 Collamer Rd., East Syracuse, NY 13057, 315-656-3988

Advanced Video Technology, Inc., 1310 S. Dixie Hwy., Ste. 18W, Pompano Beach, FL 33060, 305-785-2490

Albany Microcomputer Services, 12553 San Pablo Ave., Richmond, CA 94805, 415-253-5935

Alternative Services, 8003 Castlewa Dr., Indianapolis, IN 46250, 317-845-0018

Amcom Corp., 6205 Bury Dr., Eden Prairie, MN 55346, 612-949-9400 or 800-328-7723

American Computer Repair, Inc., RD6 Farm Bureau Rd., Allentown, PA 18106, 215-391-0100

American Computer Engineers, 11175 Flintkote Ave., Ste. F, San Diego, CA 92121, 619-587-9002

American Digital, 82 Winchester St., Newton, MA 02161, 617-964-5270

Amtec Computer Systems, 8515 Douglas, #17, Des Moines, IA 50322, 515-270-2480

Analog Technology Center, 62B Route 101-A, Amherst, NH 03031, 603-673-0404

Area TV & Computers, 561 E. 12 St., Erie, PA 16503, 814-453-4200

Avnet Computer Technologies, Inc., 10000 W. 76th St., Eden Prairie, MN 55344, 800-877-2285

BBS, 10649 Haddington #180, Houston, TX 77043, 800-683-2044

Broder Enterprises, 2648-A Brenner Dr., Dallas, TX 75220, 214-350-0501

C3, Inc., 460 Herndon Pkwy., Herndon, VA 22070, 703-471-6000

Century Computer Marketing Service Div., 4755 Alla Rd., Marina Del Rey, CA 90292, 213-827-0999

Century Data Systems, 506 N. Harrington St., Raleigh, NC 27603, 919-821-5696

Circuit Test, Inc., 12749 W. Hillsborough Ave., Tampa, FL 33635, 813-855-6685

Cirdata Corp., 1175 Tourmaline Dr., Newbury Park, CA 91320, 800-829-4379

Cirvis, Inc., 5082 Bolsa Ave., Ste. 112, Huntington Beach, CA 92649, 714-891-2000

CJF Enterprises, Inc., 4834 NE 12 Ave., Ft. Lauderdale, FL 33334, 305-491-1850

CNS, 21 Pine St., Rockaway, NJ 07866, 201-625-4056

Coastal Electronics, 8 Mall Ct., Savannah, GA 31406, 912-352-1444

Comptronics, 313-A&B Highway 70E, Garner, NC 27529, 919-779-7268

CompuCare Microsystems, 11-22 45th Road, Long Island City, NY 11101, 718-361-5546 (Goldstar Parts)

Compufix, Inc., 4 W. Chimney Rock Rd., Bound Brook, NJ 08805, 201-271-0020

Compupair, Inc., 7808 Cherry Creek So. Dr., #102, Denver, CO 80231, 303-368-4541

Computer Technology Services, Inc., 15801 Rockfield Blvd. Ste. L, Irvine, CA 92718, 714-855-8667

Computer Doctor, 4801A Burnet Rd., Austin, TX 78756, 512-467-9355

Computer Maintenance Co., 1636 Wilshire Blvd., Los Angeles, CA 90017, 213-483-2400

Computer Services Group, 22 West 38th St., New York, NY 10018, 212-819-0122

Computer Care, Inc., 1116 Smith St., Room 213, Charleston, WV 25301, 304-340-4283

Computer Service Supply Corp., P.O. Box 673, Londonderry, NH 03053, 800-255-7815

Computer Parts Interchange, 5272 Fulton Dr. NW, Canton, OH 44718, 216-494-4074

Computer Maintenance Service, 7930 Alabama Ave., Canoga Park, CA 91304, 818-347-3588

Computer Repair Co., 225 Water St., Quincy, MA 02169, 617-786-7405

Comstar, Inc., 5250 W. 74th St., Minneapolis, MN 55435, 800-735-5502

Conversion Systems, Inc., 8333 Clairemont Mesa Blvd., San Diego, CA 92111, 619-571-9088 or 800-346-4380

Cosmic Enterprises, Inc., 84 South St., Hopkinton, MA 01748, 508-435-6967

Cosmic Services, Inc., 3750 Hacienda Blvd. Ste. F, Ft. Lauderdale, FL 33314, 305-797-0143

CPR, 641 E. Walnut St., Carson, CA 90746, 213-538-1900

Digital Repair Corp., 8918 Tesoro Drive, Suite 108, San Antonio, TX 78217, 512-828-2256

ETI, Electro-Tech Industries, 101 State Pl., Bldg. B, Escondido, CA 92029, 619-745-3573

Federated Consultants, Inc., 2306 Country Valley Rd., Garland, TX 75041, 800-443-6400

FRS, Inc., 1101 National Dr., Sacramento, CA 95834, 916-928-1107

GE Computer Service, 6875 Jimmy Carter Blvd., Norcross, GA 30071, 800-GESERVE

General Diagnostics, Inc., 1515 W. 190th St., Ste 20, Gardena, CA 90248, 213-715-1222

Genicom Corp., Genicom Dr., Turner #3, Waynesboro, VA 22980, 703-949-1000

Golden Coast Electronics, Inc., 4343 Viewridge Ave., San Diego, CA 92123, 619-268-8447

Gorrell's Computer Services, 2341 Fortune Dr., Lexington, KY 40509, 606-299-8468

Hanson Data Systems, Inc, 734 Forest St., Marlboro, MA 01752, 617-481-3901

Hardware Services NW, 13429 SE 30th St., Ste. A, Bellevue, WA 98005, 206-746-6030

Hayes Instruments Service, 530 Boston Rd., Billerica, MA 01821, 508-663-4800

HB Computer Tech. Co., 12704 Yukon Ave., Hawthorne, CA 90250, 213-644-2602

Hi-Tek Services, Inc., 32970 Alvarado-Niles Rd., #720, Union City, CA 94587, 415-489-8909

Hyland/Rice Business Systems, 112 River St., Valley W. Plaza, Fitchburg, MA 01420, 617-342-9707

Iicon Corp., 16040 Caputo Dr., Morgan Hill, CA 95037, 408-779-7466

Images-Ink, 14180 E. Firestone Blvd., Santa Fe Springs, CA 90670, 213-926-6842

Independent Computer Services, Inc., 400 Devon Park Dr., Wayne, PA 19087, 215-687-0900

Instrument Repair Labs, Inc., 2100 W. 6th Ave., Broomfield, CO 80020, 303-469-5375

INTEC, 1008 Astoria Blvd., Cherry Hill, NJ 08003, 800-225-1187

Integrated Computer Services, Inc., 14180 Live Oak Blvd., Ste. B, Baldwin Park, CA 91706, 818-960-1921

International Computer Service, Inc., 13256 S. Brandon Ave., Chicago, IL 60633, 312-731-1000

Jadtec Computer Group, 546 W. Katella Ave., Orange, CA 92667, 714-997-8927

JC Enterprises, P.O. Box 4172, Dept. 363, Woodland Hills, CA 91364, 818-773-0296

KCS Computer Service, Inc., 7462 Talbert Ave., Huntington Beach, CA 92647, 714-848-7971

Lupac Computer Parts & Services USA, Inc., 21345 Lassen St., Chatsworth, CA 91311, 818-709-2621

Magnetic Data, Inc., 6978 Shady Oak Rd., Eden Prairie, MN 55344, 612-944-0842

Manufacturers Equipment Repair Group, 3860 Trade Center Dr., Ann Arbor, MI 48104, 313-429-4028

Mark McCloud Associates, 165-F Cristich La., Campbell, CA 95008, 408-559-7888

Micro Products Repair Center, Inc., 405 Murray Hull Pkwy., E. Rutherford, NJ 07073, 201-896-1810

Micro Clinic, 105 State St. Schenectady, NY 12305, 518-370-8092

Micro Medics, 7041 Jackson, Warren, MI 48091, 313-759-0231

Micro Medic, Inc., 22515 Aspan, Ste. G, El Toro, CA 92630, 714-581-3651

Microlife Corp., 537 Olathe, Ste. F, Aurora, CO 80011, 303-367-8333

Midwest Service Management, 26 N. Park Pl., Newark, OH 43055, 614-345-9843

Monitech, 2 Caesar Pl., Moonachie, NJ 07074, 201-933-6484 or 800-332-9349, FAX 201-933-5301

Monterey Computer Consulting, 149 Bonifacio Pl., Monterey, CA 93940, 408-394-5980

Morrow Microcomputer Service, Inc., 1232-D Village Way, Santa Ana, CA 92705, 714-834-1351

NBSS, 8639 Loch Raven Blvd., Baltimore, MD 21204, 301-665-8870

Northeast Technical Services, 146 Londonderry Tpke., Hooksett, NH 03106, 800-537-0359

Northstar MatrixServ, 8055 Ranchers Rd., Minneapolis, MN 55432, 800-969-0009

Nova Technology Services, 7509 Connelle Dr., Hanover, MD 21076, 800-523-2773

Novadyne Computer Systems, Inc., 1775 E. St. Andrew Pl., Santa Ana, CA 92705, 714-566-4965

On Board Electronics, 250 Main St., Beacon Falls, CT 06403, 203-729-4503

PC Repair Corporation, 2010 State St., Harrisburg, PA 17103, 717-232-7272 or 800-727-3724

PCSI, 104 E. 23rd St., New York, NY 10010, 212-475-5575

Peripheral Maintenance, Inc., 16 Passaic St., Fairfield, NJ 07006, 201-227-8411

Peripheral Parts Support, Inc., 219 Bear Hill Rd., Waltham, MA 02154, 617-890-9101

Power Clinic, 1510 Randolph, Ste. 202, Carrollton, TX 75006

Premier Computer Corp., 8200 Normandale Blvd., Minneapolis, MN 55437, 612-835-2586

Princeton Computer Support, P.O. Box 7063, Princeton, NJ 08540, 609-921-8889

Print-Com Services Co., 440 Kirkwood Ave., Iowa City, IA 52240, 319-337-3845

Pro Computer Service, 10054 E. Haven Ct., Santee, CA 92071, 619-562-8546

PTS Corporation, 5233 S. Hwy 37, Bloomington, IN 47401, 800-999-2723

Quality Repair Services, 45973 Warm Springs Blvd., Ste 1, Fremont, CA 94539, 415-651-8486

R&M Associates, 330 Phillips Ave., S. Hackensack, NJ 07606, 201-440-8585

Raynet, 16810 Barker Springs Rd., Ste. 200, Houston, TX 77084, 713-578-3802

RBB Systems, Inc., 8767 T.R. 513, Shreve, OH 44676, 216-567-2906

Repair Pro/D.S. Walker, 11210 Steeplecrest Dr., Houston, TX 77065, 800-262-7339

Resource Dynamics, Inc., 17304 N. Preston Rd. #800, Dallas, TX 75252

Restorr Magnetics, 1455 McCandless Dr., Milpitas, CA 95035, 408-946-9207

Retail Control Systems, 412-776-5544

Rodax, Inc., 12366 Northup Way, Bellevue, WA 98005, 206-885-9999

Service 2000, Inc., 5301 E. River Rd., Suite 108, Minneapolis, MN 55421, 800-338-6824

Servitech, Inc., 1509 Brook Dr., Downers Grove, IL 60515, 708-60515

SMH Electronics Co., 16 Kendrick Rd., Wareham, MA 02571, 508-291-7447

Solutronix, 7255 Flying Cloud Dr., Eden Prairie, MN 55344, 800-875-2580

Sprague Magnetics, Inc., 15720 Stagg St., Van Nuys, CA 91406, 800-3225-4243

SRM, Inc., 2231 S. Oneida, Green Bay, WI 54304, 414-497-7863

Synergy Computer Services, Inc., 755 Queensway E., Unit 26, Mississauga, ONT, CN L4 4C5, 416-273-9565

Systems Support, Inc., 5879 W. 34th St., Houston, TX 77092, 713-683-6824

Systems Diagnosis, Inc., 3 Richmond Sq., Providence, RI 02906, 401-331-8980

T&W Computer Service, 10278 Page, Saint Louis, MO 63132, 314-569-2200

Technical Sales & Service, 2820 Dorr Ave., Fairfax, VA 22031, 703-698-0347

Telford Technical Service, Inc., 9213 Fairview, Boise, ID 83704, 208-322-1434

Test Point Enterprise, 405 Unit F, River St., Warwick, RI 02886, 401-739-7900

The Repair Co., 1585 McCandless Dr., Milpitas, CA 95035, 408-946-5015

The Eighth Bit, Inc., 19701 Detroit Rd., Rock River, OH 44116, 216-333-5010

Total Maintenance Concepts, 746 Industrial Dr., Elmhurst, IL 60126

Unicomp System, 11362 Westminster Ave., Ste. U, Garden Grove, CA 92643, 714-534-5092

Victor Computer Service, Inc., 8125 Westglen Drive, Houston, TX 77063, 713-789-1888 or 800-999-1827

Visalia Computer Technology, Inc., 125 S. Church, Visalia, CA, 209-625-1480

Warner Electronics, Inc., 1240 Valley Belt, Cleveland, OH 44131, 216-661-0304

Welling Electronics, 529 No. 33, Omaha, NE 68131, 402-342-6564

Wisk Computer Services, Inc., 1605 Watt Dr., Santa Clara, CA 95054, 408-748-9891 or 800-688-9701

Yaltronics, Inc., 650 W. Smith Rd., Medina, OH 44256, 216-723-HELP

NETWORK PRODUCTS (BOARDS AND CONNECTIVITY EQUIPMENT)

3-Com Corporation, 408-764-5000 or 800-638-3266

Accton Technology Corporation, 46750 Fremont Blvd. #104, Fremont, CA 94538, 800-926-9288, FAX 510-226-9833

Allied Telesis, 575 East Middlefield Road, Mountain View, CA 94043, 415-964-2771 or 800-424-4284, FAX 415-964-0944

Alloy Computer Products, Inc., 165 Forest St., Marlborough, MA 01752, 508-481-8500 or 800-544-7551, FAX 508-481-7711

Anixter Bros., Inc., 4711 Golf Rd., Skokie, IL 60076, 312-677-2600

Artisoft, 691 East River Rd., Tucson, AZ 85704, 800-846-9726, FAX 602-293-8065

Asante Technologies, 404 Tasman Dr., Sunnyvale, CA 94089, 800-662-9686

Axis Communications, 130 Centre St, Danvers, MA 01923, 508-777-7957

Black Box Corporation, P.O. Box 12800, Pittsburgh, PA 15241, 412-746-5500

Cabletron Systems, 35 Industrial Way, Rochester, NH 03867-5005, 603-332-9400

Castelle, Inc., 3255-3 Scott Blvd., Santa Clara, CA 95054, 408-496-0474 or 800-359-7654, FAX 408-496-0502

Cubix Corporation, 2800 Lockheed Way, Carson City, NV 89706, 702-883-7611, FAX 702-882-2407

Eagle Technology, 1160 Ridder Park Drive, San Jose, CA 95131

Farallon Computing, Inc., 2000 Powell St., Suite 600, Emeryville, CA 94608, 510-596-9100, FAX 510-596-9020

Gateway Communications, Inc., 2941 Alton Ave., Irvine, CA 92714, 714-553-1555 or 800-367-6555

Intercomputer Communications Corp., 8230 Montgomery Road, Cincinnati, OH 45236, 800-274-6633

Legacy Storage Systems, Inc. 200 Butterfield Dr., Unit B, Ashland, MA 01721, 508-881-6442 or 800-267-6442, FAX 508-881-4116

Microdyne Corp., 207 South Peyton St., Alexandria, VA 22314, 703-739-0500 or 800-255-3967

MOD-TAP System, 285 Ayer Rd., P.O. Box 706, Harvard, MA 01451-0706, 508-772-5630

Network General, 4200 Bohannon Dr., Menlo Park, CA 94025, 800-952-6300

NetWorth, Inc., 8404 Esters Road, Irving, TX 75063, 214-929-1700 or 800-544-5255, FAX 214-929-1720

Newport Systems Solutions, Inc., 4019 Westerly Place, Newport Beach, CA 92660, 800-368-6533, FAX 714-752-8389

Persoft, Inc., 465 Science Dr., Madison, WI 53744, 608-273-6000 or 800-368-5283, FAX 608-273-8227

Racal-Datacom, 508-263-9929 or 800-526-8255

SMC (Standard Microsystems Corp.), 35 Marcus Blvd., Hauppauge, NY 11788, 516-273-3100 or 800-762-4968, FAX 516-273-1803

South Hills Electronics, 1936 W. Liberty Ave., Pittsburgh, PA 15226, 412-341-6200 or 800-245-6215

Thomas Conrad Corporation, 1908-R Kramer Lane, Austin, TX 78758, 512-836-1935 or 800-332-8683

Xircom, 26025 Mureau Rd., Calabasas, CA 91302, 818-878-7600

PARTS—NEW, USED AND REFURBISHED

7-Sigma, Minneapolis, MN, 612-722-5358, FAX 612-722-0493

Amcom Corp., 6205 Bury Dr., Eden Prairie, MN 55346, 612-949-9400 or 800-328-7723, FAX 612-949-0750

American Computer Repair, Inc., Allentown, PA, 215-391-0100

Barrister Information Systems Corp., Buffalo, NY, 716-845-5010, FAX 716-845-0077

Bell Atlantic Computer Technology Services, Hayward, CA, 415-732-3000, FAX 415-732-3061

Big Blue Products, Northport, NY, (516) 261-1666, FAX 516-261-1566

Bottom Line Industries, Chatsworth, CA, 818-700-1922, FAX 818-700-0836

Century Computer Marketing, 4755 Alla Road, Marina del Rey, CA 90292, 213-827-0999, FAX 213-578-2160

Computer Service Supply Corp., Londonderry, NH, 800-255-7815, FAX 603-622-0128

Computer Parts Unlimited, 5321 Derry Ave. Suite F, Agoura Hills, CA 91301, 808-879-1100, FAX 818-879-1199

Computrs, Inc., Butler, NJ, 800-637-4832, FAX 201-482-7725

Data Exchange, Camarillo, CA 93012, 805-388-1711, FAX 805-482-4856

Dataserv, 12125 Technology Dr., Eden Prairie, MN 55344-7399, 612-829-6500 or 800-245-7378, FAX 612-829-4258

Decision Data, Horsham, PA, 215-956-6867, FAX 215-443-0857

DMA, Inc., Amery, WI, 800-548-4073, FAX 715-268-6432

Electroservice Laboratories, Ventura, CA, 805-644-2944, FAX 805-644-5006

Exsel, Inc., 2200 Brighton-Henrietta Townline Rd., Rochester, NY 14623, 716-272-8770 or 800-624-2001

Heritage Computer, Minneapolis, MN, 612-881-0333 or 800-828-8266, FAX 612-888-8979

Hi-Tech Computer Products, Inc., Ft. Lauderdale, FL, 305-977-6991, FAX 305-977-0047

Logicare, 2297 Lansdowne Pl., Merrick, NY 11566, 516-868-0499

National Parts Depot, 3 Elkay Dr., Chester, NY 10918, 914-469-4800 or 800-524-8338, FAX 800-331-4829

PC Parts Express, 1420 Valwood Pkwy. #204, Carrolton, TX 75006, 214-406-8583 or 800-727-2787, FAX 214-406-9081

Repair Pro, 5161 Langfield Rd., Houston, TX 77040, 713-744-8300, FAX 713-744-8322

Selecterm, Inc., 153 Andover St., Danvers, MA 01923, 800-676-4944, FAX 508-777-2098

POWER PROTECTION AND BACKUP

American Power Conversion, P.O. Box 278, 132 Fairgrounds Rd., W. Kingston, RI 02892, 800-541-8896

DataShield, 269 Mt. Herman Rd., Scotts Valley, CA 95066, 408-439-6600

EFI Electronics Corporation, 2415 South 200 West, Salt Lake City, UT 84119, 801-977-9009

Emerson Electric Co., 800-222-5877

Kalglo Electronics, Inc., 6584 Ruch Rd., Bethlehem, PA 18017, 215-837-0700 or 800-524-0400

Para Systems, Inc., 1455 LeMay Dr., Carrollton, TX 75007, 214-466-7363 or 800-238-7272, FAX 214-446-9011

Perma Power, 5601 West Howard Ave., Chicago, IL 60648, 312-648-9414

Tripp Lite, 500 North Orleans, Chicago, IL 60610, 312-329-1777, FAX 312-644-6505

Upsonic, 1392 Industrial Dr., Tustin, CA 92680, 714-258-0808

POWER SUPPLIES AND FANS

Jameco Electronics, 1355 Shoreway Rd., Belmont, CA 94002, 415-592-8097

PC Power & Cooling, Inc., 31510 Mountain Way, Bonsall, CA 92003, 619-723-9513

POWER SUPPLY REPAIR

Abex Data Systems Inc., 1 Barnida Dr., East Hanover, NJ 07936, 201-887-2600

Accram, Inc., Computer Repair Center, 2901 W. Clarendon, Phoenix, AZ 85017, 602-264-0288

Accu-tek Service, Inc., 25365 Dequindre, Madison Heights, MI 48071, 313-542-9960

Albany Microcomputer Services, 12553 San Pablo Ave., Richmond, CA 94805, 415-253-5935

Amcom Corp., 6205 Bury Dr., Eden Prairie, MN 55346, 612-949-9400 or 800-328-7723

American Digital, 82 Winchester St., Newton, MA 02161, 617-964-5270

American Computer Engineers, 11175 Flintkote Ave., Ste. F, San Diego, CA 92121, 619-587-9002

American Computer Repair, Inc., RD6 Farm Bureau Rd., Allentown, PA 18106, 215-391-0100

Amtec Computer Systems, 8515 Douglas, #17, Des Moines, IA 50322, 515-270-2480

Analog Technology Center, 62B Route 101-A, Amherst, NH 03031, 603-673-0404

Area TV & Computers, 561 E. 12 St., Erie, PA 16503, 814-453-4200

Avnet Computer Technologies, Inc., 10000 W. 76th St., Eden Prairie, MN 55344, 800-877-2285

BBS, 10649 Haddington #180, Houston, TX 77043, 800-683-2044

BEC, Inc., 945 Horsham Rd., Horsham, PA 19044

Broder Enterprises, 2648-A Brenner Dr., Dallas, TX 75220, 214-350-0501

C3, Inc., 460 Herndon Pkwy., Herndon, VA 22070, 703-471-6000

Century Data Systems, 506 N. Harrington St., Raleigh, NC 27603, 919-821-5696

Century Computer Marketing Service Div., 4755 Alla Rd., Marina Del Rey, CA 90292, 213-827-0999

Circuit Test, Inc., 12749 W. Hillsborough Ave., Tampa, FL 33635, 813-855-6685

Cirvis, Inc., 5082 Bolsa Ave., Ste. 112, Huntington Beach, CA 92649, 714-891-2000

CJF Enterprises, Inc., 4834 NE 12 Ave., Ft. Lauderdale, FL 33334, 305-491-1850

CNS, 21 Pine St., Rockaway, NJ 07866, 201-625-4056

Coastal Electronics, 8 Mall Ct., Savannah, GA 31406, 912-352-1444

Compufix, Inc., 4 W. Chimney Rock Rd., Bound Brook, NJ 08805, 201-271-0020

Compupair, Inc., 7808 Cherry Creek So. Dr., #102, Denver, CO 80231, 303-368-4541

Computer Parts Interchange, 5272 Fulton Dr. NW, Canton, OH 44718, 216-494-4074

Computer Maintenance Service, 7930 Alabama Ave., Canoga Park, CA 91304, 818-347-3588

Computer Service Supply Corp., P.O. Box 673, Londonderry, NH 03053, 800-255-7815

Computer Care, Inc., 1116 Smith St., Room 213, Charleston, WV 25301, 304-340-4283

Computer Commodities, 7573 Golden Triangle Dr., Minneapolis, MN 55344, 612-942-0992

Computer Maintenance Co., 1636 Wilshire Blvd., Los Angeles, CA 90017, 213-483-2400

Computer Field Services, Inc., 197 Main St., N. Reading, MA 01864, 508-664-2828

Comstar, Inc., 5250 W. 74th St., Minneapolis, MN 55435, 800-735-5502

Conversion Systems, Inc., 8333 Clairemont Mesa Blvd., San Diego, CA 92111, 619-571-9088 or 800-346-4380

Cosmic Enterprises, Inc., 84 South St., Hopkinton, MA 01748, 508-435-6967

Cosmic Services, Inc., 3750 Hacienda Blvd. Ste. F, Ft. Lauderdale, FL 33314, 305-797-0143

CPR, 641 E. Walnut St., Carson, CA 90746, 213-538-1900

Crisis Computer Corp., 2298 Quimby Rd., San Jose, CA 95122, 800-729-0729

CRT Systems, Inc., 3071 Research Dr., Richmond, CA 94806, 415-262-1730

CRT Corp., 15822 Arminta St., Bldg A, Van Nuys, CA 91406, 818-786-8967

Damomics Computer System, 111 N. Main St., Elmira, NY 14901, 607-732-5122

Data Systems Maintenance, 4551 Ponce de Leon Blvd., Coral Gables, FL 33146, 305-665-3626

Data Products Corp., 6219 DeSoto Ave., Woodland Hills, CA 91367, 818-887-3909

Data Exchange Corp., 708 Via Alondra, Camarillo, CA 93010, 805-388-1711

Datagate, Inc., 1971 Tarob Ct., Milpitas, CA 95035, 408-946-6222

Dataserv, 12125 Technology Dr., Eden Prairie, MN 55344, 612-829-6000

Datatech Depot, Inc., 1081 N. Shepard St., Anaheim, CA 92806, 714-632-1800

Digital Computer Service, 624 Krona Dr. Ste 195, Plano, TX 75074, 214-422-1864

Digitronix, Inc., 9005 F St., Omaha, NE 68127, 402-339-5340

DJS Electronics, Inc., 589 Bethlehem Pike, Ste. 700, Montgomeryville, PA 18936, 215-822-5515

DMA, Inc., 611 Development Blvd., Amery, WI 54001, 715-268-8106

EDP Research & Development Co., 118 W. Pond Meadow, Westbrook, CT 06498, 203-399-5018

Efficient Field Service Corp., 11 School St., N. Chelmsford, MA 01863, 508-251-7800

Electronic Products Service, Inc., 6500 McDonough Dr., Ste. E-4, Norcross, GA 30093, 404-448-0748

ETI, Electro-Tech Industries, 101 State Pl., Bldg. B, Escondidt, CA 92029, 619-745-3575

FRS, Inc., 1101 National Dr., Sacramento, CA 95834, 916-928-1107

GE Computer Service, 6875 Jimmy Carter Blvd., Norcross, GA 30071, 800-GESERVE

General Diagnostics, Inc., 1515 W. 190th St., Ste. 20, Gardena, CA 90248, 213-715-1222

Genicom Corp., Genicom Dr., Turner #3, Waynesboro, VA 22980, 703-949-1000

Hanson Data Systems, Inc., 734 Forest St., Marlboro, MA 01752, 617-481-3901

Hayes Instruments Service, 530 Boston Rd., Billerica, MA 01821, 508-663-4800

HB Computer Tech. Co., 12704 Yukon Ave., Hawthorne, CA 90250, 213-644-2602

Hi-Tek Services, Inc., 32970 Alvarado-Niles Rd., #720, Union City, CA 94587, 415-489-8909

Images-Ink, 14180 E. Firestone Blvd., Santa Fe Springs, CA 90670, 213-926-6842

Independent Computer Support Services, Inc., 400 Devon Park Dr., Wayne, PA 19087, 215-687-0900

Instrument Repair Labs., Inc., 2100 W. 6th Ave., Broomfield, CO 80020, 303-469-5375

INTEC, 1008 Astoria Blvd., Cherry Hill, NJ 08003, 800-225-1187

Integrated Computer Services, Inc., 14180 Live Oak Blvd., Ste. B, Baldwin Park, CA 91706, 818-960-1921

JC Enterprises, P.O. Box 4172, Dept. 363, Woodland Hills, CA 91364, 818-773-0296

Lupac Computer Parts & Services USA Inc., 21345 Lassen St., Chatsworth, CA 91311, 818-709-2621

Magnetic Data Inc., 6978 Shady Oak Rd., Eden Prairie, MN 55344, 612-944-0842

Manufacturers Equipment Repair Group, 3860 Trade Center Dr., Ann Arbor, MI 48104, 313-429-4028

Micro Products Repair Center, Inc., 405 Murray Hill Pkwy., E. Rutherford, NJ 07073, 201-896-1810

Micro Medic, Inc., 22515 Aspan, Ste. G, El Toro, CA 92630, 714-581-3651

Micro Medics, 7041 Jackson, Warren, MI 48091, 313-759-0231

Midwest Service Management, 26 N. Park Pl., Newark, OH 43055, 614-345-9843

Modumend, Inc., 30961 Aguora Rd. #311, Westlake Village, CA 91361, 818-889-5550

Monterey Computer Consulting, 149 Bonifacio Pl., Monterey, CA 93940, 408-394-5980

Morrow Microcomputer Service, Inc., 1232-D Village Way, Santa Ana, CA 92705, 714-834-1351

NBSS, 8639 Loch Raven Blvd., Baltimore, MD 21204, 301-665-8870

Nordisk Systems, Inc., 11807 E. Smith St., Santa Fe, CA 90670, 213-942-1797

Northeast Technical Services, 146 Londonderry Tpke., Hooksett, NH 03106, 800-537-0359

Northstar MatrixServ, 8055 Ranchers Rd., Minneapolis, MN 55432, 800-969-0009

Nova Technology Services, 7509 Connelle Dr., Hanover, MD 21076, 800-523-2773

Novadyne Computer Systems, Inc., 1775 E. St. Andrew Pl., Santa Ana, CA 92705, 714-566-4965

On Board Electronics, 250 Main St., Beacon Falls, CT 06403, 203-729-4503

PC Repair Corporation, 2010 State St., Harrisburg, PA 17103, 717-232-7272 or 800-727-3724

PCSI, 104 E. 23rd St., New York, NY 10010, 212-475-5575

Peripheral Solutions, Inc., 151 Harvey West Blvd., 8-B, Santa Cruz, CA 95060, 408-425-8280

Peripheral Maintenance, Inc., 16 Passaic Ave., Fairfield, NJ 07006, 201-227-8411

Peripheral Parts Support, Inc., 219 Bear Hill Rd., Waltham, MA 02154, 617-890-9101

Peripherals, 1363 Logan Ave., Costa Mesa, CA 92626, 714-540-4925

Power Clinic, 1510 Randolph, Ste. 202. Carrollton, TX 75006

Princeton Computer Support, P.O. Box 7063, Princeton, NJ 08540, 609-921-8889

Print-Com Services Co., 440 Kirkwood Ave., Iowa City, IA 52240, 319-337-3845

Quality Repair Services, 45973 Warm Springs Blvd., Ste. 1, Fremont, CA 94539, 415-651-8486

R&M Associates, 330 Phillips Ave., S. Hackensack, NJ 07606, 201-440-8585

Raynet, 16810 Barker Springs Rd., Ste. 200, Houston, TX 77084, 713-578-3802

RBB Systems, Inc., 8767 T.R. 513, Shreve, OH 44676, 216-567-2906

React Computer Services, Inc., 865 N. Ellsworth, Villa Park, IL 60181, 708-832-1181

Repair Pro/D.S. Walker, 11210 Steeplecrest Dr., Houston, TX 77065, 800-262-7339

Restorr Magnetics, 1455 McCandless Dr., Milpitas, CA 95035, 408-946-9207

Rodax, Inc., 12366 Northup Way, Bellevue, WA 98005, 206-885-9999

Service 2000, Inc., 5301 E. River Rd., Ste. 108, Minneapolis, MN 55421, 800-338-6824

Serviceland of Upstate NY, Inc., 3259 Winton Rd., S. Rochester, NY 14623, 716-427-0880

Servitech, Inc., 1509 Brook Dr., Downers Grove, IL 60515, 708-620-8750

SMH Electronics Co., 16 Kendrick Rd., Wareham, MA 02571, 508-291-7447

Solutronix, 7255 Flying Cloud Dr., Eden Prairie, MN 55344, 800-875-2580

Sprague Magnetics, Inc., 15720 Stagg St., Van Nuys, CA 91406, 800-325-4243

SRM, Inc., 2231 S. Oneida, Green Bay, WI 54304, 414-497-7863

Synergy Computer Services, Inc., 755 Queensway E., Unit 26, Mississauga, ONT, CN L4 4C5, 416-273-9565

Systems Diagnosis, Inc., 3 Richmond Sq., Providence, RI 02906, 401-331-8980

Technical Sales & Service, 2820 Dorr Ave., Fairfax, VA 22031, 703-698-0347

Telford Technical Service, Inc., 9213 Fairview, Boise, ID, 83704, 208-322-1434

Test Engineering Services, Inc., 5653 Stoneridge Dr., Ste. 104, Pleasanton, CA 94588, 415-463-8146

The Repair Co., 1585 McCandless Dr., Milpitas, CA 95035, 408-946-5015

Total Maintenance Concepts, 746 Industrial Dr., Elmhurst, IL 60126

Trans Datacorp, 1200 O'Brien Dr., Menlo Park, CA 94025, 415-327-2692

Unicomp System, 11362 Westminster Ave., Ste. U, Garden Grove, CA 92643, 714-534-5092

Victor Computer Service, Inc., 8125 Westglen Drive, Houston, TX 77063, 713-789-1888 or 800-999-1827

Welling Electronics, 529 No. 33, Omaha, NE 68131, 402-342-6564

Wisk Computer Services, Inc., 1605 Watt Dr., Santa Clara, CA 95054, 408-748-9891 or 800-688-9701

Yaltronics, Inc., 650 W. Smith Rd., Medina, OH 44256, 216-723-HELP

PRINTER BUFFERS, SWITCHES, SHARING DEVICES

ASP Computer Products, Inc., 160 San Gabriel Drive, Sunnyvale, CA 94086, 408-746-2965 or 800-445-6190, FAX 408-746-2803

Buffalo Products, Inc., 2805 19th St. SE, Salem, OR 97302-1520, 503-585-4336 or 800-345-2356

Data Spec, 20120 Plummer St., Chatsworth, CA 91313, 818-993-1202

PRINTERS AND PLOTTERS

Advanced Matrix Technology, 765 Flynn Rd., Camarillo, CA 93012, 800-637-7898 or 800-992-2264

Alps America, 3553 North First St., San Jose, CA 95134-1803, 408-432-6000 or 800-825-2577

Apple Computer, Inc., 20525 Mariani Ave., Cuppertino, CA 95014, 408-973-2222

Brother International Corp., 200 Cotontail La., Somerset, NJ 08875, 201-981-0300

C. Itoh Electronics, Inc. (CIE), 2515 McCabe Way, Irvine, CA 92714, 714-833-8445 or 800-877-1421

C-Tech Electronics, Inc., 2515 McCabe Way, Irvine, CA 92714, 714-833-1165 or 800-347-4017, BBS 714-660-1656

Cal-Comp, P.O. Box 3250, Anaheim, CA 92803, 800-CAL-COMP

Canon USA Printer Div., P.O. Box CN 11250, Trenton, NJ 08650, 800-848-4123

Centronics, 603-881-0111

Citizen America Corp., 2450 Broadway, Suite 600, Santa Monica, CA 90404-3060, 213-453-0614 or 800-556-1234

Data General Corp., 4400 Computer Dr., Westboro, MA 01580, 800-345-3577

Dataproducts Corp., 6200 Canoga Ave., Woodland Hills, CA 91367, 818-887-8000

Datasouth, P.O. Box 240947, Charlotte, NC 28224, 704-523-8500 or 800-438-5050

DCS/Fortis, 1820 W. 220th St., Suite #220, Torrance, CA 90501, 213-782-6090 or 800-736-4847

Desktop Systems, Inc., 48431 Milmont Dr., Fremont, CA 94538, 415-683-4725

Epson America, Inc., 20770 Madrona Ave., Torrance, CA 90503, 213-782-2600 or 800-922-8911

Facit, Inc., 400 Commercial St., Manchester, NH 03108, 800-879-3224 or 603-647-2700

Fortis Information Systems, Inc., 6070 Rickenbacker Rd., Commerce, CA 90040, 800-241-0947

Fujitsu America, Inc., 3055 Orchard Dr., San Jose, CA 95134, 408-432-1300 or 800-826-6112, BBS 408-944-9897

Hewlett-Packard Co., 19310 Pruneridge Ave., Cupertino, CA 95014, 800-752-0900

Houston Instruments, 8500 Cameron Rd., Austin, TX 78753, 800-444-3425

IBM Co., 101 Paragon Dr., Montvale, NJ 07645, 800-426-2468

Juki Office Machine Co., 23844 Hawthorne Blvd., Ste. 101, Torrance, CA 90505, 800-325-6134

Kyocera Unison, Inc., 1321 Harbor Bay Pkwy., Alameda, CA 94051, 415-748-6680

Lexmark Corp. (IBM Printers), 740 New Circle Rd., Lexington, KY 40503, 606-232-3000 or 800-537-2540

Mannesmann Tally Corp., 8301 S. 180th St., Kent, WA 98032, 206-251-5524 or 800-843-1347

NCR Corp., 3718 North Rock Rd., Wichita, KS 67226, 316-636-8570

NEC, 1414 Massachusetts Ave., Boxborough, MA 01719, 508-264-4300 or 800-325-5500, BBS 508-264-8816

Okidata, 111 Gather Dr., Mount Laurel, NJ 08054, 609-235-2600

Packard Bell, 9425 Canoga Ave., Chatsworth, CA 91311, 818-773-4400

Panasonic Communications & Systems Co., 2 Panasonic Way, Secaucus, NJ 07042, 800-222-0584, BBS 201-863-7847

Panasonic, 425 E. Algonquin Rd., Arlington, IL 60005, 708-364-7900

Personal Computer Products, 11590 West Bernardo Court, Suite 100, San Diego, CA 92127, 619-485-8411

QMS, Inc., One Magnum Pass, Mobile, AL 36618, 205-633-4866, 800-438-4473

Qume Corp., 2350 Qume Dr., San Jose, CA 95131, 408-942-4000 or 800-223-2479

Seikosha America, Inc., 10 Industrial Ave, Mahwah, NJ 07430, 201-327-7227 or 800-477-7468

Sharp Electronics Corp., Sharp Plaza, Mahwah, NJ 07430, 201-529-9500

Shinwa of America, 5915 Lincoln Ave., Morton Grove, IL 60053

Star Micronics America, Inc., 420 Lexington Ave., Suite 2702, New York, NY 10170, 714-768-3612 or 800-227-8274

Texas Instruments, Inc., P.O. Box 202230, Austin, TX 78720, 800-527-3500

Toshiba, 9740 Irvine Blvd., Irvine, CA 92718, 714-380-3000 or 714-583-3961 or 800-624-5932 or 800-334-3445

PRINTHEAD REPAIR

7-Sigma, Inc., 2843 26th Ave. Minneapolis, MN 55406, 612-722-5358

Abex Data Systems, Inc., 1 Barnida Dr., East Hanover, NJ 07936, 201-887-2600

Accram Inc. Computer Repair Center, 2901 W. Clarendon, Phoenix, AZ 85017, 602-264-0288

Amcom, 6305 Bury Dr., Eden Prairie, MN 55346, 800-328-7723

American Digital, 82 Winchester St., Newton, MA 02161, 617-964-5270

American Computer Hardware, 2205 S. Wright St., Santa Ana, CA 92705, 714-549-2688

Amtec Computer Systems, 8515 Douglas, #15, Des Moines, IA 50322, 515-270-2480

Avnet Computer Technologies, Inc., 10000 W. 76th St., Eden Prairie, MN 55344, 800-877-2285

BRC Electronics, 3361 Boyington, Ste. 160, Carrollton, TX 75006, 214-385-3561

C. Hoelzle Associates, 2632 South Croddy Way, Santa Ana, CA 92704, 714-850-9191

Compufix, Inc., 4 W. Chimney Rock Rd., Bound Brook, NJ 08805, 201-271-0020

Compupair, Inc., 7808 Cherry Creek S. Dr., #102, Denver, CO 80231, 303-368-4541

Computer Care, Inc., 1116 Smith St., Rm 213, Charleston, WV 25301, 304-340-4283

Comstar, Inc., 5250 W. 74th St., Minneapolis, MN 55435, 800-735-5502

Cosmic Services, Inc., 3750 Hacienda Blvd., Ste. F, Ft. Lauderdale, FL 33314, 305-797-0143

Cosmic Enterprises, Inc., 84 South St., Hopkinton, MA 01748, 508-435-6967

CPE, Inc., 220 Mavis, Irving, TX 75061, 214-259-6010

Data Exchange Corp., 708 Via Alondra, Camarillo, CA 93010, 805-388-1711

Data Products Corp., 6219 DeSoto Ave., Woodland Hills, CA 91367, 818-887-3909

Datatech Depot, Inc., 1081 N. Shepard St., Anaheim, CA 92806, 714-632-1800

Depot America, Inc., 562 Lincoln Blvd., Middlesex, NJ 08846, 201-560-8584

DH Serv, 15070 Ave. of Science, San Diego, CA 92128, 619-487-7112

DMA, Inc., 611 Development Blvd., Amery, WI 54001, 715-268-8106

General Diagnostics, Inc., 1515 W. 190th St., Ste. 20, Gardena, CA 90248, 213-715-1222

Impact Printhead Services, 8701 Cross Park, #101, Austin, TX 78754, 512-832-9151

Juno Technical Services, Inc., 721 Sandoval Way, Hayward, CA 94544, 415-487-7601

Lone Star Data Corp., 500 Sandan, San Antonio, TX 78216, 512-340-6811

Lupac Computer Parts & Services USA, Inc., 21345 Lassen St., Chatsworth, CA 91311, 818-709-2621

Micro Products Repair Center, Inc., 405 Murray Hill Pkwy., E. Rutherford, NJ 07073, 201-896-1810

Northstar MatrixServ, 8055 Ranchers Rd., Minneapolis, MN 55432, 800-969-0009

Repair Pro/D.S. Walker, 11210 Steeplecrest Dr., Houston, TX 77065, 800-262-7339

Servonics Corp., 14 Kendrick Rd., Wareham, MA 02571, 508-295-6372

Trilogy Magnetics, 424 N. Millcreek Rd., Quincy, CA 95971, 916-283-3736

Voltura Enterprises, Inc., P.O. Box 251, Chester, NJ 07930, 201-879-5803

SCANNERS

Microtek Lab, Inc., 680 Knox Street, Torrance, CA 90502, 213-321-2121, 800-654-4160

SCHEMATICS AND SERVICE MANUALS

Howard W. Sams & Co., 4300 West 62nd Street, Indianapolis, IN 46268, 800-428-SAMS

Maintenance Information Technologies, 1275 Experiment Farm Rd., Suite B, Troy, OH 45373, 513-339-8095

Schematic Solutions, Inc., 11120 Wurzbach Rd. #206, San Antonio, TX 78230, 512-696-0404

SOFTWARE AND OPERATING SYSTEMS

Abacus Software, 5370 52nd St. SE, Grand Rapids, MI 49512, 616-698-0330

Access Technology, Two Natick Executive Park, Natick, MA 01760, 508-655-9191

Aldus, 411 1st. Ave. S., Ste. 200, Seattle, WA 98104, 800-33-ALDUS

Alpha Software Corp., 1 North Ave., Burlington, MA 01803, 800-451-1018

American Small Business Computers, Inc., 327 South Mill St., Pryor, OK 74361, 918-825-4844

Ashton-Tate, 20101 Hamilton Ave., Torrance, CA 90509-9972, 213-329-8000

Auto Desk, 415-332-2344

BMU Softworks, 2457 Perkiomen Ave., Reading, PA 19606, 800-333-7582, FAX 800-678-9850

Borland International, 1800 Green Hills Rd., Scotts Valley, CA 95066, 408-438-5300 or 800-331-0877

Brown Bag Software, 2155 S. Bascom Ave., Ste. 105, Campbell, CA 95008, 800-523-0764

Business Vision Management Systems, 140 Allstate Pkwy., Ste. 401, Markham, Ontario L3r 5Y8, 416-475-2767

C&S Consultants, 8205 Old Deer Trail, Raleigh, NC 77615, 919-847-9997

Central Point Software, Inc., 15220 NW Greenbriar Pkwy., Suite 200, Beaverton, OR 97006, 503-690-8090 or 800-888-8199

Clarion Software, 150 E. Sample Rd., Pompano Beach, FL 33064

Computer Associates International, Inc., 1240 McKay Dr., San Jose, CA 95131, 408-432-1764 or 800-645-3003 or 800-531-5326

Contact Software International, 1625 W. Crosby Rd., Carrollton, TX 75006, 214-418-1866

Cross Communications Company, 303-444-7799, FAX 444-4687

DacEasy, 17950 Preston Rd., Suite 800, Dallas, TX 75252, 214-248-0205 or 800-322-3279, FAX 214-250-3752, BBS 900-370-2322

DataEase International, 7 Cambridge Dr., Trumbull, CT 06611, 203-374-8000

DiagSoft, Inc., 5615 Scotts Valley Dr., #140, Scotts Valley, CA 95066, 408-438-8247

Digital Research, Inc., 60 Garden Ct., Monterey, CA 93942, 800-274-4374, FAX 800-955-3676

East Coast Software, 2300 Peachford Rd., Suite 1150, Atlanta, GA 30338, 404-455-9200

Enable Software, 313 Ushers Rd., Northway 10 Executive Park, Ballston Lake, NY 12019, 518-877-8236

Feldstar Software, P.O. Box 871564, Dallas, TX 75287, 214-407-1006

Fifth Generation Systems, Inc., 10049 N. Reiger Rd., Baton Rouge, LA 70809, 504-291-7221 or 800-873-4384

FormalSoft, P.O. Box 1913, Sandy, UT 84091, 801-565-0971

Funk Software, Inc., 222 Third St., Cambridge, MA 02142

Geoworks, 2150 Shattuck Ave., Berkeley, CA 94704, 415-644-0883

Gibson Research Corp., 22991 La Cadena, Laguna Hills, CA 92653, 714-830-2200

Haven Tree Software, Ltd., P.O. Box 1093, Thousand Island Park, NY 13692, 800-267-0668

Informix Software, Inc., 16011 College Blvd., Lenaxa, KS 66219, 913-599-7100

Intuit, 66 Willow Pl., Menlo Park, CA 94026, 800-624-8742

Landmark, 703 Grand Central St., Clearwater, FL 34616, 813-443-1331

Lotus Development Corp., 55 Cambridge Pkwy., Cambridge, MA 02142, 617-577-8500, BBS 900-454-9009

Management Information Software, Inc., 3301 Grandy Blvd., Tampa, FL 33611, 813-832-3449

Mathematica, Inc., 402 S. Kentucky Ave., Lakeland, FL 33801, 813-682-1128

MathSoft, Inc., 201 Broadway, Cambridge, MA 02139, 617-577-1017 or 800-628-4223

MECA Ventures, Inc., 355 Riverside Ave., Westport, CT 06880

Microcom, Inc., 500 River Ridge Dr., Norwood, MA 02062, 617-551-1000 or 800-822-8224

Micropro, 33 San Pablo Ave., San Rafael, CA 94903, 800-227-5609

Microsoft Corp., One Microsoft Way, Redmond, WA 98072-6399, 206-882-8086 or 800-541-1261 or 800-426-9400

Microway, P.O. Box 79, Kingston, MA 02364, 508-746-7341

Mosaic Software, Inc., 1972 Massachusetts Ave., Cambridge, MA 02140, 617-491-2434

Novell, Inc., 122 E. 1700 S., Provo, UT 84601, 801-379-5900

OnTrack Computer Systems, Inc., 6321 Bury Dr., Eden Prairie, MN 55346, 612-937-1107 or 800-752-1333

Open Systems, Inc., 7626 Golden Triangle Dr., Eden Prairie, MN 55344, 612-829-0011 or 800-328-2276

Paper Software, Inc., P.O. Box 567, New Paltz, NY 12561, 914-255-0056 or 800-551-5187

Peachtree Software, 800-554-8900

Personics, 63 Great Road, Maynard, MA 01754, 508-897-1575 or 800-445-3311, FAX 508-897-1947

Polaris Software, 17150 Via Del Campo, Suite 307, San Diego, CA 92127, 619-674-6500

Powerline Technologies, 4101 N. Stiles, Oklahoma City, OK 73105, 405-521-1203

Proteo Technology, 210 Carnegie Centre, Suite 101, Princeton, NJ 08540, 609-520-9880

Qualitas, Inc., 7101 Wisconsin Ave., Suite 1386, Bethesda, MD 20814, 301-907-6700

Quarterdeck Office Systems, 150 Pico Blvd., Santa Monica, CA 90405, 213-392-9851, FAX 213-399-3802

QUE, 800-992-0244

Quicksoft, Inc., 219 First Ave. N. #224, Seattle, WA 98109, 206-282-0452 or 800-888-8088

Santa Cruz Operation, 408-425-7222 or 800-626-8649

Simon & Schuster Software, Route 59 at Brookhill Drive, West Nyack, NY 10995, 800-223-4022

SitBack Technologies, Inc., 9290 Bond, Suite 104, Overland Park, KS 66214, 913-894-0808 or 800-873-7482

Software Publishing Corp., 1901 Landings Dr., Mountain View, CA 94039, 408-988-4005

SourceMate Information Systems, 20 Sunnyside Ave., Mill Valley, CA 94941, 415-381-1011

Spinnaker Software Corp., 201 Broadway, Cambridge, MA 02139, 617-494-1220 or 800-323-8088, FAX 617-494-1219

Stac Electronics, 5993 Avenida Encinas, Carlsbad, CA 92008, 619-431-7474

Storage Dimensions, Inc., 1656 McCarthy Blvd., Milpitas, CA 95035, 408-954-0710

Sundog Software Corp., 264 Court Street, Brooklyn, NY 11231, 718-855-9141, FAX 718-855-5844

Symantec, 10201 Torre Ave., Cupertino, CA 95014, 408-253-9600 or 800-441-7234

Teknon Corp., 8603 East Royal Palm Rd., Scottsdale, AZ 85258, 602-569-1500

Traveldata Company, 5266 Hollister Avenue, Suite 114, Santa Barbara, CA 93111, 800-325-0511

Traveling Software, Inc., 18702 North Creek Parkway, Bothell, WA 98011, 206-483-8088, 800-343-8080

Trius, Inc., P.O. Box 249, North Andover, MA 01845-0249, 508-794-9377, BBS 508-794-0762

Ventura Software, 15175 Innovation Dr., San Diego, CA 92128, 800-822-8221

Westbrook Technologies, Inc., 22 Pequot Park Road, P.O. Box 910, Westbrook, CT 06498-0910, 203-399-7111, 800-874-1495, FAX 203-399-7137

Westlake Data Corp., P.O. Box 1711, Austin, TX 78767, 512-328-1041

Wordperfect Corp., 1555 Technology Way, Orem, UT 84057, 801-226-2690 or 800-321-3248, BBS 801-226-5555

XyQuest, 44 Manning Rd., Billerica, MA 01821, 508-671-0888

ZSoft, 450 Franklin Rd., Ste. 100, Marietta, GA 30067, 404-428-0008

STATIC BAGS AND MATS

Static Control Components, Inc., P.O. Box 152, Sanford, NC 27331-0152, 800-356-2728

SYSTEMS AND TERMINALS

3E Electronic Purchasing, Inc., 38 W. 32nd St., #1410, New York, NY 10001, 212-967-2866 or 800-222-3237

A-Tronic Computer, 15703 E. Valley Blvd., Industry, CA 91744, 818-330-7528

Aberdeen, Inc., 1125 South Maple Ave., Unit P, Montebello, CA 90640, 800-552-6868

Abtech, Inc., 1431 Potrero Ave., Suite B, S. El Monte, CA 91733, 818-575-0007

Access Computer Technologies, 2225 El Camino Real, Santa Clara, CA 95050, 408-247-4990

Acer America Corporation (Acer, Inc.), 401 Charcot Ave., San Jose, CA 95131, 408-922-0333 or 800-733-2237

Acma Computers, Inc., 48501 Warm Springs Blvd., Fremont, CA 94539, 510-623-1212 or 800-456-8898, FAX 510-623-0818

Acron Technology, Inc., 182-H Dayton-Jamesburg Rd., Dayton, NJ 08810, 908-274-0300

Acumen Computer Systems, 12116 Severn Way, Riverside, CA 92503, 714-371-2992 or 800-876-0486, FAX 714-371-2993, BBS 714-371-2993

Advanced Logic Research, Inc., 9401 Jeronimo, Irvine, CA 92718, 714-581-6770, 800-444-4257, FAX 714-581-9240

Advanced Micro Computer Systems, 13933 N. Central Expwy., Suite #208, Dallas, TX 75243, 214-644-8850, FAX 214-644-8880

Allegro Computer Corp., P.O. Box 675, Troy, OH 45373, 800-326-7015

Altec Technology, 18555 E. Gale Ave., Industry, CA 91748, 818-912-8688 or 800-255-9971

Altima, 800-356-9990

American Mitac, 410 E. Plumeria Dr., San Jose, CA 95124, 408-432-1160 or 800-648-2287, BBS 408-954-9275

Ameritek International, Inc., 1061 N. Shepard St., Bldg. C, Anaheim, CA 92806, 714-666-0210

Amkly Systems, 60 Technology Dr., Irvine, CA 92718, 800-367-2655

Andrex Corp., 356 S. Milpitas Blvd., Milpitas, CA 95035, 408-263-3993 or 800-886-3993

Apex Computer, Inc., 1279 S. Willow St., Manchester, NH 03103

Apple Computer, Inc., 20525 Mariani Ave., Cuppertino, CA 95014, 408-973-2222

Arche Technologies, Inc., 48502 Kato Rd., Fremont, CA 94538, 510-623-8100 or 800-322-2724

Ares Microdevelopment, Inc., 23660-A Research Dr., Farmington Hills, MI 48335, 800-322-3200

Argonaut Network Systems, 1030 Calle Sombra #H, San Clemente, CA 92672, 714-361-0665 or 800-274-6638

Ariel Design, Inc., 45 Pond St., Norwell, MA 02061, 617-982-8800, 800-552-7435

AST Research, 16215 Alton Pkwy., Irvine, CA 92713-9658, 800-876-4278 , FAX 714-727-4773, BBS 714-727-4723

AT&T, 800-922-0354

Austin Computer Systems, 10300 Metric Blvd., Austin, TX 78758, 512-339-3500 or 800-752-4171, BBS 800-339-3582

Automated Computer Technology Corp., 10849 Kinghurst, Houston, TX 77099, 713-568-1778 or 800-521-9237

Auva Computer, 960 Industrial Dr., Elmhurst, IL 60126, 708-832-0160

Binary Technology, Inc., 2657 Beltline Rd., Carrolton, TX 75006, 214-417-0777 or 800-776-7990

Bitwise Designs, Inc., Rotterdam Industrial Park #50, Schenectady, NY 12306, 518-356-9741 or 800-367-5906

Blackship Computer Systems, Inc., 2031 O'Toole Ave., San Jose, CA 95131, 408-432-7500 or 800-231-8324, FAX 408-432-1443

Blue Circle Group, 6101 Baker Rd., #206, Minnetonka, MN 55345, 612-945-9144 or 800-747-9069, FAX 612-945-9170

Blue Star Computer, 2312 Central Ave. NE, Minneapolis, MN 55418-3764, 612-788-3711 or 800-950-8894, FAX 612-788-3442

Blue Dolphin Computers, Inc., 890 Cowan Rd., Suite F, Burlingame, CA 94010, 415-259-9890 or 800-345-0633

Boxlight Corp., 19689 7th Ave. NE, Suite 143, Poulsbo, WA 98370, 206-697-4008

C2 Micro Systems, 47560 Seabridge Dr., Fremont, CA 94538, 510-651-6432

Cad One Computer Design, Inc., 270 Communication Way #4D, Hyannis, MA 02601, 508-778-1897, FAX 508-778-1887

CCT, Inc., 15100 SW Koll Pkwy., Beaverton, OR 97006, 503-626-8126 or 800-944-8686

Centrix Computer Systems, 15316 E. Valley Blvd., Industry, CA 91746, 818-777-9187 or 800-777-9187

Club American Technologies, 3401 W. Warren Ave., Fremont, CA 94539, 415-683-6600

Comp & Soft Computers, 12037 Dorsett Rd., St. Louis, MO 63043, 314-298-1900 or 800-327-8486

Compaq Computer Corp., 20555 FM 149, Houston, TX 77070, 713-370-0670

Compuadd Computer Corp., 12303 Technology Blvd., Austin, TX 78727, 512-250-1489 or 800-999-9901, BBS 512-250-3226 or 900-990-0111

Computer Market Place, Inc., 1101 Sussex Blvd., Broomall, PA 19008, 215-690-6919 or 800-545-7397

Computer Systems West, 545 High St., Eugene, OR 97401, 503-342-4153 or 800-342-4153

Computers A La Carte, 190 Hampshire St., #102, Lawrence, MA 01840, 617-687-4681

Computrend Systems, Inc., 1306-1308 John Reed Ct., Industry, CA 91745, 800-568-6388

Comtrade Electronics USA, Inc., 1016-B Lawson St., City of Industry, CA 91748, 818-964-6688 or 800-969-2123

Continental Resources, Inc., P.O. Box 9137, Bedford, MA 01730, 617-275-0850 or 800-937-4688, BBS 617-275-4121

Copam, USA, 45875 Northport Loop E., Fremont, CA 94538, 800-828-4200

Cordata - Daewoo, 1055 W. Victoria St., Compton, CA 90220, 213-603-2901 or 800-233-3602

Corporate Triangle, 1350 Ridder Park Dr., San Jose, CA 95131, 408-453-8310 or 800-288-2180, FAX 408-441-8825

CPC Computer Products, 278 State St., North Haven, CT 06473, 203-281-6705 or 800-272-7281, FAX 203-776-3958

CSS Laboratories, Inc., 1641 McGraw Ave., Irvine, CA 92714, 714-852-8161 or 800-966-2771

CUI, 1680 Civic Center Dr. #101, Santa Clara, CA 95050, 408-988-2703 or 800-457-7298

Cumulus Corp., 23500 Mercantile Rd., Cleveland, OH 44122, 216-464-2211, BBS 216-464-3012

Datamedia Corp., 20 Trafalgar Sq., Nashua, NH 03063, 603-886-1570 or 800-832-4362

Datom Technologies, Inc., 511 Baddour Pkwy., Lebanon, TN 37087, 615-449-2434 or 800-874-1795

Dell Computer Corp, 9505 Arboretum Blvd., Austin, TX 78759-7299, 512-338-4400 or 800-624-9896, FAX 800-950-1329, BBS 512-338-8528

Designer Systems, 714 South Pascack Rd., Chestnut Ridge, NY 10977, 914-735-0559, FAX 914-735-0702

Digital Equipment Co., 146 Main St., Maynard, MA 01754, 800-344-4825

Digitech Microsystems, 800 Monterey Pass Rd., Monterey Park, CA 91754, 213-267-1638 or 800-999-7957

DTK Computer, Inc., 17700 Castleton St. Suite #300, City of Industry, CA 01748, 818-810-0098 or 800-925-7318

Dyna Micro, 30 West Montague Expwy., San Jose, CA 95134, 408-943-0100 or 800-336-3962

Eltech Research, Inc., 47266 Benicia St., Fremont, CA 94538, 800-365-8355

Empac International Corp., 47560 Seabridge Dr., Fremont, CA 94538, 510-651-6432

Epson America, Inc., 3415 Kashiwa St., Torrance, CA 90505, 213-539-9140

Ergo Computing, One Intercontinental Way, Peabody, MA 01960, 508-535-7510 or 800-633-1925, FAX 508-535-7512

Essence Group, Inc., 17815 Newhope St., Suite #203, Fountain Valley, CA 92708, 714-546-3111, BBS 714-455-0425

Everex Systems, Inc., 48431 Milmont Dr., Fremont, CA 94538, 800-356-4283

Fail-Safe Technology Corp., 5757 W. Century, #645, Los Angeles, CA 90045, 310-417-4988

Falco Data Products, 440 Potrero Ave., Sunnyvale, CA 94086, 408-745-7123 or 800-325-2648

First Computer Systems, Inc., 6000 Live Oak Pkwy., Suite 107, Norcross, GA 30093, 404-441-1991

Frontier Systems, Inc., 2819 N. Hamline Ave., Roseville, MN 55113, 800-926-6788

Fujikama U.S.A., Inc., 865 N. Ellsworth, Villa Park, IL 60181, 800-883-8830

Futuretech Systems, Inc., 6 Bridge St., Hackensack, NJ 07601, 201-488-4414 or 800-275-4414

Gateway 2000, 610 Gateway Dr., North Sioux City, SD 57025, 800-523-2000

Grand Technology, Inc., 4019 Clipper Ct., Fremont, CA 94538, 510-659-1002

GRiD Systems Corp., 47211 Lakeview Blvd., Fremont, CA 94538, 415-656-4700

Hast Computer Systems, Ltd., 2781 Brower Ave., Oceanside, NY 11572, 516-678-9165 or 800-253-7922

HeadStart Technologies Co., 40 Cutter Mill Rd., Suite 438, Great Neck, NY 11021

Hewlett-Packard Co., 1131 Chinden Blvd., Boise, ID 83714, 800-367-4472

Homesmart Computing, 14760 Memorial Dr., Suite #303, Houston, TX 77079, 713-589-2749 or 713-589-7100 or 800-627-6998

Hyundai, 166 Baypointe Pkwy., San Jose, CA 95134, 408-473-9200

IBC/Integrated Business Computers, 21621 Nordhoff, Chatsworth, CA 91311, 800-468-5847, BBS 818-882-9217

IBM, P.O. Box 1328-W, Boca Raton FL 33429

Imperial Computer, 31A S. San Gabriel Blvd., San Gabriel, CA 91776, 818-285-1258

Infomatic Power Systems, 9832 Alburtis Ave., Santa Fe Springs, CA 90670, 310-948-2217

Insight Computers, 2415 S. Roosevelt, Tempe, AZ 85282, 602-967-4999 or 800-488-0007, FAX 602-350-1182

Iverson Computer Corp., P.O. Box 6250, 1356 Beverly Rd., McLean, VA 22106, 800-444-7290

Kaypro Corp., 533 Stevens Ave., Solana Beach, CA 92075, 619-481-4300

Keydata International, Inc., 111 Corporate Blvd., S. Plainfield, NJ, 908-755-0350 or 800-486-4800, FAX 908-756-7359

Kris Technologies, 260 East Grand Ave., South San Francisco, CA 94080, 415-875-6729 or 800-282-5747

Lancer Research Inc., 140 Atlantic St., Pomona, CA 91768, 714-396-8100 or 800-888-9808

Lasermaster Corp., 6900 Shady Oak Rd., Eden Prairie, MN 55344, 612-944-9331 or 800-462-1891, BBS 612-835-5463

Leading Technology, Inc., 10430 SW Fifth St., Beaverton, OR 97005, 503-646-3424 or 800-999-4888

Leading Edge Products, Inc., 117 Flanders Rd., Westborough, MA 01581, 508-836-4800 or 800-874-3340

Legatech Computers, 789 South San Gabriel Blvd., Suite #1, San Gabriel, CA 91776, 818-309-2941 or 800-892-9911

Link Technologies, Inc., 47339 Warm Springs Blvd., Fremont, CA 94539, 415-651-8000 or 800-448-5465

Lodestar Computer, 18539 E. Gale Ave., City of Industry, CA 91748, 818-810-3818 or 800-875-7569, FAX 818-810-5928

Loop Technology, 15355 Barranca Pkwy., Irvine, CA 92718, 213-404-1686

Micro Express, 1801 Carnegie Ave., Santa Ana, CA 92705, 714-852-1400 or 800-782-3378, FAX 714-852-1225

Micro Generation, 300 McGraw Dr., Edison, NJ 08837, 908-225-8899 or 800-872-2895

Micro Smart, Inc., 200 Homer Ave., Ashland, MA 01721, 508-872-9090 or 800-370-9090, FAX 508-881-1520

Microlab, 23976 Freeway Park Dr., Farmington Hills, MI 48335, 313-474-0408 or 800-388-7818

Miltope Corp., 1770 Walt Whitman Rd., Melville, NY 11747, 516-420-0200

Misys, Inc., 1351 Oakbrook Dr., #160, Norcross, GA 30093, 404-448-8486 or 800-932-6936

Mitsuba Corp., 1925 Wright Ave., La Verne, CA 91750, 714-392-2000

MRC Technology, Inc., 1400 W. Lambert Rd., #D, Brea, CA 92621, 310-690-9455 or 800-878-5868

Naga Computers, 1520 W. Mineral Rd., Tempe, AZ 85283, 602-820-3294 or 800-964-3939, FAX 602-820-3294

NCI/National Computer, Inc., 7000 N. Broadway, #3, Denver, CO 80221, 800-659-5012

NCR Corp., USG-1, Dayton, OH 45479, 800-226-6627

NEC Technologies, Inc., 1414 Massachusetts Ave., Boxborough, MA 01709, 508-264-8000 or 800-388-8888 or 800-325-5500

Netis Technology, Inc., 1544 Centro Pointe Dr., Milpitas, CA 95035, 402-263-0395

New MMI Corp., 2400 Reach Rd., Williamsport, PA 17701, 717-327-9200 or 800-221-4283 or 800-233-8950, BBS 717-327-9952 or 717-327-4953

Northgate Computer Systems, Inc., 7075 Flying Cloud Drive, Eden Prairie, MN 55344, 612-943-8181 or 800-446-5037, BBS 612-943-8341

Noteable Computers, Inc., 18436 Ward St., Fountain Valley, CA 92708, 714-964-1837, FAX 714-968-4338

Oakfield Computer Manufacturing, Peekskill, NY 10566, 914-739-7400 or 800-858-7755, FAX 914-739-2889

Olivetti Office USA, P.O. Box 6945, Bridgewater, NJ 08807-0945, 908-526-8200 or 800-527-2960

Packard Bell, 9425 Canoga Ave., Chatsworth, CA 91311, 818-773-4400

Pan United Corp., 2 Ethel Rd., Suite #203-83, Edison, NJ 08817

PC Craft, Inc., 640 Puente St., Brea, CA 92621, 714-256-5026, BBS 714-256-5033

PC Ease, Inc., 5813 Main St., #10, Williamsville, NY 14221, 716-626-0315 or 800-472-3273, FAX 716-626-1541

PC Brand, 877 Supreme Dr., Bensenville, IL 60106, 800-347-8324, FAX 800-722-7392

PC Ware International, Inc., 43-35 10th St., Long Island City, NY 11101, 718-706-7770 or 800-253-9538, FAX 718-706-7864

Polywell Computers, Inc., 61-C Airport Blvd., S. San Francisco, CA 94080, 415-583-7255 or 800-799-1278

Positive Corp., 818-341-5400 or 800-252-6345

Prime Computer, Inc., Prime Park, Natick, MA 01760, 800-343-2540

Proteus Technology Corp., 377 Rt. 17 Airport Center, Hasbrouck Heights, NJ 07604, 201-288-2041 or 800-878-6462, BBS 201-288-2241

Quad Micro Systems, Inc., 60 James Way, Southampton, PA 18966, 215-322-7058

Reply Corporation, 4435 Fortran Dr., San Jose, CA 95134, 408-473-7592 or 800-955-5295

Rever Cruiser, 716-723-8820

Rose Hill Systems, 4865 Scotts Valley Drive, Scotts Valley, CA 95066, 408-438-3871 or 800-248-7673, FAX 408-438-3642

SAI Systems Laboratories, Inc., 911 Bridgeport Ave., Shelton, CT 06484, 203-929-4959 or 800-331-0488

Saint Croix Computer, P.O. Box 309, 4661 Stillwater Blvd., Lake Elmo, MN 55042

Samsung Information Systems America, Inc., 3655 North First St., San Jose, CA 95134, 408-434-5400 or 800-446-0262, FAX 408-434-5653, BBS 800-624-8999

Sceptre Technologies, Inc., 560 S. Melrose St., Placentia, CA 92670, 714-933-0800

Songtech International, Inc., 44061 So. Grimmer Blvd., Fremont, CA 94538, 415-770-9051, FAX 415-770-9060

Standard Computer, 12803 Schabarum Ave., Irwindale, CA 91706, 818-337-7711 or 800-662-6111, FAX 818-960-2926, BBS 818-338-9894

Swan Technologies, 3075 Research Dr., State College, PA 16801, 814-238-1820 or 800-468-7926, BBS 814-237-6145

Tandon, 49 Strathearn Place, Simi Valley, CA 93065, 805-581-2995

Tangent Computer, Inc., 197 Airport Blvd., Burlingame, CA 94010, 800-223-6677

Tatung Company of America, Inc., 2850 El Presidio St., Long Beach, CA 90810, 213-979-7055 or 800-827-2850

Televideo Systems, Inc., 1170 Morse Ave., Sunnyvale, CA 94088, 408-745-7760 or 800-835-3228

Texas Instruments, 800-527-3500

Toshiba America Computer Systems Division, 9740 Irvine Blvd., Irvine, CA 92718, 714-583-3000 or 800-334-3445

Touche Micro Technologies, 8205 S. Cass Ave., Darien, IL 60559, 708-810-9977 or 800-999-2486

Transcomputer, Inc., 1026 W. Maude, Bldg. #304, Sunnyvale, CA 94086, 408-733-3070

Treasure Chest, 1310 Carroll St., Kenner, LA 70062, 504-468-2113 or 800-245-3040, FAX 504-461-8095

Tri-Star Computer, 120 S. Weber Dr., Chandler, AZ 85226, 800-688-8324, BBS 602-966-3122

Trident Technologies, Ltd., 580 Washington St., Newton, MA 02158

Trisys Marketing Co., 1026 W. Maude, #304, Sunnyvale, CA 94086, 408-733-3073

Ultra-Comp, 3801 Ultra-Comp Dr., Earth City, MO 63045, 314-298-1998 or 800-828-1766

Unisys, P.O. Box 500, Blue Bell, PA 19124, 800-448-1424

Wyse, 800-438-9973

Xinergy Microsystems, 278 Daniel Webster Hwy. S., Nashua, NH 03060, 603-888-8288

Xinetron, Inc., 2338A Walsh Ave., Santa Clara, CA 95051, 408-727-5509 or 800-345-4415

Zenith Data Systems, 1000 Milwaukee Ave., Glenview, IL 60025, 312-391-8744 or 800-523-9393

Zeos International, Ltd., 530 5th Ave. NW, St. Paul, MN 55112, 612-633-7337 or 800-228-5390 or 800-848-9022, BBS 612-633-0815

TAPE BACKUP EQUIPMENT

Archive Corporation, Data Storage Division, 1650 Sunflower Ave., Costa Mesa, CA 92626, 714-966-5589 or 800-537-2248

Colorado Memory Systems, 800 S. Taft Ave., Loveland, CO 80537, 303-669-8000

Cybernetics Group, Rock Landing Corporate Center, 11846 Rock Landing, Newport News, VA 23606, 804-873-9000, FAX 804-873-8836

Emerald Systems, 12230 World Trade Dr., San Diego, CA 92128, 800-767-2587

Exabyte Corp., 1685 38th St., Boulder, CO 80301, 800-392-2983

Irwin Magnetics, 2101 Commonwealth Blvd., Ann Arbor, MI 48105, 800-348-6242

Maynard Electronics, 36 Skyline Dr., Lake Mary, FL 32746, 407-263-3500 or 800-821-8782, FAX 407-263-3638

Mountain Computer, 360 El Pueblo Road, Scotts Valley, CA 95066, 408-379-4300 or 800-458-0300

Summit Memory Systems, Inc., 100 Technology Circle, Scotts Valley, CA 95066, 408-438-2660, FAX 408-439-6725

Tallgrass Technology, 11100 W. 82nd St., Overland Park, KS 66214, 913-492-1496

Tecmar, 6225 Cochran Rd., Solon, OH 44139, 216-349-1009 or 800-422-2587, FAX 216-349-0851

TAPE DRIVE REPAIR

Digital Repair Corp., 8918 Tesoro Drive, Suite 108, San Antonio, TX 78217, 512-828-2256

TEST EQUIPMENT

AVA Instrumentation, Inc., 8010 Highway 9, Ben Lomond CA 95005, 408-336-2281

Computer Service Technology, Inc., 2546 Merrell, Dallas, TX 75229, 214-241-2662

Contact East, 335 Willow Street South, P.O. Box 786, North Andover, MA 01845, 617-682-2000

Jameco Electronics, 1355 Shoreway Rd., Belmont, CA 94002, 415-592-8097

Jensen Tools, Inc., 7815 South 46th St., Phoenix, AZ 85044, 602-968-6231

John Fluke Mfg. Co., Inc., P.O. Box C9090, Everett, WA 98206, 206-347-6100

M-Test Equipment, 118 King St., Suite 420, San Francisco, CA 94107, 415-882-4100 or 800-334-4193

MCM Electronics, 650 Congress Park Dr., Centerville, OH 45459, 513-434-0031 or 800-543-4330

NTI (Network Technologies, Inc.), 7322 Pettibone Rd., Chagrin Falls, OH 44022, 216-543-1646 or 800-RGB-TECH

Polar Instruments, 8229 44th Ave. W., Suite H, Mukilteo, WA 98275, 206-355-2554 or 800-328-0817

Print Products International Inc., 8931 Brookville Rd., Silver Spring, MD 20910, 301-587-7824 or 800-638-2020

Protek, P.O. Box 59, Norwood, NJ 07648, 201-767-7242

Proto PC, Inc., 2439 Franklin Ave., St. Paul, MN 55114, 612-644-4660

Schlumberger Technologies, Instruments Division, P.O. Box 7004, 829 Middlesex Turnpike, Billerica, MA 01821, 508-671-9710 or 800-225-5765

Specialized Products Co., 3131 Premier Drive, Irving, TX 75063, 800-527-5018

Techni-Tool, 5 Apollo Road, Box 368, Plymouth Meeting, PA 19462, 215-825-4990

Tektronix, P.O. Box 4600, Beaverton, OR 97076, 800-426-2200

Time Motion Tools, 410 South Douglas St., El Segundo, CA 90245, 213-772-8170 or 800-779-8170

United Electronic Industries, 10 Dexter Ave., Watertown, MA 02172, 617-924-1155

TOOLS

Bondhus Corp., 1400 E. Broadway, P.O. Box 660, Monticello, MN 55362, 612-295-5500 or 800-328-8310

Branson Ultrasonics Corp., 41 Eagle Rd., Danbury, CT 06813, 203-796-0400 (ULTRASONIC KEYBOARD CLEANERS)

Contact East, 335 Willow Street South, P.O. Box 786, North Andover, MA 01845, 617-682-2000

Jameco Electronics, 1355 Shoreway Rd., Belmont, CA 94002, 415-592-8097

Jensen Tools, Inc., 7815 South 46th St., Phoenix, AZ 85044, 602-968-6231

MCM Electronics, 650 Congress Park Dr., Centerville, OH 45459, 513-434-0031 or 800-543-4330

Metro Data Vac, One Ramapo Ave., Suffern, NY 10901, 914-357-1600 or 800-822-1602, FAX 914-357-1640

Mouser Electronics, P.O. Box 699, Mansfield, TX 76063, 800-346-6873

Print Products International Inc., 8931 Brookville Rd., Silver Spring, MD 20910, 301-587-7824 or 800-638-2020

Specialized Products Co., 3131 Premier Dr., Irving, TX 75063, 800-527-5018

Techni-Tool, 5 Apollo Road, Box 368, Plymouth Meeting, PA 19462, 215-825-4990

Time Motion Tools, 410 South Douglas St., El Segundo, CA 90245, 213-772-8170 or 800-779-8170

Tool Kit Specialists, Inc., 1366 Borregas Ave., Sunnyvale, CA 94089, 408-745-6020

Glossary
of Terms

8086—An Intel microprocessor with 16-bit registers, a 16-bit data bus, and a 20-bit address bus that can only operate in real mode.

8088—An Intel microprocessor with 16-bit registers, an 8-bit data bus, and a 20-bit address bus that can only operate in real mode. This processor was designed as a low-cost version of the 8086.

80286—An Intel microprocessor with 16-bit registers, a 16-bit data bus, and a 24-bit address bus that can operate in either real or protected mode.

80386—An intel microprocessor with 32-bit registers, a 32-bit data bus, and a 32-bit address bus that can operate in either real, protected, or virtual mode.

80386SX—An Intel microprocessor with 32-bit registers, 16-bit data bus, and 24-bit address bus that can operate in real, protected, or virtual mode. The 80386SX was designed as a low-cost version of the 80386.

AC (Alternating Current)—A current that swings from negative to positive in a cyclic pattern, measured in cycles per second (cps) or hertz (Hz).

accelerator board—An add-in board that replaces the computer's CPU (and sometimes the clock), allowing the system to run faster.

access time—The time needed from the point where information is requested until the information is delivered, usually measured in nanoseconds for electronic components (RAM), and milliseconds for mechanical access (hard drives).

active device—In current loop applications, a device capable of supplying current for the loop.

active high—A digital signal that has to go to a high value (binary 1) to produce an effect. Same as positive or true.

active low—A signal that has to go to a low value (binary 0) to produce an effect. Same as negative or false.

actuator—The device in a disk drive that moves the read/write heads across the platter surface.

adapter—A name used by IBM to describe a board or card inserted into an expansion bus slot in order to attach a device to the system.

address—The location in memory where a particular piece of data or an instruction resides. A unique sequence of bits, a character, or a group of characters that identifies a network station, user, or application; a unique designation for the location of data; used mainly for routing purposes

address bus—A group of electrical conductors used to transmit address information between the microprocessor and other devices connected to the system.

ADF (Adapter Definition File)—A configuration file that is included with an adapter used to expand a microchannel system.

alphanumeric—A character that is either a letter, number, or a punctuation mark.

analog—A continuously variable signal. In communications, transmission employing variable and continuous wave-forms to represent information values, where interpretation by the receiver is an approximation (quantification) of the encoded value; compare with Digital.

ANSI (American National Standards Institute)—The principal development standards organization in the U.S.A.; the U.S.A.'s member body to the ISO. ANSI is a nonprofit independent body that is supported by trade organizations, professional societies, and industry. (ANSI defined ASCII.)

APA (All Points Addressable)—A video mode in which all pixels can be controlled by software.

API—Application Program Interface. A set of formalized software calls and routines that can be referenced by an application program to access underlying network services.

APPC—Advanced Peer to Peer Communications. Uses Logical Unit (LU) 6.2, a network node definition by IBM, featuring high-level program interaction capabilities on a peer- to-peer basis.

AppleTalk—A proprietary computer networking standard promulgated by Apple Computer for use in connecting Macintosh computers and other peripherals, particularly LaserWriter printers. Operates at 230 kilobytes per second (Kbps).

application layer—The highest of the seven layers of the OSI model structure. Contains all user or application programs. In the IBM SNA (Systems Network Architecture), the end-user layer.

application software—A group of interrelated programs that perform a specific function in the processing or manipulation of data.

archive bit—One bit in a file's attribute byte that tells whether the file has been changed since it was last backed up.

architecture—1. Overall building wiring. 2. Local Area Network topology (bus, ring, star, etc.). 3. In a computer, the size (8-, 16-, or 32-bit) and type of bus (EISA, ISA, Microchannel)

ARP (Address Resolution Protocol)—A Transmission Control Protocol/Internet Protocol (TCP/IP) process that maps IP addresses to Ethernet addresses; required by TCP/IP for use with Ethernet.

ARPA (Advanced Research Projects Agency)—Developed the first major packet-switched network; operates within the U.S. Department of Defense.

ARQ (Automatic Request for Retransmission)—A communications feature whereby the receiver asks the transmitter to resend a block or frame, generally because of errors detected by the receiver.

ASCII (American Standard Code for Information Interchange)— A standard 7- or 8-bit code used to represent alphanumeric data, control codes, and certain graphics characters. A 7-bit plus parity character set established by ANSI and used for data communications and data processing. ASCII allows compatibility among data services; one of two such codes (see EBCDIC) used in data interchange, ASCII is normally used for asynchronous transmission.

asynchronous—Data transmission that is not related to the timing, or a specific frequency, of a transmission facility; transmission characterized by individual characters, or bytes, encapsulated with start and stop bits, from which a receiver derives the necessary timing for sampling bits; also start/stop transmission.

ATE (Automated Test Equipment)—Units such as those manufactured by Fluke and Schlumberger, used to locate a failing component on a printed circuit board.

attenuation—Deterioration of signals as they pass through a transmission media, as measured in decibels; opposite of gain.

attribute byte—A byte of information that is part of a file's directory entry describing attributes of that file such as read only, or backed up since the last change. Attributes can be set using the ATTRIB command found in MS-DOS.

AUI—Attachment Unit Interface. Most commonly used with reference to the 15 pin D-type connector and cables used to connect single- and multiple-channel equipment to an Ethernet transceiver.

AUTOEXEC.BAT—A special batch file, customized for each system, which MS-DOS will execute upon booting, containing a group of sequentially executing commands.

automatic head parking—Hard drive head parking performed automatically whenever the drive is normally powered off.

AWG—American Wire Gauge. A standard for determining wire size. The gauge varies inversely with the wire diameter.

backbone—The backbone is that part of the network that carries the heaviest traffic. It is the main trunk cable from which all connections to the network are made. A transmission facility designed to interconnect low-speed distribution of user devices.

bad sector—A disk sector that can not be used because of a flaw in the media or damaged format information.

bad track table—A label attached to a hard drive, supplied by the manufacturer (or a repair facility), listing defective tracks. This is needed for low-level formatting.

balun—Balanced/Unbalanced, an impedance-matching device to connect balanced twisted pair cabling with unbalanced coaxial cable.

bandwidth—The difference, expressed in hertz (Hz), between the highest and lowest frequencies of a transmission channel.

bank—A group of memory chips that make up a block of memory, consisting of one chip for each line in the data bus and one parity chip for each 8 bits. A machine with an 80386 processor has 36 chips (32 for the data lines and 4 parity chips) in a bank.

barrel contact—An insulation displacement type contact (see IDC) consisting of a slotted tube that cuts the insulation when the wire is inserted.

baseband—The total bandwidth or capacity of a cable is used to transmit a single digital signal.

BASIC (Beginners All-purpose Symbolic Instruction Code)—A high-level programming language that is included with MS-DOS. IBM systems have a version of BASIC in ROM, which will load if a bootable disk is not present.

batch file—A file with the extension BAT, which causes a group of MS-DOS commands to execute sequentially. See AUTOEXEC.BAT.

batch processing—A data processing technique in which data is accumulated and then processed in a large group. Opposite of interactive or on-line processing.

baud—A measure of the rate of data transmission that roughly corresponds to the number of bits-per-second being passed.

bezel—A cosmetic panel covering all or part of an opening into which a mass storage device would be installed.

binary—The base-2 numbering system where the only possible digits are 0 and 1.

BIOS (Basic Input Output System)—Programs supplied by the manufacturer in the form of Read Only Memory (ROM) that define and control the physical parts and limitations of the computer.

bisynchronous—A closely timed method of communication between computers, usually used with mainframe and minicomputers.

bit (binary digit)—One-eighth of a byte. A single digit represented by a 1 or 0, on or off, high or low, or other means.

bit duration—The time it takes for one encoded bit to pass a point on the transmission medium. In serial communications, a relative unit of time measurement, used for comparison of delay times.

block—A group of records, words, characters, RAM, or cylinders on a disk, treated as one logical entity.

boot—To load an operating system into a computer.

boot record—The first record loaded by an operating system, which interacts with the BIOS and tells the computer how to proceed from that point.

bps—Bits per second. Often preceded by K (kilo/thousands) or M (mega/million).

bridge—A device that connects different local area networks at the data-link layer.

broadband—The bandwidth capacity of a specific cable which is divided into numerous channels and can transmit various signals simultaneously.

broadcast—A method of transmitting messages to two or more stations at the same time, such as over a bus-type local area network. A protocol mechanism whereby group and universal addressing is supported.

buffer—A segment of memory used to store data temporarily while it is being transferred from one device to another. Buffers are used for transferring information from the computer to a printer, a hard disk to memory, or between devices that accommodate different transmission rates.

bus—A Local Area Network topology in which all workstations are connected to a single cable. All stations hear all transmissions on the cable. Each workstation then selects those transmissions addressed to it based on address information contained in the transmission.

byte—A unit of information (character). A group of eight (sometimes seven) bits.

card—A printed circuit board, usually inserted into an expansion slot. Used interchangeably with board or adapter.

carrier—A signal upon which data signals are superimposed.

CCITT (Consultative Committee for International Telephony and Telegraphy)—An international association that sets worldwide communication standards.

CD ROM (Compact Disk Read Only Memory)—A compact disk containing up to 650 megabytes of data.

CGA (Color Graphics Array)—A video system that supports graphics with resolution of 320 X 200 in four colors or 640 X 200 in monochrome mode.

channel—A physical or logical path for the transmission of information.

character—A standard 8-bit unit representing a symbol, letter, number, or punctuation mark.

character-oriented—Describing a communications protocol or a transmission procedure that carries control information encoded in fields of one or more bytes.

characteristic impedance—The impedance termination of an (approximately) electrically uniform transmission line that minimizes reflections from the end of the line.

checksum—A technique for determining whether a package of data is valid by adding up a string of binary digits and comparing the result with a predetermined number.

chip—Another name for integrated circuit or IC, derived from the "chip" of silicon contained within the IC.

clean room—A dust-free environment rated by a "class" number that refers to the size and number of dust particles per cubic foot of space. Hard drives must be opened in a clean room so that dust is not trapped inside.

clock—A crystal that provides timing signals to the computer.

closet—Typically refers to the point on each floor of a building where workstations connect to the trunk cable or Local Area Network.

cluster—A group of one or more disk sectors, the size of which varies depending on the disk type and DOS version.

CMOS (Complimentary Metal Oxide Semiconductor)—A type of chip that requires very little power, used to store system configuration information, and powered by a battery when system power is not present.

coaxial cable—A transmission medium consisting of one central wire (two for twinaxial) surrounded by a dielectric insulator and encased in a metal sheath. Also called "coax."

cold boot—The sequence of events that takes place when power is applied to a computer.

COMMAND.COM—The MS-DOS command processor, a file that must be present in the root directory of a boot disk in order for a microcomputer system to boot and function. COMMAND.COM interprets instructions entered by the operator or contained within a program.

communications server—An intelligent device (computer) providing communications functions. An intelligent, specially configured node on a local area network that is designed to enable remote communications access and exit for LAN users.

composite video—Video information and sync. pulses combined, available on some video adapters, for feeding certain types of monitors and video equipment. The Apple II series uses composite video. Most PC class machines do not use composite video, although several Color Graphics Adapters (CGA) have a composite video connector.

compression—Any of several techniques that reduce the number of bits required to represent data for purposes of transmission or storage.

computer—A device that stores and processes data (information).

concentrator—Any communications device that allows a shared transmission medium to accommodate more data sources than there are channels currently available within the transmission medium.

conditioning—Extra-cost options that users may apply to leased, dedicated, or voice grade telephone lines to increase line quality or speed.

CONFIG.SYS—A file, customized for each system, that modifies MS-DOS and system ROM information, depending upon the needs of specific application software and physical devices.

configuration file—A file that works in conjunction with an application to tell the software information about the configuration of the printer and video system.

console—The terminal and/or keyboard that is used to communicate with the processor.

contention—In communications, a situation where multiple users vie for access to a transmission channel within a multiplexed digital facility.

controller—The card, board, or adapter used to interface a device (such as a hard drive or tape unit) with the system by way of the expansion bus.

coprocessor—An additional processor, designed to handle specific tasks in conjunction with the main processor.

core—The central region of an optical wave guide through which light is transmitted, typically 8 to 12 microns in diameter for single mode fiber and 50 to 100 microns for multi-mode fiber. A term for memory, used in mainframe environments.

CP/M (Control Program for Microcomputers)—An 8-bit operating system written by Digital Research and widely used before the advent of the PC and MS-DOS.

CPS (Cycles [Characters] Per Second)—The frequency of alternating current, formerly expressed in cycles per second, now expressed in hertz (Hz.). Comparative speed of a printer expressed as characters per second.

CPU (Central Processing Unit)—The microprocessor chip that contains the processor, arithmetic logic unit, and registers.

CRC (Cyclic Redundancy Check)—A basic error-checking mechanism for link-level data transmissions. The data integrity of a received frame or packet is checked via a polynomial algorithm based on the content of the frame and then matched by the result obtained by the sender and included in a (most, 16-bit) field appended to the frame.

cross connect—The physical connection between patch panels or punch down blocks that facilitates connection from the workstation to the host or network.

cross talk—The unwanted introduction of signals from one channel to another.

cross wye—A cable used at the host system, or network interface equipment, that changes pin/signal assignment in order to conform to a given wiring standard (USOC, AT&T PDS, DEC, MMJ, etc.).

CRT (Cathode Ray Tube)—Generic term to describe a video monitor or terminal. The glass cylinder that acts as the viewing screen in a video monitor. This tube contains and retains hazardous voltages.

CSMA/CD (Carrier Sense Multiple Access / Collision Detection)—A local area network access method in which contention between two or more stations is resolved by collision detection. When two (or more) stations transmit at the same time, they both stop and signal that a collision has occurred. Each then tries again after waiting a predetermined time period.

CSU (Channel Service Unit)—A piece of customer equipment used to terminate a digital circuit, such as a DDS or T1. It performs certain line conditioning functions, ensures network compliance with FCC rules, and responds to loopback commands from the central office.

current loop—A form of long distance serial communication that requires a constant source of current on the line.

cursor—A flashing (sometimes not flashing) mark that indicates the area on the monitor where input from the keyboard will appear.

cylinder—The total number of tracks on a disk that can be read while the platter(s) are rotating and the head(s) are stationary.

D4 framing—A T1 12-frame format in which the 193rd bit is used for framing and signaling information.

daisy chain—The connecting together of two or more devices. In a Thin Ethernet network, nodes are daisy-chained together. SCSI devices also are daisy-chained.

data—Information.

data communications—The transmission, reception, and validation of data. Data transfer between data source (origin node) and data sink (destination node) via one or more data links according to appropriate protocols.

data link—Any serial data communications transmission path, generally between two adjacent nodes or devices, and without intermediate switching nodes. A data link includes the physical transmission medium, the protocol, and associated devices and software, so it is both a physical and logical link.

data-link layer—Second layer in the OSI model. The network processing entity that establishes, maintains, and releases data link connections between (adjacent) elements in a network. Controls access to the physical medium (Layer One).

data-transfer rate—The average number of bits, characters, or blocks per unit of time, transferred from a data source to a data sink.

datagram—A finite-length packet with sufficient information to be independently routed from source to destination. Datagram transmission typically does not involve end-to-end session establishment and may or may not entail delivery-confirmation acknowledgment.

DCE (Data Communications Equipment)—The designation given to equipment that provides the functions required to establish, maintain, and terminate a data transmission connection, such as modems and multiplexers, by the Electronic Industry of America (EIA). Differs from DTE (Data Terminal Equipment) in that it transmits data on pin 3 and receives data on pin 2.

DDS (Dataphone Digital Service)—A private-line digital service offered intraLATA by BOCs (Bell Operated Companies) and interLATA by AT&T Communications with data rates typically at 2.4, 4.8, 9.6, and 56 Kbps. Part of the services listed by AT&T under the Accunet family.

DDS-SC—Dataphone Digital Service with Secondary Channel. Also referred to as DDS II. A tariffed private-line service offered by AT&T and certain Bell Operated Companies (BOCs) that allows 64 Kbps clear-channel data with a secondary channel providing end-to-end supervisory, diagnostic, and control functions.

deallocated cluster—An area of disk space, marked in the FAT as available, after the data occupying the cluster has been erased.

DECNET—Digital Equipment Corporation's proprietary network architecture that works across all of that company's machines. This network is endowed with a peer-to-peer methodology.

dedicated line—A dedicated circuit, also called a nonswitched channel or private line.

default—The configuration that is supplied by the manufacturer.

delay—In communications, the time between two events.

density—The amount of data that can be recorded on a given area of a floppy disk.

DES (Data Encryption Standard)—A scheme approved by the National Bureau of Standards that encrypts data for security purposes. DES is the data-encryption standard specified by Federal Information Processing System (FIPS) Publication 46.

destination field—A field in a message header that contains the address of the station to which a message is being directed.

device driver—Information that is loaded by the CONFIG.SYS file, which alters the configuration of a computer from the specifications supplied by the BIOS ROM.

diagnostics—Programs used to test parts or all of a computer system. Most systems have some type of ROM-based diagnostics, some require disk-based diagnostics, and some have a combination of both.

digital—Referring to communications procedures, techniques, and equipment by which information is encoded as either a binary one (1) or zero (0). The representation of any information in discrete binary form.

DIP switch—A group of either slide or rocker switches, found inside many systems and printers, named for the Dual Inline Package form factor. DIP switches are used to alter the configuration of the hardware.

disk/file server—A mass-storage device that can be accessed by several computers and enables the storage and sharing of files.

distributed processing—A method whereby two or more processors work together to perform a single task.

Distribution Frame—See MDF and SDF.

DLC (Data Link Control)—The set of rules (protocol) used by two nodes, or stations, on a network to perform an orderly exchange of information.

DMA (Direct Memory Access)—The process by which data is moved from a storage device, such as a disk drive, directly into memory without the control of the CPU.

DNA (Digital Network Architecture)—Digital Equipment Corporation's layered data communications protocol.

DNIC (Data Network Identification Code)—A four-digit number assigned to public data networks and to specific services within those networks.

DOS (Disk Operating System)—A group of programs that instruct a disk-based computer system how to manage resources and operate related equipment.

downtime—A period during which computer or network resources are unavailable to users because of a failure.

draft proposal—An ISO standards document that has been registered and numbered but not yet given final approval.

driver—A software module that, under control of the processor, manages an I/O port to an external device (e.g., a serial RS-232 port to a modem).

Drop—A cable that connects the main network cable, or bus, and the data terminal equipment (DTE).

Drop Set—All parts needed to complete connection from the drop (wall plate, coupling, MOD-MOD) to the terminal equipment. This would typically include a modular line cord and interface adapter.

Drop Side—Defines all cabling and connectors from the terminal equipment to the patch panel or punch down block designated for terminal equipment at the distribution frame.

DSU (Data Service Unit)—A piece of customer equipment used to interface a digital circuit (DDS) combined with a channel service unit (CSU). A unit that converts a data stream to bipolar format for transmission.

DTE—Data Terminal Equipment. User devices such as terminals and computers, that connect to data circuit equipment (DCE) such as modems. The RS232-C standard referring to equipment that transmits data on pin 2 and receives data on pin 3. This standard typically applies to terminals, PCs, and printers.

D-type—The standard connector used for RS232-C, RS423, and RS422 communication. It is most commonly used in 9-, 15-, and 25-pin configurations.

EBCDIC (Extended Binary Coded Decimal Interchange Code)— An 8-bit character code used primarily in IBM equipment. The code provides for 256 different bit patterns.

EEMS (Enhanced Expanded Memory Specification)—Ashton-Tate and AST's standard for utilization of expanded (paged) memory using 64K page frames.

EGA (Enhanced Graphics Adapter)—A video system that supports monochrome, color, or enhanced graphics monitors with resolutions of up to 640 × 350 with 16 colors.

EIA—1. Electronic Industries Association. 2. A commercial building wiring standard developed in 1989 by the EIA for voice and data communication.

EISA (Enhanced Industry Standards Architecture)—A 32-bit bus architecture pioneered by Compaq and several other manufacturers that allows backward compatibility with older 8- and 16-bit adapter cards.

EMI (Electromagnetic Interference)—A device's radiation leakage that couples onto a transmission medium, resulting (mainly) from the use of high-frequency-wave energy and signal modulation. Can be reduced by shielding.

EMS (Expanded Memory System)—Lotus's, Intel's, and Microsoft's (LIM) standard for expanded (paged) memory.

emulation—The process of having one entity behave like another.

encoding / decoding—The process of organizing information into a format suitable for transmission, and then reconverting it after transmission.

EPROM (Erasable Programmable Read Only Memory)—A type of ROM chip that can be erased by ultraviolet light and reprogrammed.

ESDI (Enhanced Small Device Interface)—High-speed hard disk interface with built-in cache that permits use of high-capacity 1:1 interleaved drives.

Ethernet—A local area network design that is the product of Xerox Corp. Ethernet is characterized by 10-Mbps baseband transmission over a shielded coaxial cable and employing CSMA/CD as the access control mechanism. Ethernet is standardized by the IEEE as specification IEEE 802.3.

expanded memory—Paged memory outside the 1Mb range addressed by DOS that can be used for data provided that EMS software is used and is recognized by the application.

extended memory—Memory above the 1Mb range addressed by DOS, which can be used by other operating systems or as a RAM disk, or print buffer with special software designed for that purpose. Extended memory can not be installed on 8-bit systems.

FAT (File Allocation Table)—Information on a disk, following the boot record, that tells the disk which sectors are allocated to each file.

FCC (Federal Communications Commission)—A board of commissioners, appointed by the president, with the authority to regulate all interstate telecommunications originating within the United States.

FCS (Frame Check Sequence)—In bit-oriented protocols, a 16-bit field that contains transmission-error checking information, usually appended at the end of a frame.

FDDI (Fiber Distributed Data Interface)—An ANSI specified standard for fiber-optic links with data rates up to 100Mbps.

feeder cable—The 25-pair cable that is run from the equipment location to the distribution frame. The equipment end is typically wired with a female 50 position connector, and the distribution frame end is wired with a male 50 position plug.

FEP (Front End Processor)—A dedicated computer linked to one or more host computers or multi-user minicomputers, which performs data-communications functions and serves to off-load processing from attached network computers. (In IBM SNA networks, an IBM communications controller.)

fiber loss—The attenuation (deterioration) of the light signal in optical-fiber transmissions.

fiber optics—Transmission technology in which modulated light wave signals, generated by a laser or LED, are propagated along a (typically) glass or plastic medium and then demodulated to electrical signals by a light-sensitive receiver.

file recovery—Not always successful techniques for repairing files that have been damaged due to loss of power while the file was open or defective storage media.

file server—In local area networks, a station dedicated to providing file and mass data storage services to the other stations on the network.

firmware—Code that is stored in ROM, usually referred to when speaking about printers.

flag—In communications, a bit pattern of six consecutive "1" bits (01111110) used in many bit-oriented protocols to mark the beginning (and often the end) of a frame.

flow control—The procedure or technique used to regulate the flow of data between devices. Flow control prevents the loss of data once a device's buffer has reached its capacity.

form factor—The physical dimensions of a device. Two devices with the same form factor may be physically interchangeable, but their electronic characteristics may prevent them from being compatible.

formatted capacity—The quantity of data that can be contained by a disk after it has been prepared by the operating system. This is the stated capacity of the disk minus the "overhead" and any bad sectors.

FPU (Floating Point Unit)—Another name for a floating point math coprocessor.

fractional T1 (FT1)—A flexible and upgradeable digital communications link that provides a portion of one 1.544-megabit T1 service.

framing—A control procedure used with multiplexed digital channels, such as T1 carriers, whereby bits are inserted so that the receiver can identify the time slots that are allocated to each subchannel. Framing bits may also carry alarm signals indicating specific alarm conditions.

FRD—Fire Retardant. A rating used for cable with Teflon or equivalent jacket and insulation. The cable is to be used when local fire codes call for low flame and low smoke, or when cable is run through a forced air plenum.

FTAM (File Transfer, Access, and Management)—An OSI application utility that provides transparent access to files stored on dissimilar systems.

FTP (File Transfer Protocol)—An upper-level TCP/IP service that allows copying of files across a network.

function keys—Keys that can be programmed to perform a special function or initiate a sequence of events. These usually include the F1 through F10 (or F12) keys used alone or in combination with the ALT (alternate), CTRL (control), or SHIFT keys.

gain—Increased signal power, usually the result of amplification. Opposite of attenuation.

gateway—A conceptual or logical network station that serves to interconnect two otherwise incompatible networks, network nodes, subnetworks, or devices. A gateway performs a protocol conversion operation across numerous communication layers.

GIF (Graphic Interchange Format)—One of the many "standard" formats that allows graphic images to be moved between applications.

giga—Multiplied by one billion (1,000,000,000).

ground—An electrical connection or common conductor that connects to the earth at some point.

group addressing—In transmission, the use of an address that is common to two or more stations. On a multipoint line, where all stations recognize the addressing characters but only one station responds.

harmonica—A device that is attached to the end of a connectorized feeder cable that converts the 25 pair into individual 4-, 6-, or 8-wire modular channels.

head crash—A situation where the read/write head strikes the surface of a hard disk, damaging the head, the media, or both.

head end—A passive component in a broad-band transmission network that translates one range of frequencies (Transmit) to a different frequency band (Receive). The component allows devices on a single-cable network to send and receive signals without interference.

header—The control information added to the beginning of a message. The header contains the destination address, source address, and message number.

hexadecimal—The base 16 numbering system, where numbers 0–9 and letters A–F are used to indicate 0 through 16.

hidden file—A file that is not displayed in a directory because of special settings in its attribute byte.

high-level format—The format placed on a disk by the operating system.

home run—A cable run usually consisting of two, three, or four-pair cable from a wall plate in a fixed-wall office to a termination point at the distribution frame.

horizontal—That part of the wiring grid that services the same floor of a building.

ICMP (Internet Control Message Protocol)—The TCP/IP process that provides the set of functions used for networking layer management and control.

IDC—Insulation Displacement Contact. A type of wire terminating connection in which the insulating jacket is cut by the connector when the wire is inserted.

IDE (Integrated Disk Expansion or Intelligent Drive Electronics)—A type of hard drive with an attached controller. A 40 or 44 conductor cable connects the drive to the system bus by either a direct connection to the system board or through an expansion card. This single cable carries power, data, and address signals.

IEEE (Institute of Electrical and Electronic Engineers)—An international society of professional engineers that issues widely used networking (and other) standards.

impedance—The effect of a transmitted signal of resistance, inductance, and capacitance.

inside wiring—In telephone deregulation, the customer's premises wiring. The wiring inside a building.

intelligent terminal—A programmable terminal.

interactive processing—Describing time-dependent (real-time) data communications. Conversational processing (a user enters data and then awaits a response).

interface—A physical point between two devices where the electrical signals, connectors, timing, and handshaking are defined. The interface is the procedures, codes, and protocols that enable two devices to communicate with each other.

interlaced—A method of increasing the resolution of a monitor by manipulation of the scanning process. A special video adapter and monitor are required for interlaced video.

interleave factor—The number of rotations that a disk must make in order to read a complete track.

internal command—A command contained within COMMAND.COM so that an external file does not have to be loaded for the command to function.

international standard—An ISO standards document that has been approved in final balloting.

internet—A large network comprised of several small networks.

interrupt—The suspension of a process caused by an external event such as the activation of a key on the keyboard.

I/O (Input / Output)—A circuit that permits communication between the processor and a device.

IP (Internet Protocol)—Used in gateways to connect networks at the OSI network layer (layer 3 and above).

ISA (Industry Standard Architecture)—The bus architecture used by IBM in the original PC and then expanded upon with the introduction of the 16-bit AT.

ISDN (Integrated Services Digital Network)—A project within the CCITT for the standardization of operating parameters and interfaces for a network that will accommodate a variety of mixed digital transmission services. Access channels under definition include basic rate (144 Kbps) and primary rates (nominally 1.544 and 2.048Mbps).

ISO (International Standards Organization)—An organization that promotes the development of standards for computers (and other goods). The ISO is the developer of the OSI model.

jitter—The slight movement of a transmission signal in time or phase that can introduce errors and loss of synchronization in high speed synchronous communication.

jumper—A patch cable, wire, or clamp used to establish a circuit.

kilo—Multiplied by 1,000. In the case of computers, however, a kilobyte is 1.024 bytes.

LAN (Local Area Network)—A data communications network spanning a limited geographical area. It provides communication between three or more computers and peripherals, in most cases using a high-speed media (such as coaxial cable, twisted pair wire, or optical fiber) as its backbone.

landing zone—An unused track on a disk surface that the read/write rests on when the drive is powered down normally.

LAP (Link Access Procedure)—The data link-level protocol specified in the CCITT X.2 interface standard.

LAPD (Link Access Procedure-D)—Link-level protocol devised for ISDN connections, differing from LAPB (LAP-Balanced) in its framing sequence. Likely to be used as a basis for LAPM, the proposed CCITT modem error control standard.

LAT (Local Area Transport)—A protocol unique to Digital Equipment Corporation products for virtual terminal access across an Ethernet network.

latency—The time interval between when a network station seeks access to a transmission channel and when access is granted or received.

layer—In the OSI reference model, one of seven basic layers, referring to a collection of related network processing functions.

leased line—A dedicated circuit, typically supplied by the telephone company.

LED (Light Emitting Diode)—A device that converts electrical energy into light. The main source for optical fiber transmission.

line cord—The connecting cord between the terminal device and the drop.

link layer—Layer Two of the OSI reference model, also known as the data-link layer.

LLC (Logical Link Control)—A protocol developed by the IEEE 802 committee for data-link-level transmission control. The upper sublayer of the IEEE Layer 2 (OSI) protocol that compliments the MAC protocol. IEEE standard 802.2 includes end-system addressing and error checking.

logical drive—A drive named by a DOS drive specifier. A physical drive may contain several logical drives.

low-level format—The "physical" formatting of a drive that specifies the interleave, marks defective tracks, and divides the surface into tracks and sectors.

LSI (Large-Scale Integration)—A newer type of integrated circuit chip that performs the same functions of several other types of chip, thus enabling a greater number of circuits to occupy a smaller area.

LU 6.2—In SNA, a set of protocols that provides peer-to-peer communications between applications.

MAC (Media Access Control)—A media-specific access-control protocol within IEEE 802 specifications. MAC currently includes variations for the token ring, token bus, and CSMA/CD. MAC is the lower sublayer of the IEEE's link layer (OSI), which compliments the Logical Link Control (LLC).

magnetic medium—Any data storage medium including disks and tape, where different patterns of magnetization represent bit values.

maintenance provider—An organization providing hardware or system maintenance. There are four categories of maintenance providers. First-party maintainers are the manufacturers themselves. Manufacturers will only maintain their own equipment. Second-party maintainers are Authorized Dealers. Dealers must maintain all of the items that they sell. Third-party are independent maintenance companies. They do not sell hardware and usually are not authorized by any manufacturer. Fourth-party maintainers will repair items to the component level. They are often used by second- and third-party maintainers to repair boards, drives, and so forth.

Manchester encoding—Digital encoding technique (specified for the IEEE 802.3 Ethernet baseband network standard) in which each bit period is divided into two complimentary halves. A negative-to-positive (voltage) transition in the middle of the bit designates a binary "1," while a positive-to-negative transition represents a "0." The encoding technique also allows the receiving device to recover the transmitted clock from the incoming data stream (self-clocking).

MAP (Manufacturing Automation Protocol)—A General Motors originated suite of networking protocols, the implementation of which tracks the seven layers of the OSI model.

mapping—In network operations, the logical association of one set of values, such as addresses on one network, with quantities or values of another set, such as devices on another network (e.g., name-address inter-network route, protocol-to-protocol mapping).

MAU (Multistation Access Unit)—A node on a Token-ring Network that provides eight terminal ports. The mechanical interface is the

IBM data connector. A wiring concentrator used in local area networks.

M bit—The More Data mark in an X.25 packet that allows the DTE or DCE to indicate a sequence of more than one packet.

MCA (Micro-Channel Architecture)—A new type of bus design developed by IBM and incorporated in their high-end PS/2 line.

MCGA (Multi-Color Graphics Array)—A color graphics video system that can support up to 320 X 200 resolution with 256 colors or 640 X 480 in monochrome mode.

MDA (Monochrome Display Adapter)—A video adapter for displaying monochrome text but having no graphics capability.

MDF—Main Distribution Frame. The central connecting point for both voice and data wiring. Also serves as the main location from which cross connecting and testing are done.

medium—A substance used for the propagation and transmission of signals.

mega—Multiplied by one million (1,000,000).

MFM (Modulated Frequency Modulation)—A data-encoding scheme used on hard disks.

MHS (Message Handling System)—The standard defined by the CCITT as X.400 and by the ISO as Message Oriented Text Interchange Standard (MOTIS).

micro—A prefix indicating one-millionth (1/1,000,000 or 0.000001). Abbreviated as μ.

Micro Channel—A proprietary bus developed by IBM for the PS/2 family of computers.

microprocessor—A solid-state central-processing unit that is the brain of the computer. The microprocessor interprets instructions from the software and directs the numerous activities that are performed within the system.

MIF (Minimum Internetworking Functionality)—A general principle within the ISO that calls for minimum local area network station complexity when interconnecting with resources outside the local area network.

milli—A prefix indicating one-thousandth (1/1,000 or 0.001).

Mini-MAP (Mini-Manufacturing Automation Protocol)—A version of MAP consisting of only the physical, link and application layers intended for lower-cost, process-control networks. With Mini-MAP, a device with a token can request a response from an addressed device. Unlike a standard MAP protocol, the addressed Mini-MAP device need not wait for the token to respond.

MIPS (Millions Instructions Per Second)—Gauge of a computer's raw power.

MMJ—A six-wire modular jack with the locking tab shifted off to the right-hand side. Used in the DEC wiring system.

MODEM (MOdulator / DEModulator)—A device that converts signals from a computer to a form that can be transmitted over telephone lines and then back to a form that a computer can understand.

module—An assembly that contains one or more subcircuits or a complete circuit.

MS OS/2—A single-user, multi-tasking operating system for 80286 and higher microcomputers.

MTBF (Mean Time Between Failures)—The time period in which a device will function normally before requiring service, based upon testing that is performed by the manufacturer.

MTTR (Mean Time To Repair)—The average time required to perform corrective maintenance on a failed device.

multimode—An optical fiber designed to carry multiple signals, distinguished by frequency or phase, at the same time.

multiple routing—The process of sending a message to more than one recipient, usually when all destinations are specified in the header of the message.

multipoint line—A single communications line or circuit interconnecting several stations supporting terminals in several different locations. This type of line usually requires some kind of polling mechanism, and each terminal must have a unique address. Also called a multidrop line.

multi-tasking—The ability to execute two or more applications simultaneously.

multi-user—A system in which two or more terminals are connected to one CPU.

nano—A prefix indicating one-billionth (1,000,000,000 or 0.000000001).

NCC (Network Control Center)—Any centralized network diagnostic and management station or site, such as that of a packet-switching network.

NDIS (Network Driver Interface Specification)—A standard established by Microsoft for writing hardware-independent drivers.

NETBIOS (Network Basic Input/Output System)—Software developed by IBM that provides the interface between a PC's operating system, the I/O bus, and the network. A de facto standard.

NETVIEW—An IBM mainframe network management product that integrates the functions of several earlier IBM network management products.

network—An interconnected group of nodes, able to share common resources (printers, disks, software). A series of points, nodes, or stations connected together by communication channels. The assembly of equipment through which connections are made between data stations.

network architecture—A set of design principles, including the organization of functions and the description of data formats and procedures, used as the basis for the design and implementation of a network.

network interface controller—Electronic circuitry that connects a workstation to a network, usually in the form of a card that fits into one of the expansion slots inside a personal computer. The network interface controller works with the network software and computer operating system to transmit and receive messages on the network. Also called a network adapter or network interface card.

network layer—Layer 3 in the OSI model. The logical network entity that services the transport layer. The network layer is responsible for ensuring that data passed to it from the transport layer is routed and delivered through the network.

network topology—The physical and logical relationship of nodes in a network. The schematic arrangement of the links and nodes of a network. Networks typically have a star, ring, tree, or bus topology, or a hybrid combination.

NFS (Network File Server)—An extension of TCP/IP that allows files on remote nodes of a network to appear locally connected.

NMI (Non-Maskable Interrupt)—An internally generated signal that tells the system that a parity error has occurred, which causes the system to halt and display an error message.

node—A point where one or more functional units interconnect transmission lines. A physical device that allows for transmission of data within a network. These include host processors, communications controllers, cluster controllers and terminals.

octopus—A device that is attached to the end of a connectorized feeder cable that converts the 25 pair to individual 2-, 4-, 6-, and 8-wire channels.

off-line—A condition in which a user, terminal, or other device is not connected to a computer or is not actively transmitting via a network.

on-line—A condition in which a user, terminal, or other device is actively connected with the facilities of a communications network or computer.

operating system—A group of programs which attend to utilities, housekeeping, I/O management, and interface an operator with the computer.

optical disk—A very high-density information storage medium that uses light to read and write digital information.

optical fiber—Any filament or fiber, made of dielectric materials, that is used to transmit laser or LED generated light signals. Optical fiber usually consists of a core that carries the signal and cladding (a substance with a slightly higher refractive index than the core) that surrounds the core and serves to reflect the light signal.

OS/2—A single-user, multi-tasking operating system for use on microcomputers having a "286" or greater capacity microprocessor.

OSI (Open System Interconnection)—A logical structure (model) for network operations, standardized within the ISO. A seven-layer network architecture being used for the definition of network protocol standards to enable any OSI compliant computer or device for a meaningful exchange of information. The layers are: physical, data link, network, transport, session, presentation, and application.

OSINET—A test network sponsored by the National Bureau of Standards (NBS), designed to provide vendors of products based on the OSI model a forum for performing interoperability testing.

overhead—In communications, all information, such as control, routing, and error checking characters, that is in addition to user-transmitted data. These include information that carries network status or operational instructions, network routing information, and re-transmission of user data messages that are received in error.

overlay—A part of an application program that is moved into and out of RAM as needed by the application in order to reduce memory usage.

overrun—A situation where data moves from the sending device faster than it can be accepted by the receiving device.

overwrite—Writing data to an area on a disk where other data resides, replacing the original data.

packet—A sequence of data, with associated control information, that is switched and transmitted as a whole. Packet refers mainly to the field structure and format defined with the CCITT X.25 recommendation.

PAL (Programmable Array Logic)—A type of chip that can be programmed by the user. PALs contain a fusible link that can be burned, preventing the internal code from being copied.

parallel—In computer parlance, the movement of data over several wires simultaneously.

parallel processing—Simultaneous execution of two or more processes or programs within the same processor.

parity—A method of data checking in which an extra bit is used. If odd parity is used, the parity bit is set to either 0 or 1 so that the total number of 1's transmitted is an odd number.

partition—A logical portion of a disk that is devoted to a particular operating system. Partitioning of a hard disk permits several logical drives to reside on a single physical drive or utilization of two (or more) operating systems on a single physical drive.

pass-through—The ability to gain access to one network element through another.

passive device—In current loop applications, a device that must draw its current from connected equipment.

PBX (Private Branch Exchange)—A manual, user-owned telephone exchange.

PC (Personal Computer)—A generic term for a single-user micro-computer.

peripheral—Any piece of equipment that is attached to the system by means of a cable or adapter.

PGA (Professional Graphics Adapter)—An adapter that supports up to 1024 X 768 resolution with 256 colors.

physical drive—A single drive that can be partitioned into one or more logical units. Some software can configure two or more physical drives into one logical drive.

physical layer—Level 1 (the lowest layer) in the OSI architecture below the link layer. Concerns itself with the voltage levels, cabling, speed, and signaling (handshaking) used between equipment.

pixel—The smallest addressable area in a video system, usually related to a dot on the screen.

point-to-point—Describes a circuit that connects two points directly, where there are generally no intermediate processing nodes, computers, or branched circuits, although there could be switching facilities. A type of connection, such as a phone line circuit, that links two logical entities.

polarization—The modular connector mechanical form factor.

port—A point of access into a computer, network, or other device. A physical or electronic interface.

POST (Power On Self-Test)—A series of internal tests that are performed by the computer when it is powered on.

power supply—A device within the computer or printer that converts line voltage supplied by the utility company into 5 and 12 volts DC for use by the computer (or 5, 12 and 30, volts for a printer).

premises wiring—The technology of wiring buildings and property for data, telephone, video, and other electrical/electronic functions.

presentation layer—Layer six of the OSI reference model. The presentation layer provides the standards for restructuring data into the required format, character set, or language.

presentation manager—The icon-based graphical user interface software contained within OS/2 and Windows.

print server—An intelligent device used to transfer information to a series of printers.

program—A set of instructions that tells the computer how to perform a task. Some programs stand alone, while other programs may be part of an application.

PROM (Programmable Read Only Memory)—A type of ROM chip that can be programmed once, and can not be erased.

propagation delay—The time it takes a signal composed of electromagnetic energy to travel from one point to another over a transmission channel. Propagation delay is usually most noticeable in communicating with satellites.

protected mode—The mode of operation found in 80286 and higher microprocessors that permits multi-tasking without application programs overlapping each other's RAM area.

protocol—A formal set of rules governing the format, timing, sequencing, and error control of exchanged messages on a data network. Protocols may be oriented toward data transfer over an interface, between two logical units that are directly connected, or an end-to-end basis between two users over a large and complex network.

public network—A network operated by common carriers or telecommunications administrations for the provision of circuit-switched, packet-switched, and leased-line circuits to the public.

PVC (Polyvinyl Chloride)—The material most commonly used for the insulation and jacketing of cable.

queue—A group of items waiting for service.

RAM (Random Access Memory)—Volatile memory that is used by the computer.

RAM disk—An area of RAM that simulates the function of a disk. Special software is needed for this function. Information can not be kept on a RAM disk after the system power is removed.

real mode—The mode of operation for the 8-bit processors (and the default mode for all other processors). Multi-tasking is not available with a real mode processor. Applications that are designed for the 8-bit processor can run on higher processors, but only in the real mode.

real time—Operating mode that allows immediate interaction with data as it is created. Opposite of batch processing.

redundancy—In data transmission, the portion of a message's gross information content that can be eliminated without losing essential information.

refresh cycle—The period of time needed for the computer to access all of the storage locations in RAM. Dynamic RAM (DRAM) requires frequent access or the information will fade. Static RAM does not require refreshment as frequently as dynamic RAM.

register—An area in memory that is used by the computer for specific functions.

repeater—In digital transmission, equipment that receives a pulse train, amplifies it, retimes it, and then reconstructs the signal for retransmission. In fiber optics, a device that decodes a low-power light signal, converts it to electrical energy, and then retransmits it via an LED or laser light source.

reseller—An organization that purchases hardware and software for the purpose of selling these items to the end user. Resellers often collect components from several manufacturers, interconnect the devices, and configure the system before delivery.

resolution—The ability of a screen to display characters and/or graphics. Usually expressed by the number of pixels that can be addressed by the video system, the greater the number of pixels, the smaller each pixel is and the better (higher) the resolution.

response time—For interactive sessions, the elapsed time between the end of an inquiry and the beginning of a response.

retransmissive star—In optical fiber transmission, a passive component that permits the light signal on an input fiber to be retransmitted on multiple-output fibers.

Ring—1. A Local Area Network topology in which data is sent from workstations via a loop or ring. 2. One conductor of a pair (vs. tip).

ring network—A network topology in which each node is connected to two adjacent nodes.

RISC (Reduced Instruction Set Computing)—An internal computing architecture where processor instructions are pared down so that most of them can be performed in a single processor cycle, thereby improving overall system efficiency.

RJ—Registered Jack.

RLL (Run Length Limited)—A data-encoding scheme used on hard disks. RLL permits more data to be stored on a drive than MFM encoding.

ROM (Read Only Memory)—Permanent storage. A device (usually a chip or set of chips) containing data and programs, that can not be altered.

root directory—The main directory of a disk, having a specific size and containing housekeeping information for that particular disk. If the disk is bootable, the root directory contains the necessary system files.

router—A network device that examines data addresses. The router determines the most efficient pathway to the destination and routes the data accordingly.

SAA (System Application Architecture)—A set of standards developed by IBM, providing identical user interfaces for applications running on PCs, minicomputers, and mainframes.

SCSI (Small Computer System Interface)—An interface standard, widely used by Apple, that permits several peripheral devices (disk and tape drives) to be daisy-chained provided that each is assigned a unique SCSI address (usually through a selector on the device itself).

SDF—Sub Distribution Frame. Intermediate cross-connect points, usually located in wiring or utility closets. A trunk cable or LAN backbone is run from each SDF to the MDF (Main Distribution Frame).

serial transmission—The sequential transmission of data over a circuit, one bit at a time. Compare with parallel that transmits seven or eight bits at the same time.

session—A connection between two stations that allows them to communicate. The time period that a user engages in a dialogue with an interactive computer.

session layer—Layer five of the OSI reference model. The session layer provides protocols for assembling physical messages into logical messages.

shadow RAM—An area of high-speed RAM, usually at a high-address range, into which the contents of the system ROM is copied during the boot operation. This permits ROM instructions to execute more quickly and improve overall system performance.

shell—Software (either command.com, or a menu) that permits the user to communicate with the operating system.

SIMM (Single Inline Memory Module)—A small circuit board containing a complete bank of RAM, permitting quick addition or replacement of memory and requiring less space than individual chips.

single mode—An optical wave guide that propagates light of only a single wavelength and usually a single phase. An optical fiber that allows the transmission of only one light beam, or data carrying lightwave channel, and is optimized for a particular lightwave frequency.

SIPP (Single Inline Pin Package)—Similar to a SIMM, but connects through the use of pins, rather than the edge card connector.

SMT (Surface Mount Technology)—ICs and components that are glued and soldered to the surface of a printed circuit board rather than through holes drilled into the board.

SNA (Systems Network Architecture)—The IBM network architecture for communications among IBM devices and between IBM and other machines.

soft error—An error in reading or writing data that appears sporadically because of a transient problem such as power fluctuations.

SPOOL (Simultaneous Peripheral Operation On Line)—A program or piece of hardware that controls data going to an output device.

star—A Local Area Network topology in which all workstations are wired directly to a central workstation or hub that establishes, maintains, and breaks connection to the workstations.

Starlan—A local area network design and specification, within IEEE 802.3 standards, characterized by 1 Mips baseband data transmission over two-pair, twisted-pair wiring.

station—Any DTE that receives or transmits messages on a data link, including network nodes and user devices.

step-index—A type of optical fiber with a uniform refractive index at its core and a sharp decrease in the refractive index at its core cladding interface.

System Connect—The method by which connection is physically made to the host computer or Local Area Network.

system files—A file or group of files necessary to boot an operating system. MS-DOS requires two hidden files (IBMIO.COM and IBMDOS.COM) as well as COMMAND.COM to be present in a specific area on the boot disk.

system integrator—A consultant or vendor who gathers a group of components and combines them into a system.

System Side—Defines all cabling and connectors from the host computer or Local Area Network to the cross connect field at the Distribution Frame.

T1—AT&T term for a digital carrier facility used to transmit a DS-1 formatted digital signal at 1.544 Mbps.

T carrier—A time-division-multiplexed, digital-transmission facility, typically telephone company supplied, usually operating at an aggregate data rate of 1.544 Mbps and above.

TCP/IP (Transmission Control Protocol / Internet Protocol)—A layered set of protocols that allows sharing of applications among

PCs in a high-speed communications environment. Because TCP/IP's protocols are standardized across all of its layers, including those that provide terminal emulation and file transfer, different vendors' computing devices (all running TCP/IP) can exist on the same cable and communicate with one another across that cable. TCP/IP corresponds to layers four (transport) and three (network) of the OSI reference model.

telecommunications—A term encompassing both voice and data communications in the form of coded signals over media.

TELNET—A virtual terminal service available through the TCP/IP protocol suite.

tera—A multiplier indicating one trillion (1,000,000,000,000).

terminal—A point in a network at which data can either enter or leave. A device, usually equipped with a keyboard and a display, capable of sending and receiving data over communications link. Generically the same as data terminal equipment (DTE).

terminal server—A device that allows one or more terminals to connect to an Ethernet network.

terminated line—A circuit with a resistance at the far end that is equal to the characteristic impedance of the line, so that no reflections or standing waves are present when a signal is entered at the near end.

timeout—Expiration of a predetermined period of time, at which some predefined action occurs. Timeouts are employed to avoid unnecessary delays, if a piece of equipment is unable to respond to an instruction.

token bus—A LAN standard that uses a token-passing media access method on a bus configuration.

token ring—A data-signaling scheme in which a special data packet (called a token) is passed from one station to another along an electrical ring. When a station wants to transmit, it takes possession of the token, transmits its data, then frees the token after the data has made a complete circuit of the electrical ring.

TOP (Technical and Office Protocols)—A Boeing version of the MAP protocol suite, aimed at office and engineering applications.

Topology—The architecture of a network, or the way circuits are connected to link the network nodes together.

TPI (Tracks Per Inch)—A measurement of the density of a disk. 5-1/4 inch, 360K disks have 48TPI.

Trunk Cable—Trunk Cable typically refers to a copper twisted pair backbone or vertical riser cable consisting of multiple groups of 25 pairs.

transaction—In communications, a message destined for an applications program. A computer-processed task that accomplishes a particular action or result. In interactive communications, an exchange between two devices, one of which is usually a computer.

transceiver—A device that can both transmit and receive.

transmission—The dispatching of a signal, message, or other form of intelligence by wire, radio, telegraphy, telephony, facsimile, or other means. A series of characters, messages, or blocks, including control information and user data.

transport layer—Layer four in the OSI reference model, which provides a logical connection between processes on two machines.

tree—A LAN topology that recognizes only one route between two nodes on the network. The "map" resembles a tree or the letter T.

TSR (Terminate and Stay Resident)—An application that is loaded into memory for use on demand. TSRs are activated by a particular key sequence, used as necessary, and then become "invisible" until they are needed.

twisted pair—Two insulated copper conductors that are wound around each other to cancel the effects of electrical noise. Twisted pair may or may not be shielded.

UDP (User Datagram Protocol)—The TCP/IP transaction protocol used for applications such as remote network management and name-service access. UDP lets users assign a name, such as "VAX 2," to a physical or numbered address.

UNIX—An operating system originally designed by AT&T for multiuser and minicomputer systems.

UPS (Uninterruptible Power Supply)—A device containing batteries that can supply power to a computer when utility company power fails. The size of the UPS determines how many devices can be powered and for how long a period of time.

USOC 1—1. Uniform Services Ordering Code. 2. A term originally used by the telephone company to specify installation of a standard modular jack other than RJ11W or RJ11C. More recently refers to a modular standard (tip/ring sequence).

utility software—Programs that make operation of a computer easier for the user. Utilities generally provide menus for performing operations that would otherwise require knowledge of operating system commands.

UTP—Unshielded Twisted Pair. Twisted pair cable without either individual or over all shielding.

VAN (Value Added Network)—A network whose services go beyond simple switching.

VAR (Value Added Reseller)—A reseller who adds value by providing a complete hardware and software system to perform a specific function such as CAD, Specialized Accounting, Medical Office Management, and so forth. A VAR also provides installation and training services.

Vertical—That part of a wiring grid that connects the host computer or Main Distribution Frame to equipment located on other floors.

VGA (Video Graphics Array)—Supports graphics up to 640 X 480 resolution with 16 colors.

virtual circuit—In packet switching, a network facility that gives the appearance to the user of an actual end-to-end circuit. A dynamically variable network connection where sequential data packets may be routed differently during the course of a session. Virtual circuits enable transmission facilities to be shared by many users simultaneously.

virtual memory—A technique in which parts of programs or data are moved from disk to memory and back under the direction of software. This permits use of files that are larger than the capacity of the system's memory.

virtual storage—Storage space that may be seen as addressable main storage but is actually auxiliary storage. The amount of virtual storage available depends upon the hardware and the operating system being used.

wait state—A method of slowing the speed of a system in order to use slower (less expensive) RAM chips. One wait state will reduce system performance by 20 to 25%.

wideband—A system in which multiple channels access a medium (usually coaxial cable) that has a large bandwidth, greater than that of a voice-grade channel. Wideband systems typically offer higher-speed data transmission capability.

wiring closet—A central location for termination and routing of on premises wiring systems.

Wiring Grid—Refers to the overall architecture of building wiring.

workstation—Input/Output equipment at which an operator works.

write precompensation—Variations in the timing of a read/write head from the outer tracks to the inner tracks of a hard drive to compensate for the "bit-shifting" that occurs on the inner cylinders.

X.25—The standard interface for packet switched, data communications networks, as designated by the Consultative Committee for International Telephony and Telegraphy (CCITT).

XENIX—A 16-bit multi-user operating system for microcomputers derived from UNIX.

XNS (Xerox Network Systems)—A peer-to-peer protocol developed by Xerox that has been incorporated into several local area networking schemes, including the 3Com 3+ and 3+Open network operating systems.

Laser Printer Engine Cross-Reference

The following chart lists the engines used in laser printers marketed by various manufacturers. This information is current as of January 1990.

Manufacturer	Printer	Laser Engine
AB Dick	IP-0800-SMT	Canon LBP-CX 8ppm
	2205	Canon LBP-CX 8ppm
ACOM Computer, Inc.	LX-3830	Olympus S3000
	MC-3815	Ricoh LP-4150
	MC-3820	Canon LBP-20
	LX-3820	Canon LBP-20
AEG Olympia, Inc.	Laserstar 6	Ricoh LP-1060
AGFA Compugraphic Div.	CG 400-PS	Agfa-Gevaert P400
	CG 420-XL	Canon LBP-20
	P3400 PS	Minolta SP100
ALPS America	LPX 2020	Alps LPX 2020
	LPX 600	Sharp JX-9300
ASR Research	Turbo Laser/PS	Ricoh LP4081 8ppm

Manufacturer	Printer	Laser Engine
AST Camintonn	Turbo Laser/PS	Ricoh LP4081 8ppm
	Turbo Laser/PS-Plus 3	Ricoh LP4081 8ppm
AT Systems	PC-LP1	Ricoh LP4048/4081/4150
AT&T	593	TEC LB-1305
Abaton	Quickstep	Casio LCS 130
Acer	LP-75	Ricoh PC Laser 6000
	LP-76	Ricoh PC Laser 6000
Acom Computer	LO8129	Canon LBP-CX 8ppm
	LX8219	Canon LBP-CX 8ppm
	LX3219	Canon LBP-CX 8ppm
	LX528	Canon LBP-CX 8ppm
	LX3808	Canon LBP-SX II
	LX3815	Ricoh LP4150 15ppm
Advanced Tech Int'l.	Laserprint 800	Canon LBP-CX 8ppm
	Laserprint 870	Canon LBP-CX 8ppm
	0870	Canon LBP-CX 8ppm
	LC-6026	Dataproducts LZR-2600
	Laserprint 2670	Dataproducts LZR-2600
	Laserprint 0880	Ricoh LP4080 8ppm
	DW-2	Ricoh LP4080/4081/4150
	GR-2	Ricoh LP4080/4081/4150
	RP-1	Ricoh LP4080/4081/4150
	DW-1	Ricoh LP4080/4081/4150
	Laserprint 1570	Ricoh LP4150 15ppm
Advanced Vision Rsch.	AVR-LP03	Canon LBP-CX 8ppm
Aedex Corp.	Laserbar-508	Canon LBP-CX 8ppm
	Laserbar-608	Ricoh LP4080 8ppm
	Laserbar-615	Ricoh LP4150 15ppm
Alcatel Courier	9376	Ricoh LP4150 15ppm
	9375	Ricoh LP4150 15ppm

Manufacturer	Printer	Laser Engine
Allied Linotype		Canon LBP-CX 8ppm
American Printing Tech.	8ppm	Canon LBP-CX 8ppm
	Pagewriter	Ricoh LP4120 12ppm
Ampack Bus. Systems		Canon LBP-CX 8ppm
	Laserpro	Xerox 2700 12ppm
Apollo Computer	Domain LSR 26	Dataproducts LZR2600
	Laserprint 800	Ricoh LP4081 8ppm
	Domain/Laser-26	Toshiba A-740
Apple Computer	Laserwriter Plus	Canon LBP-CX 8ppm
	Laserwriter	Canon LBP-CX 8ppm
	Laserwriter II NTX	Canon LBP-SX II
	Laserwriter II SC	Canon LBP-SX II
	Laserwriter II NT	Canon LBP-SX II
Apricot	Laser PCL	Kyocera F-1010
Atari Corp.	SLM804 Laser Printer	TEC LB-1301
Autographix Corp.	8ppm	Canon LBP-CX 8ppm
Autologic	APS-55/200	Canon LBP-CX 8ppm
	APS-55	Xerox 2700 12ppm
BDS Computer Corp.	630/8T	Canon LBP-CX 8ppm
	Laser 630/8	Canon LBP-CX 8ppm
	Laser 630/8E	Canon LBP-CX 8ppm
	2630	Dataproducts LZR2600
	2655	Dataproducts LZR2600
	2665	Dataproducts LZR2600
	LZR 2600	Dataproducts LZR2600
BDT Products	ERGOPRINT 610	Xerox 4045
BGL Technology Corp.	Mark II / Mark III	Dataproducts LZR2600
	Mark IB	Toshiba PageLaser 12

Manufacturer	Printer	Laser Engine
	Mark I	Dataproducts LZR-1200
	Mark IT	Dataproducts LZR-1200
	Mark I Plus	Dataproducts LZR-1200
	Mark IV	Dataproducts LZR-26
BLaser	Star 2	Canon LBP-SX II
BLaser Tech	BLaser II	Canon LBP-CX 8ppm
	BLaser Five	Canon LBP-CX 8ppm
	BLaser	Canon LBP-CX 8ppm
Bantec/Impac		Siemens 2300 160ppm
Bedford Computer	QMS 800	Canon LBP-CX 8ppm
	QMS 1200	Xerox 2700 12ppm
Bell & Howell		Ricoh LP4080/4081/4150
British Telecom	MP 2010	Kyocera F-1010
Brother	HL8 Laser AS	Canon LBP-SX II
	HL 8	Canon LBP-SX II
	LP 10	Kyocera F-1010
Burroughs	AP9208	Ricoh LP4080/4081/4150
	9270	Xerox 8700/9700
C. Itoh Electronics, Inc	LIPS II	Konica LP-3010
	Megaserve/30	Olympus S3000
	Megapro/30	Olympus S3000
	Megapro +/30	Olympus S3000
	Megaline/30	Olympus S3000
CAF Computer Corp.	CAF Laser	TEC LB-1305
CAMEX	3000 Bit Printer	Canon LBP-20
CDC	5870	Xerox 8700/9700
CDS	4300	Canon LBP-CX 8ppm
	2300	Canon LBP-CX 8ppm

Manufacturer	Printer	Laser Engine
CPT	LP-6	Canon LBP-CX 8ppm
	LP-8S	Canon LBP-CX 8ppm
	PS-8	Canon LBP-CX 8ppm
	LP-8GS	Canon LBP-CX 8ppm
	CPT LP-8	Canon LBP-SX II
	Pageprinter 1	Ricoh LP4120 12ppm
	CPT LP-15	Ricoh LP4150 15ppm
CSS Laboratories, Inc.	O.A. Writer Color Magic	Colorocs 4007
Canon	LBP-8A2	Canon LBP-CX 8ppm
	LBP-8A1	Canon LBP-CX 8ppm
	LBP-8 II	Canon LBP-SX II
	LBP-8III	Canon LBP-8III
	LBP-8III R	Canon LBP-8III R
	LBP-4	Canon LBP-4
	LBP-8III T	Canon LBP-8III T
Casio Computer Co.	LCS 240	Casio LCS 240
	LCS 300	Casio LCS 300
Compugraphic	CG300-PS	Canon LBP-CX 8ppm
	CG500-PS	Canon LBP-CX 8ppm
	EP308	Canon LBP-CX 8ppm
	CG408	Canon LBP-SX II
Computer Language Res.	Formwriter 2X	Canon LBP-SX II
	Formwriter 2	Canon LBP-SX II
	Formwriter 4	Ricoh LP4080/4081/4150
	Formwriter 6	Xerox 4045 10ppm
Concept Technology	Conceptwriter	Canon LBP-CX 8ppm
	Laser 8	Canon LBP-CX 8ppm
Continental Systems	L-2060	Ricoh LP-1060
	L-2060	Ricoh PC Laser 6000
Cordata, Inc.	LP-300	Canon LBP-CX 8ppm

Manufacturer	Printer	Laser Engine
	LP-300X	Canon LBP-CX 8ppm
	Intellipress Printer	Canon LBP-CX 8ppm
Corporate Data Sciences	CDS 4300	Canon LBP-CX 8ppm
	CDS 2300	Canon LBP-CX 8ppm
DEC	LN 03	Ricoh LP4081 8ppm
	LN 03 Plus	Ricoh LP4081 8ppm
	LN 03R Scriptprinter	Ricoh LP4081 8ppm
	LN 01	Xerox 2700 12ppm
DTP Systems	DTP Laser Printer	TEC LB-1301
	Desktop Printer	TEC LB-1305
Data Card	Troy 308	Ricoh LP4080/4081/4150
Data General	4557	Canon LBP-CX 8ppm
	4558	Canon LBP-CX 8ppm
	6454	Canon LBP-SX II
	6479	Dataproducts LZR2600
	6474	Toshiba A-739
	6475	Toshiba A-739
	6480	Toshiba A-739
	6477	Toshiba A-739
	6476	Toshiba A-739
	4425	Xerox 2700 12ppm
	4426	Xerox 2700 12ppm
	LDP-12	Xerox 2700 12ppm
	6479	Toshiba A-740
Data Terminals & Comm.	Laser Octave	Canon LBP-CX 8ppm
Datagraphix	9835	Siemens 2300 160ppm
	9810	Siemens 2300 160ppm
	9820	Siemens 2300 160ppm
	9845	Siemens 2300 160ppm
	9825	Siemens 2300 160ppm
	9830	Siemens 2300 160ppm

Manufacturer	Printer	Laser Engine
	6800	Siemens 2300 160ppm
Datapoint	7410 Starbeam	Canon LBP-CX 8ppm
Dataproducts	LZR 2600	Dataproducts LZR2600
	LZR 2655	Dataproducts LZR2600
	LZR 2665	Dataproducts LZR2600
	LZR 2610T	Dataproducts LZR2600
	LZR 2620	Dataproducts LZR2600
	LZR 2630	Dataproducts LZR2600
	LZR-650	Sharp JX-9500
	LZR-1219	Toshiba A-739
	LZR-1230	Toshiba A-739
	LZR-1260ESS	Toshiba A-739
	LZR-1260I	Toshiba A-739
	LZR-1274	Toshiba A-739
	LZR-2620	Toshiba A-740
	LZR-2665	Toshiba A-740
	LZR-2655	Toshiba A-740
	LZR-2630	Toshiba A-740
	LZR 1260	Toshiba PageLaser 12
	LZR 1200	Toshiba PageLaser 12
	LZR 1230	Toshiba PageLaser 12
Datasource	M7001 Laser Printer	Mita LP-X1
Decision Data	6408-2	Ricoh LP4080/4081/4150
	6408	Ricoh LP4080/4081/4150
	6415 Laserprinter	Ricoh LP4150 15ppm
	6424	Kentek K-3
Delphax Systems, Inc.	3030G	Olympus S3000
Derex, Inc.		Canon LBP-CX 8ppm
	12 PDR	Ricoh LP4120 12ppm
Desktop Systems, Inc.	DSI Laser Printer	TEC LB-1305
Destiny	Laser ACT II	Ricoh PC Laser 6000

Manufacturer	Printer	Laser Engine
	Laser Act I	Ricoh PC Laser 6000
Develop	1200	Kyocera F-1010
	1000	Kyocera F-1010
E.L.T.	Labelmaster 20	Ricoh LP4080/4081/4150
	Labelmaster 10	Ricoh LP4080/4081/4150
Eastman Kodak	Ektaprint 1308	Canon LBP-CX 8ppm
	Ektaprint 1320	Canon LBP-20
Electronic Form Systems	Formwriter 10XD	Canon LBP-20
	Formwriter 10X	Canon LBP-20
	Formwriter 10	Canon LBP-20
	Formwriter 2X	Canon LBP-CX 8ppm
	Formwriter 2EX	Canon LBP-RX
	Formwriter 2EXD/MX	Canon LBP-SX II
	Formwriter 2E	Canon LBP-SX II
	Formwriter 4	Ricoh LP4081 8ppm
	Formwriter 8	Ricoh LP4150 15ppm
Epson	GQ-3500	Ricoh PC Laser 6000
	EPL-6000	TEC LB-1305
Facit	OPUS 2E	Ricoh LP4080/4081/4150
	OPUS 3	Ricoh LP4080/4081/4150
	P7080 (OPUS 2E)	Ricoh LP4080R
	P7150 (OPUS 3)	Ricoh LP4080R
	P4580 (OPUS 1)	Ricoh LP4120 12ppm
	OPUS 1	Ricoh LP4120 12ppm
	P6080 (OPUS 4)	Ricoh PC Laser 6000
	6010-P	Ricoh PC Laser 6000
	OPUS 4	Ricoh PC Laser 6000
	P6060	TEC LB-1305
Fontex Technology, Inc.	SYSLASER	TEC LB-1305
Fortis Infromation Sys.	DP-600S	Casio LCS 130
	DP-600W	Casio LCS 130

Manufacturer	Printer	Laser Engine
	DP-600P	Casio LCS 130
	DP-800	Casio LCS 130
Four Phase	PT365	Xerox 2700/3700
	8165	Xerox 2700/3700
Fujitsu America, Inc.	RX7100PS	Fujitsu RX7100
	RX7200	Fujitsu RX7200
	RX71000	Fujitsu RX7100
	RX7400	Fujitsu RX7400
General Business Tech.	6630DW	Canon LBp-CX 8ppm
	6630LS	Canon LBP-CX 8ppm
	6630XP	Canon LBP-CX 8ppm
	6633XP	Canon LBP-CX 8ppm
	6636PM	Canon LBP-CX 8ppm
	6634	Canon LBP-CX 8ppm
	6635	Canon LBP-CX 8ppm
	6636LX	Canon LBP-SX II
	6840Xp	Delphax S3030G
	6615XP	Kentek K-2+
	6624XP	Kentek K-3
	6824XP	Kentek K-4
	6640XP	Olympus S3000
	6620XP	Ricoh LP4120 12ppm
	6600XP	Xerox 2700 12ppm
	6600PC	Xerox 2700 12ppm
	6637	Canon LBP-20
	6638	Canon LBP-20
	6639	Canon LBP-20
GCC Technologies	PLP II	Oki Electric OL-400
	PLP Plus	Ricoh LP-1060
	Personal Laser Printer	Ricoh LP-1060
	Business Laser Printer	Ricoh LP-1060
GTC Tech	BLaser II	Canon LBP-CX 8ppm

Manufacturer	Printer	Laser Engine
	BLaserstar	Canon LBP-CX 8ppm
	BLaser Five	Canon LBP-CX 8ppm
	BLaser	Canon LBP-CX 8ppm
Genesis Computer Corp.	Laserset Printer	Canon LBP-CX 8ppm
Genicom	6100 Series	Canon LBP-SX II
	6145	Canon LBP-SX II
Genigraphics	8707 8ppm	Ricoh LP4080/4081/4150
Gestetner	8ppm	Canon LBP-CX 8ppm
	800 GLS/02	Canon LBP-SX II
	800 GLS/04	Canon LBP-SX II
Goldstar Telecomm Co.	GLP-1000	Goldstar GLP-1000
Hanzon	LP-5000	Ricoh LP4080/4081/4150
Harris Corp.	H165-01	Ricoh LP4080 8ppm
Harris/Lanier	LS-8	Ricoh LP4080/4081/4150
	LS-6	Ricoh PC Laser 6000
	LS-15	Ricoh PC Laser 6000
Hermes	F1010/F1200	Kyocera F-1010
Hetra	3024	Xerox XP-24
Hewlett Packard	LaserJet Plus	Canon LBP-CX 8ppm
	2686 LaserJet	Canon LBP-CX 8ppm
	2686TZ	Canon LBP-CX 8ppm
	1686TA	Canon LBP-CX 8ppm
	LaserJet 500 Plus	Canon LBP-CX 8ppm
	LaserJet	Canon LBP-CX 8ppm
	LaserJet 2000	Canon LBP-SX II
	LaserJet Series II	Canon LBP-SX II
	2687A	Ricoh LP 4120 12ppm
	2688A	Ricoh LP 4120 12ppm
	LaserJet Series 2000	Canon LBP-20

Manufacturer	Printer	Laser Engine
	LaserJet IIP	Canon LBP-4
	LaserJet IID	Canon LBP-RX
Honeywell Bull	Model 80	Ricoh LP4080/4081/4150
IBM Corporation	4019 Laserprinter	IBM 4019
	4216 Pers. Pageprinter	Ricoh LP-1060
	3812 Pageprinter Mod. 2	Kentek K-2
	3816 Pageprinter M. 01S	Kentek K-3
	3816 Pageprinter M. 01D	Kentek K-4
	3820 Pageprinter	Minolta SP50B
	4216 Per. Pagepr. II	Ricoh LP-1060
IDEA Courier	9375	Ricoh LP-4150
	9376	Ricoh LP-4150
Imagen	Image Station	Canon LBP-CX 8ppm
	8/300	Canon LBP-CX 8ppm
	3308	Canon LBP-CX 8ppm
	2308	Canon LBP-CX 8ppm
	2308/S Imageserver XP	Canon LBP-SX II
	Imagestation/S	Canon LBP-SX II
	12/300	Ricoh LP-4120 12ppm
	24/300	Xerox 3700 24ppm
	4324 Image Server XP	Xerox 3700 24ppm
Imprint Tech	Lightwriter	Canon LBP-CX 8ppm
	VideoPrint 300	Xerox 2700 12ppm
Informer Comp. Terminals	287-LP	Canon LBP-CX 8ppm
Interleaf, Inc.	LPR-308	Canon LBP-CX 8ppm
	LPI-308	Canon LBP-CX 8ppm
	OPS-2000	Canon LBP-CX 8ppm
	LPR-326S	Dataproducts LZR2600
	LP-306	Dataproducts LZR2600
	LPR-326S	Canon LBP-20
Itek Composition Sys.	Digitek Laser	Canon LBP-CX 8ppm

Manufacturer	Printer	Laser Engine
JPS Microsystems	MAXX/8	Canon LBP-SX II
JRL Systems, Inc.	340G High Res Laser Sys	Minolta SP340
Jasmine Technologies	Directprint	Casio LCS 130
Kanematsu-Gosho USA	M5311	Canon LBP-20
Kentek Information Sys.	K-2+	Kentek K-2+
	K-3	Kentek K-3
	RT4324 Duplex Pg Printr	Kentek K-4
Kienzle	271	Kyocera F-1010
Konica Corporation USA	LP-3015	Konica LP-3015
	LP-3110	Konica LP-3110
Kyocera	F-2010	Kyocera F-1010
	F-1200	Kypcera F-1010
	F-1010	Kyocera F-1010
	F-1000A	Kyocera F-1010
Kyocera Unison, Inc.	F-1000A	Kyocera FBP-01
	F-2000A	Kyocera FBP-01
	F-2010	Kyocera FBP-01
	F-3010	Kyocera FBP-02
LEXI Corporation	1087 II	Kyocera F-1000A
	1019 II	Kyocera F-1000A
	1012	Kyocera F-1000A
	2012	Kyocera F-2000A
	2019	Kyocera F-2000A
	2087 II	Kyocera F-2000A
	2087	Kyocera F-2000A
	2019 II	Kyocera F-2000A
	3019	Kyocera F-3010
	3012	Kyocera F-3010
	1019/1087	Kyocera F-1010

Manufacturer	Printer	Laser Engine
	3087	Kyocera F-3010
Laser Barcode Systems	Barcode Printer	Canon LBP-CX 8ppm
Laserdata, Inc.	Laserview Printer	Rocoh LP4080/4081/ 4150
Lasermaster Corp.	LM XT/RP4081	Ricoh LP4081 8ppm
	Lasermaster 1000	Canon LBP-SX 400
Lasersmith, Inc.	PS-415/PS-830 GT	Canon LBP-CX 8ppm
	PS-300/PS-415+	Canon LBP-CX 8ppm
	PS-415 GT	Canon LBP-CX 8ppm
	PS-830/PS-600	Canon LBP-CX 8ppm
Lee Data	1323	Dataproducts LZR2600
Legend	Blazer	Canon LBP-CX 8ppm
Linotype Co,	Linotype Laser Pr. 8/4	Canon LBP-CX 8ppm
Management Graphics	MGI Laserprinter	Canon LBP-CX 8ppm
Mannesmann Tally	MT 920	Kyocera F-1010
	MT 910SL	Kyocera F-1010
	MT 910 Univ. Publ. Sys.	Kyocera FPB-01
	MT 910	Kyocera FPB-01
	MT 905	TEC LB-1305
Megacom	4050 Plus	Xerox 4505 50ppm
Memorex	MRX 408	Canon LBP-CX 8ppm
	15ppm	Ricoh LP4080/4081/4150
Metaphor Comp. Sys.	Laserprinter 5200	Canon LBP-CX 8ppm
Microtek	Turboprint	TEC LB-1305
Miltope Business Prod.	30M	Olympus S3000
	30L	Olympus S3000
Minemos	6000	Ricoh LP-4120 12ppm

Manufacturer	Printer	Laser Engine
Minolta Corp.	SP101	Minolta SP101
	SP130	Minolta SP130
	Sp340	Minolta SP340
	340G	Minolta SP340
Mita Copystar America	LP-2080	Mita LP-X2
Mitek Systems	100T	Canon LBP-CX 8ppm
	2125	Canon LBP-CX 8ppm
	110T	Canon LBP-CX 8ppm
	120T	Canon LBP-CX 8ppm
	115T	Canon LBP-CX 8ppm
	125T	Canon LBP-SX II
	2150	Ricoh LP-4150 15ppm
	150T	Ricoh LP-4150 15ppm
	130T	Canon LBP-SX
Mohawk	Laserprinter	Xerox 4045 10ppm
Motorola Computer Sys.	8165	Xerox 2700 12ppm
NBI, Inc.		Canon LBP-CX 8ppm
	908	Ricoh LP-4080 8ppm
	Oasys MOd 12	Xerox 2700 12ppm
	Oasys 10	Xerox XP-10E
	Oasys Mod 24	Xerox XP-24
NBS Southern	3815	Ricoh LP 4150 15ppm
NCR	6406	Canon LBP-CX 8ppm
	6416	Canon LBP-CX 8ppm
	6480	Siemens 2200 80ppm
	6435	TEC 1305B
	6426	Xerox 4045 10ppm
NEC Technologies, Inc.	Silentwriter LC 890XL	NEC LC 800
	Silentwriter2 290	Canon LBP-UX
	Silentwriter2 260	Canon LBP-UX

Manufacturer	Printer	Laser Engine
National Computer Prod.	DW-X2700	Xerox 2700 12ppm
Newgen Systems Corp.	TURBOPS/400	Canon LBP-SX
	TURBOPS/480	Canon LBP-SX
	TURBOPS/300	Canon LBP-SX
Nissho Electronics USA	LN-2248B	Minolta SP348
	LN-2248	Minolta SP348
Nokia	10/1000/2020	Kyocera F-1010
North Atlantic Tempest	Smartwriter	Canon LBP-CX 8ppm
	Laser 8	Canon LBP-CX 8ppm
	KISS	Canon LBP-CX 8ppm
	Big Kiss M	Canon LBP-CX 8ppm
	Smartwriter 80+	Canon LBP-CX 8ppm
	PS800	Canon LBP-CX 8ppm
	PS800+	Canon LBP-CX 8ppm
	Laser II	Canon LBP-CX 8ppm
OCE/CPT	6015	Canon LBP-CX 8ppm
	6010	Canon LBP-CX 8ppm
	6017	Canon LBP-CX 8ppm
Oasys	Mod 805	Canon LBP-CX 8ppm
	Mod 812	Canon LBP-CX 8ppm
	Laserpro 820-C	Canon LBP-CX 8ppm
	Mod 810	Canon LBP-CX 8ppm
	Laserpro 810-C	Canon LBP-CX 8ppm
	Laserpro 805-R	Ricoh LP4080/4081/4150
	Laserpro 820-R	Ricoh LP4080/4081/4150
	Laserpro 810-R	Ricoh LP4081 8ppm
	Laserpro 1510	Ricoh LP4150 15ppm
Octave Systems	Laser Octave	Canon LBP-CX 8ppm
Office Automation Sys.	Laserpro 810-R	Ricoh LP-4081
	Laserpro 5215	Ricoh LP-4150

Manufacturer	Printer	Laser Engine
	Laserpro 1510	Ricoh LP-4150
	Laserpro Silver Express	TEC LB-1301
	Laserpro Gold Express	TEC LB-1301
	Laserpro Express Ser II	TEC LB-1301
	Laserpro Exec	TEC LB-1305
	Laserpro 5287	TEC LB-830
	Laserpro 2200	Minolta SP330
Okidata	Okilaser 400	Oki Electric OL-400
	Laserline 6	Ricoh LP-1060
	Laserline Elite	Ricoh PC Laser 6000
	Laserline Elite Plus	Ricoh PC Laser 6000
Olivetti	101	Canon LBP-CX 8ppm
	PG 208/M1	Canon LBP-SX II
	PG 108	Canon LBP-SX II
	PG 208/M2	Canon LBP-SX II
	PG 1260	Toshiba A-739
	PG 1230	Toshiba A-739
Olympia	Laserstar 6	Canon LBP-CX 8ppm
		Ricoh PC Laser 6000
PCPI	Laserimage 1030-LN03=	Ricoh LP-1060
	Laserimage 1034	Ricoh LP-1060
	Laserimage 1000-PS	Ricoh LP-1060
	Laserimage 1030	Ricoh LP-1060
	Laserimage 1032	Ricoh LP-1060
	Laserimage 1035	Ricoh LP-1060
	Laserimage 2022	Ricoh LP-4081
	Laserimage 2024	Ricoh LP-4081
	Laserimage 2020	Ricoh LP-4081
	Laserimage 2025	Ricoh LP-4081
	Laserimage 3020-LN03+	Ricoh LP-4150
	Laserimage 3000-3X	Ricoh LP-4150
	Laserimage 3020	Ricoh LP-4150
	Laserimage 3024	Ricoh LP-4150

Manufacturer	Printer	Laser Engine
	Laserimage 3022	Ricoh LP-4150
	Laserimage 3025	Ricoh LP-4150
Packard Bell	PB-83PS	Canon LBP-CX 8ppm
	PB-8300DB	Canon LBP-CX 8ppm
	PB-8300	Canon LBP-CX 8ppm
	PB-9000 Plus	Ricoh PC Laser 6000
	PB-9500	TEC LB-1305
Panasonic	KX-P4450	Panasonic KX-P4450
Pentax Teknologies	Laserfold 240	Pentax PL-F0242
Perg Systems	PLP-CX	Canon LBP-CX 8ppm
Personal Computer Prod.	DaisyLaser 1000	Canon LBP-CX 8ppm
	DaisyLaser 2000	Ricoh LP4080/4081/4150
	Laserimage 2000	Ricoh LP-4081 8ppm
	Laserimage 3000	Ricoh LP-4150 15ppm
	Laserimage 1000	Ricoh PC Laser 6000
Phillips Info. Systems	Laserprinter	Canon LBP-CX 8ppm
	PLP-15	Ricoh LP4080/4081/4150
Prime Computer, Inc.	8ppm	Canon LBP-CX 8ppm
	12ppm	Xerox 2700 12ppm
	24ppm	Xerox 3700 24ppm
Printer Systems Corp.	Model 106	Ricoh PC Laser 6000
	Intelliprint Model 106	Ricoh LP-1060
	Intelliprint 218	Fujitsu RX7300
Printronix	L2324-S	Kentek K-3
	L1212	Mita LP-X1
	L1012	Mita LP-X1
Printware, Inc.	720IQ/1200HD	Printware 720IQ
	720 IQ Professional	Printware 720IQ
Q/Cor	Quadlaser I	Ricoh LP-4080R

Manufacturer	Printer	Laser Engine
	Quadlaser Postscript	Ricoh LP-4081
QMS	Big Kiss	Canon LBP-CX 8ppm
	Smartwriter 8/3X	Canon LBP-CX 8ppm
	Smartscript 800	Canon LBP-CX 8ppm
	PS 800 II	Canon LBP-CX 8ppm
	Conceptwriter	Canon LBP-CX 8ppm
	Big Kiss II	Canon LBP-CX 8ppm
	Lasergrafix 800 II	Canon LBP-CXD 8ppm
	Smartwriter 20 Plus	Canon LBP-SX II
	Smartwriter 30 Plus	Canon LBP-SX II
	PS-810	Canon LBP-SX II
	Lasergrafix II 800	Canon LBP-SX II
	Kiss Plus	Canon LBP-SX II
	Smartwriter Plus	Canon LBP-SX II
	PS-1500	Ricoh LP-4150 15ppm
	Smartscript 150	Ricoh LP-4150 15ppm
	Lasergrafix 1510	Ricoh LP-4150 15ppm
	Lasergrafix 1200	Xerox 2700 12ppm
	Lasergrafix 2400	Xerox 3700 24ppm
	6320 Imageserver XP	Canon LBP-20
	3320 Imageserver XP	Canon LBP-20
	5320 Imageserver XP	Canon LBP-20
	7320 Imageserver XP	Canon LBP-20
	2308/S Imageserver XP	Canon LBP-SX
	PS 810 Turbo	Canon LBP-SX
	Imagestation/S	Canon LBP-SX
	3308/S Imageserver XP	Canon LBP-TX
	PS 820	Canon LBP-TX
	PS 820 Turbo	Canon LBP-TX
	PS 2200	Panasonic FPL-301
	Lasergraphix 2200	Panasonic FPL-301
Quadram	QuadLaser DP8	Ricoh LP4080/4081/4150
	QuadLaser WS8	Ricoh LP4080/4081/4150
	QuadLaser FP8	Ricoh LP4080/4081/4150

Manufacturer	Printer	Laser Engine
	QuadLaser I	Ricoh LP-4080R
	QuadLaser Pastscript	Ricoh LP-4081 8ppm
Qume Corporation	Crystalprint Wp	Casio LCS130
	Crystalprint Publisher	Casio LCS130
	Crystalprint Super SerII	Casio LCS130B
	Crystalprint Series II	Casio LcS130B
Radio Shack	LP1000	Ricoh PC Laser 6000
Raster Devices Direct	Trendsetter 1000	Canon LBP-SX
	RD2 Impression	Ricoh 6000/EX
Ricoh	PC Laser 6000	Ricoh LP-1060 6ppm
	LP4080	Ricoh LP-4080 8ppm
	LP4080R	Ricoh LP-4080 8ppm
	LP4081	Ricoh LP-4081 8ppm
	LP4120	Ricoh LP-4120 12ppm
	LP4150	Ricoh LP-4150 15ppm
	PC Laser 6000/PS	Ricoh LP-1060 6ppm
	PC Laser 6000/EX	Ricoh LP-1060 6ppm
	PC Laser 15/EX	Ricoh LP-4150 15ppm
Rise Tech	EPT-1	Canon LBP-CX 8ppm
Rosetta Technologies	RT3105 Page Printer	Fujitsu RX7100
	RT4115 Page Printer	Kentek K-2+
	RT4224 Page Printer	Kentek K-3
	RT4324 Duplex Page Pr.	Kentek K-4
Seikosha America, Inc.	OP-215	Seikosha OP-200
Sharp Electronics, Inc.	JX-9500	Sharp JX-9500
Siemens	2200	Siemens 2200 80ppm
	2300	Siemens 2300 160ppm
Sony	OA-P5108 8ppm	Ricoh LP4080/4081/4150
Sperry	0777	Siemens 2200 80ppm

Manufacturer	Printer	Laser Engine
Star Micronics	Laserprinter 8	Canon LBP-SX II
Stoll	ST-10/20	Kyocera F-1010
Storage Tecnology Corp	6100	Siemens 2200 80ppm
Sun Microsystems	Sun Laserwriter	Canon LBP-CX 8ppm
TAB	Series 1000	Canon LBP-CX 8ppm
TAXAN Corp.	Crystaljet	Casio LCS 300
TEC America, Inc.	LB-1306C	TEC LB-1306
	LB-1306	TEC LB-1306
TGV Data	Laser I	Ricoh LP4080/4081/4150
Talaris Systems	T-812	Canon LBP-CX 8ppm
	T-802	Canon LBP-CX 8ppm
	T-820+	Canon LBP-CX 8ppm
	T-610	Canon LBP-CX 8ppm
	T-810	Canon LBP-CX 8ppm
	T-800	Canon LBP-CX 8ppm
	T-812H	Canon LBP-CXD
	T-811/2/3/4	Canon LBP-SX II
	T-1502	Ricoh LP-4150 15ppm
	T-1500	Ricoh LP-4150 15ppm
	1590 Printstation	Ricoh LP-4150 15ppm
	T-1200	Xerox 2700 12ppm
	T-2400	Xerox 3700 24ppm
	T-2492B	Xerox XP-24
Tandem Computers	5573 Laser-LX	Canon LBP-SX II
Tegra	Genesis XP-800	Canon LBP-SX II
	Genesis XP-1000	Canon LBP-20
Telefile Computer Prod.	T7467 L2	Xerox 3700 24ppm
	T3487 L2	Xerox 4045 10ppm

Manufacturer	Printer	Laser Engine
Texas Instruments	OmniLaser 2108	Ricoh LP-4081 8ppm
	OmniLaser 2115	Ricoh LP-4150 15ppm
	OmniLaser 2015	Ricoh LP-4150 15ppm
	LP2106	Ricoh PC Laser 6000
	Microlaser/Microlaser PS	Sharp JX-9500
	OmniLaser 2106	Ricoh LP-1060 6ppm
Texet	IP-300	Canon LBP-CX 8ppm
Toshiba America	2600 26ppm	Dataproducts LZR2600
	PageLaser 12 12ppm	
Toshiba Pagelaser 12		
	PageLaser 6	TEC LB-1305
Triumph/Adler	SDR 7710/7720	Kyocera F-1010
Troy	TROY 315	Ricoh LP-4150
	308 MICR Printer	Ricoh LP-4081
UNISYS	Model 37	Kyocera FBP-01
	AP 9206	Ricoh LP-1060
	27/37	Kyocera F-1010
	Laser 37	Kyocera F-1010
	AP 9208 MOD I 8ppm	Ricoh LP-4080 8ppm
	AP 9215 MOD I	Ricoh LP-4150 15ppm
	AP 9215-1 MOD I	Ricoh LP-4150 15ppm
	AP 9415	Ricoh LP-4150 15ppm
Varityper	VT600P	Panasonic FPL-130
	LP2300	Ricoh LP4080/4081/4150
Viewtech	Viewwriter	Canon LBP-CX 8ppm
Wang	LPS-8	Canon LBP-CX 8ppm
	LCS-8	Canon LBP-SX
	LDP-8	Canon LBP-SX II
	LCS-15	Ricoh LP-4150 15ppm

Manufacturer	Printer	Laser Engine
	LPS-12	Xerox 2700 12ppm
	LPS-24	Xerox 2700/Xerox 3700
	LIS-12	Xerox 2700/Xerox 3700
	LIS-24	Xerox 3700 24ppm
	LIS-24	Xerox XP-24
Wordplex	XP 12E	Xerox 2700 12ppm
XPOINT Corp.	6219-26	Dataproducts LZR2600
	6219-12	Toshiba A-739
Xerox	2700	Xerox 2700 12ppm
	2700 II	Xerox 2700/Xerox 3700
	3700	Xerox 3700 24ppm
	4045 Model 20	Xerox 4045 10ppm
	4045 Model 50	Xerox 4045 10ppm
	4090	Xerox 4050 50ppm
	4650	Xerox 4050 50ppm
	4050	Xerox 4050 50ppm
	8790	Xerox 8700/Xerox 9700
	8700	Xerox 8700/Xerox 9700
	9700	Xerox 9500/9700 120ppm
	9500	Xerox 9500/9700 120ppm
	9790	Xerox 9500/9700 120ppm
	4045 Model 160	Xerox XP-10
	4045 Model 150	Xerox XP-10
	4045 MOdel 120	Xerox XP-10
	NS3700	Xerox XP-24
	3700 LPS	Xerox XP-24
Xyvision	6408	Canon LBP-CX 8ppm
Zygal	KF1010	Kyocera F-1010

Index